GERMANY and EUROPE

GERMANY and EUROPE:

Historical Essays by HAJO HOLBORN

Doubleday & Company, Inc.

Garden City, New York

1970

"Moltke and Schlieffen" is reprinted by permission of Princeton University
Press from MAKERS OF MODERN STRATEGY, edited by Edward M.
Earle. Copyright © 1943 by Princeton University. "Russia and the European
Political System" by Hajo Holborn, is from RUSSIAN FOREIGN POLICY,
edited by Ivo J. Lederer. Copyright © 1962 by Yale University. Reprinted
by permission of Yale University Press. "Diplomats and Diplomacy in the
Early Weimar Republic" is from THE DIPLOMATS, 1919–1939, edited
by Gordon A. Craig & Felix Gilbert. Copyright © 1953 by Princeton
University and reprinted here by permission of Princeton University Press.
"Origins and Political Character of Nazi Ideology" is reprinted with permission from the *Political Science Quarterly*, Vol. LXXIX (December
1964), pp. 542–54.

To Dietrich Gerhard
and
Felix Gilbert

CONTENTS

I   GERMAN IDEALISM IN THE
LIGHT OF SOCIAL HISTORY

———◆———

(Translated by Robert Edwin Herzstein)

THE CONTRAST between Germany and Western Europe in modern history has long been a subject of historical interpretation and research. The split in Europe, which has existed since the French Revolution and shook the continent to its foundations in the Industrial Revolution, had profound consequences. In two world wars it led not only to the political collapse of Germany as a great power but also to the end of Europe's hegemony in the world. Thus, the split between Germany and the West will of necessity always be an important theme for historians. At the same time we should beware of exaggeration. The entire world situation cannot be explained by this split. The rise of America and of Russia probably would have occurred anyway, and a certain weakening of England's position was most likely unavoidable once the nationalism of the Occident spread to the Orient. There were also powerful historical trends and movements outside the German-West European area.

The fact that the contrast between Germany and the West has tended to fade away, in large measure due to the far vaster East-West conflict, should make it possible for us to view it more objectively than before. The last sixty years have on all sides been witness to propagandistic abuses concerning defamatory comparisons of German and Western ideas and institutions. We do not have to unravel this confusion once more, but on the other hand we must keep in mind the results of serious studies of responsible statesmen and citizens. Fortunately we can say with certainty that the propaganda of the Second World War has not made as deep or as lasting an impact upon the scholarship of the countries of the West as did that of the First World War and the subsequent years.

The only question of concern to us here is the origin of the separation of Germany from Western Europe and America. This split occurred, as Friedrich Meinecke and Ernst Troeltsch have shown, during the age of German idealism, by which is meant the great intellectual movement in Germany during the years 1770–1840. It was at this time that Germany departed from the mainstream of European political thought. This mainstream had always centered around the doctrine of natural law. Germany went on to develop a new, philosophically revolutionary concept of history and the state, one of peculiar greatness and danger. This concept did not altogether predestine Germany's modern development, but it did point it in new directions. Troeltsch and Meinecke were not engaged in an attack upon German idealism, in whose tradition they were brought up and whose unique artistic and philosophical works they attempted to understand through their critical analyses. Troeltsch remarked upon many occasions that German idealism would increase its influence even upon Western Europe and America. Events have vindicated this viewpoint. Troeltsch, however, often warned us to beware of seeking the roots of German political thought of the later nineteenth and early twentieth century exclusively in German idealism. The wild exaggeration of national sentiment in the era of the First World War and its apocalyptic transformation into National Socialism were also rooted in causal factors that did not exist in Germany alone. At the same time we must freely acknowledge that the peoples of Western Europe were better able to limit the baleful effects of pseudo-science in politics. Social Darwinism is an example of this fact. In any event, it will be necessary to limit the study of the influence of German idealism to the period before 1848 lest we jump unprepared into the era of full-grown capitalism and nationalism.

The attempt to understand what differentiated the German intellectual tradition from the Western European one has mostly been made by an examination of patterns of thought and ideas. Ernst Troeltsch approached the problem in this way, though he was of course aware that this methodology overlooked other, less thoroughly researched aspects of the problem. Thus, in his last great interpretive address on "Natural Law and Humanity in World Politics" Troeltsch acknowledged that he approached these theories and their development purely "from their logical and dialectical side." He further stated that "In reality, the rise and development of such theories cannot be detached from the concrete needs and interests of their contemporary environment . . . They are intellectual structures that cannot be torn from the practical needs and circumstances that create them. They are therefore justified not only from the point of view of pure theory but mainly from that of their practical contributions and effects." The study of the political and social history of German idealism is just as important as that of the history of its leading ideas. Only in this way can we fulfill the requirement outlined by Friedrich Meinecke in his *German Catastrophe:* one can only arrive at a real understanding of modern German history if one first grasps the meaning of the spiritual, political, and social transformations that have made the modern German.

German idealism was the creation of a specific social stratum. The situation and position of this class was determined by the prevalent structure of contemporary German society. It is obvious that the representatives of idealism formed their views of the social and political aspects of life against the background of this environment. The nexus of relationships that made up German society in turn influenced the German idealists in their ideas about the future of society. No matter how much they may have estranged themselves from their roots, regardless of how much their fantasies and ideas may have removed them from the hustle and bustle of "the common life," they still had to find a general answer to a most important question: What social authorities were necessary for the life and continued cultivation of the new spirit, and what social circumstances could be disregarded? Naturally, their answer was rejected by those whose approach to life grew out of different spiritual and sociopolitical circumstances. Too little attention has been paid to the church as the focus of the intellectual and spiritual integration of society. There is no doubt that German idealism failed to elevate itself to the level of a national culture and guide even in the Protestant areas of Germany. It could not solve the practical and intellectual problems of all classes. Partially as a result of this, it tragically became a factor in the widening of class divisions in German society. The political theory of German idealism, which assigned such an important role in state and nation to power, did not overcome the inner class divisions of the German people. On the contrary, this doctrine ended by giving these divisions a sharp ideological rigidity. This lack of a larger moral and social unity contributed to Germany's later attempts to use the strength of its people for goals of political conquest. This, in turn, was the road to dictatorship—over other peoples and over Germany itself.

I

The development of a conflict between Germany and Western Europe is strictly a fact of the last two centuries. The entire course of German history before then was part and parcel of a common European history. Certainly, even in this earlier time we can seek and find national peculiarities of political and social organization, as well as of religion, art, and intellectual creativity. Yet this national differentiation of peoples was something of general European character. Germany seemed to have found the possibility of an independent position with the advent of the Protestant Reformation. Let us never forget, however, that the Protestantism of Germany revealed itself as less self-conscious than that of England, Holland, or Sweden. Furthermore, Germany as a whole did not become a Protestant country. Although the collapse of religious unity contributed to the destruction of a common European feeling, Germany even in this respect was no more or less remarkable than the rest of the continent.

Germany's location between East and West did not cause profound differences to arise between her and the West either. Before the mid-nineteenth century Germany was never "a land in the middle," but rather the great eastern borderland of Western civilization. The relations of Germany with the Slavic world were never those of mutual transmitter, but rather those of a bellicose or peaceful bearer of Western civilization to the East. The German nation extended Western civilization eastward, and in so doing secured it. We do not mean to detract from the importance of Poland, Bohemia, and Hungary if we say that without German influence on the Elbe, the Oder, the eastern shores of the Baltic Sea, and the lands bordering the Danube the history of the Western world would have remained a simple continuation of the history of the lands comprising the western half of the Roman Empire. If this had been the case, it is quite possible that the history of the West would have been very short. Without the strength that the Germanic world gave to the West it is by no means certain that the West would have survived so successfully. Further, the German contribution to the history of the West was not limited to securing its external survival. From the beginning it proved to be a fertile force in Western culture, for example in political and legal concepts and in intellectual and artistic expression. With a few exceptions, of which the German Reformation was the last and the most important, the great cultural factors that molded the West came mostly from the older world of Western and Southern Europe. Scholasticism, mysticism, and Gothic art were not native to Germany. Some German historians have asserted that at least Gothic art and mysticism found their highest creative expressions only in Germany, but such a claim cannot be objectively settled. Let us more accurately say that, despite a certain time lag, Germany never became a mere imitator of foreign models but rather filled these alien forms with new meaning. Germany participated in the general life of Europe fully and spontaneously.

It was only around the middle of the sixteenth century that the contrast between Germany and the West became more obvious. At the same time we observe a lowering of the cultural level in the East. Where England and France were entering the great ages of their national histories, Germany found it impossible to remake her constitution of the Empire. The lives of most Germans remained enclosed within the various territorial states. Most of these had been the results of accidental and forgotten past circumstances. The Thirty Years' War sharpened the miseries of this utterly fragmented state system and brought wide areas of the old Empire under foreign rule. At the same time, this war prepared the way in some of the states for new types of government and administration. These tended to imitate the French, though on a much reduced scale. Theoretically there was a possibility—most unlikely when one considers the trend of German history since the end of the fifteenth century—that the German dualist territorial states in which power was divided between the princes and estates might develop as did their Dutch and English analogues. In fact, however, these German states, in which the estates participated in the government, proved to be the predecessors of an ultimate absolutism.

As in France—and in England as early as under the Tudors— in Germany the development of absolutism was the result of internal wars. In addition, the impact on Germany of foreign invasions was overwhelming. Nevertheless, the development of absolutism in Germany after 1648 cannot, as such, be viewed as representing a severe break with the West. Contemporaries on both sides of the Rhine saw no evidence of such a break. The early generation of the French Enlightenment viewed Frederick the Great as a champion of its ideas, and he in turn was dazzled by France.

Even when we acknowledge these truths, however, this seeming unity should not confuse the real issue. Under the surface of a common European civilization wide-ranging forces were preparing the way for new sources of national differentiation. From the point of view of constitutional history France in the eighteenth century was closer to Prussia than to England, yet socially it approximated England more than Germany. Since the middle of the sixteenth century the German economy had been at a relative standstill. Germany then had suffered the frightful bloodletting of the Thirty Years' War, and it only slowly began to recover during the next century. France, on the other hand, played a respectable role in the expansive "Atlantic age." Under the umbrella of French absolutism there developed a richly variegated national society full of profound tensions and dynamism. Under certain circumstances these might be turned against the regime. Germany's social organization had become rigid and unproductive. In many ways one can make a case for the view that the sixteenth century in Germany was more bourgeois than the eighteenth.

Otto Hintze defined the threefold meaning of feudalism as a political, military, and social system. As a political and military system of organization it belonged to the Middle Ages, although it is obvious that the constitution of the German Empire of the early modern period cannot be understood without some knowledge of the constitutional aspects of medieval feudalism. Even in the officer corps of the new armies the old function of military feudalism did not quite disappear. As an economic and social manifestation feudalism continued to dominate everywhere on the continent even in the modern period. The French Revolution destroyed the power of the landholding aristocracy west of the Rhine. This was the forceful work of a strong third estate such as did not exist on the other side of that river. The economic and social aspects of feudalism ruled Germany until well into the nineteenth century, and we can even see traces of this domination in the unhappy history of the Weimar Republic. The role of feudalism in modern Germany was thus much greater than in Western Europe. Feudalism was all played out in the West by the early nineteenth century.

The absolutist German territorial state [of the early modern period] rested upon the social and economic position of the landowning nobility. In addition the state guaranteed these nobles a privileged position in the body politic. Although the noble was obliged to serve the state in different ways, he had secure claims to many of the highest positions in the government. On his own lands and in his local sphere he enjoyed almost total authority. In contrast with this, the influence of the bourgeoisie upon the politics of the territorial states was quite limited. The general situation in various parts of Germany differed toward the end of the eighteenth century, but one may generalize and say that the artisan and the small merchant tended to be preponderant in the towns. Large entrepreneurial undertakings and high finance were rare, and a good many of the "manufactures," predecessors of modern industry, were state-owned factories in that age of German mercantilism. Germany did not have a strong, self-conscious middle class that, proud of its abilities and of its contribution to the national welfare, sought political rights. Even the municipal reforms of Baron Stein were well ahead of their time. And the difficulty in the beginning of finding independent burghers who were willing to serve as elected officials in the new municipal administrations is well known.

The civil servants were the burghers who had the greatest influence upon public life, comparatively speaking. The civil-

servant caste included, in the broadest sense, professors, second-
ary-school teachers, and pastors, for schools were state institutions, and the churches—including the Catholic—were closely
bound up with the courts and the aristocracy. Among the cultivated members of the middle class there was, at the very
most, an enlightened enthusiasm for reform, but never the sense
of outright political opposition. This reformist tendency never
went much further than that of the enlightened princes. The
center of this burgher world was to be found in Germany's institutions of higher learning. Thus, the political "demand" that
was closest to the hearts of the burgher state servants concerned
the security of these institutions of learning and training. "Freedom of thought" therefore came to be viewed as absolutely
necessary. Social and political rights, on the other hand, might
be seen as desirable, but hardly of such primary concern. In
general, the attitude of the enlightened burgher was that the
ideal organization and administration of government could be
achieved through the progressive training of better civil servants.
The entire intellectual bent of eighteenth-century Germany was
in the direction of the education and cultivation of the individual. All political demands were secondary, if they were
considered at all.

The course of history ran quite differently in Western Europe.
France experienced a revolution followed by various socio-politi-
cal experiments. All of these, however, show a steady evolution
toward liberal and democratic forms. The French thinker who
most influenced German idealism was Rousseau. His criticism of
rationalistic civilization as the suppression of human feeling and
will in favor of mere reason found a passionate echo in Germany.
Rousseau saw two great needs if the future was to be saved:
the creation of a basically altered order of society and state,
and a new form of education for the individual. Rousseau's educational ideal, the expression of a new view of man, was en-
thusiastically taken up by certain Germans as early as the time

of *Sturm und Drang* and Kant. The entire German-idealist view of culture and education is drenched in Rousseau's pedagogic ideology. Rousseau's political radicalism, however, which for Western Europeans was only the other side of the same problem, received but scant attention in Germany. After a short period of hesitation upon the outbreak of the French Revolution, the Germans returned to their cultural ideal of inwardness. It was the French invasion and the rule of Napoleon that finally led German intellectuals to the problem of the state. The classic historical treatment of this development is to be found in Friedrich Meinecke's *Cosmopolitanism and the National State*.

It is important that we note the lack of truly revolutionary thought in Germany in this period. Rather, there was the desire to reform the old system while retaining the absolutist upper structure. One can, of course, reply that any other course would have been unrealistic, but thinkers need not necessarily be "realistic"—as Rousseau and Marx demonstrated. Deeply committed to absolutism, the German middle class did not dream of revolution but rather was content to pursue the path that led to reform of the authoritarian state, not to its destruction. Many of the reforms that were enacted after 1807 were in the general spirit of the old absolutist order. This is especially true of the abolition of special rights pertaining to regional political units and to social privileges. And yet the reforms of this period went far beyond absolutism, because they were filled with a new spirit.

The real aim of the German middle class, and of some nobles, was the creation of a state based upon justice and culture, but at the same time having great political power. Significant inequalities of rights remained after 1815, but the ideas of equality before the law and an independent judiciary made great strides forward. Perhaps even more novel in German history was the conscious ideal of the state as the bearer of culture. The theory was that the abstract, mechanistic, and institutional state of Frederick the Great would be replaced by the living community of the nation. The organs of this state were to represent and further the riches of the new national culture. That the securing of the state based upon law and culture demanded popular representative bodies was realized by few men and resolutely demanded by even fewer. The struggle for a Prussian constitution ended with the defeat of early German liberalism and for some time left no trace of a strong, internal opposition group. Similarly, the beneficent creation of constitutions in the medium-sized German states before 1848 did not yield the results it might have because of the attitude of two great powers in the German Confederation.

The dominance of the bureaucratic spirit was demonstrated by the prevalent acceptance of the idea that the authoritarian order could be reformed simply by securing government by law and supporting national culture. The authoritarian state, after all, represented administrative rule by the bureaucracy. The civil servants who staffed it were "the selection of the ablest men of the whole nation who with great effort had mastered the difficult art of administration and government," an art that "demanded deep insight into present realities, but also complete freedom of mind so that what does not yet exist will be brought to life," to quote Leopold von Ranke on the ethos and political position of the German civil-servant class of the period of the Restoration and the *Biedermeier*. These statements appeared in his *Dialogue on Politics* of 1836,[1] and the overwhelming majority of German burghers would have agreed with him at that time. German law and German culture were in the hands of authorities who constituted an experienced and cultivated élite. The monarchy would see to it that "the right man would be placed in the right position. . . ."

Without denying the great accomplishments of the German bureaucracy in this period—and many of their deeds, such as the Prussian-German Customs Union, were not merely technical facts, but first-rate political achievements—it remains true that

this bureaucracy did not of itself have the resources to bring
into being a state built on law and culture. There were too many
arbitrary police arrests, too many special courts, too much censorship. The monarchy, moreover, was only partially occupied
with these middle-class German ideals of the day. There was so
much tolerance of aristocratic privilege that at times the state-
building work even of early modern absolutism seemed to be
called into question. Still more serious was the continued separation of the army from civil society. What was so significant
here was not merely that the princes retained complete control
of the armies while the officer corps continued to have the Junkers as its social base, but that many of these officers never attended any sort of civil school. The training centers for cadets
outlived the reforms of Scharnhorst and Humboldt.

If the German middle classes could tolerate all this, the reason
lies not only in their total respect for inherited authority, but
also in the prevalent view that the state was a power among
powers. For a generation that had experienced the impact upon
the old Empire of the French Revolution and Napoleon, nationality was not only a cultural possession, but the physical guarantee of independence. Thus, while the domestic militarization of
the state appeared to be molded by these circumstances, there
was actually nothing that predetermined a further result: the
acknowledgment that the military held the first rank within
the state, with the concomitant separation of the civil sphere
from the military. The introduction of compulsory military service, which could have led to increased bourgeois influence in
the army, ended with a lame compromise. The theoretical right
of burghers to enter the officer corps was acknowledged, as was
the shorter military obligation of well-educated youths. Nothing
says more, however, of the peculiar class nature of German
society than the historically unique institution of the one-year
volunteers [*Einjährige*] on the basis of education rather than
wealth. The establishment of the national militia and its inte-

gration into the organs of the new state administration were the single greatest concession made by the old order to the bourgeoisie. Nevertheless, the national militia remained the stepchild of the Prussian state, without, one might add, this causing any serious popular conflict before 1848.

II

This rather brief survey shows the close relationship that existed between the social position of the German bourgeoisie and its practical and theoretical political goals as of the beginning of the nineteenth century. It would, however, be a gross simplification to assert that this relationship was purely the result of determining social factors. Ideas are never mere projections of a concrete external situation, but are in themselves creative acts that attempt in a most subtle manner to bring the real circumstances of life into harmony with the inner needs of men. When we inquire into the deeper spiritual longings of the educated German bourgeoisie, we come up against the problem of the religious sentiment of German idealism. Recently, there has been a great deal of discussion of this point. But it has not touched upon its social and political significance to any great extent, aside from occasional forays involving the nature of romantic concepts of the corporative state, etc. In reality, the secularization of religion brought about by the German idealists involved much more fundamental attitudes with regard to society.

This is not the place to reexamine the great historical controversy as to whether German idealism was the natural modern form of Protestantism or the transformation of Protestantism into a neo-gnosticism. Everyone would admit today that the liberal Protestantism of the nineteenth century was not aware of the difficulties involved in this weighty problem. Again and again liberal German Protestants insisted that Kant's concepts of "radi-

cal evil" and the categorical imperative were the direct successors
to the religion of Luther, ignoring the gulf between Luther's
time and the era of Kant. Kant believed that "You can because
you should," while Luther insisted that human reason alone
would not prove sufficient to a man attempting to act by the
dictates of morality. On the other hand, the modern followers
of Kierkegaard underestimate the symbiosis that has often occurred between Christianity and ancient ideas. This relationship
in ever new forms has helped mold the character of Western
Christianity.

In any case, the main point of contrast between the German
Enlightenment and that of Western Europe was religion. Few
anti-religious ideas were found in Germany. Anti-clericalism took
on a milder form than in France and England. There was no
philosophical materialism in Germany until after the deaths of
Hegel and Schelling, and what practical materialism there was
existed in the courts and among nobility rather than in the
homes of the middle class. The German burgher had not lost
his respect for religion as such. Nevertheless, the substance of
Lutheran faith was constantly diluted by the growing influence
of rationalism and of secular culture. Pietism and Lutheran orthodoxy could not stem the tide.

German idealism of the late eighteenth and the early nineteenth century represented a passionate attempt to realize a
new "religious" meaning in life. Christianity was still strong
enough in Germany to influence every idealist in one way or
another. Certainly, between Winckelmann on one side and Ha-
mann and Jacobi on the other we find all sorts of combinations
of Christian and classical intellectual tendencies. For our purposes let us note that both German idealism and the later German "historical school" rejected the mechanistic rationalism of
the Western Enlightenment and, in this respect at least, remained closer to Christian thought. But at the same time the
predominant pantheism and panentheism simply disregarded

essential tenets of the historical faith, such as the concepts of a personalistic God and consciousness of sin.

At the same time, German idealism changed the sphere of ethical and spiritual action in human history. Despite his uniqueness, Hegel is a typical example. For Hegel the state was the realization not only of law, but also of morality. If this is the case, the church loses any vital role it had in history. Hegel did not wish to do away with the churches, and he took great satisfaction in the knowledge that his philosophical system could vindicate the basic dogmas of Christianity. But just as the practical influence of his philosophy upon religion was a two-edged sword, so his recommendation that the churches limit themselves to the cultivation of an attitude suitable for the community was a dubious service.

Even Luther, of course, did not worry greatly about the "visible" church. He always viewed the structural guidelines that he bequeathed to his church as a temporary structure, nothing more. Luther's concept of the church placed most emphasis, as Karl Holl has shown, upon the "invisible" church, the community of saints, and the word of God. The "visible" church could only lead one to the path, for the road of the individual believer was one of private and public penitence, isolated and communal prayer, study of the Holy Book, and partaking of the activities of brotherly love. In this interpretation the church was the place where God revealed himself to man and fulfilled His noblest cosmic goal—the assumption of man, childlike, to the bosom of the Father. Certainly, God had established secular authority, and it was the duty of Christians to obey its laws. But the true church had a higher and more independent role in history than the state. And since the church included more than preaching, Luther's ideal church left room for active participation by the laity. Actually, most of Calvin's ecclesiastical views in this area did not contradict those of Luther.

The Lutheran Church in Germany did not fulfill many of the

possibilities that Luther's ideas suggested. The rule of the territorial princes over the church imposed upon it a high degree
of supervision and control as well as the early forms of the
absolute state. The princes gained control of the churches at the
top, though the nobility still exercised a great deal of influence
upon clerical life through its rights of patronage. With these
reservations, the church became an institution under the direction of an academically educated clerical estate. The orthodoxy
that followed Luther's era narrowed the founder's faith to a
rigid dogma in which the word of God was preserved for all
eternity. Reforming initiative was therefore prevented even in
the narrow theological sphere. Beyond the purely theological
realm, change and renewal were all but impossible. The laity
did not have a role in governing the church. The churches
played hardly any role in watching over public mores. The
schools were institutions of the state, and to the state belonged
the duty of fostering social welfare. To be sure, pastors could
awaken the consciences of princes and civil servants to these
problems, but they could not attempt to solve them by direct
church action.

Pietism broke down the fences of orthodoxy in many ways. It
freed itself from the narrowness of orthodox Lutheranism. It
played down the significance of the rigid confessional creed and
made emotional experience the touchstone of its religious view.
In this way, ideas dating from pre-Lutheran mysticism flowed
into Protestantism. At the same time, the Pietists revolted against
the institutionalized character of the Lutheran Church. They
wanted to see the Christian faith put into practice not only
by ministers, but also by every humble member of the church.
These "quiet ones in the land" desired a church that was a true
community of spiritual and practical piety. They created a new
popular and largely undogmatic literature, poetry, and music of
edification and distinguished themselves through their practical
Christian deeds in the areas of welfare and education.

Pietism did not, however, succeed in taking over the Lutheran Church and overthrowing orthodoxy. Its role was more that of a leaven in the ecclesiastical and popular life of the nation. We know of its influence upon German idealism through the lives of the great idealists. Pietism as a religious and ecclesiastical movement became partially reconciled with orthodoxy through a common hostility to the Enlightenment and later to idealism. By the beginning of the nineteenth century, Pietism and orthodoxy appeared to be almost one and the same. Yet neither Pietism nor orthodoxy were yet in any condition to roll back the steady advance of the Enlightenment in the intellectual and political life of Germany. German idealism was to accomplish this deed, but not necessarily to the good of the Lutheran Church.

In order to understand this development, we have to return to politics once more. Enlightened despotism had tended to treat the schools and churches as mere institutions of the state. The reforms brought about after 1806 perfected this policy. There are no examples of replacing the state governments of the churches by popular ecclesiastical constitutions. It is astounding that what occurred was the expansion of the government-controlled Lutheran Church organization even to churches in lands ruled by Catholic princes. Almost everywhere, autonomous ecclesiastical authorities disappeared as the churches became organs of the state bureaucracy. After 1815 the princes gave the churches a thoroughly authoritarian aspect as they themselves decided upon questions of faith and liturgy. "Throne and altar" were practically united thereafter in the history of Protestant Germany. The church, essentially restricted to the sermon, recognized obedience to the monarchical state as an important part of religious sentiment. The Protestant churches remained people's churches in the superficial sense that every subject in a Protestant state was born into one of them. In a deeper sense, however, this was not true, for the Protestant churches did not have a democratic leadership and were not dealing with the vital problems of the people, which, after all, had as much religious significance as did the theology of the confessional creed. The introduction of councils and synods in the second half of the century was a case of too little, too late. Earlier, this innovation had not been welcomed in the Reformed Churches of Germany. Wichern and his "Inner Mission" movement did not develop within the official churches, but fought them and failed to reform the churches as a whole. Nevertheless the Inner Mission, the most important lay movement in nineteenth-century German Protestantism, was an indication of the significant popular forces the Protestant churches could have mobilized.

After 1815 the Protestant churches found most of their support among the groups that were most interested in preserving traditional forms of state and economy: the nobility, the peasants, and, with less certainty, the artisans. It was only in Swabia that Pietism showed a more democratic aspect, and there only because the "good, old rights" of the various estates were still respected. It should not be overlooked that in the rural areas of Germany the local churches retained strong folk characteristics. The common prayer and bible sessions, still maintained by many Junkers and their laborers, deepened the ties between classes. It is probable that even in the First World War the Junker officer knew the common soldier (at least if he was of rural origin) better than did the bourgeois officer. Besides, the latter did not distinguish himself by any great appreciation of the emotional life of the industrial workers.

Nevertheless, the definite subordination of the Protestant churches under the various monarchical states, the limitation they put on the cultivation of the confessional creed, and the narrowing of active church membership to traditional social groups were all caused to some extent by the intellectual development of German idealism. This brings us to an area of subtle relationships which often seem paradoxical. The revival of religious feeling in Germany drew much of its strength from German idealism and its victory over mechanistic rationalism as a glance at Schleiermacher and the whole romantic school shows. We cannot say that a revival of religion in Germany would have been unthinkable without idealism, for Western Europe experienced a similar return to religion even earlier. For this reason we must look for the influence of German idealism not in the simple reassertion of religion, but in the peculiar form that this revival took on in Germany.

As we have mentioned earlier, German idealism did not have any great place for the church in its intellectual house. Ranke, for example, was a devout Christian who made the struggle between church and state as two independent authorities a focal point of his historical writing. At the same time, in his *Dialogue on Politics*, he asserted that the church unites man with a mysterious community that transcends all else. This highest community establishes an unchanging religious rule for mankind, and tries to hold off everything that might violate it. "However," he adds, "there also is the limit to her authority. In a positive way she does not have any influence on things human. Whatever degree of secular power she claims, that much she loses in spiritual power. She has no immediate connections with the institutions of the state. . . ." Ranke gives the "spirit of the church" a universal position that is beyond the concrete individual state. The idea of the state would be destroyed "if it were to include the entire world." But obviously the universal spirit of the church must not attempt to realize itself through secular means. It suffices to say that, "By nature each church claims to be the universal one." An ecumenical movement never arose in German Protestantism, and, perhaps even more surprising, there was not even a strong movement for the creation of a German national Protestant Church. For over a century, after the demise of the *corpus evangelicorum* of the Holy Roman

Empire, German Protestantism did not possess even the shadow of a common political organ.

Ranke represented his generation's more religiously inclined and pro-clerical type of German idealism. There is no special need to emphasize the contrast with Hegel. However, in the practical application of their ideas the difference between the two was not so meaningful. Even Ranke stated that, "Essentially our activity belongs chiefly to society." On the whole, though, the future generally belonged more to the type of thought about church and state that Hegel articulated. The modern age did not share Ranke's profound fear that the province of the church would be violated if men attributed "so many elements of spiritual unity" to the state and demanded from the individual such a complete devotion to it. Yet even a Schleiermacher was hardly in a position to found anew the true idea of the community of the church. Taken broadly, German idealism viewed the church as had the Enlightenment; this explains some of the sympathy that many romantics had for the Catholic Church.

III

The state's ascendancy over the church, which had been a European phenomenon since the later medieval period, was closely related to the rise of the doctrine of natural law. Obviously, the ancient theory of natural law did not take into consideration the concept of "church and state." Regardless of whether natural-law philosophy was predominantly more pantheistic or deistic, its concept of the individual endowed man with reason and the rational ability to overcome his sensuous nature. Reason is of divine origin; thus it becomes a moral commandment that man follow its dictates. The first human beings were good; that is, their reason was capable of controlling their passions. Sadly, however, this primeval idyll soon ended. Out of the temptations of the senses, rule and servitude, private property and poverty came into the world and destroyed the kingdom of equality and fraternity. Since then it has been the important task of those few who still hear the voice of divine reason to work together. The end of their efforts will be to create those institutions in state and society that subjugate the destructive powers, thereby restoring man's dignity and a unified world order of equality and fraternal freedom.

Occidental Christianity took over this doctrine of natural law in a somewhat changed form. The Christian dogma of original sin made it necessary that state and laws be seen not as works of men endowed with reason but as God's penalties for human sins. Generally, the Christian view held that the church was the interpreter of divine intentions and thus of divine justice, whose realization all political and social institutions must serve. No one disputed, however, that man himself had the ability of rationality and morality, which God had raised to a more elevated plane through the church. Thus, the ancient doctrine of natural law continued to exist throughout the Middle Ages, though on the lower level of social ethics.

The modern era brought with it a gradual renaissance of this ancient theory, adding to it and broadening it. The growth of the modern state and the weakening of the churches after the split in Christianity made secular authority visibly more independent of the decrees of the church. The state became the real bearer of rational progress. In the earlier version of this new secular doctrine of natural law, which to some extent still reflected the old concept of human sin, it was assumed that the subjects of a state had surrendered their original rights to the prince. This viewpoint shows the continued prevalence of the Christian idea of original sin and the fall from grace. In more modern versions certain rights of the subject are viewed as inalienable and specifically protected by constitutional precedent. In the end politics was based entirely upon the individual, and the sovereignty of the people was proclaimed. This whole evolution paralleled great changes in the intellectual world-view. The idea of religious tolerance was one of the strongest levers in the struggle for the establishment of constitutionally guaranteed rights. In addition, the new scientific world-view was carried over into the realm of social theory, and the individual was seen as the "atom" of the entire social process. Society, like nature, must conform to rational laws. All of this strengthened the trend toward democratic attitudes. By the same token, thoughts about the afterlife and sin tended to fade as they were replaced by optimistic ideas such as the perfectibility of man and society. This newer tradition was carried on without a break by the liberalism of nineteenth-century Western Europe.

While these events in no wise diminished the role of the state in the modern age in Western Europe, the relationship there between church and state was not to become that of Germany. The forms that the doctrine of natural law took in nineteenth-century Western Europe had many colorings. The Catholic Church continued to adhere to its modified form of the doctrine. The intellectuals, indifferent to religion, supported radically rationalistic dogmas based upon a secularized theory. Intermediate versions of the doctrine were to be found in the Protestant churches, for example, within both the High Church and the evangelical groups of the Anglican Church especially, but also in the Calvinist churches and in Methodism. All churches in Western Europe agreed, however, that political institutions should be merely the agents of a divine or natural reason. In other words, the state had no absolute moral value in itself, but was rather a tool to be used in the realization of the pragmatically reasonable moral goals of society. In contrast to Hegel, this approach held that the state was the realization of legality but not of morality. Morality must be brought into the state through the activity of its citizens or through the churches.

Given these developments, it was logical that the churches would give up most of their political rights. In the case of

America they wound up with no political privileges. The churches gained something, however, which has tended to make up for their losses: an independent role in society that has enabled them to become the leaders of new moral and political movements in the name of Christian morality. Even the Established Church of England has fought off all attempts on the part of the state to encroach upon the ecclesiastical domain. The historical importance of the modern relations between church and state in Western Europe was revealed most clearly in the case of the Methodists and related religious groups in the late eighteenth century. John Wesley and his followers succeeded in achieving a seeming rapprochement between Christianity and the new proletariat that the Industrial Revolution had begun to spawn. It has been said with justice that Wesley prevented a great social and political revolution in England by his popular and passionate methods of reconversion of the suffering masses. Another effect of Wesley's work was that nineteenth-century English social movement and Socialism never departed from the bedrock of Christian ideas. Even today pure Marxism is a relatively weak power in Britain. The fact that Sunday schools and Bible societies made such an impression upon the life of the English people in the early nineteenth century is of tremendous historical significance. The Overseas Mission and the abolitionist movement caught the imagination of the nation and demonstrated the power of voluntary Christian social action.

It is certainly true that the Anglo-Saxon churches endangered themselves by basing themselves on individual social classes and supporting the social aims of these classes. At times they became simple organs of humanitarian politics, and what Christian theology they retained often seemed to be on the verge of disappearing. On the other hand, Christianity became the true religion of the masses and maintained its influence upon all social groups, although it was weakened later in the century.

France was a somewhat different case. The Catholic Church

had been closely tied to the *ancien régime* and the Restoration, and democratic freethinkers wanted to make the cult of reason the religion of the state. This fundamental split tended to exacerbate the wounds in the social structure of the nation. France, however, was another nation in which the state was subordinate to the moral judgment of its citizens. The most important French social programs of the first half of the century, such as those of Saint-Simon and Comte, treated religion and church in the context of the social question.

It was during this same period that German idealism, particularly in its last, romantic manifestation, rejected natural law, the profane form as well as the Christian. To be sure, Christian natural law had always played a more modest role in German Lutheranism than it had in Catholicism. It is also a fact that German natural law had always appeared in an authoritarian version. From this point of view the German romantic influence upon the theory of the state and the philosophy of history represented a noticeable step in the direction of greater freedom. Generally speaking, German idealism often had a strong tinge of political liberalism, particularly in the case of Kant, and even more in that of Wilhelm von Humboldt. What is much more significant, however, is the political direction that German idealism took in the post-Kantian period. It not only rejected the democratic natural-law theory of the French Revolution, but also the more moderate constitutionalism that was typified by the English experience. The basic idea in the new German romanticism was the idea of individuality. In the place of a generally valid reason whose general laws govern and exalt the world, it put a "world spirit" which did not express itself in eternal values, but rather in history, in a variety of individualistic forms. The characteristic political view held by the German idealists was not a world of equal states that can preserve peace, but a world of different nations which live in tension and struggle. Some emphasized the slow and quiet radiation of the folk spirit [*Volksgeist*]; others, the creative genius of the great personality; still others, the revolutionary power of individual ideas. Whatever the form of expression, German idealists rejected the idea of general laws and reason.

Thus they viewed existing states not only as the real vessels of history, but also as the highest possible embodiment of the Absolute Idea in the present, not as stages in an evolution toward some ultimate moral order. To be sure, Hegel intended to save the idea of progress in history philosophically, but even in his system the dialectic of progress served only to interpret the past. The philosopher has no vision of the nature of future progress. The positive law of the individual states was thereby made absolute and could not be corrected by the application of abstract moral norms. Its validity could in the end be tested only in world power struggles. The ideal of the culture-state demands that national culture pervade the entire state. But the culture of a nation is not the equal product of all classes within the state. It is ultimately the work of genius and creative intellectuals, and of those who follow in their footsteps, the educated individuals. To transpose a saying of Hegel's, the ideal is the progress of the consciousness of freedom, understood entirely as a phenomenon of the inner growth of the personality.

Such a world-view leads to a pluralistic ethic in terms of individual development, but to no meaningful *social* ethic. Since the duty of obedience to the positive law of a state was absolute, no problems of social ethics remained. In addition, there was no longer any room for Christian charitable activity outside the realm of the state. Since the state was the highest embodiment of the social community, one could logically expect that the state would do everything within its power for the common welfare. Even if, as in the case of Schleiermacher, one adds a religious element to artistic and intellectual education, the result remains essentially individualistic. For Schleiermacher, too, the church was a union composed of individuals. It became a congregation only in the sense that all of its members sat at the feet of the same pastor. The same aristocratic concept of culture that animated German idealism was also noticeable in liberal theology.

IV

The pronounced aristocratic character of German idealism not only prevented the German educated classes from assuming a fully committed role in terms of social problems but also, in the purely intellectual realm, shifted the relationship between religion and intellect. With very few exceptions the Lutheran Church had equated religion with the acknowledgment of the literal truth of its confession. If religion was to be grasped in such a cerebral manner, the next logical step would be to ask whether it was not merely a backward aspect of philosophy, lacking the clear and valid view of the truth that pure philosophy might offer. As early as Hegel we see the idea that the man of culture would have to progress from the mere "representation" that was religion to the logical "notion" that was philosophy. Others, echoing Goethe's "these realms are a closed book to us," went even further and abandoned both religion and philosophy in favor of a purely aesthetic culture. In this way the deep split between the mainstream of German culture and the churches became irrevocable. There is no question that the authoritarian constitution of the Protestant churches contributed mightily to this outcome. When we note, however, that these churches kept the allegiance of the traditionalistic, though not of the educated, classes, we must look back to the very nature of German idealism for an explanation. The predominantly intellectual and aesthetic character of German idealism stood for the concept of an individualistic culture based on the inner personality of man. It was thus as far removed from the life of the various German classes desirous of participating in the community as was the upper-echelon civil servant from a mere underling.

This is not to say that all educated people rejected the churches. The theological students of Kant, Hegel, and Schleiermacher struggled to build a synthesis of Christian faith and German idealist culture which they hoped would appeal even to the most aesthetic and idealistic heirs of Goethe and Schiller. But although liberal theology was to make unforgettable contributions to understanding the nature of religion, particularly in historical research, it failed to overcome the cleavage between the churches and the educated class, whose members, if not satisfied with an individualistic cultivation of science and art, served the state with devotion, for they saw their social ideas become reality under its aegis. One of the major reproaches these intellectuals began to hurl at the churches was that confessional differences had hindered the development of a uniform national spirit. The Wartburg Festival of 1817 represented an early effort to create a common religious expression for the German national spirit, and many attempts to found a "national religion" occurred thereafter. These were strange artificial counterparts to the French attempt at a religion of reason, which the Germans had ridiculed.

A glance at the Catholic Church in the nineteenth century shows clearly the historical tasks that Protestantism was not able to solve. One would suppose that the Catholic Church had been deeply wounded in Germany by the loss of its traditional forms of organization during the Napoleonic period. Its close ties with the nobility were compromising. Furthermore, the biting attacks of the Enlightenment had been aimed more at Catholicism than at Protestantism. The new age of nationalism seemed to endanger a universal church particularly. Yet despite all these threats and conflicts, a renewed Catholic Church was able to secure a strong place for itself in the nineteenth century, revealing a truly extraordinary ability for social and political integration. The first half of the nineteenth century saw the Catholic Church undergo a profound transformation. At first this internal revolution went on almost unnoticed. Outwardly the church appeared to be working hand in glove not only with conservatives but even with reactionary forces, though its hierarchical and universal order always guaranteed it a certain freedom from state control. Within the church, however, a far-reaching social democratization was occurring. A new type of priest emerged, one who was no longer tied mainly to the nobility, which before 1815 had been interested chiefly in directing the secular role of the German church. The end of the ecclesiastical principalities was a blessing for the church, for it could now choose its clergy from all classes and thereby transcended what remained the norm in the socially narrower Protestant clergy. Just as the split between culture and religion was not as pronounced in the Catholic Church, so its roots went deeper and more broadly into the life of the people. The Catholic Church had obviously never given up its claim to be the judge of the political and social policies of secular states. Now it was more capable than ever of inaugurating, or at least tolerating, social action and policy, on the practical as well as the theoretical level. The unity of the majority of Catholics from all classes in Germany gave the church its political strength. Later on, this Catholic unity would include large numbers of the working class, as Germany became ever more industrialized in an age of fully developed capitalism.

German Protestantism and the German idealism that grew on its soil were not capable of achieving such heights of social integration. They were intellectually and socially divided among themselves and unprepared to absorb new class tendencies or give them an independent direction and meaning. It is not surprising that all attempts to found a Christian Socialist movement in Germany failed, or that it was Karl Marx who gave an ideology to the German workers' movement. Marx based much of his work upon French and English sociology and economics and thus owed something to the Western European tradition of natural law. The style and direction of his philosophy, however, cannot be grasped unless one realizes how much Marx owed to the social and intellectual influence of German idealism.

The oft-repeated assertion of Marx and Engels that German Socialism "is child and heir of German idealistic philosophy" is true in many ways, no matter how unpleasant this sounds to many. Above all, Marx agreed with German idealism's belief about the highest cultural values for man. The absolute ideal for both was the free realization of the intellectual and affective strength of man through the autonomous development of personality. For this reason the concept of "progress in consciousness of freedom" was for Marx the real goal of knowledge and education. Marx differentiated himself most clearly from German idealism in believing that man's consciousness is devoid of freedom so long as the economic mode of production is determined by a ruling class, and that only the destruction of a class society by the proletariat will provide the opportunity for the intellectual autonomy and freedom of the human personality. The means of production must be transformed from tools of class domination into tools for the common welfare. While the messianic expectations of Marxism are completely rooted in the tradition of German idealism, Marx's theory of history differs radically.

Pushing the goal of history into the future did not mean the denial of the immanent necessity of past history, but the latter appears imperfect, or at least unfinished. The philosopher and historian must not be content quietly to contemplate the past and the present but must help lead them to their ideal goal. Thus, historical materialism also became a guide and goad to revolutionary strategy. The doctrines of historical materialism (which in its origins was not philosophical naturalism, though the later Engels began to turn it into such) were prepared in many particulars by idealism. Idealism had already done much to replace religion with philosophy and had in its philosophy of history viewed the historical religions as mere expressions of different cultures and periods. Nor did it rebel against the authoritarian state's using the existing churches as institutes for the preservation of obedience to the state among its people. When Marx began his programmatic battle against the authoritarian state, he immediately directed his fire at the churches as well. His dictum, that religion is a private matter for the individual to decide, is proof of this.

Marx's struggle, however, became a total conflict with the state as a whole, and in Germany this meant the culture-state, the state founded upon law, and the state based on power. Marx's concept of power was highly ambivalent. Power over other human beings was evil and would have to be stamped out. At the same time, however, in order to accomplish the desired goals of history, which consisted in brotherly love and world peace, the most unscrupulous use of force was necessary. Up to this point Marx, as the leader of the revolution, remained a Hegelian. As a prophet of the blissful end of history he was a pacifist, a man who foresaw the withering away of the power-state together with the authoritarian state. Marx could not accept the idea of a state based upon law and culture in the strict sense. For Marx, law was always the expression of the ruling classes, and the culture of the bourgeois society was not the true expression of a free spirit but merely an ideology. True justice and autonomy of culture can blossom only when the state as we have known it has been abolished and the rule of the proletariat has been secured. Marx talks about society, but he does so as one might speak of a church with all attendant attributes. It is the common consciousness of a class that will bring it to life.

When Marx was developing the fundamentals of his philosophy of history and his theory of society in the 1840's, in which he already placed his faith in the industrial workers as a revolutionary class, Germany was still a predominantly agrarian country. The proletariat played but a small role in the revolution of 1848–49. But Marx proved correct in his assumption that a future German proletariat would hold high the banner of his ideas. He could justify his expectation simply by the assumption that in his theoretical program the industrial proletariat gained the self-consciousness of its economic and social position. But even if we grant that there is a certain natural affinity between the social aspirations of this class and its Socialist demands, there is still reason to doubt that Marxism was the predetermined reaction of the working class. The example of America illustrates this point. Here was a land that never knew feudalism and therefore possessed almost limitless potentialities of social expansion within a libertarian and egalitarian system. It demonstrated that many different historical causes have determined the direction of social movement. Likewise, the development of the working classes in England and even France did not dispose them to be particularly inclined toward Marxism. Even in Germany the policies of the trade unions and of the Catholic working class show that Marxism was far from the predetermined expression of the feeling of the masses.

If Karl Marx dominated the German proletariat's struggle to so great an extent, the reasons for this are to be found in the peculiar social and intellectual history of Germany. The constitution of the workers' movement as a class party apart from other political and intellectual groupings consummated the inner split in the German nation, the inheritance of the authoritarian German power-state. German idealism lacked the strength and will to overcome this baneful inheritance. Idealism on its part had been the product of a specific social setting which it never completely overcame. Its rejection of natural law and its simultaneous neglect of the church endowed the bureaucratic and military state with a nimbus which not only furthered the pursuit of power politics but also made the integration of the old and new German social classes well nigh impossible. As Germany entered the new age of nationalistic state building and industrial capitalism after 1848, it was divided in more than a superficial political sense in its fundamental thinking on subjects such as church and state, intellect and society, universal humanity and nation. This intellectual outlook hardened class conflicts instead of abolishing or at least toning them down.

When Ranke published his *History of England* in 1859 he wrote that a French historian—he was referring to Guizot—would have put the major emphasis in such a work upon the constitutional viewpoint and "would have sought a guide or model for a political doctrine." "Germans on the other hand will attempt . . . to grasp an event in its political and religious totality as well as its universal historical relationships." It is no doubt true that Germany could have well used a Guizot and a Tocqueville alongside Ranke, but it is also a fact that Ranke did more than transcend the purely national viewpoint in his concept of world history. He was also conscious of the religious substance of political decisions. In all of this, however —and here he was not without blame—Ranke did not greatly influence his immediate successors. In the year 1859, Germans were no longer speaking of any "political and religious totality." They were now talking about *Realpolitik*.

II   BISMARCK'S REALPOLITIK

IN VIEW of the close connection of Bismarck's work with the rise
and defeat of Germany as a world power and, even more
important, with Europe's loss of leadership in world affairs,
it is not surprising that even sixty years after his death the
figure of the German chancellor has remained shrouded in controversies.[1] These controversies cannot be easily settled, but
we cannot hope for progress as long as we do not clearly define
the historical ideas and the political and social movements that
molded his nature and the configuration of objective historical
powers in which he acted. Bismarck has often been described,
particularly by German writers, as a man who was not truly
a member of his own age, but rather belonged to an earlier
historic age if not to a timeless age of heroes.[2] Foreign students
have been inclined to neglect the time-bound conditions of his
growth, with the result that he has appeared more modern
than he was.

Obviously it is quite impossible to place Bismarck outside
the century on the political fortunes of which he had a greater
impact than almost any other person. At the same time, uniquely
personal as his historical role was, Bismarck was to some extent
the beneficiary of prior historic decisions. If it seemed in the
early part of the nineteenth century that liberalism might
steadily spread from Western to Central Europe, the success of
Bismarck's policies in the 1860's brought this movement to a
standstill. But the weakness of the forces of liberalism in Central
Europe had already been revealed by the course of the revolu-

tions of 1848–49, and some effective methods for subverting
liberalism had been practiced by Louis Bonaparte and Prince
Felix Schwarzenberg at a time when Bismarck was still in a
largely meditative stage of his career.

In a famous letter to Leopold von Gerlach, Bismarck expressed his belief that "nobody ever loses the stamp which the
age of youthful impressions has imposed on him,"[3] and he dis-
tanced himself from the older man who had formed his ideals
during the war of liberation from Napoleon. Friedrich Meinecke
already had called attention[4] to the relatively cool attitude which
Bismarck always displayed with regard to the period of Prussian reform and liberation. To be sure, the struggle against
foreign domination seemed to him a worthy cause, but he
denied that the simultaneous attempt of the Prussian reformers
to establish an ideal German state had made an essential contribution to eventual liberation. The philosophical idealism of
the age of Kant, Fichte, and Schleiermacher, in which a Stein,
Humboldt, Scharnhorst, Gneisenau, and Boyen had found the
expression of their own ideal longings, was alien to Bismarck.

Bismarck grew up when German philosophy of the classic
age ceased to satisfy the hearts of the young. In the years after
1815, German philosophy had grown more scholastic, and the
deep human experiences which had once led to its creation
were largely hidden under a crust of abstract logical thought.
The generation which began to take the stage after 1835, the
year in which David Friedrich Strauss published his *Life of
Jesus,* criticized idealism for its failure to understand the new
reality and to give a positive direction to life. Strauss, and those
after him, Ludwig Feuerbach, Bruno Bauer, and Karl Marx,
all manifested the gathering trend toward realism, which with
these young Hegelians, however, assumed at first an even more
intensely rationalistic tinge than with the old Hegel.

It was this rationalism that Bismarck resented. As a youth he
had received religious instruction from Schleiermacher, the warm-

hearted philosopher and patriotic preacher whose vindication of religion and emphasis on sentiment and feeling had meant to an earlier generation the release from the exclusive rule of reason. Bismarck discovered in Schleiermacher's teachings only an intellectualistic pantheism, which he proceeded to combine with a skepticism that denied the possibility of any human knowledge of God's plan of the world and of the place of the individual in it. This agnosticism, which according to Bismarck derived chiefly from Spinoza and the Stoics, always welled up as one important element in Bismarck's thinking, and particularly in his late years.

Bismarck's search for the concrete beauty of life never fully relieved the boredom and melancholy that his skepticism produced. He was always close to nature. His wide readings in German classic literature and most of all in Shakespeare, as well as the music of Beethoven, gave his imaginative mind models of heroic men and great tragic situations. Shakespeare had been declared the poetic genius by Herder and the young Goethe. Bismarck fully accepted the modern German outlook that originated with the literary revolution of *Sturm und Drang*. He desired passion and sentiment, and therefore found much of the work of the romantic writers to his liking. Yet it was not the romanticism which looked for an escape from reality into a realm of artificial beauty or of religion that attracted him, but those romantic efforts that led to a clearer grasp of reality. Through its devotion to the unique value of individuality, romanticism, indeed, prepared the ground for a more realistic study of the world, as the growth of modern historical studies in Germany showed. With sharp and piercing eyes the young Bismarck looked around in his own personal world and early revealed an extraordinary gift for literary narration and characterization.

In the school of romanticism the cult of personality flourished to excess, and in this respect also Bismarck was a true child of his age. For some time Byron was dearer to him than Shakespeare. The young Bismarck gave free reign to his pugnaciousness in dozens of duels, and he plunged headlong into stormy love affairs. Eventually he refused to enter, as a Prussian of his class was expected to do, the government services or make the army his career. "I do not like superiors," he exclaimed, and another time, "I want to make music as I like it or not at all." Thus he withdrew to the family estates, which he managed very effectively. But only part of his energies were engaged. There was time left to resume the search for the meaning of life, and even more to parade his self-confidence before the neighbors by audacious acts of sportsmanship or by extravagant pranks. The unbridled cult of individuality was threatening to corrode any serious purpose of his existence. It was his conversion to a positive theistic Christian view and his marriage, in 1847, that ended this period in the life of the "mad Junker," as he had been called.

Bismarck's religious conversion has been much studied.[5] Practically no one has questioned the sincerity of his religious feelings, though many have pointed out that Bismarck's adoption of a theistic faith was closely related to his wish to be accepted by his devout future bride and her Pietistic family. The sudden death of a close friend, Marie von Blankenburg, and the love for her friend Johanna von Puttkamer naturally gave his questions about life a new urgency, and the religion of his friends made a serious impression on him. Still, there was a strong voluntaristic side to Bismarck's decision. By embracing a personal God he set an end to his drifting in doubts. At the same time his marriage gave him a firm anchorage in Prussian society, in which he had his natural roots, but from which so far he had longed to flee into a world of free and heroic action. Together with his pantheism he dismissed what he occasionally called his republicanism. In the same breath he won a wife and a religious and political faith. He had chosen his fundamental position when a little later the revolution drew him into the political arena, first as a parliamentarian, subsequently as a diplomat, and finally as a minister of state.

Yet before appraising his statecraft we must stress that Bismarck did not become a Pietist in 1847. He placed his trust in a personal God, whom he accepted as the creator and king of the universe, but he obviously cared little for Christian dogmas. He prayed to God, whose ways he considered unfathomable and whom he did not think to move by his prayer. But he said—probably unaware that the words could be found in Schleiermacher's *Glaubenslehre*[6]—that the usefulness of prayer lay in submission to a strong power. His new belief in a personal God was actually still compatible with much of Bismarck's original skepticism. Though less general, it was almost as subjective as his earlier notions. As a matter of fact, in his later years he seems to have moved even closer to his early ideas.

It was probably impossible in nineteenth-century German Protestantism to find any conception of the Christian church as a divinely ordained community which possessed a moral authority independent of the state.[7] The Protestant churches were essentially state-controlled institutes for preaching. The Pietists were critics of this state-system and often opposed to ministers. But all they could do was to form small conventicles such as those in which Bismarck had come in contact with Pietistic orthodoxy. Bismarck never cultivated any group worship after his conversion and favored the state-church, though he himself, as he put it, did not wish to be "edified by mouth of ministers." Yet since he suspected ministers of being desirous of power, he preferred having them under the supervision of the state. Another observation can be made. The new faith helped to give Bismarck's whole thinking a firm orientation. It also made him act not only with greater determination but also with a heightened sense of moral responsibility. Yet it did not change his relations with his fellow-men. He remained the cavalier,

normally polite to his equals, well-mannered and benevolent
even to members of the lesser classes, but on the other hand
reckless in forcing people to serve him or humiliating them if
they refused, or were suspected of refusing, cooperation. The
man who lay awake whole nights "hating," who could perhaps
forget but not forgive—all this according to his own testimony
—had not through his conversion become a new man.

Friedrich Meinecke has suggested that the decline of German
idealism in the 1830's might be responsible for Bismarck's
turning away from idealism to orthodoxy and thereby from
liberalism to conservatism.[8] He thought that if Bismarck had
found a philosophy which would have answered the burning
questions of his personal growth, he might have become a more
liberal statesman like Cavour. Although I agree with Meinecke
that the formation of Bismarck's personal convictions cannot be
explained outside of his age, the question raised by Meinecke
defies a solution because it is impossible to visualize different
historical circumstances while assuming that the person involved
would remain the same. Bismarck actually absorbed certain
influences of German idealism, and the subjective and voluntaristic religion which he adopted was clearly "post-idealistic,"
but the liberal and humanitarian elements of the classic German philosophy found no response in him.

In 1838 the young Gladstone wrote his first book in which he
pleaded for the closest relation between church and state.[9]
Without a sanctifying principle, he argued, the state would
become a mere machine with no other function than that of
registering and executing opinions of the popular will like the
hands of a clock. Gladstone was then still an ardent Tory,
and his theses were warmly applauded by Friedrich Wilhelm
IV of Prussia and his conservative friends. It is well known how
greatly Gladstone's political views changed in his later years,
when he became a liberal out of Christian convictions. But as
little as he gave up his Christian belief did he deviate from

his early demand that creative politics called for "sanctifying principles." Bismarck saw in Gladstone more than in any other statesman on the contemporary European scene his ideological opposite. He was wrong, however, in asserting that Gladstone —or, as he labeled him with one of his strongest vituperative expressions,[10] *"Professor"* Gladstone—was ruining England, nor could he know that a Gladstonean Professor Wilson was destined to become the foremost destroyer of the German monarchy.

What made Bismarck a fiery enemy of Gladstone was both Gladstone's liberalism and his insistence on a Christian program in politics. Bismarck soon parted company with his early conservative associates, the members of the so-called Christian Germanic circle,[11] with regard to the application of Christian principles to practical politics. In Bismarck's view, the world and its orders were created by God and the course of history directed by Him. The existing political institutions, consequently, were not made by men nor could they be altered by ideal constructions of human reason, as the liberals proposed. But the concrete plan of God was unknown to man, except that it was clear that in all history the decisions had been reached by power used for selfish interests, and that this *raison d'état* could be studied and acted upon. This nature of the political life of the world was to him divinely instituted and, therefore, essentially immutable, although life was a continuous conflict and struggle. To hope that men could change the nature of politics would be sinfully arrogant and would mean to meddle in divine government. The statesman might gain, however, at rare moments a fleeting adumbration of divine action on a higher plane.

These ideas excluded the possibility of Christianizing the state and the international life. There was no ideal state, let alone an ideal international order, but only the concrete order of history which demanded from everybody obedience to the positive law. The Bismarckian attitude has been called Lutheran

by historical students of Bismarck, and it is quite true that his
political conceptions showed the earmarks of the political thinking that had developed in German Lutheranism. But it would
be erroneous to assume that Bismarck's and Luther's opinions
were identical.[12] The world of states was for Luther not the
arena for the realization of the Kingdom of God. Luther admitted
that statecraft required special political knowledge though to
him this was not identical with the *raison d'état*. And while
Luther did not believe that the state as such was a Christian
institution, he considered it the duty of every individual Christian
to assert within the public life a special moral attitude derived
from his Christian faith. In this respect Bismarck's early conservative companions, particularly Friedrich Julius Stahl, were
closer to Luther than Bismarck.

But Bismarck did not deny that at least the statesman himself,
if he was a Christian, was bound by certain specific principles.
The exercise of power was not to aim at personal ends but was
a calling to preserve the natural order of things and to serve
the state. No doubt, these were important moral restraints which
reflected genuine ideas of Luther, though in somewhat weaker
fashion. Luther justified war only in self-defense and recommended that Christian princes should rather suffer some occasional injustice and forget about their own "reputation" than
go to a war that would bring calamitous suffering to their
people. Bismarck repeatedly condemned preventive wars and
never accepted war lightheartedly, but he did accept it as a
means for accomplishing his political aims. Also, he ruled out
wars for prestige, but not for the honor of the state.

The outlook on life and history with which Bismarck entered
politics endowed the prevailing political conditions of Prussia
with an aura of sanctity. Not only the monarchy but also the
traditional class society of Prussia, with the Junker estate as the
dominant social group, was in his eyes the God-willed order of
things, and its maintenance by all means of political cunning

the unquestionable duty of the statesman. Liberalism, which for him comprised every movement derived from the ideas of the American and French Revolutions, was the sworn enemy of a healthy political life, since it attempted to replace historically developed forms of life by an arbitrary system of man-made institutions. In Bismarck's thought any kind of liberalism was bound to lead to government by parties, and this weakening of the authority of the state would bring forth the chaos of a social republic, from which a people could be freed only by a regime of fire and sword. On the other hand, a regime of naked force was disliked by Bismarck, although many governmental measures which he recommended or adopted were of highly doubtful legality. He was not even a champion of an unrestricted absolute monarchy. He objected to the suppression of the independent rights of the nobility by rulers. Moreover, absolutism fed that "boa constrictor," bureaucracy, which was tyrannical but at the same time a breeding ground of liberal notions.

These Bismarckian conceptions might have made this Junker a radical reactionary after the breakdown of the German revolution, radical to the extent of demanding the suppression of those moderate German-national and liberal trends that had existed in Prussia before 1848, and even more of the concessions made during the revolution, of which the Prussian constitution of 1850 was the most important grant. But in spite of his brazenly contemptuous attitude toward democracy and liberalism during the revolution, Bismarck was not found among the extreme die-hards in the 1850's. A parliament, in particular, seemed to offer many potential advantages. Through it the conservatives could assert their views—if need be even against crown and bureaucracy—and Bismarck never forgot that the king had faltered in the early months of the revolution. But the chief value of a parliament was the chance it provided for entering into a contest with the liberal forces. Bismarck realized that these forces could not be conquered by mere repression and that the ideological errors and the political futility of modern democracy would have to be shown up by word and deed.

While Bismarck, therefore, accepted a parliament, he remained a deadly foe of parliamentary government. The monarchical government was always to retain a basis of power of its own and for this reason never surrender its exclusive control of the army and foreign affairs. During the revolution of 1848–49 Bismarck had seen that the Austrian and Prussian monarchies recovered their strength because their armies remained loyal to the dynastic cause. He had also observed the weaknesses in German liberalism, how the fear of social revolution had impaired its aggressive spirit, how the political moderates and radicals had divided, and how the ideas about the forms of the desired national union, *gross-deutsch* vs. *klein-deutsch*, had produced further splits in German liberalism. He had also noticed that the social and economic program of the liberals failed to keep its early large following united, and that individual groups could be bought rather cheaply by the old governments. It had not escaped his attention that the majority of the German people, especially the peasant and working classes, were still politically quiescent and that it might be feasible to mobilize them for the support of monarchical government, as Louis Bonaparte had done.

These were Bismarck's formative experiences as he rose to become the leading statesman of the Prussian state. His supreme goal was and remained the preservation and the elevation of the Prussian military monarchy. He was convinced that the power of Prussia in Germany and Europe could be enhanced once her policies were freed from the shackles which the Christian principles of the old conservatism imposed. This applied not only to foreign affairs but also to domestic politics. As long as the sanction of force remained firmly in the hands of a sovereign king, he saw no danger in adopting some of the aims of what he called "the revolution." Jacob Burckhardt proved his gift of divination when, in 1872, he wrote in a letter to a friend: "Bismarck took only into his own hands what would have happened eventually, albeit without him and against him. He saw that the growing democratic social tide would somehow produce a state of absolute violence. . . . Said he: 'I shall do it myself,' and conducted the three wars of 1864, 1866, and 1870."[13]

"Only the kings make revolution in Prussia," Bismarck once said to Napoleon III,[14] and on this premise he was willing to play with the devil. He felt strong enough to see to it that "God will remain master in the house and the devil can only show himself in the entrance hall, even though he may sometimes pretend there to be the lord."[15] These words of Bismarck revealed the springs of his political actions. He freely cooperated in the diplomatic field not only with governments of revolutionary origins, if this seemed advantageous to him, but equally with revolutionary forces at home. The principle of legitimate monarchy was boldly violated by him when he dispossessed the dynasties of Hanover, Hesse-Kassel, and Nassau, in 1866, and introduced Bonapartist devices such as universal suffrage into German politics. The most crucial issue was the problem of nationalism. Bismarck's Prussian patriotism originally far outweighed his German-national sentiments. Nationalism to him smelled too much of the democratic *volonté générale* and he saw the political world grounded on historic states. But German unification offered the greatest single opportunity for the growth of Prussian power; it could not be achieved without some cooperation with the popular national movement, which might imperil the monarchical structure of the Prussian state. Only insofar as national unification could be accomplished without subordinating the Prussian crown to the rule of parties did it become a practical policy. On the other hand, if the royal government succeeded in fulfilling the national dream which the German liberals had failed to realize in 1848–49, the national principle would strengthen conservatism, and liberalism would lose its appeal.

The political order that Bismarck created in Germany fully confirmed these fundamental thoughts and convictions. The new German Empire was built on the balance of a union of the German princes and states, represented in the chief federal organ, the Bundesrat, or Federal Council, on the one side, and the popular national movement represented in the Reichstag on the other. The Prussian government was still in undisputed control of the royal army and of the conduct of foreign policy; besides, it was capable of manipulating the balance between the German princes and the parties. In the decade after 1866 Bismarck leaned heavily on the largest political party, the Liberal Party, because he was apprehensive of the attitude of the non-Prussian particularist forces and equally of the fierce opposition of his former friends, the Prussian conservatives, to which he was exposed in this period. In order to gain the support of the liberals Bismarck made very important concessions not only in economic policy but also in the establishment of fundamental political institutions. But in the management of military and foreign affairs he brooked no interference with the absolute prerogatives of the crown. When he gained the impression that liberals might eventually gather sufficient strength to impose parliamentary government, he broke up the Liberal Party by buying the continued backing of the right wing with the gift of industrial protection and maneuvering the remaining left liberals into a forlorn opposition.

After 1878 the balance between the particularist and the nationalist forces was shifted. The states as represented in the Bundesrat as well as the Prussian government were used as a shield to stop the further development of the central parliament. The coalition with the Prussian conservatives was thus restored and was cemented by the grant of protective import duties on agrarian products. After 1878 Bismarck also began to relax in the war which he had conducted against the Center Party in the years after 1872. Since the political movement of German Catholicism was linked up with the particularist forces and could rely on an autonomous and universal authority, the Roman Catholic Church, he had fought both the political aspirations of the German Catholics and the claims of the Roman Church. A compromise over state-church relations was developed in the course of the 1880's, and though the German government and the Center Party continued to look at each other with deep distrust, they cooperated in a good many political actions.

After national unification had been achieved, Bismarck was quick to brand everybody who opposed or criticized the new constitutional order an unpatriotic citizen, or as he expressed it, a *Reichsfeind*. While the leaders of the center remained at least under the suspicion of being "enemies of the Empire" and the left liberals remained marked men, Bismarck saw the chief danger for the Empire after 1878 in the growing working-class movement. To be sure, he met it not only by repressive measures against the Social Democratic Party but also by legislation that aimed at the alleviation of the conditions of the industrial worker. But when these positive social policies, which were conceived in a paternalistic spirit, failed to produce immediate results, he prepared for a showdown with the Social Democrats in 1890. In the expectation that the Reichstag might make the suppression of the Social Democratic Party impossible, Bismarck began to consider concrete plans for a *coup d'état* which was intended to create a docile federal parliament.[16] German constitutionalism was certainly on unsafe grounds, and Max Weber's description of the Bismarckian system as "pseudo-constitutionalism" seems historically correct.

Bismarck's fall in 1890 was connected with these issues, though it was essentially caused by the desire of Wilhelm II to rule by himself. By one simple stroke the young emperor was able to remove not only the founder of the Empire but also with him the leading role of the ministers, which Bismarck had considered necessary for the formulation of prudent policies in a modern monarchy. But he had overrated his personal capacity for keeping the trust of the monarch and never contemplated the problem of his succession earnestly enough. In the years after his dismissal Bismarck began to clamor for the strengthening of the parliament which, while in power, he had done his best to make impotent. Another major weakness of his policies became apparent only in the era of Wilhelm II. As mentioned before, Bismarck deeply resented the power of bureaucracy in government. He saw in bureaucracy a force that tended to disregard traditional class lines and regional differences in the light of a concept of law applicable to every citizen of the state. Actually, Bismarck's semi-absolutist state could not have existed without a bureaucracy, and the extension of governmental functions to many new fields in the absence of a marked increase of self-government was bound to proliferate bureaucratic rule. Bismarck's critical attitude toward bureaucracy resulted merely in the weeding out of men of liberal character, and the personal regime of Wilhelm II inherited a civil service of unusually servile and spineless behavior. Bismarck himself knew quite clearly the foundation of power on which he had placed the Prussian kings. At the last meeting with Wilhelm II in 1897 the old man remarked, pointing to the military officers of the imperial entourage, that the emperor would be able to act as he pleased just as long as he had such an officer corps behind him.[17] Indeed, the Empire of Bismarck and Wilhelm II collapsed only when the German army was defeated.

Bismarck's statecraft was called *Realpolitik*[18] already by his contemporaries, particularly by those German liberals who after 1866 were eager to make their peace with Bismarck even if this implied the abandonment of most of their political faith. There was great comfort in having been shown wrong not by a straight-line conservative partisan but by a man above ideologies. Bismarck himself promoted such sentiments. He was quite sincere when he made many confessions like the following: "If I had to go through life with principles, I would feel as though I had to walk a narrow path in the woods and had to carry a long pole in my mouth." He never tired of emphasizing that the statesman could not impose his will on the course of history, but that on the contrary the general developments forced his hands. Realistic observation of existing political conditions and the ability to wait for the right moment of intervention were absolute prerequisites of any political action. Moreover, since the counteraction of others and the fluctuating configuration of political forces could never be predicted with certainty, it was always advisable to hold more than one policy ready in order to be prepared for shifting circumstances.

Bismarck possessed the ability of keeping two or more irons in the fire as well as an acute sense of timing, and he was masterly in recognizing and analyzing the power factors of any given situation. He was profoundly conscious of the fact that the political craft was "the art of the possible." This goes far to explain his great success as a statesman, but it does not explain the character of his policies. Bismarck was not a mere opportunist who simply responded to events as they unfolded. It is quite wrong to assume that he had a fully developed plan of German unification, roughly identical with his subsequent policies, when he became Prussian prime minister in 1862. Actually he considered various solutions as late as 1866, and he hesitated for a long time to play for the high stakes which were involved in the war with Austria. But all his policies, the ones contemplated and the ones enacted, had their general unity and ultimate purpose in firm principles which were to him unchangeable ideals. While he denied any human capacity to improve the nature of politics by the application of Christian or liberal ideas, he believed religiously in the duty of the statesman to conserve a state independent of popular forces.

Bismarck applied these principles not only to national but also to international policies. In the preservation of the Hapsburg monarchy as a great power after Sadowa and the close cooperation with Russia, it was his chief objective to stem the progress of the movement of nationalities in Eastern Europe.[19] He was afraid that these national states would be of revolutionary character. The existence of the three historic empires seemed to him also a necessity for the maintenance of peace in Europe. Under parliamentary government a stable foreign policy was continuously imperiled by shifting majorities. But the three emperors still held full control over foreign and military affairs. To bring them into a lasting league was the chief endeavor of Bismarck after 1871, and perhaps already after 1866.[20] In the chapter of his memoirs in which he epitomizes the intention of his policy of alliances, he describes his attempt to build a league of the three emperors as having been motivated by the expectation of an imminent struggle between the two European movements, named by Napoleon the Republican and the Cossack parties. He goes on to say that he would rather describe them in present-day terms as "the system of order on a monarchical basis in opposition to the social republic into which the anti-monarchical movement, slowly or by leaps, usually sinks."[21]

The historian can point out that successful as Bismarck's diplomacy was up to 1890, it did not solve all the problems of the future. Monarchical succession may produce even greater freakishness than varying parliamentary majorities. As a matter of fact, diplomatic relations between Germany and Russia grew more difficult under Alexander III than they had been under Alexander II, and the rising Pan-Slavism was having greater influence on the decisions of the czarist regime in foreign affairs. In

Austria-Hungary the imperial government proved powerless to check the continuous growth of national movements. Bismarck, although not unaware of the developments in Russia and Austria-Hungary, tended rather to minimize their significance. He persuaded himself too easily that the Austrian monarchy still had the power, through a *coup d'état*, to curb the nationalities by abrogating the constitutional rights which it had conceded after 1861. These were signs that his diplomatic aims rested not only on the realistic appraisal of events but also on strong political convictions.

In contrast to classical liberalism Bismarck did not conceive of the state as the representative of the nation. Nor did he follow Hegel, who accepted absolutist governments but saw in the state the embodiment of a national culture. This view presupposed at the very least some causal interaction between the progress of a national civilization and the life of the state. Bismarck's concept of the state excluded all forces which might interfere with the independent authority vested in the king. The state was for him identical with the monarch and those men needed to maintain and exercise his sovereignty, primarily the noblemen serving in the king's army and councils. Such an authoritarian political philosophy could gain popular support as long as the churches preached obedience to the established social and political order and the people readily accepted Christian teachings. But the Roman Catholic social theory, though anti-revolutionary, was far from anti-critical, and vis-à-vis the Prussian monarchy the German Catholics had good reasons to keep a reserved attitude even before the *Kulturkampf*. The Protestant churches, on the other hand, had lost their hold over the German urban population.

Bismarck's theory of state and government was ill-suited to serve as the political creed of the non-Prussian groups included in the new Empire, and even less of the new classes which the modern industrial expansion created. Bismarck himself was in-

capable of understanding the yearnings for a higher human
dignity which expressed themselves in liberalism and social
democracy as well as in the political ideas of German Catholicism. To him all these political theories were subversive. He
denied to the parties any participation in the government and
kept them divided among themselves by fomenting antagonism
over economic interests. The founder of the unified Empire
failed to unify the people. Bismarck knew about this lack of
integration. Conscious of the need for mass support he turned
to nationalism. In a letter written to Prince Wilhelm half a
year before the latter's accession to the imperial throne, he said:
"The national idea is stronger than the Christian idea, even
among Social Democrats and other democrats, maybe not in
the country, but in the cities."[22] From 1871 on, Bismarck
used increasingly national tones in his public utterances.[23] He
did not use the language of liberal nationalism but liked to
talk of the perennial qualities of the German race which he discovered in all of German history and Teutonic prehistory.[24]
Here it was demonstrated that the Germans had always prospered when they followed their kings and exhibited their best
virtues, such as supreme bravery, to support their leaders. There
was also the reverse side, the stories about the endemic party
spirit that every so often had spelled disaster to the nation.
Bismarck was far removed from the biological materialism of
the National Socialist racial theory. He drew distinctions between "masculine" and "feminine" races and asserted that the
best people were those produced from a mixture of the two.
Happily, the Prussians, with their strong Slav admixture, fitted
into such a pattern. Also Bismarck's anti-Semitism was rather
undogmatic and derived largely from class-consciousness and
Christian antipathy. Yet he was already affected by the new
naturalism or Social Darwinism when he described the world
of political power as mirroring nature, in which eternal war
went on among lower and higher animals and the stronger

prevailed. Ernst Troeltsch has shown how easily such naturalistic views could be grafted on the social teachings of Lutheranism.[25] Lutheranism declared it to be the divine will that governmental authority in this world had to rest on power and since the individual had no recourse from the abuse of power to ethical principles, it was tempting to describe secular history in naturalistic terms.

Thus the lack of political ideas on which the loyalties of the large masses of the modern age might have been built aided the promotion of political ideologies, ideologies which did not represent the full scope of Bismarck's thinking. A new German generation was quick to fasten upon the nationalist ideas of Bismarck and expand on them. At the same time a legendary Bismarck grew up and was immortalized in the innumerable statues of him, erected between 1890 and 1914 on German city squares and hill sites. In these monuments Bismarck appears as the fearless military Empire builder and stony Teutonic hero, but they reveal nothing of the spiritual German heritage which helped to form his personality.

III MOLTKE AND SCHLIEFFEN

———◆———

I

FOR HALF a century after the peace of Vienna, Prussia abstained from active participation in European wars. When in the sixties the Prussian army emerged as the most powerful force on the continent, it had had for almost two generations no practical experiences of war. It had undertaken some insignificant campaigns during the revolution of 1848–1849 and had been mobilized repeatedly between 1830 and 1859 in anticipation of conflicts which did not materialize. In the same period the Russian, Austrian, French, and British armies had been fighting wars. The superiority of the Prussian army in the sixties was made possible only by its organization, by its peacetime training, and by the theoretical study of war which had been brought to perfection in the half century before Sadowa and Sedan.

The Prussian army of the nineteenth century was created by four men: Frederick the Great, Napoleon, Scharnhorst, and Gneisenau. Frederick bequeathed precious memories of victory and endurance in adversity, which are so essential for the pride and self-reliance of an army. In addition, he impressed upon his military successors the knowledge that even the peacetime life of an army consists of hard labor and that battles are won first on the training ground. There was undoubtedly in the Prussian army an overemphasis on the minutiae of military life, which was originally counterbalanced by the strategic genius of the king. He did not train younger strategists, however, and it was a foreign conqueror who reminded the Prussians of the role which strategy plays in warfare, and two young officers, both non-Prussian by birth, had to remold the Prussian army, which they did largely along the modern French pattern. Thus Napoleon became the second taskmaster of the Prussian army, and—after Jena—Scharnhorst and Gneisenau adapted the Prussian army to the new type of warfare.

The Prussian military reformers knew that new methods of war were an expression of the profound social and political changes which the French Revolution had produced. The army of Frederick the Great had been a force of mercenaries isolated from civilian society. Only the noble-born officer's sense of honor and loyalty was glorified while the rank and file were kept together by a brutal discipline. The Prussian military reformers undertook to transform the army of the age of despotism into a national army. To this end they introduced universal conscription of a more radical type than had ever been attempted before. Napoleon's Treaty of Tilsit hampered the immediate realization of Scharnhorst's ideas, but in the Prussian military law of 1814, drafted by his pupil, Boyen, his plan became the permanent order of Prussia's military system.

Conscription became the rule in practically all countries on the continent, but outside of Prussia it amounted merely to the conscription of the poor, since the well-to-do were allowed to make money payments or purchase substitutes. In Prussia, all groups of the population actually served. In this respect, the Prussian army was more clearly a citizens' army than that of any other country. Unfortunately, the Prussians were not democratic citizens, but remained subjects of a bureaucratic absolutism. There was also a recrudescence of the privileged position of the Prussian gentry in government and army, and the Junker class continued to monopolize the officers' positions. National service, the logical outcome of national and liberal thought in America and France, became in Prussia a device for strengthening the power of an absolutist state.

The dream of the Prussian military reformers of creating a true citizens' army was frustrated by the political reaction after 1815. The legacy of their strategic and tactical knowledge fared better, though even here the old school scored certain successes. The Prussian field-service regulations of 1847 tried to revive Frederickian tactics which Scharnhorst's order of 1812 had wisely excluded. Still Scharnhorst's and Gneisenau's strategic ideas were not forgotten in the Prussian army.

Among the contemporaries, these two officers from Hanoverian and Austrian families were the only equals to Napoleon in the art of war. An early death in the summer of 1813 kept Scharnhorst from ever assuming high command in the field. Gneisenau, as the chief of staff of the Prussian army from the fall of 1813 to the summer of 1815, was destined to prove that the new Prussian school of military thought could produce not merely a new philosophy, but also men to translate their insight into action.

There has been much controversy about which of the two was the greater general. Clausewitz, friend and pupil of both, gave the crown to Scharnhorst because he combined a profound contemplative mind with a deep passion for action. Schlieffen found Gneisenau superior because he seemed to have higher perspicacity and determination on the battlefield. From a historical point of view, however, it is most important to remember that both officers, the calm and self-possessed Scharnhorst and the impetuous and generous Gneisenau, represented a new type of general. Both were born leaders of men, the one possibly greater in educating them for war, the other in directing them on the battlefield, but both these children of Germany's philosophical age, of the epoch of Kant and Goethe, believed that thought should lend wings to action.

The new Prussian strategy sprang from an original interpretation of Napoleon's art of war. To most nineteenth-century students of war before Sadowa and Sedan, Jomini's writings seemed the last word on Napoleonic strategy. Had not Napoleon himself said that this man from Switzerland had betrayed the innermost secrets of his strategy? Napoleon, however, though admiring Jomini, had also remarked that he set down chiefly principles, whereas genius worked according to intuition. Jomini's cold rationalism was not capable of doing justice to the spontaneity which was the hidden strength of Napoleon's actions. The interpretation of Napoleon's strategy, which Scharnhorst found and which animated Gneisenau's conduct of the campaigns of 1813–1815, was based on a historical and inductive method which gave full credit to the creative imagination of the commander and the moral energy of his troops. In Clausewitz' work *On War*, the new philosophy found its classic literary expression.

The new Prussian school of strategy created its own organ in the Prussian general staff, which became the brains and nerve center of the army. The origins of the general staff go back to the decade before 1806, but not before Scharnhorst's time did it receive its characteristic position. When, in 1806, Scharnhorst reorganized the ministry of war, he created a special division which was charged with the plans for organization and mobilization and with the peacetime training and education of the army. Under the jurisdiction of this section came also the preparation of military operations by intelligence and topographical studies, and finally the preparation and direction of tactics and strategy. As minister of war, Scharnhorst retained the direction of this section and exercised a strong influence on the tactical and strategical thought of the officers in it by training them in war games and staff maneuvers. It became customary to assign these officers as adjutants to the various army units, which went far to extend the control of the chief of staff over all generals. The young men with the purple-striped trousers carried strategic thought into all sections of the army.

Under Scharnhorst, the general staff was still a section of the war ministry, under which it would have remained if Prussia had received a parliament. The absolutist structure of the Prussian government, however, made it possible to divide military responsibility under the supreme command of the king. In 1821, the chief of the general staff was made the highest adviser of the king in matters of warfare, while the ministry of war was restricted to the political and administrative control of the army. This decision was of far-reaching consequence, since it enabled the general staff to take a leading hand in military affairs, not merely after the outbreak of war, but also in the preparation and initial phase of a war.

II

Moltke was destined to take full advantage of the traditional ideas and institutions which were created during the wars of liberation. Like Scharnhorst and Gneisenau, he was not a Prussian by birth, but came from the neighboring Mecklenburg. His father was an officer of the king of Denmark, who, as the Duke of Schleswig and Holstein, was then still a German prince. Moltke was brought up as a Danish cadet, becoming a lieutenant in 1819. His experiences at school had been unhappy, however; his relations with his father were not close; nor did service in the Danish army hold out great prospects. In 1822, Moltke applied for a commission in the Prussian army, in which his father had started his military career before transferring to the Danish army.

The Prussians put the young lieutenant through a stiff examination and made him begin at the very bottom of the military ladder again. After a year, however, he was favored by admission to the war college which was under Clausewitz' direction. Clausewitz gave no lectures, however, and Moltke did not come under his spell before 1831, when Clausewitz' work was posthumously published. From his studies at the war college, Moltke gained his lasting interest in geography, physics, and military history, which were well presented at the school. In 1826, Moltke returned to his regiment for two years, but most of his time was again given to theoretical work, this time to the teaching of the officers of his division. In 1828, he was assigned to the general staff, to which he belonged for more than sixty years.

With the exception of five years as a lieutenant in the Danish and Prussian armies, Moltke never served with the troops. He had never commanded a company or any larger unit when, at the age of sixty-five, he took virtual command of the Prussian armies in the war against Austria. The years from 1835 to 1839, which he spent in Turkey as a military adviser of the Sublime Porte, gave him some actual war experiences in the futile campaign against Mehemet Ali of Egypt. The Turkish commander threw the good advice of the young captain to the winds, and Moltke saw war at its worst among defeated troops.

When he returned to Berlin, the hardest period of his life was over. As a lieutenant, he never had a penny to spend. Dire need dictated his writing a short story for a popular magazine, or historical essays. In order to purchase mounts, without which he could not accept a commission on the general staff, he translated six volumes of Gibbon's history only to discover that his publisher was insolvent. It is impressive to see how the young Moltke wrestled with such materialistic problems and yet acquired an Attic education in such a Spartan setting. His chief work in his early years was concerned with topography, but he went beyond into all the other aspects of geography and penetrated deep into history as well. His learning and education were remarkably well rounded, and with them grew his power of expression. Moltke became one of the foremost writers of German prose.

He did not become, however, a statesman or original political thinker. Scharnhorst and Gneisenau had been statesmen as much as generals and their military reforms aimed directly at a reform of the whole life of the nation. This had made them suspect in the conservative atmosphere of the Prussian or, for that matter, of the Austrian and Russian courts. As soon as the French Revolution and Napoleon seemed defeated, they were called Jacobins, and Gneisenau and the younger reformers were retired. Moltke was conscious of the natural interrelation of generalship and statesmanship, and took a lively personal interest in politics. He abstained from active participation in political affairs, however, and never questioned the powers that be. He was convinced of the superiority of monarchical government and found its special justification in the fact that it allowed the officers to manage army affairs without interference from nonprofessional elements. The defeats of German liberalism in the revolution of 1848–1849, and again in the sixties, were highly gratifying to him.

An officer of his quiet manner, conforming political views, and wide learning was well received at court. In 1855, Friedrich Wilhelm IV made him aide-de-camp to his nephew, Prince Friedrich Wilhelm, the future emperor Friedrich III. This appointment brought Moltke into contact with the prince's father, known as the soldier-prince, and Wilhelm I apparently discovered in Moltke talents which seemed to recommend him for the position of chief of the general staff.

One of Wilhelm's first actions when in 1857 he became regent of Prussia was to appoint Moltke to the post. Still Wilhelm I was immediately more interested in the political and technical reorganization of the army, and the figure of the minister of war, Roon, overshadowed the silent chief of staff in the councils of state. What Roon and Wilhelm proposed was a decided improvement in the efficiency of the army, but it meant at the same time the ultimate abolition of those militialike sections of the army in which a more liberal spirit had survived. The popular *Landwehr* (territorials or national guard) was curtailed in favor of a greatly expanded standing army. This gave the professional royalist officer corps unchallenged control over all military establishments of the nation. The Prussian parliament fought this measure, but the reorganization became effective under Bismarck even without parliamentary consent. The ensuing constitutional conflict was still raging when the battle of Sadowa was fought. The parliamentary opposition, however, broke down when the Bismarckian policy and Moltke's victories fulfilled the longing for German national unity. Moltke's successful strategy, therefore, decided two issues: first, the rise of a unified Germany among and over the nations of Europe; second, the victory of the Prussian crown over the liberal and democratic opposition in Germany through the maintenance of the authoritarian structure of the Prussian army.

The role which Roon, as minister of war, played in the years of political conflict made him the most influential figure in the army before 1866. Wilhelm I was so used to taking military advice from him that the chief of the general staff was almost forgotten. The unpretentious Moltke was little known in the army, and even during the battle of Sadowa, when an officer brought an order from him to the commander of a division, the latter replied, "This is all very well, but who is General Moltke?" Moltke's rise to prominence among the advisers of the king was sudden and unexpected, though it was the logical outcome of Prussian military history following the days of Scharnhorst and Gneisenau.

His aloofness from the political scene in the years from 1857 to 1866 allowed him to give his undivided attention to the preparation of future military operations. The revolutions of 1848–1849, the rise of the Second Empire in France, and the Crimean War had already shown that a new epoch of European history had opened in which military power was freely used. Moltke began at once to overhaul the plans which the Prussian general staff had drawn up. His predecessor, General Reyher, incidentally one of the few Prussian generals who had come up from the ranks, had been a man of great vision and a remarkable teacher of strategy. Moltke could count on the ability of the Prussian officer to find original solutions for the tactical problems of war. In fact, the officers silently dropped the official service regulations of 1847 as soon as they crossed the Bohemian frontier in 1866 and followed largely their own ideas.

The peacetime formation of the Prussian army was a more highly developed system than that of any country. With the exception of the guard troops, the regiments drew their recruits and reservists from their local districts. The Hapsburg Empire with its nationality problems could not use such a system. Moreover, after 1815, the Prussian army had retained an organization in army corps which Napoleon had created during his campaigns, but which had been given up by France under the Bourbons. With the exception of Prussia, army corps were formed on the eve of war, which again acted as a brake upon rapid mobilization and upon the capacity of troops and leaders in the performance of large-scale operations.

Rapid as the mobilization of the Prussian army was, comparatively, Moltke accelerated it still further. The unhappy geographical structure of the Prussian monarchy of this period, with its far-flung east-west extension from Aix-la-Chapelle to Tilsit severed by Hanover, aggravated Prussia's military problems. The railroad age offered a remedy which Moltke exploited to the full. Moltke had begun to study railroads before a single line had been built in Germany. He apparently believed in their future, for when in the early forties railroad building got under way, he even risked his savings by investing in the Berlin-Hamburg railroad. His speculative interest was enhanced by his matrimonial concern, namely to cut down the distance which separated him from his young bride in Holstein! But his military thinking was always awake. In 1847–1850, troops of various nations were for the first time moved by rail. In 1859, when Prussian mobilization was pending during the Italian war, Moltke could test the facilities for the rail transportation of the whole army and could introduce important improvements.

The railroads offered new strategic opportunities. Troops could be transported six times as fast as the armies of Napoleon had marched, and the fundamentals of all strategy—time and space—appeared in a new light. A country which had a highly developed system of rail communications gained important and possibly decisive advantages in warfare. The speed of the mobilization and of the concentration of armies became an essential factor in strategic calculations. In fact, the timetable of mobilization and assemblage, together with the first marching orders, formed in the future the very core of the strategic plans drawn up by the military staffs in expectation of war.

In addition to making use of the modern railroads, Moltke proposed to employ the dense road system which had come into being in the course of the Industrial Revolution. Napoleon had already pointed the way by dividing his army on marches and had set, in the campaign of 1805 which led to the surrender of the Austrian army at Ulm, a classic example for the strategic use of separate marching orders. An army column is, however, not ready for battle, and it takes a full day to deploy a corps of 30,000. The changeover from marching to battle formation was accordingly a time-consuming process, and armies had, therefore, to be massed days before the battle. After 1815, road conditions improved greatly and new tactics became possible. In 1865, Moltke wrote: "The difficulties in mobility grow with the size of military units; one cannot transport more than one army corps on one road on the same day. They also grow, however, the closer one gets to the goal since this limits the number of available roads. It follows that the normal state of an army is its separation into corps and that the massing together of these corps without a very definite aim is a mistake. A continuous massing becomes, if merely on account of provisioning, embarrassing and often impossible. It makes a battle imperative and consequently should not take place if the moment for such a decision has not arrived. A massed army can no longer march, it can only be moved over the fields. In order to march, the army has first to be broken up, which is dangerous in the face of the enemy. Since, however, the concentration of all troops is absolutely necessary for battle, the essence of strategy consists in the organization of separate marches, but so as to provide for concentration at the right moment."

It is probable that Moltke already envisaged operations in which the concentration of the army would take place on the battlefield itself, thus discarding the Napoleonic principle that the army should be concentrated well before the start of a battle. Still Moltke's direction of operations in the weeks before Sadowa did not disregard the Napoleonic rule from the very beginning. He could have drawn the armies together before the battle but he decided at a late date to continue their separation and to achieve their union on the battlefield. After Sadowa, he summed up his ideas thus: "It is even better if the forces can be moved on the day of battle from separate points against the battlefield itself. In other words, if the operations can be directed in such a manner that a last brief march from different directions leads to the front and into the flank of the enemy, then the strategy has achieved the best that it is able to achieve, and great results must follow. No foresight can guarantee such a final result of operations with separate armies. This depends, not merely on calculable factors, space and time, but also often on the outcome of previous minor battles, on the weather, on false news; in brief, on all that is called chance and luck in human life. Great successes in war are not achieved, however, without great risks."

The last remarks permit a glimpse at Moltke's philosophy of war. As a loyal student of Clausewitz, Moltke was anxious to extend the control of reason over warfare as far as possible. He knew, however, only too well that the problems of war cannot be exhausted by calculation. War is an instrument of policy and, though Moltke maintained that a commander should be free in the actual direction of military operations, he admitted that fluctuating political aims and circumstances were bound to modify strategy at all times.

While the impact of politics on strategy confronted a general with an element of uncertainty, Moltke felt that the mobilization and initial concentration of the army was calculable since it could be prepared a long time before the outbreak. "An error," he said, "in the original concentration of armies can hardly be corrected during the whole course of a campaign." The necessary orders, however, can be deliberated long before and, assuming that the troops are ready for war and transportation is properly organized, they will inevitably lead to the desired results.

Beyond this stage, war becomes a combination of daring and calculation. After actual operations have begun, "our will soon meets the independent will of the enemy. To be sure, we can limit the enemy's will if we are ready and determined to take the initiative, but we cannot break it by any other means than tactics; in other words, through battle. The material and moral consequences of any larger encounter are, however, so far-reaching that through them a completely different situation is created, which then becomes the basis for new measures. No plan of operations can look with any certainty beyond the first meeting with the major forces of the enemy. . . . The commander is compelled during the whole campaign to reach decisions on the basis of situations which cannot be predicted. All consecutive acts of war are, therefore, not executions of a premeditated plan, but spontaneous actions, directed by military tact. The problem is to grasp in innumerable special cases the actual situation which is covered by the mist of uncertainty, to appraise the facts correctly and to guess the unknown elements, to reach a decision quickly and then to carry it out forcefully and relentlessly. . . . It is obvious that theoretical knowledge will not suffice, but that here the qualities of mind and character come to a free, practical, and artistic expression, although schooled by military training and led by experiences from military history or from life itself."

Moltke denied that strategy was a science and that general principles could be established from which plans of operations could be logically derived. Even such rules as the advantages of the inner line of operation or of flank protection seemed to him merely of relative validity. Each situation called for a definition in terms of its own circumstances, and for a solution in which training and knowledge were combined with vision and courage. In Moltke's opinion, this was the chief lesson to be derived from history. Historical study was also of the greatest usefulness in acquainting a future commander with the complexity of the circumstances under which military actions could take place. He believed that no staff or army maneuvers, indispensable as they were for the training of staff officers, could put before their eyes as realistic a picture of the significant aspects of war as history was able to do.

The study of military history was made one of the central responsibilities of the Prussian general staff and not left to a subordinate section. Moltke set the style by his classic monograph on the Italian war of 1859, first published in 1862, which aimed at an objective description of the events in order to draw from them valid practical conclusions. The histories of the wars of 1866 and 1870–1871 were later written in a similar manner under his direction.

Moltke took the view that strategy could benefit greatly from history, provided it was studied with the right sense of perspective. His own practice exemplifies the benefits which he derived from historical study. He knew, of course, of Napoleon's occasional use of detached corps for attacks against the flank or rear of the enemy. These operations with detailed units, however, had not affected Napoleon's general principle of strong concentration of the gross of the army, and his belief in the irresistible power of central attack. The advantages of such a strategy had been great in the age of Napoleon, but they had not shielded him against ultimate defeat. The battle of Leipzig had shown the possibilities of concentric movements of individual armies which Scharnhorst had predicted in his advice that one should never keep an army aimlessly massed, but always fight with concentrated forces. In Moltke's opinion, the progress of technology and transportation made it possible to plan concentric operations on a much larger scale than had been used half a century before.

Important as history was for the officer, Moltke pointed out that it was not identical with strategy. "Strategy is a system of ad-hoc expedients; it is more than knowledge, it is the application of knowledge to practical life, the development of an original idea in accordance with continually changing circumstances. It is the art of action under the pressure of the most difficult conditions."

Accordingly, the organization of command held a prominent place in Moltke's ideas on war. He treated the subject with great clarity in his history of the Italian campaign. No war council could direct an army, and the chief of staff should be the only adviser of the commander with regard to the plan of operations. Even a faulty plan, provided it was executed firmly, was preferable to a synthetic product. On the other hand, not even the best plan of operations could anticipate the vicissitudes of war, and individual tactical decisions which must be made on the spot. In Moltke's view, a dogmatic enforcement of the plan of operations was a deadly sin and great care was taken to encourage initiative on the part of all commanders, high or low. Much in contrast to the vaunted Prussian discipline, a premium was placed upon independent judgment of all officers.

Moltke refrained from issuing any but the most essential orders. "An order shall contain everything that a commander cannot do by himself, but nothing else." This meant that the commander in chief should hardly ever interfere with tactical arrangements. But Moltke went beyond this. He was ready to condone deviations from his plan of operations if the subordinate general could gain important tactical successes, for, as he expressed it, "in the case of a tactical victory, strategy submits." He remained unmoved when certain generals in the first weeks of the Franco-Prussian War, by foolhardy though gainful enterprises, wrecked his whole plan of operations.

Moltke did not wish to paralyze the fighting spirit of the army or to cripple the spontaneity of action and reaction on the part of subordinate commanders. The modern developments had placed a greater responsibility upon them than was the case in former ages. One of the chief reasons why Napoleon kept his army close together was his wish to keep all troops within the reach of his direct orders. Moltke's system of disposition in breadth made the central direction of the battle itself extremely difficult, although the marches prior to the battle could be easily arranged by telegraph. Moltke directed most movements in the war of 1866 from his office in Berlin, and arrived in the theater of war just four days before the battle of Sadowa. He confined himself very wisely to general strategic orders. To ensure an adequate, and this meant free, execution of strategic ideas, army commands were created while the authority in tactical questions rested with the commanders of corps and divisions.

Moltke's strategic thought and practice met its first and greatest test in the Austrian campaign of 1866. His role in the war which Austria and Prussia conducted against Denmark in 1864 had been modest. In the latest phase of the war he had quickly stopped the bungling which characterized the regime of the old Field Marshal Wrangel, and his critical counsel established him in the eyes of Wilhelm as a prudent strategist. In the discussion of war plans against Austria he became increasingly prominent so that Wilhelm I, on June 2, 1866, directed that all orders to the army should be issued through him. Since the king henceforth accepted Moltke's advice almost unconditionally, the sixty-five-year old general, who had thought of retirement, found himself the virtual commander in chief of the Prussian army.

The first test of his generalship was at the same time the greatest one in his career. The forces were more evenly matched than later in the Franco-Prussian war, and Moltke had to over-come more obstinate geographical and political problems. The war of 1866 and particularly the Bohemian campaign also illus-trate the strategic side of war in a much clearer form than the Franco-Prussian or for that matter most other wars.

Wilhelm I wished to avoid the war with Austria into which Bismarck ultimately pushed him. The Prussians thus began their mobilization much later than the Austrians and even then it remained doubtful whether the king could be persuaded to de-clare war, thereby enabling the army to take the offensive. The original strategic problems were accordingly very delicate. From Bohemia and Moravia the Austrians could have operated against either Upper or Central Silesia or marched into Saxony to threaten Berlin, possibly after effecting a union with the Ba-varian army in northern Bohemia or Saxony. Whether one or the other of these possibilities could be realized depended en-tirely upon the date of the actual opening of war. Naturally enough, Moltke supported Bismarck in urging the king to act soon, but he avoided prejudicing the political issue by military measures—in contrast to his nephew, who as chief of staff had to inform Wilhelm II in August 1914 that the strategic plans of the general staff had deprived the government of its freedom of action.

2-G. F. BUSH-1943

1. Bohemian battle area, 1866, showing main railroads and the
advance of the Prussian armies.

Key: I First Silesian Army
II Second Silesian Army
E Army of the Elbe

The elder Moltke's moves were aimed in the first place at
making up for the delay caused by the belated start of the
Prussian mobilization. In addition, he wished to cope with a
possible Austrian advance against Saxony and Berlin or against
Breslau in Central Silesia while Upper Silesia remained originally unprotected. Whereas the Austrians could employ only
one railroad line for their mobilization in Moravia, Moltke used

five to transport the Prussian troops from all over Prussia to the
neighborhood of the theater of war. As a consequence, on June
5, 1866, the Prussian armies were spread over a half circle of 275
miles from Halle and Torgau to Görlitz and Landshut. The
original placement of the Prussian troops was safe as long as the
Austrian forces were far to the south. In point of fact, they were
not even in Bohemia, as Moltke assumed, but still in Moravia.

Moltke, of course, never planned to leave his troops at their
points of disembarkation but began at once to draw them closer
toward the center around Görlitz. At all times he refused,
however, to order a full concentration in a small area as was
advocated by most Prussian generals and even by members of
his own staff. On the other hand, he too felt somewhat worried
when he ultimately learned that the main Austrian forces were
assembling in Moravia and not in Bohemia, a fact which seemed
to point to a contemplated Austrian offensive toward Upper
Silesia. Reluctantly he allowed the left wing to extend toward
the Neisse river, thus again spreading the Prussian armies over a
distance of more than 270 miles from Torgau to Neisse. His
hesitation was chiefly caused by uncertainty about the policy of
Wilhelm I and not by military considerations. In Moltke's opinion, everything would be well if he did not miss the opportunity
of achieving the ultimate concentration of the Prussian armies
along the shortest route, which meant by a forward move into
Bohemia.

Moltke had chosen Gitschin as the point for such a concentration—not because it offered important strategic advantages
of itself, but merely on account of distances. It was about
equally close to the two main Prussian armies, the Second Army
under the Crown Prince, Friedrich Wilhelm, which formed the
left wing in Silesia, and the First Army under Prince Friedrich
Karl, which had its base around Görlitz. At the same time,
Gitschin was equally distant from Torgau and Olmütz, that is,
from the Prussian Elbe army and from the Austrian main army.

Provided the Prussian armies could begin marching on the same day on which the Austrian army left Moravia, their concentration should have been completed before the Austrians arrived at Gitschin.

It was not before the twenty-second of June that officers of the Prussian vanguard handed Austrian officers notification of the Prussian declaration of war, but Prussia had opened hostilities against other German states on June 16. Thus the Elbe army began to occupy Saxony on the same day on which the Austrian army started its march from Olmütz to Josephstadt at the upper Elbe.

The Austrian army was worthy of the best traditions of Austrian military history. Its morale and enthusiasm were high; its officers, among them some of the best generals of the period, had great ability and practical experience. Certain branches of the services, namely cavalry and artillery, were definitely superior to those of the Prussian army. The strength of the latter was in its infantry which excelled both in tactics and arms. The Prussian needle-gun by itself, however, could not have achieved victory as was proved in the war against France, where the Prussians fought against an infantry armed with superior rifles. It was the outmoded shock tactics of the Austrian infantry together with its old-fashioned guns which put the Austrians at a decided disadvantage.

The scales were turned, however, by the lesser strategic ability of the Austrian high command. Benedek was a fine soldier with a distinguished record of war service to the Hapsburg Empire. He was at his best in battle; fearlessly and correctly he directed even the retreat of his beaten army on the battlefield of Sadowa. But he had grown up in the classic school of strategic thought and his chief strategic adviser, General Krismanic, whom he had not selected, lived largely in the operational thought of the eighteenth century. These elements determined the strategic conduct of the war by the Austrian high command. They meant formation in depth and emphasis upon the maintenance of naturally strong positions. Moltke, on his part, showed that space could be conquered by time.

The Austrian army moved from Moravia in three parallel columns. Though the strain of such marching arrangements was considerable, the Austrians reached their goal quickly and in good order. But after the arrival of the vanguards in Josephstadt on June 26, at least three days were needed to mass the army again. This loss of time probably saved the Prussian armies.

In spite of Moltke's continuous warnings, the First Army had made slow progress, since Prince Friedrich Karl wanted to wait for the Elbe Army, which, after occupying Saxony, was to be joined to his command. This gave Benedek an opportunity to use the inner line of operations. Which of the two about equally strong Prussian armies Benedek should have attacked has been an interesting controversy among students of military history. Probably Benedek's judgment was right when he considered chiefly an attack on the First Army. He failed, however, to recognize in time that he had only one or possibly two days in which he could have taken the offensive against one of the Prussian armies without having to fear the other in his rear. Since the Austrian high command believed rather in the tactical advantage of strong positions than in the priceless value of time, and since the early concentration of the army hindered its mobility, the opportunity slipped by. When Benedek discovered the mistake, it was even too late to retreat behind the Elbe at Josephstadt and Königgrätz, and he had to accept battle with the river at his rear.

The danger of an Austrian attack against one of the two Prussian armies having passed, Moltke began to delay the concentration of the armies, keeping them at one day's distance from each other in order to achieve their union on the battlefield. During the night of July 2, the last orders were given. They were actually bolder than their execution made them appear.

According to Moltke, the left wing of the Second and the right wing of the First Armies were supposed to operate not merely against the flanks but also against the rear of the enemy. Moltke conceived of Sadowa as a battle of encirclement. But the Prussian generals did not follow him and the Austrian army got away—though losing a fourth of its strength. An immediate pursuit was impossible since the troops of the Second Army had run into the front of the First, thus causing a mix-up of all army units which could not be easily disentangled. Four years later, the battle of Sedan proved that the Prussians had learned their lesson, although they fought a smaller French army on that occasion.

Moltke had shown by his strategy that the much-vaunted inner line of operations was merely of relative significance. He summed up his experiences in these words: "The unquestionable advantages of the inner line of operations are valid only as long as you retain enough space to advance against one enemy by a number of marches, thus gaining time to beat and to pursue him, and then to turn against the other who is in the meantime merely watched. If this space, however, is narrowed down to the extent that you cannot attack one enemy without running the risk of meeting the other who attacks you from the flank or rear, then the strategic advantage of the inner line of operations turns into the tactical disadvantage of encirclement during the battle."

These sentences have often been interpreted as a definite condemnation of operations along the inner line and a recommendation of concentric maneuvers. This was not Moltke's opinion. During the Franco-Prussian War of 1870–1871, he used both concepts freely and successfully, depending chiefly upon the actions of the enemy. Moltke's strategy was characterized by his openness of mind and by the elastic changes from one device to the other.

It has been suggested that Moltke's strategy reflected the superior military strength which Prussia enjoyed at that time, but such a statement is true only within certain limitations. In 1866, Moltke had to create the slight superior strength of the Prussian armies in Bohemia, which, incidentally, was not to be found in manpower. He took the risk of denuding all Prussian provinces of troops and of leaving only an extremely small army to deal with Austria's German allies. If the Bohemian campaign had dragged on or turned into a deadlock, Napoleon III could have used the chance to take the Rhineland and to settle the fate of the continent. Nor were possibilities of this sort entirely lacking during the war of 1870–1871.

After the treaty of Frankfurt, Prussia-Germany could breathe more freely, provided the government succeeded in preventing the military cooperation of her foremost neighbors, France and Russia. Moltke had considered this eventuality for the first time in 1859, but it had been a passing cloud on the political horizon. From 1879 on, the possibility of a Franco-Russian coalition loomed larger and larger in the thoughts of the general staff. With the conclusion of the Franco-Russian alliance in the early nineties, it became the major strategic consideration.

Moltke's plans in this situation were in line with his strategy in the past, namely to fight one enemy with as little as possible in order to make available superior forces with which to crush the other. His advice was to stay on the defensive in the west and to take the offensive against Russia. Germany, in possession of Alsace-Lorraine, could defend her western frontier with small forces whereas she could not hope to achieve rapid decisions against the rising line of French fortifications. Greater results could be hoped for in Russia. Moltke's second successor as chief of the general staff, Count Schlieffen, reversed the sequence in 1894; from that time on, the German plans for a two-front war envisaged making the first offensive in the west.

III

Count Alfred Schlieffen, born in 1833, was the descendant of a noble family which had given many outstanding civil servants and officers to the Prussian monarchy. His reticence, his limited eyesight, and his genuine interest in studies seemed to predestine him for civil rather than military service, and it was not until he was serving his year in the army that he decided to become an officer. From 1858 to 1861 he attended the war college, and his subsequent appointments indicate clearly that his superiors had earmarked him for high staff positions. At due intervals he changed from posts in the great general staff to staff work with the troops until in 1876 he became for seven years commander of the First Uhlan Guard regiment at Potsdam. From 1883 to his retirement in 1906, he was again with the general staff, first as head of various sections and after 1891 as its chief.

Schlieffen's career prior to his last fifteen years in the general staff brought him somewhat more into contact with the life of the troops than had been the case with Moltke. He had also acquired more practical war experience than Moltke had gained before 1864. During the war of 1866, Schlieffen was a member of the staff of a cavalry corps. In this capacity he saw the battle of Sadowa which made a great impression upon him. To his regret, he did not participate in the frontier battles of the Franco-Prussian War. But he had opportunities to demonstrate his talent when he served on the staff of an army during the Loire campaign and collected variegated impressions and ideas about war and generalship.

Compared to Moltke's early struggles, Schlieffen's rise to prominence was fairly easy. Nor did he have to fear that his advice as chief of the general staff would not be accepted. Before 1866 the influence of the general staff had not been unchallenged, but the supreme authority which the office inspired after Sadowa and Sedan fell to Schlieffen with Moltke's toga. Schlieffen was thus able to concentrate even more than Moltke on military problems and to ignore their political implications. The increasing professionalization which was a characteristic of life in the late nineteenth century was reflected in the history of the German army command. When Schlieffen studied at the war college in the fifties, specialists and technicians were already beginning to overshadow that older philosophical and historical universalism which had been Moltke's spiritual food and which explained to a large extent his Olympian calm and serenity. Schlieffen had a Promethean nature, which drove him by an unending zeal to achieve the impossible, but his efforts were restricted to his professional sphere. On the political causes and consequences of war, he did not speculate very much. Moltke, too, had kept from meddling in politics, but he had been very conscious of political forces and tried to adapt his strategy to them. Schlieffen's whole life and thought were devoted to strictly military problems.

The sudden death of his young wife after a brief marriage left Schlieffen oblivious to everything but his duties as chief of staff. Every phenomenon of life was immediately examined for its war potentialities. There was something inhuman in his ascetic devotion to his military tasks although it seemed superhuman to his loyal students. To those anxious to pierce the secrets of modern generalship his mind exercised a compelling fascination.

Though the membership and sections of the Prussian general staff expanded after 1891, it did not alter as an institution. Its functions continued to be the education of the army for war and the preparation of operations. Schlieffen's chief technical contributions were the further development of railroad transportation, the creation of mobile heavy artillery—carried through against the staunch opposition of the army conservatives—and the introduction of certain new branches such as the army railroad engineers and the air corps. He was keenly interested in the progress of modern technology, but was not too successful in convincing the semi-feudal officer corps of the necessity of making full use of new discoveries. The officers remained extremely suspicious of modern technology and were not willing to assign to scientists and engineers a major role in the management of military affairs. During the First World War only the heavy artillery and the military railroad engineers were equal to their task. The German air force and signal corps were inadequate and, what was worse, the army command was unprepared to employ the new technical possibilities. The tank battles of 1918 produced a change of heart, the results of which can be seen in the coordination of military and technical services in Hitler's army.

Schlieffen gave so much thought to modern technology, not because he believed that technology would dethrone strategy but because he saw in it a new challenge to military leadership. In his sarcastic manner he once remarked of the progress of modern technology: "Dividing its precious gifts among all evenly and impartially, it created the greatest difficulties and considerable disadvantages for all." Of the two chief results of the industrial age, speed and mass production, only the latter seemed to affect warfare. Modern mass armies with their tremendously increased firing power apparently eliminated the strategy of mobile warfare as it had been developed by Napoleon and Moltke. But Schlieffen criticized those officers who meekly accepted this loss of mobility and maneuver and could not think of other solutions for it than defensive positions or frontal attacks. "The Russo-Japanese War," he wrote, "has proved that mere frontal attacks can still be successful in spite of all difficulties. Their success is, however, even in the best case only small. To be sure, the enemy is forced back, but after a little while he renews his temporarily abandoned resistance. The war drags on. Such wars are, however, impossible at a time when the existence of a nation is founded upon the uninterrupted progress of commerce and industry. . . . A strategy of attrition will not do if the maintenance of millions of people requires billions." In Schlieffen's opinion only a strategy of annihilation could preserve the existing social order.

Schlieffen was not a prophet of total war, although he feared that fundamental social changes would become certain in the course of a long war. The anxiety that the contemporary strategists might fail added a somber shade to all his thought and teaching. It was as a thinker and teacher of strategy that he gained his place in history. Whether he would also have proved himself a great commander in war cannot be said. He possessed qualities which seemed to qualify him singularly well for the high command in war. His thought was never confused by minor considerations nor perturbed by mere incidents, and in spite of his cool remoteness of manner his personality radiated a sovereign strength which electrified all around him. His students were convinced that he would have become as great a master on the battlefield as at the map table, and that none of the generals of the First World War measured up to his greatness. Like Scharnhorst, however, Schlieffen died on the eve of great decisions, occupied to his last moments in January 1913 with the solution of Germany's military problems. His shadow hung over the First, as it is still over the Second World War, and his influence on German military thought can hardly be overestimated. As late as 1938 General Beck, the chief of the German general staff in the period of German rearmament, called him the "first among the classic teachers of strategy," though General von Fritsch added to his own praise the warning that "the enormous progress of technology since Schlieffen's death may make some of his rules appear as no longer strictly valid."

The Franco-Russian alliance of 1893 made it certain that in case of a European conflict Germany would have to fight a two-front war. It seemed hopeless to compete with the Franco-

Russian bloc in numbers. For political reasons Austria-Hungary was unable to expand her armaments considerably. Italy could not be counted on as an ally, while as time progressed Britain became more clearly a potential military adversary. On the other hand, Germany still held the advantage of the central position on the continent, and, if she took the risk of an uneven distribution of her troops, of greater striking power in one theater of war during its initial phase. In Schlieffen's opinion this temporary German superiority had to be employed where it was most likely to result not merely in victorious battles but in a speedy decision of the war. Moltke's recommendation of defensive warfare against France and an offensive against Russia did not seem to promise this success. Operations in the east would be time-consuming, since the vast eastern plains permitted the Russians to employ evasive tactics. A stalemate in the west and protracted warfare in the east would make Britain the arbiter of Europe. Even without expecting British intervention Moltke had warned that in contrast to the wars of 1859, 1864, or 1870–1871, future wars were likely to last for many years. To overcome the danger of protracted warfare, Schlieffen decided in 1894 that, in the event of war, offensive action should be undertaken first against France.

Schlieffen's reasoning was based on the fact that France was the more powerful military enemy of Germany and the one whose concentrated strength could be met and disposed of at an earlier date of war. Control of France would make a British intervention improbable or ineffective. However, in order to achieve a supreme decision of the European war through a campaign in France it would not be enough to force the French army to retreat into the interior or even to capture Paris. It would be necessary to annihilate the total armed strength of Germany's western enemy.

The first Schlieffen plan for an offensive against France, drawn up in 1894, was hardly adequate for the achievement of such a super-Sedan; it still rested almost completely upon frontal attack from Lorraine, and the growing strength of French armaments made it a costly and precarious scheme. Between 1897 and 1905 Schlieffen evolved his grandiose plan of a German offensive which was to gain its irresistible momentum from the weight of a powerful German right wing wheeling through Luxembourg, Belgium, and southern Holland. The famous memorandum of 1905 gave these strategical ideas for a western campaign their classic form, though Schlieffen continued to his death to re-examine and reformulate its problems. The decision to open a two-front war with a lightning offensive against France was accepted by both the German general staff and the German government in spite of the great political risks which the violation of Belgian and Dutch neutrality imposed. The east was to be guarded only by small forces, and up to eight-ninths of the German army was to be used to eliminate the armed might of France. However, the German army of the east, according to Schlieffen's hopes, was not to fall back at once behind the fortresses of the Vistula, but should first attempt to attack the Russian armies which would be forced by the Masurian lakes to divide their forces in invading East Prussia. The inner line coupled with a strategy of encirclement might enable the numerically inferior army to achieve a victory.

This dream of an eastern victory was realized in the battle of Tannenberg of August 28, 1914, in which the Rennenkampf army was annihilated. The plan for such a battle was originally conceived by Schlieffen and was often tried out with his officers. In 1914 Hoffmann and Ludendorff executed an oft-posed Schlieffen war game problem in a manner which would have delighted their military teacher. Schlieffen had never expected that an eastern battle of this type would be decisive in terms of the strategy of the war. He had only hoped that such a victory would gain time for the completion of the great operations in the west.

However, as the strategy of a battle the eastern or Tannenberg type seemed to Schlieffen the highest achievement of generalship. In the first volume of Hans Delbrück's *History of the Art of War*, published in 1900, which dealt with the strategy of antiquity, he found the prototype of this form of battle in the Carthaginian victory at Cannae. In 216 B.C. Hannibal had annihilated a vastly superior Roman army by boldly accepting temporary defeat in the center in order to be strong enough to crush the enemy's wings and to encircle his legions. Schlieffen judged that all the great commanders of history had aimed at the Cannae scheme. Frederick the Great did not have forces powerful enough to perfect such annihilating blows, but in Schlieffen's opinion Frederick's important victories were incomplete Cannaes. Napoleon at the height of his career had shown the Hannibal touch, as for example in the great campaign of 1805 which culminated in the capture of Mack's army at Ulm. The defeat of Napoleon, in turn, was the result of a Cannae strategy, particularly in the battles of Leipzig and Waterloo. The same was true in the case of Sadowa, which was well conceived but not too brilliantly executed. In recent times Sedan had constituted a true Cannae.

Schlieffen was prone to simplify military history. He had formed his strategical concepts in studying modern tactics and too easily projected modern ideas into the historical past. It is questionable whether Napoleon's strategy of central breakthroughs illustrated the lesser form of his military genius. It was correct to emphasize, however, that as a consequence of modern firing power frontal attack had become exceedingly costly and less effective. This had already been the case in the epoch of Moltke, but the progress of military technology in the half century after Sadowa made tactical defense even more powerful. On the other hand, the lines of communication of modern armies grew more vulnerable since ammunition was a vital necessity in maintaining the fighting quality of modern mass armies. A thrust into the enemy's rear was, therefore, the real aim of a flanking attack. It was not enough to roll the enemy's wings toward the center of his position. This latter method would only lead to what Schlieffen, using an expression of Napoleon's, called an "ordinary" victory; the thrust into the rear would mean a battle of annihilation.

Schlieffen was convinced that the encirclement battle, preferably conducted as an attack against both wings of the enemy, was the highest achievement of strategy. To master the problems of such a strategy was imperative for a numerically weaker army, since in it was to be found the only hope for victory. Frederick the Great's statement that there was no need to despair in the face of a superior enemy, provided the dispositions of the general made up for numerical shortcomings, expressed Schlieffen's own confident hope which he tried to infuse into the German officer corps.

It was difficult enough to use a Cannae strategy in a situation where space for maneuver was available, as in East Prussia where single armies were expected to fight in the initial stage of the German-Russian war and the railroad could be used for surprise operations of relatively small armies. But the growth of mass armies and the space which they needed as a result of modern firearms made the scheme inapplicable to the western European theater of war. Armies of millions would cover all available space along the Franco-German frontier and possibly extend from the Channel to Switzerland. A simultaneous assault against the two wings of the French army was impossible since the French right wing was protected by Belfort and the Swiss Jura fortifications. Only an offensive through Belgium against the left wing of the French army held out the chance for a thrust into the enemy's rear. The Schlieffen plan has been compared to Frederick's oblique battle order of Leuthen in 1757, when 70,000 Austrians were defeated by an army of 35,000. However, Frederick's forces were too weak to allow him the full exploitation of his flanking tactics for a strategy of encirclement. Schlieffen could assemble sufficient strength for a battle of annihilation by temporarily ignoring the Russian threat to Germany's eastern provinces.

In his memorandum of 1905 Schlieffen counted on using against France eight armies comprising altogether 72 divisions, 11 cavalry divisions, and 26½ *Landwehr* brigades. In addition he intended to use eight *Ersatz* corps as soon as they could

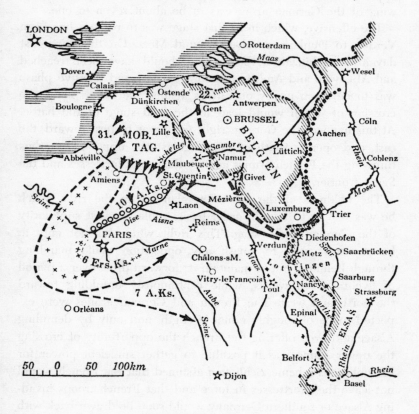

2. Schlieffen's plan of operations (1905)

be mobilized. The overwhelming mass of these armies was to be concentrated between Metz and Aix-la-Chapelle with the greatest power again assigned to the right wing. An army of only nine divisions, three cavalry divisions, and one *Landwehr* brigade was to be placed between Metz and Strasbourg while southern Alsace was to be left unprotected with merely three and a half *Landwehr* brigades covering the right bank of the upper Rhine. The ratio of strength between the right and left wing of the German army was to be about seven to one.

The offensive, which in its first stage was to reach a line from Verdun to Dunkirk, revolved around Metz. On the thirty-first day after mobilization the Somme should have been reached and Abbéville and Amiens passed. The next and decisive phase was to be taken up by operations against the lower Seine, the crossing of which would lead to the final stage of the battle. At this moment the German right wing was to turn toward the east, and operate south of Paris against the upper Seine, thus throwing the French armies against their own fortresses and the Swiss frontier.

The boldness of the Schlieffen plan lay in the risks which he was willing to take in order to assemble the vast superiority of the German right wing. This right wing was not only to be strong enough to smash any opposition while marching through Belgium, but to maintain its forward drive over a period of five to seven weeks, while continuously unfolding toward the north and west. The French and German armies were expected to be of roughly equal strength, and only by denuding Alsace and even offering the French the opportunity of crossing the upper Rhine was it possible to gather sufficient power for his ambitious scheme. Schlieffen assumed that the French would not leave their fortresses in force and that French troops invading Alsace or southern Germany would soon be drawn back with magnetic power by the threat of the wheeling German right wing. If so, they would probably be too late to affect the decision of the campaign.

In reviewing war games in 1901 Schlieffen pointed to the contrast between his and Moltke's strategical concepts in the following terms: "In 1870 we were able to attack the front of the enemy. Our numerical superiority then enabled us after making contact with the enemy to wheel around his extended wing and strike his flank. Now, we can never count on numerical superiority, only at best on equal numbers. Ordinarily, we shall have to be satisfied with being considerably inferior in numbers. Necessity compels us to think of a way in which to conquer with numerically weaker forces. There is no panacea, not just *one* scheme, but one idea seems to be well founded: if one is too weak to attack the whole, one should attack a section. There are many variations of this. One section of the enemy's army is its wing, and consequently one should attack a wing. This is difficult in the case of a company, a battalion, or a detachment, but it grows simpler the stronger the enemy is, the farther his lines extend, the more time it takes to support the attacked wing by the other one. How is the enemy's wing to be attacked? Not with one or two corps, but with one or more armies, and the march of these armies should be directed, not against the flank, but against the enemy's line of retreat, in emulation of what was demonstrated at Ulm, in the winter campaign of 1807, and at Sedan. This leads immediately to a disturbance of the enemy's line of retreat and through it to disorder and confusion which gives an opportunity for a battle with inverted front, a battle of annihilation, a battle with an obstacle in the rear of the enemy."

These words contain the essence of Schlieffen's strategic thought, which wrestled with the problem of how to fight brief and decisive wars against a stronger enemy. He did urge the expansion of the army, and this took place at various times between 1891 and 1906, though at the time of his resignation

Germany trained only 54 percent of her registered young men compared to France's 78 percent. But he never advocated the full mobilization of German manhood, only the provision of enough troops for operations of the contemplated character. Strategical thought and ability meant to him more than sheer superiority in mass and numbers.

It was in this spirit that Schlieffen tried to train the members of the general staff, aiming throughout the years for ever greater perfection. The first two volumes of his official military writings, published by the German general staff in 1937 and 1938, make it possible to study the progress of his strategical concepts and teachings in the fifteen years during which he held Scharnhorst's and Moltke's position in the German army. Most of Schlieffen's ideas were the logical continuation of the classic tradition of Frederick, Napoleon, and Moltke, and their adaptation to modern war conditions. Schlieffen, however, went beyond his great predecessors by planning beforehand not merely the mobilization, transportation, first concentration, and direction of the offensive, but also the decisive battle itself. This gives the so-called "Schlieffen plan" of 1905 its place in the history of strategy. It should be noted that it is not quite correct to speak of a Schlieffen plan of 1905 since the document was only the sketch of a plan counting on forces which were not yet at the disposal of the German high command.

Napoleon occasionally boasted of having worked out beforehand the total course of his campaigns. But opposing statements and the actual practice of his generalship contradict this. On the whole, he would have agreed with Moltke's statement that the "independent will of the enemy" made it impossible to predetermine the course of war. In contrast, Schlieffen believed that the will of the enemy could be immobilized by forcing him from the outset into the defensive. This required the highest speed in all operations, though this was hardly new in military history. Higher mobility has been at all times one of the fundamental prerequisites of military success. Schlieffen merely applied the old principle to countries with highly developed systems of transportation and communication.

In addition, however, Schlieffen insisted that the success of such strategic operations depended on the full control of all available space in order to keep the enemy from launching strategic operations of his own. His plan for an invasion of northern France through Belgium and southern Holland was largely dictated by the desire to hold the French army within the predictable and inescapable line between the Channel and the Swiss Alps. He warned again and again that it was essential for the German army to reach the Channel and Abbéville, since otherwise outflanking moves by the enemy could hardly be avoided. Faced by a German army with its right wing safely protected by the French coast the French army would find it extremely difficult to extend its left wing in time and in sufficient strength to halt the German offensive, particularly if the center of the French army was at the same time locked in battle.

The Schlieffen plan left the French hardly any strategical choice except one which was bound to increase their troubles. The French could take the offensive against Alsace-Lorraine but they could not gain decisive results from this; on the contrary, they would have removed troops even farther from the crucial area of northern France. Schlieffen was not willing to count on such errors, which he liked to call a "favor" (*Liebesdienst*) of the enemy. Naturally he hoped that mistakes of the enemy would facilitate successful operations, but he expected them to occur as the result of hasty countermoves to the unexpected German dispositions. He was bold and ready to run risks, but he was no gambler and therefore refused to anticipate a faulty French plan in drawing his own strategical blueprint.

If Schlieffen was to turn a whole war into a single battle, preconceived and prepared simultaneously with the plans for the mobilization, transportation, and first concentration of the army, he needed a fully integrated organization of the army command. Early, he envisaged the commander in chief as the First World War saw him: "The modern commander in chief is no Napoleon who stands with his brilliant suite on a hill. Even with the best binoculars he would be unlikely to see much, and his white horse would be an easy target for innumerable batteries. The commander is farther to the rear in a house with roomy offices, where telegraph and wireless, telephone and signaling instruments are at hand, while a fleet of automobiles and motorcycles, ready for the longest trips, wait for orders. Here, in a comfortable chair before a large table, the modern Alexander overlooks the whole battlefield on a map. From here he telephones inspiring words, and here he receives the reports from army and corps commanders and from balloons and dirigibles which observe the enemy's movements and detect his positions."

He explained, however, to his officers: "It will be impossible always to issue a specific order of battle. In any case, the order of attack has been replaced by the marching order, and by this is meant not the marching order which leads directly to the battlefield, but the marching order which starts the army moving after its first concentration has been achieved, and which leads only in the end to an encounter with the enemy. Assuming a smooth and normal course of events, army corps meeting the enemy will simply have to form a battle line and attack. Out of the direction of their marching orders follows the envelopment, the breakthrough, etc., in brief, the form of the battle which the commander in chief has planned. But it is unlikely that everything can be anticipated so that such a simple course can be assumed. Various incidents may happen which may necessitate a certain deviation from the original plan here and there. It will not be possible to ask the commander for orders in this case, since telegraph and other communications may not work. The corps commander will be faced with the necessity of arriving at a decision of his own. In order that this decision should meet the ideas of the commander in chief he must keep the corps commanders sufficiently informed, while, on the other hand, the latter must continuously strive to keep in mind the basic ideas of all the operations and to enter into the mind of the commander in chief."

In contrast to Moltke, whose flexible plans of operations had made allowance for considerable mistakes in execution, Schlieffen's strategy called for a high degree of exactness. To be sure, Moltke was not in a position to impose his will to the same extent as his fortunate heirs. In any event, however, modern mass armies needed stricter coordination if they were to remain manageable in mobile operations and particularly in circumstances where maneuverability was supposed to make up for the relative weakness in numbers.

Schlieffen, therefore, laid an even sharper emphasis on strategy in training the members of the general staff. Many officers were surprised to see how even the youngest officers of the general staff were permitted to direct maneuvers of large army units. This did not lead to a disregard of tactical knowledge in the German army since its mastery was widespread, but often enough it produced a lack of respect for the older front-line commanders who were far removed from the source of strategic wisdom. The fateful role which Lieutenant Colonel Hentsch played during the battle of the Marne by ordering the retreat of the German armies on the right wing against the better judgment of the commander and chief of staff of the First Army illustrates the point. However, the whole state of the German high command under Schlieffen's successor, the younger Moltke, had changed so completely that a direct comparison is impossible. Schlieffen, in speaking about the future command, had always assumed that the army would have a real leader as its chief, not a man who would vacillate in his own strategical concepts and would, at a crucial moment, let a junior member of his staff make historic decisions in his place.

Nor was the French campaign of August 1914 a test of the Schlieffen plan. The situation of 1914 was different from the one existing in 1905, which Schlieffen tried to solve in his memorandum. Since 1905 Russia had gained fresh strength, while in France, under the influence of Colonel Grandmaison's teaching, the idea of offensive warfare had been firmly established in the general staff. The younger Moltke followed Schlieffen in planning for a weak defense in the east and strong offensive operations in the west. In the latter, however, Schlieffen's conception of the wheeling right wing was greatly changed. Whereas Schlieffen had postulated a ratio of seven to one between the right and left wing of the German army, Moltke accepted three to one. Moltke was worried about the expected French drive into Alsace-Lorraine and rightly so, but there was no justification for strengthening the southern wing of the German army excessively, since it enjoyed in the defensive the advantage of strong fortifications. In fact, Moltke himself would have made different dispositions if he had not believed that a French offensive would afford the opportunity for a decisive battle in Alsace-Lorraine. If the French left their fortresses and sent half of their army into Lorraine, their southern wing could be driven against the Vosges and the Rhine and its annihilation would have shattered all hopes for further French resistance. Moreover, the Lorraine battle could be fought three to four weeks before a decision could be expected under the Schlieffen plan of 1905.

Thus, the right wing of the German army assumed a different meaning in Moltke's view; its chief task was to induce the French to launch their offensive into Lorraine. In this case the German armies had to make their way through Belgium, but the continuation of their march toward Paris might become less important if the German left wing was meanwhile able to strike. In vague emulation of his uncle, Moltke chose an open system

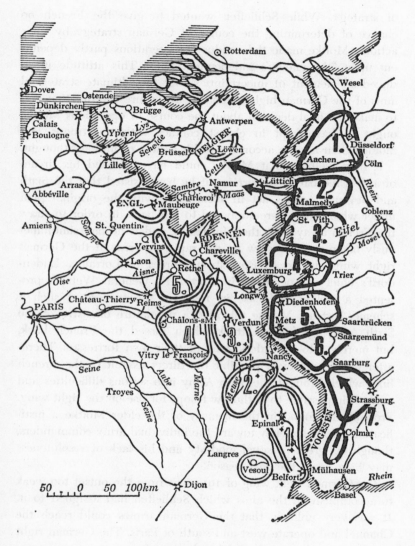

3. Deployment in the west.

of strategy. While Schlieffen wanted to give the French no chance of determining the course of German strategy by their actions, Moltke made the conduct of operations partly dependent upon "the enemy's independent will." This attitude introduced an element of uncertainty about the ultimate strategical aims of the German high command. To ensure coordination and to make the final decision about the course of operations Moltke ought to have kept in closest contact with the troops and molded their actions according to his system of military thought.

It may well be that Moltke could have realized his dream of a decisive battle in Lorraine if he had insisted that the Sixth and Seventh Armies act in accordance with the original plan under which they were supposed to fall back, in order to draw the French away from their fortresses, and if he had simultaneously taken steps to slow up the rapid progress of the German right wing and to transfer strong forces to Lorraine. Ludendorff's chief of operations in 1917–1918, General Wetzell, presented a well-argued case in 1939 for the success of such a scheme. Instead, Moltke tolerated a premature offensive of the Sixth Army by frontal attack which forced the French back, but merely into the safety zone of their own fortresses. Thereafter he did not even prohibit the direct assault of the French lines which brought the Sixth Army into serious difficulties and made it impossible to withdraw troops for use on the right wing. Probably he found in the memory of the elder Moltke a justification for his leniency toward the individual army commanders, though his great personal modesty and his lack of resoluteness may have been the real reason.

The German right wing of 1914 was from the outset too weak to accomplish all the aims which Schlieffen had assigned to it. It was very unlikely that the German armies could reach the Channel and operate west and south of Paris. The German right wing was further weakened by the transfer of two army corps from Belgium to East Prussia on August 25. They were miss-

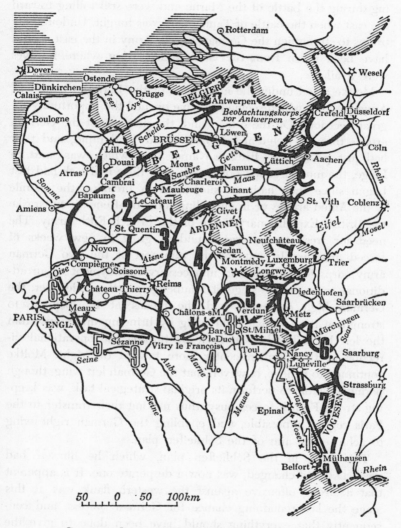

4. German advance in the west to September 5, 1914.

ing during the battle of the Marne and were still rolling toward the east when the battle of Tannenberg was fought. Undoubtedly troops to strengthen the German Eighth Army in the east should have been taken from the German left wing where reserves were available.

Moltke acted under the impression of the Lorraine battles of August 20–23, which seemed to have opened the opportunity for great decisions. On the other hand, the progress of the German armies through Belgium had been steady and rapid, and they had just passed the Brussels-Namur line, which was, next to Liège, the most dreaded bottleneck. Still their real task had just begun since they had not succeeded in breaking the morale of the Allied armies or in encircling individual enemy units, like the British Expeditionary Force or the French Fifth Army. The need for fresh troops was bound to grow in new weeks of forced marches. In spite of the transport of the two German army corps to the east and unnecessary employment of an additional corps for the siege of Maubeuge a little while later, the German high command had the means at its disposal to strengthen the German right wing by bringing up troops from the left by railroad or at least by turning the operational direction of the German center more toward the right. Moltke continued to believe, however, that the German left wing, though perhaps unable to perform its original strategical task, was keeping strong French forces busy, thus making their transfer to the Paris region impossible, and enabling the German right wing to achieve the aim of the Schlieffen plan.

This faith in the Schlieffen plan, which he himself had weakened and changed, was now a desperate one. It is apparent that a strong offensive against the western flank was at this stage the last remaining chance for German success, and consequently that everything should have been done to give the First, Second, and Third German Armies the overwhelming strength that they needed for delivering a decisive blow.

Moltke could even have given those armies a brief period of badly needed rest, provided he had taken all measures to ensure the superior strength for the coming battle. In the meantime, however, the French high command was maintaining a firm direction of the operations of all its armies even in the general retreat, and the railroad system of France was being used to the best advantage to equalize the odds and to prepare an offensive for the right moment. Moltke was out of touch with the actual situation along the front, communications were poor, railroad transportation was limited and neglected, but the chief cause of trouble was the uncertainty about the ultimate strategical plan of the German chief of staff. The commanders of individual German armies committed errors of both omission and commission, but they could not be blamed severely since the commander in chief left them largely in the dark about the meaning of the operations as a whole.

Finally the First Army succeeded in achieving the impossible by extricating itself from supreme danger by sheer boldness. It seemed just about ready to harvest a substantial part of the gains expected under the old Schlieffen plan, when Lieutenant Colonel Hentsch, whom Moltke sent to investigate the situation of the western flank, gave the order to retreat. Moltke, who had tried to follow an open system of strategy and to avoid the rigid premeditation and control of the Schlieffen plan, had generally accepted the initiative of the various army commanders during the early strategy of the war. Now, at the height of the crisis, he attempted to restore coordination by vesting authority in a younger member of his staff. Hentsch was an able officer who distinguished himself later as chief of staff in the Serbian campaign of 1915. His decisions of September 8, 1914, were largely the result of his surprise at finding the real battle conditions of the German right wing much more serious than the high command stationed in Luxembourg had visualized.

The Schlieffen plan, even in its emasculated form and in spite of the irresolute and ambiguous direction of German strategy, still gave the German offensive of 1914 a deadly force. It would not have fallen short of ultimate success if the German high command had from the beginning placed full faith in it instead of being diverted by the eastern Prussian war and by the notion of a decision in Lorraine. Schlieffen had been right when he predicted that it would be extremely difficult to achieve a more than ordinary victory in Lorraine since the French would be able to retire to their fortifications. He did not deny that in war new situations might arise and make fresh dispositions on the part of the chief commander necessary. However, the concentration upon the right wing would have unified all operations, and the commander in chief could have contented himself with impressing the ultimate meaning of the common operations upon the individual army chiefs. Even in the event of a breakdown of communications, the army commanders would have been likely to act in accordance with the underlying general conception of the operations.

Schlieffen's plan of 1905 was not his last answer to the problems of a future war. As has been stated before, he was inclined to assume in 1905 that the French would not leave their frontier fortifications. This was entirely correct, the French plan of mobilization No. 15 envisaging a strategic defensive. In the years of his retirement he noticed, however, the growing influence in France of the "neo-Napoleonic" school of offensive warfare. He was afraid that the French general staff would try to meet the German offensive through Belgium by an early occupation of the Namur-Brussels-Antwerp line. Schlieffen's fear was not wholly justified. It was true that in 1911 General Michel, who was then considered for appointment as chief commander by the French supreme war council, presented a plan which anticipated almost exactly the German operations of 1914. In its actual execution the Michel plan came close to the Allied operations in 1940, and one may even suspect that Gamelin was influenced by it. In 1911 the plan was not accepted and Joffre was designated as commander in chief. Plan No. 17 was adopted, which was built on the assumption that the Germans were likely to invade Belgium but would not have sufficient troops to pass beyond the Meuse. No French officer or historian has ever tried to explain this gravest blunder of French military intelligence.

It is interesting to see that Schlieffen even in his years of retirement did not become a victim of wishful thinking by counting on favors of the enemy. He continued to keep abreast of new developments in the field of tactics and technology. Fearing a French occupation of the Antwerp-Namur line and a subsequent offensive in Lorraine, he argued that this would necessitate the creation of strong reserves behind the German front. As the best countermove he proposed to use these reserves from the very beginning to strengthen the German battle forces and to take the initiative along the entire front from Belfort to Liège. He still maintained his belief that only the progress of the German right wing would bring great strategic results. At the same time he thought he discovered new strategical opportunities in the field of railroad transportation. The dictum of the older Moltke, that an error in the original concentration of the army could not be rectified during a campaign, began to lose its validity under the conditions existing in Western and Central Europe. The density of railroad lines would enable the commander to switch troops from one flank to the other, and in the last war games of the general staff which Schlieffen directed such maneuvers were practiced on a large scale. The German high command of 1914 showed, however, that these ideas had not yet affected the thought of Schlieffen's successor. The French proved far superior in using this new source of mobility, as they were also the first to discover the possibilities of motor transportation when

Galliéni requisitioned the taxicabs of Paris to move troops to the embattled Marne positions, and when Foch used motor transport to move 60,000 men to Flanders later in September 1914.

The battle of the Marne did not ruin Schlieffen's fame among German officers. On the contrary, the long and hopeless war of position in the west, with all its consequences for Germany's social and economic order, appeared to be the dire outcome of the disregard of his military genius. In the east Schlieffen's teachings had led to many striking victories, like Tannenberg and the winter battle of the Masurian lakes in 1914, or Herrmannstadt at the opening of the Rumanian campaign of 1916. Such victories enabled the German army to fight a worldwide coalition for four years and brought triumph almost within reach. Thus even the ultimate defeat of Germany in 1918 did not weaken the belief in Schlieffen's mastery of modern war which became steadily greater as Germany launched her rearmament.

Although there existed an orthodox Schlieffen school in the German army during the interwar period of 1920–1939 the strategists of the *Reichswehr* and of Hitler's army—men like Groener, Seeckt, Fritsch, and Beck—were by no means uncritical in their adaptation of Schlieffen's strategical concepts. The new German army was imbued with his belief in the power of the strategic initiative, of mobility, and of encircling maneuver. But at the same time the new lessons of the World War had been driven home by defeat. After the German offensive against France had come to a standstill in September 1914, the problem of defensive warfare had assumed great significance. Most of the fighting along the endless eastern front had also been in fact defensive fighting. After 1933 while the German army was still weak, the problem of defense ranked uppermost in the thought of the general staff. In the intellectual arsenal of the present German general staff there are probably more ideas about defense warfare than were put into practice in the early years of the Second World War. Field Marshal von Leeb's studies on defense of 1937–1938 shed some light on these efforts. It is also clear that the German officers are now inclined to put greater reliance on fortifications than formerly.

Of much greater importance was the experience gained in the use of frontal attacks. The trench warfare of 1914–1918 compelled the German high command to seek a new strategic approach to a decisive battle. The tactical frontal assault merely confirmed Schlieffen's prediction that the enemy would be forced to retreat but would be free to resume the fight in new positions. For decisive results the lines of the enemy had to be pierced to such an extent as to endanger his rear communications and to destroy his freedom of action. The first example of a successful strategy of breakthrough was the battle of Gorlice-Tarnow in May 1915 which had been planned by Seeckt. The results were considerable and would have been greater if the operations had been more fully prepared. A week later the Allies launched their assault against the German positions at Arras and Labassée. Thereafter both the Allied and the German generals worked on the problem of a breakthrough with subsequent strategic exploitation. The most ambitious attempt was Ludendorff's offensive in France during the spring of 1918, undertaken with the aim of forcing a decision of the war before Germany's strength gave out. No strategic success was obtained, however. A deep bulge was driven into the Allied front, but no deadly rupture occurred.

The failure of the spring offensive of 1918, together with the breakdown of the Schlieffen plan in 1914, were the chief subjects of critical military discussion in Germany after 1920. Two years before the Second World War the chief artillery expert of the Ludendorff era, Krafft von Dellmensingen, summed up the debate in his comprehensive book *The Breakthrough* for the use of Hitler's army. In a way he still reiterated Schlieffen's doctrine that "the breakthrough always remains the most difficult form of a decision," that it is "only a preparatory move, which may inflict heavy penalty upon the enemy," but that "the final victory can only be achieved by subsequent operations of encirclement." However, the author added that the necessity of attempting a breakthrough could hardly be avoided in future. "No army will consequently be as one-sided as to cultivate exclusively theories of encirclement."

The solution seen here, as in similar German studies, was the restoration of surprise and mobility through mechanized and motorized forces. It was in this field more than in any other that the German army learned from its enemies. It was not forgotten that those "black days" of July 18 and August 8, 1918, when Allied tanks rolled forward at Soissons and Amiens, had sealed the defeat of Germany. These tank assaults were great tactical achievements even though their strategic scope was limited. The German general staff of the 1930's endeavored to expand such tactical possibilities, in particular by combining them with the use of aerial weapons. But its major aim was to develop tactics that would lead to the resurrection of Schlieffen's strategy of encirclement and annihilation, which seemed to have lost its edge in the war of position from September 1914 to 1918.

In this sense the German offensive against France in 1940 was still animated by Schlieffen's ideas. The Schlieffen plan itself was not revived, however. The plan of 1940 called for a breakthrough of the center of the Allied front, which was achieved at Sedan on May 14, 1940. Two battles of encirclement were to follow, the first one to be fought against the French and British armies of the north which were to be driven to the Belgian coast and the English Channel. The second battle of encirclement was to be launched from the Sedan-Abbéville line and was aimed at forcing the southern

French armies against the Maginot fortifications and the Swiss frontier. Hitler was right, therefore, in stressing before the Reichstag the distinction between the campaign of 1940 and that of 1914. The second phase of the French war offered certain parallels to the Schlieffen plan, while the first phase, the battle of Belgium, resembled in some measure the strategy of the elder Moltke against MacMahon at Sedan. However, both phases of the battle of France were dependent upon the initial breakthrough, which was made possible by the tremendous superiority of the offensive over the defense at that particular moment of history.

This rare opportunity affected the general character of German strategy profoundly, but it was Schlieffen's teachings which had helped to guide German military thought toward a new faith in mobile warfare. His influence on the last half century of German military history was unique. Still, though the military tradition of Germany reached a new height through his activities, there were already signs that the German school of strategy had lost the idealistic energy and realistic strength of earlier times. Scharnhorst and Gneisenau had been military as well as national reformers. They had wished to reform the Prussian army not merely for the war of liberation from Napoleon but to build a more liberal Prussia as well. These two reformers considered the problems of war with a view to the peace to follow, knowing that the social implications of any military organization were far-reaching. In full harmony with their ideas, Clausewitz taught that war was a political act and that politics and warfare had "the same logic although they were using a different grammar."

The period of reaction after the Congress of Vienna frustrated all attempts to maintain a close contact between the army and the new social and political forces. The Prussian gentry regained full control over the army, which became the chief bulwark of monarchical conservatism in Germany. Outside of the preservation of the existing monarchical institutions and particularly the royal prerogatives in army affairs, the officers took no part in political matters and kept aloof from the new ideas of the century.

Moltke the Elder still had a great deal of Clausewitz' universal intellectual interest, and the stormy decades of European history between 1848 and 1871 stirred his thoughts deeply. His own political answers to the political problems of his time were all strictly on the conservative side, however, even more so than was the rather opportunistic policy of Bismarck. Moltke strongly asserted his authority against the chancellor in military affairs, but he accepted Bismarck's political leadership. Bismarck's successes at home and abroad enabled the army to fall back into its reactionary lethargy, for they freed it from all fear of parliamentary or popular control. Consequently the army was willing to follow the imperial government blindly even after 1890 when Wilhelm II took over the functions which Wilhelm I and Bismarck had held.

Schlieffen, as the chief military adviser of the crown, should have raised his voice against the dangers to German security which Wilhelm's policies created. The naval program of Wilhelm II and Tirpitz drove Britain into the opposite camp, but Schlieffen did not warn the government, although the state of German armaments and war plans made it impossible to disregard the threatening character of the international situation. Schlieffen's plan of operations, as has been seen, was based upon the expectation that the complete defeat of France would induce Britain to make peace. This was, however, not more than a hope since the Prussian general staff never considered an invasion of England. If the German-Russian war had continued after a defeat of France, Britain could at least have crippled German commerce and industry and thus forced that complete change of the German economic and social system which Schlieffen dreaded so much.

It was even more surprising that Schlieffen was unconcerned about the role of the German navy in a national program of defense. It could have no part in the type of war Schlieffen had planned for, and the building of a navy of such a size was, therefore, a waste of money and manpower. The army felt this all the time, for it was unable to procure enough funds and officer candidates for the formation of the new divisions which were needed for the implementation of the Schlieffen plan. Schlieffen did not complain, however, nor did he seem worried about the international aspects of the naval building program whose ultimate effect would be to bring a British army to the continent. He pondered even less the problems of the existing system of German government, in particular whether the army might not need a closer contact with the new social forces in order to reach the peak of its effectiveness in days of national emergency.

Schlieffen never questioned the autocratic rule of Wilhelm II. Even in his own military domain he abstained from intimating that the emperor's display of military ineptitude might be ruinous to the monarchy of Frederick the Great. Wilhelm II liked to gain maneuver victories by colossal cavalry charges, which he would lead himself, and his subsequent critiques of staff performances betrayed a similar lack of dexterity in military affairs. Such practices caused fear and resentment among the officers, which Schlieffen would parry with the statement that criticism of the emperor would undermine the monarchical authority upon which the morale of the Prussian army rested. His blind faith in monarchy was not even shaken by the appointment of the younger Moltke as chief of staff, though it led Schlieffen to voice grave admonitions that the serious character of Germany's strategical situation would allow no false military steps.

Schlieffen's blind faith in monarchy kept him from recognizing that the deepest problems of war transcend the realm of mere military proficiency. No modern general can hope to emulate Marlborough, Prince Eugene, Frederick the Great, or Napoleon in combining political with military command. Military and political affairs have grown too complex, and their mastery requires long professional experience in either field. Still, the fact that war is an act of politics has not changed. The highest form of strategy is the outcome of military excellence enlightened by critical and constructive political judgment. This truth, of which the founders of the Prussian school of strategy were well aware, was forgotten by Schlieffen and his students.

The failure of the war of movement in the west succeeding the battle of the Marne confronted the military leaders of the Second German Empire with the full impact of politics, international and national, upon the conduct of war. It became necessary to improvise a total war mobilization and war economy. The outcome of the war became dependent upon an amphibious rather than a land strategy. The pupils of Schlieffen were ill prepared for the reality of a worldwide war, which had to be fought as much with political, economic, and psychological weapons as with infantry and artillery. Ludendorff thought that he could direct those forces as easily as the army, and by subordinating the government to the orders of the high command turned Germany into a virtual military dictatorship. But the army failed to hold the home front.

The German revolution of 1918 made the officers the logical target of popular indignation and, though the army never forgot its humiliation and remained a reactionary and subversive power in the short lifetime of the German Republic, the best brains of the German army had become convinced that Ludendorff's error should not be repeated. This did not mean in their opinion that the army should ally itself with the new popular forces. It meant that they should cooperate with any political movement that would permit them to concentrate, as in Schlieffen's day, on strategy as a professional, or as they liked to call it, "unpolitical" task. This theory led even the most intelligent members of the German general staff to tolerate Hitler's rise to power in Germany. The German generals received from Hitler all the tools for renewing the war of 1914 to 1918, but they are learning again in our day that "war is an act of politics." This time, however, the logic of Nazi politics is dragging them to defeat in a war for which they had worked out the plans of a brilliant Cannae strategy. Schlieffen and his followers always disregarded the historical fact that Carthage was defeated in spite of Hannibal's victories.

IV RUSSIA AND THE EUROPEAN POLITICAL SYSTEM

———◆———

THE DRIVE toward the open sea brought the Muscovite state upon the European scene at about the same moment when another non-European empire began to retreat from the European continent. But whereas the Turks had come to Europe as mere military conquerors unwilling to learn from the Christians whom they had subjected or from the free European nations, the Russia of Peter the Great was anxious to adopt Western forms. The German nobility of the newly acquired Baltic provinces was at once used by the Russian rulers in building up the officer corps of the army, the diplomatic service, and the domestic officialdom. Beginning with Peter's own travels in Euope, Western technical inventions as well as Western ideas and institutions were transplanted into Russia on a large scale. The adoption of European features was not unlimited, and the significance of many of them changed when grafted on a civilization of heterogeneous historical origin and structure. Moreover, during the eighteenth and nineteenth centuries European influences operated almost exclusively on the small upper classes. Even Westernized Russia retained a character distinctly different from that of the European nations.

Therefore it is surprising to see how soon the Russians on their part claimed to be Europeans. As early as the eighteenth century Russia west of the Ural mountains and river was declared to be part of Europe, while the vast but sparsely populated lands from the Urals to the Pacific were labeled Asiatic Russia. This novel geographical circumscription of Europe demonstrated the desire of Russia, or at least of official Russia, to be counted among the European nations. Even today the Soviet government likes to stress the European character of Russia.[1]

In the two centuries after Peter the Great, Europe stood in the center of Russian foreign policy. Only Europe potentially possessed the power that might have undone the work of Peter the Great. Turkey, though in the eighteenth century not a negligible opponent of Russian expansion toward and along the Black Sea, was partly a European power. In the nineteenth century Turkey was a barrier to Russian progress in the Near East largely to the extent to which it was sustained and supported by one or more of the great European powers. In the Middle East and even in the Far East the real opposition to Russia during the nineteenth century came almost exclusively from European powers. The rise of modern Japan and the appearance of the United States in Asia changed the nature of Far Eastern politics. But the defeat of Russia in the war with Japan induced czarist Russia after 1906 to assign to European affairs the highest priority. Only the growth of a dynamic Chinese state, the independence of India, and the withdrawal of Britain and France from Southeast Asia in our time have created a new configuration of political forces around the Pacific. But the profound transformation that World War II and its aftermath produced in the Russo-European relationship should not be overlooked either. Historic Europe was torn asunder. One-third lies within the Russian orbit, while the other two-thirds would not by themselves be capable of maintaining their independence if the United States had not intervened and invested a substantial part of its strength in the building of a permanent coalition with free Europe. Russian foreign policy vis-à-vis Europe after 1945 does not constitute a subject that lends itself to historical analysis in relative isolation, but can only be treated as a part of Russo-American relations. On the other hand, Russian policy in Asia must be viewed today as a competing element in the formulation of over-all Russian policy.

I

The westward movement of Russia and its assumption of an imposing stature among the European powers was caused by the divisions among the major states of Europe. Foremost among them was the worldwide conflict between England and France.[2] By defeating Sweden, Russia knocked out France's chief ally in Northern Europe, and in the War of the Polish Succession of 1733–35, together with Austria, it broke the hold of French diplomacy on Poland. The wars against Turkey, in which Russia originally seemed to strengthen the fight of the Hapsburg monarchy against the infidels only to turn out to be a superior competitor for national gains, were directed against another traditional ally of France.

The decline of French influence in Europe enhanced the power of England. The English also had good reason to derive satisfaction from the removal of Sweden from the southern and eastern shores of the Baltic Sea. The Baltic region not only had become one of the most profitable trade areas of England but also delivered those raw materials that were vital for the maintenance of English sea power. Therefore England could not wish to see a single power acquire exclusive control of the Baltic. It could not desire to have Russia acquire the *dominium maris Baltici* in Sweden's place. Therefore England shielded Sweden from complete destruction. Russian access to the Baltic Sea was held in bounds. Finland remained Swedish, and Stettin and the Oder estuary, conquered by Russia, were given to Prussia.

England also became the chief beneficiary of the commercial opportunities Russia itself had to offer. The Anglo-Russian trade treaty of 1734,[3] the only trade treaty concluded by Russia in a long time, gave the English merchants a dominant role in the development of the Russian economy. This trade treaty worked well for half a century. Even during the Seven Years' War, when England supported the Prussian king against the coalition of Russia, Austria, and France, the trade treaty remained in operation, and Pitt always refused Frederick the Great's request to send naval forces into the Baltic in order to assist him in his war with Russia. Later on, England actively contributed to the Russian war against Turkey that gave Russia its first access to the Black Sea between the estuaries of the Bug and the Dnieper and, moreover, the use of all Turkish seas (including the straits) for its shipping. The Russian navy that sailed into the Mediterranean and annihilated the Turkish fleet at Chesme in 1770 was largely built and provisioned in England and had a strong complement of British sailors. The English government believed that the extension of Russian power into the eastern Mediterranean would countervail French strength in this area. Later, at the time of the American war as well as temporarily during the Napoleonic wars, England even tried to draw Russia into the western Mediterranean.

But Anglo-Russian relations became more ambiguous in the years thereafter. Although the Russians knew they could not do without foreign merchants and needed the influx of English capital, they wanted to curtail the privileges and high profits of the English in Russia. Most of all, they intended to acquire the direction of their own economic development. "We do not want to become another Portugal," it was said in St. Petersburg. The growing ambition of Russia to assert its national sovereignty found expression in the Armed Maritime Neutrality of 1780, an association of states brought together by Russia for the forceful defense of the rights of neutrals against the methods of sea warfare practiced by England in its war with the American colonies, France, and Spain. It was followed by the conclusion of a number of trade treaties chiefly with Mediterranean states. The conditions on which the Russian government made a renewal of the trade treaty with England dependent were unacceptable to the English, and they chose to forgo their legal privileges and exemptions. Although the actual superiority of the English merchants was great enough to survive the damage done by the lapse of the treaty, the event marked the beginning of a more critical stage in Anglo-Russian relations. The Russian advance to the Dniester and the seizure of the Crimea in 1783, which placed Russian vessels within two days' distance of the Bosporus, were watched by England with mixed feelings.

In the 1790's Pitt was ready to meet by force Russia's policy aiming at the total destruction of Poland. But internal opposition in England forced Pitt to abandon this plan. The subsequent twenty years showed an amazing ambivalence of political alignments. Czar Paul I (1796–1801) originally involved Russia deeply in the war against France only to land finally in the French camp. Alexander I seemed willing after 1807 to align Russia on the side of France. The grim prospect of a continent united against it led England to destroy the Danish fleet at Copenhagen in order to retain access to the Baltic Sea. Actually, Russia did not, and probably could not, enforce the continental system, since its trade with England was of vital importance. Quarrels over the anti-English blockade were largely responsible for the collapse of Franco-Russian cooperation and for the War of 1812. In alliance with England, Prussia, Sweden, and Austria, Russia defeated Napoleon in a war that saw Russian troops marching to Paris.

Before discussing the new phase of Anglo-Russian relations opened by the Congress of Vienna, we must look at the relations of Russia and its immediate neighbors during the eighteenth century. The defeat of Sweden made Russia a Baltic power, and it remained Russian policy after 1721 to strengthen its position on the Baltic. The wish to annex (East) Prussia made Russia the ally of Austria and France in the Seven Years' War. But in 1762 Peter III threw away all the military gains Russia had made and saved Frederick the Great from certain disaster. Catherine did not resume the anti-Prussian policy of Empress Elizabeth, but concentrated on Poland and Turkey. Frederick, in his Political Testament of 1768, said that Russia, with a growing population, was likely to become the most dangerous power and that its westward march had been greatly helped by the mutual enmity of Austria and Prussia, the two states that might have set limits to the Russian advance. This insight came rather late to Frederick and was not reflected in his foreign policy, even after the end of the Seven Years' War.

After 1763, Austria and Prussia started what came close to being a race for Russia's favors, and the jealousy of the two German states as well as their need of foreign support enabled Catherine to carry through the vast expansion that resulted from her Turkish wars and the three Polish partitions. The cooperation of the three Eastern powers in this period affected their relations in the Napoleonic period. Austerlitz stands out as an example, and also the protection extended by Alexander I to Prussia in 1807. It was his work that Prussia was not wiped off the map but survived, though seriously crippled, after the peace of Tilsit. Prussia was to serve as a buffer between the French and Russian empires, although until 1813 Prussia was so much dependent on France in its foreign policy that a Prussian corps had to join Napoleon's invasion of Russia in 1812. Even the destruction of the *grande armée* in the winter of 1812 did not convince the Prussian king, Friedrich Wilhelm III, that the moment for liberation from the French had arrived. The general in command of the retreating Prussian corps, von Yorck, on December 30, 1812, concluded a convention with the Russians at Tauroggen that made the Russians enter East Prussia as liberators rather than as conquerors and made the province rise in support of the Russian war against Napoleon. This patriotic movement forced Friedrich Wilhelm III into the war against France. But at this moment the foundation was laid for the close relationship between Russia and Prussia that was to exist for practically a century. Neither Friedrich Wilhelm III nor his two sons and successors, Friedrich Wilhelm IV (1840–59) and Wilhelm I (1859–88), ever forgot the service rendered by Russia to Prussia at Tilsit nor the war of liberation of 1813–14.

The decision to continue the war against Napoleon beyond the frontiers of Russia and Poland was made by Alexander I against a great deal of internal opposition.[4] The commander of the Russian armies, the old Kutuzov, was the chief speaker for the conservative and isolationist Russian sentiment. He declared that Napoleon was no longer a danger for Russia and that, by destroying Napoleon's European empire, Russia would only install England as the major world power. Alexander I, brought up on the ideas of the French Enlightenment, was surrounded by many foreign advisers, among whom at this moment Baron Stein was probably the foremost figure. Of the six Russian delegates at the Congress of Vienna only one was a Russian by birth, and Count Razumovskii, ambassador in Vienna and friend of Beethoven, was a man of European outlook. But even from a Russian nationalistic point of view it was hard to deny that Russia had an interest in removing Napoleon's domination at least from Central Europe. Otherwise Russia would have made itself strongly dependent on England as the sole great power opposed to Napoleon. Moreover the czar wanted to indemnify Sweden for its loss of Finland, annexed by Russia in 1809. Should Sweden take Norway from Denmark, German territories had to be found for the latter.

If such an advance of Russian frontiers already had far-reaching repercussions in the center of Europe, this applied with even greater force to the czar's plan of restoring the kingdom of Poland, with himself as king. This scheme, which placed Russia in a formidable position vis-à-vis Germany and Austria, could only be realized if Austria and Prussia were restored to great-power status. Although it is true that after the winter of 1812 Alexander I began to think of himself in messianic terms as the liberator of the European nations, he did not forget even then the stark interests of Russian power. Eventually he had to compromise on his aims. Metternich and Castlereagh were determined to cut the Russian gains and left no doubt that if necessary they were prepared to fight. Russia did not receive the full westward extension in Poland coveted by the czar. The Congress of Vienna stabilized the East European frontiers for a whole century. Russian expansionist moves in Europe during that period were confined to the Balkans, and the fluctuations of Russian boundaries in this area, which became a region of intense power conflict, were not of great significance.

The years after 1815 witnessed the rather rapid change in Alexander I from liberal to reactionary thinking as well as from deism to theistic mysticism. As early as 1815 his proposal for a "Holy Alliance" gave the first proof of the new direction of his thought, although his own original draft still had a certain liberal ring. Metternich made the final document a mere proclamation of paternal absolutism, and the czar, who had been largely responsible for the French *charte* of 1814 and who gave Poland a constitution in 1815, actually soon became an absolute ruler at home and abroad. He eagerly pressed the concert of the five great powers to intervene in other countries against revolutionary upheavals. The Polish constitution was originally intended simultaneously as a means for collecting experiences valuable for the subsequent launching of political reforms in Russia. Yet brakes were very quickly put on the constitutional development of Poland, and no step toward reform was undertaken in Russia. Alexander I's domestic and foreign policies were closely interwoven, and it is interesting to contemplate whether his foreign policy might have remained more daring if after 1815 he had not undergone a change of heart. As long as he played for the sympathies of the liberals of Europe, he might have tried to extend Russian influence in Europe in alliance with the liberals of Western Europe and of Germany. At one time in 1814 he boldly attempted to place his intimate, Bernadotte, on the throne of France. It is possible that he might have challenged the western frontiers of Poland after 1815 again if he had followed a liberal course in Russia and Poland.

It is against this background that Russian foreign policy in the last years of Alexander I and in the reign of his brother, Nicholas I (1825–55), must be seen. The Decembrist rising of 1825 and its defeat as well as Nicholas I's military character, so devoid of all mysticism and sentimentality, hardened the despotic system and also gave Russian foreign policy great rigidity. There was no Russian challenge of the Polish western boundaries. In 1836 Nicholas I agreed to the incorporation of the free Polish city of Cracow into Austria, which took place ten years later without any Russian misgivings. The common interest of the three Eastern monarchies in maintaining the results of the "fourth" Polish partition of 1814 became an effective cement for holding Russia, Austria, and Prussia together. But the unity of the five great powers, on which diplomacy by conference and the application of the principle of intervention rested in the aftermath of the Congress of Vienna, had already broken down by the time of Alexander's death. Canning had raised the banner of nonintervention, and even the France of Charles X opposed Russian foreign policy more than once.

Conflicts during the 1820's were largely confined to colonial

and maritime questions, and, as far as they included the problems
of the Mediterranean, we shall have to come back to them
later. But the Belgian, French, and Polish revolutions of 1830
seemed to explode the continent itself. Nicholas I wanted to
intervene in Belgium, but the Polish revolution made it impossible to march a Russian army to Western Europe. In spite
of substantial Prussian assistance, the Russian army needed
almost a year to subjugate Poland, and Czar Nicholas had to
accept the monarchy of Louis Philippe as well as the independence of Belgium, both the products of revolution. As a
consequence, the ties with Austria and Prussia were strengthened as much as possible. The alliance, usually called by its
liberal critics the "Holy Alliance," was designed to protect not
only the military security of Russia but also, in Nesselrode's
words, the "internal tranquillity" of Russia. As Baron Brunnow
wrote in a memorandum to the czar in 1838: "If Austria and
Prussia are for us, this single fact will stop the ambitious projects
of France and frustrate the evil designs of England." But he
added: "The triumph of revolutionary ideas on the banks of
the Danube and Oder concerns us more immediately than the
[English] reform bill and the July barricades [in Paris]. Here
is the reason why we must consider the cause of monarchy
in Prussia and Austria not as foreign to us, but as a question
that concerns Russia directly." The alliance with the two
monarchies "solidly founded on principles analogous to our own"
was thought to be necessary as a "moral barrier" between Russia
and France.[5] For this reason Russian diplomacy was also
continuously active to admonish the monarchical governments
of Vienna and Berlin not to swerve from the right path of
despotism.

The Russian policy in favor of international reaction aroused
the hatred of the liberal movements in Europe. Among German
liberals and democrats the belief was widely held that no progress toward a national and constitutional German state could

be expected as long as Russian influence was not removed from Central Europe. Enthusiasm for the Polish revolutionaries temporarily reached a high level. After 1848, Karl Marx and Friedrich Engels were convinced that only a war against Russia and the restoration of Poland would clear the way for the world revolution.

The revolutions of 1848, which enveloped practically all of Europe except England and Russia, seemed for a moment to place Russia in the danger of having to meet a liberal crusade. But actually the Russian government soon succeeded in inflicting a grave diplomatic defeat on the Frankfurt National Assembly, the main organ of the liberal revolution in Germany. It was a tragic error that the German liberals at this moment tried to bring Schleswig-Holstein fully into Germany. Any change of the Vienna settlement with regard to Denmark was frowned upon not only by Russia but also by England. And although England was favorably disposed toward the formation of a constitutional German state, it was not willing to tolerate any disturbance of the equilibrium created by the Vienna Congress in the Baltic between itself and Russia. This was the only major cause in which England and Russia, irrespective of their political and ideological enmity, were bound to cooperate.

The revolution in Germany subsided, but in 1849 Friedrich Wilhelm IV of Prussia, after rejecting the German crown offered to him by the Frankfurt Assembly, launched the project of reform of the Germanic Confederation, which would have integrated the non-Austrian German states under Prussian leadership. This Prussian policy, for which General von Radowitz was responsible, took advantage of the continuing weakness of the Austrian Empire. By the spring of 1849 the Hapsburg government had succeeded in restoring its authority in Bohemia, Austria, and Italy, though it failed to subdue the Hungarian revolution. Austria requested Russian military assistance, and Nicholas I, by sending an army of 120,000 men into Hungary, forced the surrender of the Hungarians at Vilagos on August 13, 1849. The Russian army returned to Russia without having demanded any price.

With the subjection of Hungary accomplished, the Austrian government of Prince Felix Schwarzenberg was able to intervene in Germany, and he imposed his will on the hesitant Prussian king, who sacrificed Radowitz. At Olmütz Prussia dropped its German reform plans, thereby opening the way for the full restoration of the Germanic Confederation with its Diet in Frankfurt. The intervention of the Russian czar in Hungary had led to the full restoration of the internal and external conditions of Central Europe as they existed before the revolutions of 1848–49. Nicholas I was satisfied not only that the revolution, which had enveloped practically all the European states except England, had not raised its head in Russia but also that Russia had succeeded in defeating the national and liberal movements of Central Europe with which England sympathized. On the occasion of the twenty-fifth anniversary of the czar's accession to the throne, in November 1850,[6] Count Nesselrode could assure him that "since 1814 the position of Russia and her sovereign has not been so good and great."

Actually Russia's position was soon revealed as being much weaker than Nesselrode and Nicholas I assumed in 1850, but it should not be forgotten that Russian policy during the years of the European revolutions had produced results that profoundly affected the course of European history for the rest of the century. While the failure of the revolutions of 1848–49 did not have its exclusive cause in Russian policy and intervention, but was largely determined by the inner weaknesses of Central European liberalism, the actions of czarist Russia contributed decisively to the breakdown of the liberal and democratic movements in 1848, from which they never fully recovered. The "constitutionalism" introduced into Germany and Austria-Hungary in the 1860's was only a pseudo-constitutionalism. While it

set the Hohenzollern and Hapsburg monarchies apart from autocratic Russia, it also kept them separate from the mainstream
of Western European political life. From this division of Europe
imperial Russia derived great advantages in the subsequent
sixty years.

The strength that Russia had shown at home and abroad
during the years of European revolutions emboldened Nicholas I to advance claims for Russian control of the straits even at
the risk of a war with the Western European powers. In the
early years of his reign Nicholas I had already conducted a war
against Turkey. The war of 1828–29 was a means to consolidate
czarist Russia, just badly shaken internally and externally by
the Decembrist conspiracy. War in Asia did not, as the European
war of 1812–15 had done, infect the Russian army with revolutionary ideas, and a victory of czardom fighting for the protection of the Orthodox faith was likely to strengthen the czarist
regime. During the Russo-Turkish War of 1828–29 Russia did
not encounter the outright hostility of England and France. In
the liberation of Greece the three powers cooperated to a large
extent, and England did not object to the actual protectorate
over the Christian Balkan provinces which, together with other
great gains, Russia won as the result of the war in the peace of
Adrianople (1829). Yet Russia avoided exploiting the military
helplessness of the Turkish Empire in a radical way. Although
it might have removed Turkey from the Balkans altogether,
Nesselrode advised the czar that Russia was ill prepared to
assume such a heavy responsibility, which in addition would
bring on a big European war. Nesselrode declared the existence of a weak Turkish Empire, open to Russian influence, as
most advantageous. Thus open war between England and Russia was avoided.

But English suspicion of Russian expansion in the Near East
had been aroused and even in these years occasionally expressed
itself rather forcefully. When Russia attempted to extend its

hold over the straits in the Russo-Turkish treaty of Unkiar-
Skelessi in 1833, British policy turned definitely hostile. Napoleon's expedition to Egypt had created a new vision of the
political significance of the great land bridge between the eastern Mediterranean and the Indian Ocean. When the building
of the "second" British Empire tended to center largely around
India after 1815, England grew sensitive to the spread of any
foreign influence and also to the penetration by any foreign
power of countries bordering on India. In all these areas, however, there was only one power, namely Russia, that posed a
threat to British interests. Anglo-Russian conflict over the Near
and Middle East became one of the major determining factors in
international affairs. However, it did not carry over into the
Baltic, which, as we have seen, had been the chief area of Anglo-
Russian contact. The international order that had come into
being in this area by 1815 was not only not questioned by either
of the two powers, but was even jointly defended, as the
Germans learned to their dismay in 1848–49.

The rise of Anglo-Russian tension, which in the early 1850's
was fanned by Louis Napoleon, who wished to humble Russia,
the chief guarantor of the Vienna settlement, also changed the
position of other powers. Austria had viewed the Russo-Turkish
War of 1828–29 with alarm. It had been Metternich's hope that
conflicts with Russia over Balkan problems, as they had occurred as early as the days of Catherine II and Joseph II,
might be more easily settled once the Eastern monarchies were
pledged to preserve the status quo. But Metternich underrated
Russia's determination to acquire control of the Turkish straits.
It was also difficult to make the conservative ideology that justified the policies of the monarchies in Europe workable in the
Near East. While it was possible to consider scrupulous adherence to existing treaties and to the principle of monarchical
legitimacy as a Christian commandment, it was highly dubious
whether the preservation of the Turkish Empire, and especially

of the sultan's rule over Christian peoples, could be considered equally sacrosanct.

The Russo-Turkish War led to a temporary eclipse of the alliance of the three Eastern monarchies. The Austrians saw in Russian progress in the Balkans a grave threat to their own vital interests. But Metternich could do little but complain about the breakdown of his hallowed diplomatic system. Active opposition to Russia would have promised practical results only if England had joined with Austria.

At the time of the Crimean War, Russia was faced with the determination of the Western powers to force its retreat in the Near East. Austria was bold enough to defend its own interests in the Balkans. By his intervention in Hungary, Czar Nicholas had just helped to reestablish the power of the Hapsburg Empire. Naturally the Austrian policy of Baron Buol that compelled Russia to evacuate the Danube principalities and keep a large army in Volhynia appeared to the czar an act of utter ingratitude and perfidy. But this decade after the revolution was a period when ideology and sentiment counted for little. It is questionable, however, whether the leaders of Austria were realistic in their political decisions. The alliance of the three Eastern monarchies based on a uniform ideology broke down, and the sympathies of the new czar, Alexander II, went to Prussia rather than Austria. The stage was thereby prepared for Bismarck. But, like Austria, Russia departed drastically from the traditional solidarity of the divine-right monarchies by moving closer to France after 1856. It was this Franco-Russian rapprochement that made possible the Italian War of 1859, in which Austria lost all its major Italian possessions except Venetia to the new kingdom of Italy. Yet the new policy was soon seen to contain serious dangers. The national unification of Italy stimulated other national revolutionary movements in Hungary, Germany, and Poland. The sympathy shown by Napoleon III for the Polish cause during the Polish revolution of 1863 ended all cooperation between Russia and France, whereas the unstinted help of Prussia in the defeat of the revolution, offered by its new prime minister, Bismarck, added new warmth to Russo-Prussian friendship.

II

The year 1855—the year of the death of Nicholas I, the succession of Alexander II, and the recognition of the loss of the Crimean War—marked the arrival of a new age of Russian history and of Russia's relations with Europe and the world. The Crimean War had demonstrated the weakness of the political, military, and social institutions of the Russia of Nicholas I. Alexander II began great internal reforms. The liberation of the peasants was the most fundamental, because in one way or another it affected every group and class of Russian society. The impoverishment of large sections of the gentry and the growth of a bourgeoisie created a half-noble, half-bourgeois layer of society that was receptive to nationalist ideas and, though not monarchical, was pressing its sentiments on the czar. Whereas Nicholas I could still formulate his foreign policies autocratically, Alexander II was greatly influenced by the nationalism of the upper groups. "As far as I am concerned, I am a Russian before I am a Slav," he could say in 1864, and he often pointed out that Pan-Slavism was likely to lead to a presumably republican federation of Slav nations.

It is true that Slavophilism and Pan-Slavism, in practice even more than in theory, merged after the Slav Congress of 1867 into a neo-Russian nationalism which clashed less openly with monarchical absolutism. The influence of nationalistic trends on Alexander was greatest in times of internal stress, as after the Russo-Turkish War of 1877–78. At that time, which saw the first rising tide of the popular revolutionary activity to which Alexander was to fall victim in 1881, another motive for the connivance of the government with the Russian nationalists became apparent. An anxious desire to retain some popular support in the face of the revolutionary movements was a handicap to the rational management of foreign policy to the very end of the czarist regime.

Alexander II's personality undoubtedly was partly to blame for the loss of the full independence of governmental policy. He possessed neither an incisive mind nor strong will-power. For example, he could have forbidden Russian generals in the Caucasus, in Central Asia, and in the Far East to advance almost continually southward, which was keeping alive the tension between Russia and England. But Alexander tolerated the refractory attitude of his colonial proconsuls even in the early years of his great reforms, when he knew that Russia would have to be extremely cautious. This colonial expansion appealed to him.

The most important change in Russia's international position in the days of Alexander II was the founding of the new German Empire. Bismarck made it impossible for Russia in 1864 to repeat its opposition to a revision of the status of Schleswig-Holstein. He had maneuvered Denmark into a political position incompatible with existing international treaties, and he had Austria on his side. It would have been difficult for England to find an excuse for intervening in favor of Denmark, even if it had been in a mood to do so. The same was actually true of Russia. Therefore, Bismarck gained his first major diplomatic victory, although in the final phase he dropped any pretext that he was aiming at maintaining the status quo.

Bismarck's success in 1864 was only the prelude to the final showdown with Austria in 1866. In the first decisive phase of the war Russia was a benevolent neutral. It did not wish to see Austria win and extend its rule in Germany, nor France use the opportunity for interfering in Germany. But after Sadowa the czar felt apprehensive about the great increase of Prussian power that at once excluded the traditional Russian influence from German affairs and even appeared to change the European equilibrium in an ominous way. Bismarck's deposition of the old dynasties of Hanover and Hesse-Kassel was vigorously protested as a flagrant violation of the monarchical principle. Bismarck was careful not to hurt those German dynasties which, like the princes of Hesse-Darmstadt or Württemberg, were directly related to the Russian imperial house, but he insisted on Prussian annexation of Hanover and Hesse-Kassel and threatened that any Russian intervention would force him to form a closer alliance with the liberal national movement in Germany so that he could fight foreign interference in German affairs. This threat caused some resentment in St. Petersburg, although it was finally decided to swallow any discontent with events in Germany. Intervention in Germany was bound to bring the French to the Rhine, and this was undesirable. There was some comfort in the reflection that Bismarck, while momentarily committing grave sins through the removal of legitimate rulers, still remained the statesman who, by his struggle with the Prussian parliament, had proved himself the strongest German foe of liberalism.

The same painful embarrassment was felt in St. Petersburg during the Franco-Prussian War. By threatening intervention, the Russian government kept Austria from using the opportunity for renewing the battle for the hegemony of Germany. Bismarck had assured the Russian government that he was ready to assist Russia in freeing itself of the worst imposition of the Paris peace of 1856, the banning of Russian naval forces from the Black Sea. Russia renounced the so-called Pontus clause of the Paris peace during the Franco-Prussian War. But this gain was small comfort in view of the sudden rise of Prussia-Germany as the most powerful state on the continent. So far Russia had always faced a divided Germany on which it could exercise strong influence through many channels. Now Russia could not hope to have greater influence than its diplomatic relations with the Berlin government might give it. Moreover apprehension was felt that the new German Empire might still expand further and particularly might aim at including Germans living outside the German borders of 1871, among them possibly the Germans in the Baltic provinces of Russia.

The process of German unification caused an important change in Russian-German relations. The growth of Slav nationalism as exemplified by Danilevskii[7] cannot be discussed here, where we are chiefly concerned with official policies. Actually the nationalist reaction was at once reflected in domestic Russian politics by the abrogation of the privileges which the German minority in the Baltic provinces had enjoyed. In the Russian government service, too, the number of Germans was decreasing.[8]

In foreign affairs the new feeling did not produce an immediate change, unless greater emphasis on Franco-Russian relations is taken into consideration. Bismarck sensed the danger of a Franco-Russian alliance from the beginning. It was the chief reason why, in spite of his own royalism, he supported the republican forces in France after 1871. A French republic, he argued, would be less *bündnisfähig* than a French monarchy. Although Alexander II, and originally even Alexander III, were averse to any form of fraternization with the French Republic, even after 1871 Russia made it clear in Berlin that it would not tolerate any further diminution of French power. In 1875, when rightly or wrongly[9] it seemed that Bismarck intended to start a preventive war against France in order to restrain its rearmament, Russia publicly announced its disapproval of any repressive German policy vis-à-vis France. Russia also avoided giving direct recognition to the German annexation of Alsace-Lorraine.

But otherwise Bismarck succeeded after 1871 not only in maintaining close and friendly relations with Russia but also in reestablishing diplomatic cooperation between Russia and Germany on the one side and Austria-Hungary on the other. In Bismarck's opinion, the Three Emperors' League, which came into being in 1872–73, constituted the ideal grouping of powers. Of all the misfortunes that might possibly befall Germany, Bismarck judged a Russo-German war the most calamitous. The losses that such a war might inflict upon Germany would be enormous, while even the defeat of all the Russian military forces would hardly diminish Russia's national strength, which rested in the many millions of robust people settled over a vast continent. On the other hand, Bismarck was afraid that in a bilateral Russo-German alliance Germany was likely to be exposed to Russian demands conflicting with vital German interests. Whereas Bismarck found that a Russian advance toward the straits and the Balkans was unobjectionable or, as he once expressed it, "was not worth the bones of a single Pomeranian grenadier," a Russian thrust into Central Europe could not be tolerated. The preservation of the Hapsburg Empire was a major German interest, and thus it was logical that the defense of the boundary that the Congress of Vienna had set to Russia's westward march should be undertaken together with Austria-Hungary.

The reason for Russia's willingness to accept the Hapsburg Empire in a renewed alliance of the Eastern monarchies lay chiefly in its desire to keep Austria-Hungary from cooperating with England. The early 1870's were the years of active Russian conquest of those regions that now form the major part of Turkestan. Anglo-Russian tension over these developments reached a high pitch. As seen from St. Petersburg, Austria-Hungary was most likely to join England in an anti-Russian policy, and therefore it was desirable to attract it to the Eastern camp. Austria on its part did not wish to serve as Britian's foot soldier in the defense of the frontier of India, but it was not inclined to write off its concern with the Balkans. This became the chief weakness of the Three Emperors' Alliance. Once the Hapsburg Empire gave up any idea of regaining its traditional leadership in Germany, Balkan problems were bound to become the chief focus of Austrian foreign policy. The growing weight of Hungary in the councils of the dual monarchy strengthened this tendency. Thus the triangular relationship of the Eastern empires functioned well only as long as Russia did not actively pursue its aims in the European parts of the Turkish Empire.

The Three Emperors' Alliance was grounded on an ideological basis to a much lesser extent than the alliance of the three Eastern monarchies in the age of Nicholas I and Metternich. A realistic appraisal of their political interests was the major motive that brought the three empires of Bismarck, Franz Josef, and Alexander II together. Even in the first half of the century the recognition of power interests had never been completely submerged in the sentiment of monarchical solidarity. Still, in the second half of the century the rational evaluation of the interests of state both in Russia and in Austria was somewhat blurred by strong internal pressures. In Austria the growing intensity of the struggle of nationalities, in Russia the anxiety over keeping some popular support of czardom made a sober evaluation of the interests of state precarious. Moreover the ideology of monarchical conservatism had not lost its appeal after 1871. Bismarck was clearly under its influence. In 1871–73 and again toward the end of his career he proposed to the monarchs international arrangements "to fight socialism and republicanism." Such "anti-Comintern pacts" were not concluded, although Bismarck's steady emphasis on monarchical solidarity and his warnings that a war between the great monarchies would end in revolution and the breakdown of all monarchical regimes found an echo in the thoughts of the Russian and Austrian rulers.

The first crisis of the Three Emperors' Alliance occurred in 1876–79. Revolts in Bosnia, beginning in the fall of 1875, led to

stormy popular sympathy with the suppressed Slav brethren in
Russian society, and Alexander II was slowly lured into a war
with Turkey. Yet before going to war the czar and Gorchakov
tried to elicit from Bismarck a promise that Germany would
protect Russia against the intervention of other powers, and this
meant chiefly Austria-Hungary. They declared that they could
claim such assistance, since by its friendly attitude in 1866 and
1870–71 Russia had made the Prussian-German Empire possible.
But Bismarck replied that Germany could tolerate the curtail-
ment of Austria's position as a great power as little as a serious
weakening of the Russian Empire. As a consequence Russia
had to negotiate with Austria, toning down its own potential
war aims and pledging important concessions to Austria in the
Balkans as the price for Austrian neutrality.

When after long fighting the Russian army forced the passes
of the Balkan mountains and approached the Turkish capital in
the last days of January 1878, Constantinople was without defense. But Alexander II accepted the advice of Gorchakov and
of the minister of war, Miliutin, not to court war with England
and Austria. The Russian army reached the Marmara Sea ten
miles west of Constantinople. On February 13, a strong British
fleet passed the Dardanelles. Russian peace negotiations with
Turkey were entrusted to Count Ignatiev, who as Russian ambassador in Constantinople since 1864 had proved himself the
most radical nationalist. The peace of San Stefano of March 3,
1878, repudiated in many important respects the assurances
that Austria and also England had received from Russia before
the opening of the war. Under the threat of war with England
and Austria-Hungary the czar agreed to have the treaty reviewed by a European conference. Before the conference,
which became the Congress of Berlin, was convened, England
and Russia reached an accord on the major revisions of the San
Stefano treaty. England and Austria agreed on a common
policy at the Congress. Finally England made the Porte cede

Cyprus to it in recognition of the protection given to Turkey at this moment.

The Congress that met under the presidency of Bismarck in Berlin from June 13 to July 13 was largely predetermined in its results. Bismarck described his role at the Congress as that of an "honest broker," and this applied particularly to his mediation between Russia and the Hapsburg Empire, which worked closely together with Britain. Lord Salisbury took the impression away from Berlin that Bismarck leaned to the Russian rather than to the English side. It was generally commented that the German chancellor showed no consideration for the hapless Turks. The concessions that Bismarck won for Russia by prodding England and Austria or imposing on Turkey were not insignificant. Yet the final Berlin treaty was deeply resented by Russian society. A flood of accusations was leveled against Russian diplomacy, because it had allowed foreign powers which had not fought to make big gains, while Russia had been deprived of what its soldiers had conquered with their blood. Actually the treaty of Berlin gave Russia very great accessions in Europe and Asia, but this counted little with the Russian public in view of the defeat of the Russian plan of a large Slav state in the Balkans. Only half of Bulgaria became autonomous, whereas the land south of the Balkan mountains received merely a tenuous form of autonomy and saw Turkish troops move in again. Russia seemed thereby rolled back from Constantinople a far distance. Meanwhile Austria-Hungary, without having fired a shot, could occupy Bosnia and Herzegovina and thereby expand its influence far into the western parts of the Balkan peninsula.

Russian feeling against Austria-Hungary ran high, but this time it turned even more violently against Germany. "The way to Constantinople leads through the Brandenburg Gate" became the new slogan. What was causing serious apprehension in Berlin and Vienna was the unwillingness of the czarist government to stop the vicious press campaign. Obviously the government was pleased that the ire of the Russian public over the misfortunes of Russian warfare and diplomacy did not have to be borne by the Russian government but was deflected toward foreign scapegoats. Yet in words and actions there were also barely veiled official threats. Bismarck's reply was the conclusion of an alliance with Austria-Hungary by which the two powers pledged their full mutual support in the event of an unprovoked Russian attack on either of them.

The alliance, which was renewed at regular intervals and lasted till 1918, has been widely interpreted as an option of Bismarck between Austria-Hungary and Russia. But although the dual alliance became the road to growing separation between the Central Powers and Russia after 1890, for Bismarck it was a means for the restoration of the Three Emperors' Alliance. He hoped that the isolation of Russia would bring the czarist government to its senses. The German-Austrian alliance did in fact have a sobering effect on the czarist government at once. In January 1880 Russian-German negotiations on a renewal of close political ties were begun in an auspicious atmosphere. In June 1881, the three empires formally signed the new Three Emperors' Alliance. The secret treaty, valid for three years, committed each signatory to benevolent neutrality if one of them should get into war with a fourth great power. This rule was also to apply to a war of one of the three empires with Turkey, with the proviso, however, that the three powers had reached a prior agreement on the results of such a war. The three powers finally assumed the obligation to respect each other's interests in the Balkans, to act jointly in questions relating to all the Turkish possessions, and to recognize the closure of the straits.

The alliance was approved by Alexander III, the son and successor of Alexander II, who had been assassinated in March 1881. Alexander III was affected much less than his father by the traditional dynastic bonds between Russia and Prussia. The pupil of Pobedonostsev, he was a Russian nationalist. But while Pobedonostsev's ideas found forceful expression in the czar's domestic policies, they did not dominate his foreign policies. Autocracy was tightened, the Russification of Poland, of the Baltic provinces and, to a lesser degree, of Finland were intensified, and the persecution of the Jews was systematically launched. Yet although Alexander III was particularly suspicious of Germans and attempted to limit their numbers in the army and in government service,[10] he cooperated rather trustingly with Bismarck in foreign affairs. His autocratic instincts led him to acknowledge that the despotic Russia was more naturally grouped with Germany than with France.

There were, however, quite realistic reasons for joining the Three Emperors' Alliance. In the discussion of the value of the tripartite alliance in the Russian foreign ministry, Saburov, the ambassador in Berlin, argued that the treaty was making any Russian action in the East dependent on the prior approval of Germany, whereas Germany had complete freedom of action. Therefore, he demanded that in a renewed treaty Germany and Austria-Hungary should promise neutrality in the case of such Russian involvement. Foreign Minister Giers and his immediate advisers took the view that such a revision was not only unattainable but also undesirable. Russia was only then beginning to build a new Black Sea navy. It would not be able to take the straits for a long time even if it had to meet only England's opposition. In these circumstances it would be unwise to focus attention upon this Russian aim. The treaty was actually renewed unchanged for another three years in 1884. The relative military as well as financial weakness was the major cause for Alexander III's conciliatory policy in these years, which made it possible for Bismarck to round out his system of alliances by building up the Triple Alliance of Germany, Austria, and Italy of 1882 and the agreements of these three powers with Rumania in the following year. Bismarck's eagerness to extend his alliances was a sign that he no longer completely trusted the strength and continuity of the policy of the czars. In 1880 he remarked: "It is true that the Russian power is no longer fully integrated; a treaty with the emperor and even with him and the heir to the throne today commits only one part of the Russian power; the other remains refractory and makes a policy of its own."[11]

The gravest fissure of the Three Emperors' Alliance, however, lay in the lack of mutual confidence between Austria-Hungary and Russia and in their continuous friction in the Balkans. In 1881 Austria-Hungary had concluded an alliance with Serbia that made the latter a virtual satellite of the dual monarchy. Russia on its part had been given by the Congress of Berlin the mandate to organize the government and administration of Bulgaria, and Russian troops were occupying the country. Bismarck tried strenuously to persuade the two allies to reach a permanent agreement on a division of the Balkans into spheres of interest that would place Bosnia, Herzegovina, and Serbia in an Austrian zone and Bulgaria and Eastern Rumelia in a Russian one. He attempted in vain to convince the Austrian statesmen that Russian occupation of the eastern Balkans, nay even of the straits, would not be a threat to Austria-Hungary, since the Russians, in such an overextended position, would be forced to come to terms with Austria.

By 1885 the Balkans were again seething with unrest, while at the same time they were the victim of the struggling great powers of Europe. The most important events took place in Bulgaria, where Russian officers and administrators had alienated the population, and the newly appointed prince, Alexander von Battenberg, had fallen out with the Russians in Bulgaria and with the St. Petersburg government. A nationalist coup in 1885 proclaimed the merger of Eastern Rumelia with Bulgaria as envisaged by the peace of San Stefano. Although von Battenberg obtained the diplomatic backing of Austria, England, and Italy, this made him as well as the whole new development in Bulgaria absolutely unpalatable to the czar. Whereas England and Austria now actually defended the peace of San Stefano, Russia insisted on the treaty of Berlin and threatened to intervene in Bulgaria. Finding Austria-Hungary on the other side of the fence, Russia announced in Berlin in late 1886 that while it was prepared to continue some sort of treaty relationship with Germany, it was not going to renew the Three Emperors' Alliance in 1887. The necessity of an option between Russia and Austria-Hungary seemed inevitable. This time Russia seemed to hold the trump cards, since in 1887, owing to the rise of General Boulanger, a grave danger of war between France and Germany developed.

The years 1887–89 witnessed the zenith of Bismarckian diplomacy, in the words of an American historian.[12] It reached, indeed, an astounding level of subtlety and complexity that cannot be described here, although fundamentally it was only an elaborate projection of Bismarck's earlier policies. Germany's complete disinterestedness in all the Near Eastern questions was the basis of Bismarck's policies. He warned Austria-Hungary that the German alliance, while protecting the integrity of the Hapsburg Empire, gave no support to Austrian policies in the Near East which were likely to result in acute conflict with Russia. As far as Austria-Hungary felt that it had to defend vital interests in the Balkans, Bismarck advised it to seek the assistance of Britain. Bismarck actually went as far as to help actively in creating the so-called Mediterranean Entente of 1887, which united Britain, Austria-Hungary, and Italy in a guarantee of the status quo in the Mediterranean, i.e., of the Turkish Empire, including the straits.

On the other side, Bismarck could assure Russia that Germany did not object to Russian progress toward the straits or to the exertion of Russian preponderance in Bulgaria. He offered to embody these promises of German policy in a written Ger-

man-Russian agreement. After a long period of diplomatic
fencing, in which Russia threatened to form a Franco-Russian
alliance, Alexander III accepted the secret "reinsurance treaty"
of June 18, 1887, in which Russia and Germany promised each
other benevolent neutrality in any war with a third power,
except one caused by either German aggression on France or
Russian aggression on Austria-Hungary. Germany recognized
the "historically acquired rights of Russia in the Balkan peninsula"
and particularly in Bulgaria. It also declared its willingness to
assist in the enforcement of the closure of the straits, and, in a
very secret article, to maintain benevolent neutrality in the
event the czar considered it necessary to take "the keys of his
empire" into his own hands.

It is clear that the reinsurance treaty was not concluded by
the Russians because they seriously intended to move against
the straits within the three years of the validity of this treaty.
Bismarck had made known to them the contents of the German-
Austrian alliance treaty of 1879, and they knew, of course, the
preparedness of Britain, Austria-Hungary, and Italy to defend
the Turkish Empire. Even an alliance with France did not hold
out much hope that Russia would be able to change the status
quo. Thus the German treaty was immediately useful for the
Russians chiefly because it gave them German diplomatic help
in extricating themselves without too great a loss of prestige
from their disappointing involvement in Bulgaria. The German
commitment with regard to a Russian seizure of the straits was
concerned with an eventuality in an indefinite future. In 1887–
90 Russia could see in it mainly a guarantee that Germany
would give neither its alliance with Austria-Hungary nor the
Triple Alliance with Austria and Italy nor the Mediterranean
Entente an offensive character.

In spite of the reinsurance treaty the years 1887–90 were
characterized by a great deal of Russo-German friction, although the Bulgarian crisis passed by in this period. In 1890

the Russians began to turn their major attention to the Far East. The building of the Trans-Siberian Railway was begun in 1891. The wish not to be exposed to hostile pressure from the West grew. The czar still found security in the reinsurance treaty, but Bismarck's successors refused its renewal. They did not really intend to steer an anti-Russian course, although a good many German statesmen were inclined to think that a war with Russia was in the end inevitable and to give the German-Austrian alliance the central place in German diplomacy. But the chief reason for the German refusal to renew the reinsurance treaty in 1890 was the belief that the Bismarckian system of alliances contained serious contradictions and that Germany's treaty ties could be reduced, since Germany was strong enough to conduct a policy of the "free hand," which meant that in view of the permanent Anglo-Russian enmity it could side with one or the other power according to what would seem most profitable in any given situation.

It is doubtful whether the Russian government recognized the motives and intentions of Wilhelm II and his advisers correctly. Apparently the Russian government saw in the German rejection of the reinsurance treaty a fundamental reorientation of German policy. The Anglo-German treaty concerning Helgoland and Zanzibar of 1890 and the renewal of the Triple Alliance in 1891, which was greatly applauded by England, was seen to point in this direction. The government of Russia would probably not have been satisfied, however, if it had understood German policy rightly, because it wanted to have assurance that the German "free hand" would not suddenly change into a mailed fist in its direction. In any event, Russia almost at once decided on an alliance with France.

In the Three Emperors' Alliance of 1881 and 1884, Germany was left without any treaty obligations with regard to France. The reinsurance treaty of 1887 specifically spelled out that Russia would not have to act as a benevolent neutral in case of a German war against France. But from the end of the 1870's on there were not only political but also strong economic forces driving a wedge between Russia and Germany, while pulling Russia and France closer together. After the Crimean War and the peasants' liberation Germany exported more industrial goods to Russia than any other country.[13] In exchange, Germany received from Russia grain and other agrarian commodities as well as certain industrial raw materials. For a good while Germany was also the chief banker of the Russian state and of Russian industries. But at the end of the 1870's both Russia and Germany introduced protectionist measures. The German agrarians demanded the exclusion of cheap Russian grain and cattle from the German market, while the German industrialists pressed the German government to fight against the high duties Russia levied on imported industrial goods. The export of grain, however, was of vital importance to the Russian economy, and tariffs on manufactured goods were not only used for the protection of the infant industries of Russia but also for the Russian treasury. The conflict of economic interests was serious and bound to affect political relations as well.

This had happened for the first time in the crisis of 1879 when Bismarck had stopped the import of Russian cattle for allegedly sanitary reasons. Conflicts increased in the following decade and after 1890 led to an open economic war, which was only uneasily settled by the commercial treaty of 1894.[14] It was of even greater consequence that in November 1887 Bismarck blocked the German financial market for Russian government loans by having the German *Reichsbank* refuse to accept Russian bonds as collateral security for loans.[15] This *Lombardverbot*, which Bismarck had intended to be temporary, became practically permanent. Except for a few loans granted for political reasons the Russian government received no German funds between 1887 and 1914.[16] German capital investment in Russia grew till 1914, although it took mainly the form of the establishment of subsidiary branches of German industrial firms (e.g., Siemens in St. Petersburg) or German participation in Russian industrial ventures.[17]

From 1888 on France assumed the financing of the Russian government. By 1914 about 9 billion rubles had been loaned to the Russian government, to which more than 2 billion other French capital investments in Russia should be added. Altogether a quarter of the total foreign lending of France prior to World War I went to Russia. It would not have been possible for the Russian government to borrow such a large amount of capital without the active political cooperation of the French government. The state of the Russian budget hardly justified these extensive loans, and the intervention of French cabinets was often needed to persuade French bankers. In these circumstances French governments were able to impose political conditions on the loans. Apparently this happened as early as 1891, when the Russian government was told there would be no loan without an alliance. In 1906 the French insisted that a substantial part of a pending loan was to be used for the building of certain railroads that would speed up the deployment of the Russian army against Germany. According to Count Witte, more than one-third of the French funds was diverted from economic development to the construction of strategic railroads.

Although the decisive motive in Russia's turning toward France was strictly political and military, the French loans contributed to solidifying Franco-Russian relations. In 1906 the French government agreed to grant the Russian government a loan before the imminent convention of the Duma, thereby strengthening Russian autocracy against constitutionalism. In return, the czarist government strongly supported the French position at the conference of Algeciras.

III

The Franco-Russian alliance of 1893 afforded the protection Russia considered necessary when it began to give its major attention to the Far East. The Bulgarian experiences had been deeply disappointing, because they had shown that an autocratic Russia would win little gratitude for the liberation of Slav peoples. All these nationalities had democratic inclinations and did not wish to build their states in the image of Russian autocracy. The years 1890–1905 showed Russian government circles to be less susceptible to Pan-Slavist ideas and slogans. The drive toward the Pacific was carried out with a strong sense of a Russian mission in Asia, accompanied by a still unbroken hope that the Asiatic world could be made to conform to the Russian model. The Russo-Japanese War of 1904–5 was to shatter this confidence.

Russia's decision to turn to the East and place the chief concern of its policies on the Trans-Siberian Railway, built in 1891–1901, and on the expansion of its position on the Pacific decreased its pressure on its European neighbors, but made the Russian alliance less valuable for the French. If Russia concentrated on its Asiatic interests and, further, if Russia got involved in a major conflict, France could be exposed to severe treatment from Germany. This actually happened in 1905, when Russia fought its losing war with Japan and was crippled by internal revolution. Germany attempted at that moment to make France retreat in the Moroccan question, and it might have tried even sterner methods if France had not had England's support in its Moroccan policies after 1904. The Anglo-French entente proved its strength even at a moment when France's ally Russia was at war with Britain's ally Japan.

The years between 1890 and 1904 were years of rapidly changing diplomatic constellations. The split of the continental powers into two groups of seemingly equal weight gave England relative freedom of action. Actually this isolation was not as splendid as it appeared in the beginning, when it was expected that Britain could play off the Triple Alliance against the Franco-Russian alliance and vice versa. But in reality the continental states often cooperated, or at least followed a parallel political course, against England. During the Boer War, Britain faced the enmity of all the continental nations. In the Far and the Middle East Britain had to meet the expansionist activities of Russia. In Egypt and in the Sudan it found itself at odds with France, while German schemes for the acquisition of colonies or dependencies proved a continuous annoyance. Serious incidents occurred, such as Wilhelm II's telegram to President Krueger in 1896 or the Anglo-French crisis over Fashoda in 1898. The British government decided to ease its burden. In 1902 it concluded an alliance with Japan, which allowed Japan to go to war against Russia a few years later. In 1904, England and France settled their colonial differences. The Anglo-French entente was no alliance, but the German challenge of 1905-6, which was designed to demonstrate the weakness not only of the Franco-Russian alliance but also of the new Anglo-French entente, resulted in a broadening of the scope of the entente and even in the beginnings of close political cooperation.

German diplomacy after 1893 had endeavored to break up the Franco-Russian alliance by many maneuvers. Maybe this would not have been impossible if at the end of the century German foreign policy had been conducted with greater continuity of purpose and sense of reality than the flighty Wilhelm II and most of his advisers possessed. But the belief that Russia and England—"the bear and the whale," as Baron Holstein said—could not get together and that Germany was strong enough to follow a policy of the free hand was right only as long as Germany did not oppose simultaneously vital interests of both Russia and Britain. This, however, Germany managed to do after 1898 with the building of a big navy and the massive support given to the modernization of the Turkish Empire. The latter consisted not merely of the construction of the Baghdad Railway but also of many other financial and economic enterprises as well as the reorganization of the Turkish army. German activities in Turkey, though resented chiefly by Russia, were in certain respects disliked by the British as well.

Sir William White, the shrewd British ambassador in Constantinople at the time when German capitalists for the first time became active in Turkey, had favored the investment of German capital in Turkey, because in due course it would create conflicts between Germany and Russia. Therefore he had helped in 1888 to facilitate the Turkish grant of the concession for the building of the Anatolian Railroad, the direct forerunner of the Baghdad Railway, to the *Deutsche Bank*.[18] Twenty years later the actual execution of the great Baghdad project by their common competitor tended to make Britain and Russia think less of their own conflicts in the Near East.

Japan's victory over Russia in 1905 also eased Anglo-Russian discord in the Far East. Thereafter the chief region of contention, which in 1906 threatened to flare up into acute strife, was the Middle East. But Britain was subordinating its Middle Eastern interests to its supreme need of isolating Germany. On the other side, Izvolskii, the new Russian foreign minister (1906–10), was worried, not without good reason, that the Japanese might reopen hostilities against Russia.[19] The best way to countenance such a possibility, in his opinion, was to win the diplomatic intercession of Japan's ally, England, which would require a settlement of Middle Eastern tensions. Such a settlement, Izvolskii hoped, would also bring nearer the day when Russia could seize the Turkish straits. Thus the Anglo-Russian agreement on Persia, Afghanistan, and Tibet of August 1907 came into being. It should be emphasized that this agreement was no alliance but at best an entente. Mutual suspicions over Middle Eastern problems were not fully allayed. Nor had every possibility of a Russo-German rapprochement necessarily disappeared. The idea of monarchical solidarity by now had grown somewhat threadbare. Moreover the international treaties that had come into existence, as well as internal pressures, limited the freedom of action even of absolute monarchs. Proof of this had been the history of the treaty that Wilhelm II had persuaded Nicholas II to sign in the summer of 1905. The czar found no minister to countersign this Björkö treaty, which would have been a clear break with the Franco-Russian alliance, and rather meekly had to inform Wilhelm II of his failure.

Yet the liaison between "Nicky" and "Willy" went on to the end, and with the grim reaction that followed the first Russian revolution after 1907 the coalition with the liberal Western powers seemed to a good many members of the Russian ruling class unnatural. But on both sides of the Russian-German frontier conservatism was too deeply permeated with nationalism to be capable of reasserting itself with great force.

The Russian Revolution of 1905 had enabled the nationalities of Russia to show that they had not succumbed to Great Russian suppression. The liberal Russia that for a while appeared to be the result of the revolution at the same time had established many fresh connections with Slavs outside the Russian borders. In 1907 the grant of universal manhood suffrage in Austria gave the Slavs a tremendous opportunity for organizing their full strength. The event could not fail to have an enormous impact on the southern Slavs of Hungary as well. As a matter of fact, the Russian Revolution and the near culmination of the Slav struggle for equality was bound to have a profound effect on the Balkan Slavs, and this effect was to be heightened when in 1908 the Young Turk revolution opened up the prospect of a complete liberation of the European parts of the Turkish Empire.

Even before the Young Turk revolution Austria-Hungary had decided on an active policy to fight the dangers likely to arise with Serbian desires to absorb Croats and Slovenes into a Great Serbian or Yugoslav state. Izvolskii gave Baron Aehrenthal the excuse for the annexation of Bosnia-Herzegovina, which Austria-Hungary had occupied since 1878. This action proved a terrible shock to Russia, but its demand to take the matter to an international conference met finally not only with Austria's refusal but also with an ultimatum from Germany that backed Aehrenthal's action to the hilt. A Russia still not recovered from the Japanese War had to give in, and even in subsequent years the more moderate Russian leaders, to whom Izvolskii's successor Sazonov belonged, were acutely aware of Russia's weakness. Subsequent increases in Russian armaments were expected to produce an army ready to meet the German army by 1917. Still, attempts to gain the straits, which had miscarried in 1908, were made again in 1911 during the Italo-Turkish War and again during the Balkan wars. On the other hand, Sazonov began his tenure in office in 1910 by an effort to lessen Russian-German tensions. It was an important concession that Russia declared its willingness not to oppose the building of the Baghdad Railway thereafter, but all other issues remained unresolved, and Russia was greatly agitated in November 1913 when the Germans sent to Turkey a large group of officers who were to reorganize the Turkish army and whose chief, General Liman von Sanders, was to become the commander of the Turkish forces in and around Constantinople. Russian protests did not prevent the assumption of military command by the Germans over this strategic area so hotly coveted by Russia.

The successful fathering of a league of all the Balkan states served in the beginning chiefly the wish to remove Turkish rule from Europe altogether and thereby to facilitate a Russian move to the straits. Still, the Balkan League was at the same time an attempt to create an additional counterweight against the Central Powers. The Balkan states, united in the League, launched war against the Turkish Empire in 1912. Only two facts deserve mention here. The Balkan wars did not lead to a general European war. This was largely the work of British diplomacy, which for the last time played with great skill the role of arbiter between two competing European groups, Russia-France on the one side and Austria-Germany on the other. Yet whether Sir Edward Grey would have succeeded in his endeavors if Russia had been more advanced in its armaments is an unanswerable question.

The other remarkable fact is to be found in the ultimate split of the Balkan League into the coalition of Serbia, Greece, and Rumania looking to Russia for the furtherance of their national aims and an isolated Bulgaria preparing for cooperation with the Central Powers and Turkey. Thereby the Balkans became the barometer for the tenuous equilibrium of Europe, and in July 1914 the threatened changes in the balance of the Balkan states led to the outbreak of a general European war. This time Austria-Hungary's intention to humiliate Serbia and to destroy its political independence was resisted by Russia at the risk of war. The Russian reaction to the blind Austrian challenge seemed quite natural and was expected particularly by Austria itself. But it was a bold action on the part of the Russian statesmen, especially since the decisive move, the order of general mobilization of July 30, was taken at a time when Britain's attitude was still in doubt. The courage of the Russian statesmen, who also knew the shortcomings of the Russian army, was to a large extent born of fear. They believed the czarist regime could not stand another diplomatic defeat. Against this they entertained the hope that in war the regime would gain the popular mass support it was so sadly lacking.

IV

The war aims which the czarist government developed were the breakup of the Turkish and Hapsburg Empires as well as the drastic reduction of the German Empire. Russian diplomacy in 1915–16 made some headway toward these goals. Its allies promised Russia the straits in March 1915, and the treaties which it, together with Great Britain and France, signed in 1915–16 in order to bring Italy and Rumania into the war were more than an adumbration of the future partition of Austria-Hungary. With regard to Germany, Sazonov contemplated not only the annexation of the Polish provinces but also of East Prussia. It is interesting that he also wanted to weaken the Prussian monarchy internally by the restoration of the kingdom of Hanover and by the return of Schleswig-Holstein to Denmark. In addition to Alsace-Lorraine the French were to receive the Palatinate and parts of the Prussian Rhineland.[20] Although some of these Russian war aims, for example those applying to the future of the Rhineland, were opposed by the British, there can be little doubt that England and France could not have seriously hindered the realization of the Russian program in Eastern and Southeastern Europe if there had still been a czarist Russia at the time of Allied victory.

Carrying speculation for a moment even a step further, one may doubt whether a czarist Russia might have successfully digested all of Poland and kept control of Central Europe in competition with the Western powers over any length of time. Nicholas I, who as we have seen was careful not to extend Russian frontiers westward beyond the lines of 1815, exercised a powerful influence over Central Europe through the alliance of the three Eastern monarchies. But the Central Europe of, let us say, 1835 still lived in a pre-industrial age, and its ruling groups, dynasties, noblemen, and bureaucrats, though standing in a political tradition very different from that of Russia, could see in Nicholas I a guarantor of their way of life. The Russia of Nicholas II, if victorious in the war, would have entered a highly industrialized Central Europe with a mobile and dynamic society. Not even in its Slav countries could Central Europe have identified itself with a czarist order. As it was, the Russian autocracy did not even adequately reflect the state of Russian society, nor was it able to harness modern forces to make its own power secure. Thus czardom perished in and by the war, and its war aims proved idle dreams.

The Soviet Union had to give up practically all the European annexations that Russia had made since the days of Peter the Great. Moreover, Belorussian groups came under Polish rule, while many Ukrainians were left in Poland and Rumania and also in Czechoslovakia. The Russian defeat in the war with Poland in 1920–21 proved all these losses to be irrecoverable. But it was not the recovery of these territories that became the major concern of the foreign policy of the Soviet Union. Its inner and outer weakness made the Soviet government chiefly fear foreign intervention. In the League of Nations the Bolshevist leaders saw an alliance of the capitalist powers that was directed mainly against the Soviet state. To block any military move of the great powers against Russia was the supreme aim of Soviet diplomacy.

But Lenin and Trotsky hoped that the Soviet Union would gain security not by the methods of traditional diplomacy but by the advance of world revolution, which the Soviet Union was to propagate and lead through the Third International. Lenin's chief target was Germany. Centrally located in Europe, once it had been revolutionized it would wreck capitalism in all of Europe. Thus Communist propaganda and subversive activities were centered on Germany. Yet the Comintern failed to produce revolution in this country. By 1924 the Weimar Republic had emerged from its first period of tribulations. Even

Lenin's successor, Stalin, in spite of his emphasis on building up Socialism in Russia, did not give up hope that the world revolution was not too far off, and although he used the Communist parties of non-Russian countries more recklessly than Lenin for Russian security needs or power ambitions, international Communist activities were not relaxed; in Europe, Germany, with the strongest Communist Party, continued to be the major target.

Actually, however, during the whole interwar period conventional diplomacy paid higher dividends than international revolutionary activities, although it should not be forgotten that the latter contributed to a good many of the rich political profits reaped by the Soviet Union after World War II. Russo-German military cooperation was launched in 1921.[21] In 1922 the Rapallo treaty was concluded, to be followed by a trade agreement later on. The ties between the Soviet Union and Germany did not amount to an alliance and it is doubtful whether the relationship can even be called an entente. But as seen from Russia it kept Germany from joining an aggressive anti-Bolshevist front and enabled the Soviet Union to win assistance in building up the Red army as well as to gain important help for developing the Russian economy through German credits, deliveries, and technicians. The relationship survived the grave crisis brought on by Germany's conclusion of the Locarno treaty and its entrance into the League of Nations. The concession made to Germany by the Western powers in actually exempting it from any possible participation in future League sanctions eventually sufficed to persuade the Soviet government that Germany had not joined the West. The Russo-German treaty of Berlin of 1926 continued Russo-German relations as they had developed since Rapallo, though perhaps in a somewhat lower key.[22]

The rise of National Socialism led to a reversal of the methods of Russian foreign policy. The general aim, to keep

the major powers of Europe divided, remained the same when
the Soviet Union joined the League of Nations and concluded
a pact with France. With the rearming of Germany, however,
the mere division of the European powers was not enough.
Direct cooperation with the Western powers, which presumably
should have taken the form of the common enforcement of
the rules of the covenant, was necessary in order to stop
Hitler. But the Ethiopian War and Spanish Civil War demonstrated the unwillingness of the Western powers to take a
strong stand against the Fascist powers, and during the Czech
crisis the League of Nations was finally declared by Chamberlain
to be a car with a defunct engine. The treaty of Munich
was interpreted by Stalin as an attempt of Britain and France
to direct the aggressive intentions of Hitler toward the East
and get Nazi Germany and the Soviet Union embroiled in
combat. When the Western powers desired Russian help in
1939, Stalin's pact with Hitler enabled the latter to open war
against Poland and the West.

We may suspect that Stalin hoped the pact with Hitler would
make future German aggression against the Soviet Union unlikely. He evidently counted on a rather lengthy war in the
West that would also weaken Hitler. Meanwhile he was able
to build up Russian military might behind a greatly improved
strategic frontier. Although Stalin was disconcerted by the quick
collapse of France, to which the French Communists contributed, he failed to see the imminent danger of a German
attack on Russia. At the Berlin meeting in November 1940,
Molotov ridiculed the assertions of Hitler and Ribbentrop that
Germany had already won the war and refused to declare the
Soviet Union disinterested in the Turkish straits in exchange
for Russia's access to the Persian Gulf. In the spring of 1941
the Soviet government gave platonic support to the anti-German
coup d'état in Yugoslavia. On the other hand Russia dutifully
delivered to the last day the strategic goods promised to Germany

in the pact of 1939. Altogether the available evidence seems to indicate that Stalin considered Hitler, even after the battle of France, still too deeply involved in fighting the war in the West to be able to launch war against the Soviet Union. His profound suspicion of the Western powers must have further induced him to interpret the concrete American and British warnings against the coming German invasion of Russia as an evil scheme for steering him into a conflict with Hitler.

Soviet foreign policy during the interwar period was on the whole conducted along opportunistic and defensive lines. This is, however, only true if diplomacy by conventional means is considered, which gives a one-sided picture. The reckless fight that a Moscow-dominated German Communist Party in virtual alliance with the Nazis led against the Weimar Republic helped to create the international situation of 1933, which must have appeared sufficiently dangerous to Stalin to make him change the Communist line by adopting the tactics of the popular front. But the popular-front government of France, let alone that of Spain, became known too soon as just another device for the conquest of power. The relative diplomatic isolation of the Soviet Union was largely caused not only by the proclamation of the fundamental dogmas of Communism but also by the practical execution of Communist policies on the international scene.

From the war that Stalin's foreign policy failed to keep from Russia's doors the Soviet Union emerged as a power that might have overrun the whole European continent if the United States had not acted as a countervailing power. Yet the Soviet Union was able to achieve its national aims in Eastern and most of Central Europe. This assumed the form of annexations and of the establishment of a string of satellite states. Nowhere were the exact Russian frontiers of 1914 restored. Stalin took certain strategically vital regions such as the Baltic states, which were made even less assailable by the annexation of Königsberg and the northeastern sections of East Prussia. There is sufficient proof that Stalin desired similar control of the Turkish straits, but they proved beyond his reach. Apart from these largely strategically motivated annexations, to which the Russian gains in Finland should be added, Stalin annexed only regions containing members of nationalities represented in the Union of Soviet Republics. It is an interesting fact that he gave just these nationalities an elevated position by nominating the Ukraine and Belorussia for membership in the United Nations.

All the other nations were allowed to stay outside the U.S.S.R. Although during the war Pan-Slav slogans could occasionally be heard, this turned out to be mere phrase-making. The federative principle of the Soviet Union was not considered the right means for tying the neighboring Western states to Russia. After 1945 an outer girdle of nominally independent states was created. Except for Yugoslavia and Albania, none of these states would have adopted Communism if the Russian army had not been present, and as late as 1953 and 1956 the Red army had to intervene in East Germany and Hungary. Communism served as the major lever for enforcing the Eastern orientation not only of the liberated countries but also of the enemy countries. Through the Cominform, the Warsaw Pact, and through economic integration these states have received certain associative bonds with Moscow as well as among themselves. Economic integration has made great progress in recent years, after the radical Russian exploitation of the resources and production of the satellite states ceased.

The Soviet Union possesses absolutely and relatively more powerful tools of foreign control than czarist Russia possessed. It openly announces that Communism is expecting to replace bankrupt capitalism all over the world and that no great war will have to be fought for it. But support is offered to Communist movements all over the world, and all diplomatic and propagandistic weapons are employed to force the Western powers to retreat from vital positions. In Europe the German Democratic Republic (DDR) is the test case in how far "conventional" Russian policy—diplomatic and, maybe, military—may go to advance the date of the arrival of the millennium. The DDR is very closely economically integrated in the Eastern bloc, in which East Germany is, next to the Soviet Union, the strongest industrial state. The leaders of the East German state like to think of it as the "Piedmont" of future German unification. Whether the Soviet government thinks German unification an immediately desirable aim may be doubted, since Soviet leaders would probably not like to have as demanding a Western comrade as they have in China in the East.

The raising of the Berlin issue by Khrushchev in November 1958 constituted a probing action of a bold nature. It promised help to the DDR, greatly worried by West Berlin as the "show window of the West behind the Iron Curtain" and at the same time the only road to freedom for the people behind the Iron Curtain. At the same time any retreat of the Western powers from Berlin would make the West Germans, nay many Western Europeans, doubt American determination to defend Western Europe and thereby produce a crisis of confidence that would be the entering wedge for Communism. Thus the shadow of Soviet power falls today all over Europe, and further Soviet progress in Europe can only be blocked by the common efforts of the Atlantic community.

V THE POLITICAL COHESION
OF THE AUSTRO-GERMAN ALLIANCE
IN WORLD WAR I

————◆————

BISMARCK CONCLUDED the Austro-German alliance in 1879 in order to ban the threat of a German-Russian war, and he achieved his immediate objective.[1] Thirty-five years later the ready support given by the government of Wilhelm II to the Hapsburg Empire brought on the war with Russia and the Triple Entente that destroyed the three Eastern monarchies. By 1914 the Dual Alliance, for Bismarck only one, if the major, instrument in the search for security, had become practically the sole diplomatic combination through which Germany and Austria-Hungary defended their international position. In Bismarck's opinion the close cooperation of the three emperors was the safest guarantee of European peace as well as of Germany's vital interests. The three empires together would be able to stabilize the political and social order of Europe. For Germany it was important to keep Russia from advancing further westward in Central Europe and to be protected against the danger of a costly and senseless war along her exposed eastern frontiers. This, however, required not only a close relationship with Austria-Hungary but also an intimate understanding with Russia, which otherwise might still prefer to ally herself with France. In order to attain this understanding Germany had to convince the Russian government that, in contrast to Austria-Hungary, she had no stake in Balkan affairs and would not oppose any

Russian move in that sphere. For this reason the Dual Alliance was strictly confined to the defense of Austria-Hungary in her frontiers of 1879. Bismarck absolutely refused to back acquisitive or anti-Russian policies of Austria-Hungary in the Balkans. He told the Vienna government that for the pursuit of such policies it would have to look for support elsewhere and pointed to England as the natural ally in any attempt to stop Russian progress in Turkey. In 1887 he even assisted cautiously in persuading the British government to join with Austria-Hungary and Italy in the formation of an entente designed to maintain the status quo in the Mediterranean.

Bismarck's decision to conclude an alliance with Austria-Hungary has often been called his final option for the Hapsburg Empire. But Bismarck always hoped that the Austro-German rapprochement would have a sobering effect on the Russians and make them eager to restore the Three Emperors' League as it had existed in 1873–76. He was right. In 1881 the league was revived and renewed once more in 1884. When after 1886 new Balkan conflicts upset Austro-Russian relations, the Russo-German reinsurance treaty of 1887, spelling out the German *désintéressement* in the Near East, preserved mutual confidence between St. Petersburg and Berlin.

It is not necessary to discuss here the proliferation of Bismarck's system of alliances after 1879. The most important alliances, of course, were the Triple Alliance with Italy of 1881 and the Rumanian Alliance of 1883. With this network of alliances Bismarck had no serious difficulties in limiting the *casus foederis* of the Dual Alliance and asserting German leadership in Vienna. But with his removal in 1890 the Dual Alliance assumed a new meaning. The nonrenewal of the reinsurance treaty in that year and the subsequent formation of the Franco-Russian alliance drastically upgraded the value of the Austrian alliance for Germany. In the eyes of Bismarck's successors it became the real keystone of German foreign policy. When the

German naval, Turkish, and Moroccan policies after the turn of the century intensified the hostility of France and Russia against Germany and led England to side with them, the Austrian alliance became the only resort of German diplomacy, the more so since Italy's attachment to the Triple Alliance had become most dubious.

In this new situation the Austrian government could feel certain that Germany was bound to support Austro-Hungarian actions that might meet with strong Russian opposition. Baron Aehrenthal informed Berlin of the impending annexation of Bosnia and Herzegovina only a few days before the public declaration of October 5, 1908, and even then without showing all his cards. Chancellor Prince Bülow, though unpleasantly surprised, threw the full weight of Germany's "shining armor" behind Aehrenthal's provocative move. Bülow's announcement that Germany would fight for Austria-Hungary in *Nibelungentreue* compelled Russia to abandon the idea of intervention. It was clear, however, that Austria-Hungary had forced Germany's hand.

But it should not be overlooked that Germany's heedless involvement in world politics and her ensuing diplomatic isolation, while strengthening her ally's role within the Dual Alliance, did not improve Austria's international position. The revision of England's Balkan and Turkish policies as the consequence of the new Anglo-Russian entente of 1907 henceforth placed many hurdles into the path of Austria-Hungary's Balkan policy which formerly could count on British understanding or even collaboration.

Germany's active policies in Turkey after 1890 were welcomed by Austria-Hungary insofar as they deepened the gulf between Germany and Russia. But, inevitably, they got Germany more interested in the Balkans as the bridge to Turkey. German activities took the form of the stimulation of trade and industrial development, the latter being greatest in the Rumanian oil industry. Austria-Hungary began to complain about the trade competition of her ally in what she considered her own commercial hunting grounds. But the Austrians could not very well openly oppose this German trade expansion. Moreover, German banks and industrial firms were a powerful influence within the Austro-Hungarian economy itself.

Another change had occurred in the relationship of the Central Powers between 1879 and 1914. Bismarck was not unhappy that the alliance with Austria-Hungary was popular with practically every political group in Germany, and he would have liked for a time to turn it into a federation, anchored in the constitutions of the two empires. But he knew that the reasons for the popularity of the alliance in Germany rested on doubtful assumptions, chiefly on the belief that Austria-Hungary, or at least the Cis-Leithanian monarchy, was controlled by the German element and that the Magyars were Germany's loyal friends. Bismarck thought of the alliance essentially in cool diplomatic terms. In looking at the Austrian problem he probably overrated the freedom of choice that the monarchy possessed in international affairs and, incidentally, also the power of the monarch in molding the internal development of the multi-national empire. He was deeply suspicious of the clericalism of the Hapsburg dynasty and its close supporters as well as of the anti-German sentiment of the Slavs, particularly the Poles, and had reservations about even the chief supporters of the alliance, the Magyars. He thought least of those Germans who saw in the alliance the first step toward a reunion of the German Austrians with the German empire. Bismarck did not wish to admit them to his empire. In his opinion, they were disloyal to their duty to assist the Hapsburg dynasty in maintaining Austro-Hungary as one of the great powers on which the European state system rested.[2]

Bismarck described at some length his critical attitude toward Austria-Hungary in his memoirs. By the time they were published, however, his successors had already moved away from it. To be sure, none of Bismarck's ideas about the Hapsburg Empire was entirely forgotten by them. But in their public statements they fell in with the sentimental popular approach that found its epitome in Bülow's *Nibelungentreue*. The German governments between 1890 and 1914, which knew better, tried at least to strengthen the influence of the German element in Vienna. Occasionally, as in the case of the Badeni language law of 1897, German diplomatic pressure verged on direct intervention in the internal affairs of the allied empire. German statesmen watched with apprehension the growing debilitation of the Hapsburg Empire as a result of the grave national struggles. Yet the German statesmen saw in these conflicts chiefly another front of the war between Germans and Slavs that to many of them seemed imminent and inevitable, a belief that greatly contributed to the decision of the German government in July 1914 to accept the risk of war with Russia.

The use of racist terminology did not mean that the government of Wilhelm II thought of eventually incorporating the Austro-Germans into the German Empire. To the end of the Second Empire the official policy remained opposition to the inclusion of nine million Roman Catholics who would jeopardize the Protestant predominance in Germany. Among the German people almost no champions of *Gross-deutschtum* existed. But at least two rather strong organizations, the Deutsche Schul-Verein and the Gustav-Adolf Verein, helped maintain German schools and churches endangered by the progress of foreign nationalities.

The strong cohesion of the Dual Alliance was clearly demonstrated by the events following June 28, 1914. Beginning with the so-called blank check of July 6 the German government did everything to encourage Austria-Hungary to make war on Serbia, assuring her of full German military assistance in the case of Russian intervention. The Germans believed that by forceful

action Austria-Hungary would "rehabilitate" herself as a great
power and thereby restore the position of the Central Powers
vis-à-vis the Entente. They also thought that Germany could
defeat Russia and France, since both powers were not yet
adequately armed. Germany would have liked Austria-Hungary
to act more quickly against Serbia, but the differences over
diplomatic tactics did not affect the close collaboration of the
two monarchs and their cabinets that led to the outbreak of
the Great War.

A certain resentment, however, was noticeable on both sides
on account of the Italian issue. The Germans, anxious to keep
Italy as an ally, urged the Vienna government to offer Italy the
Trentino. The Austrians were annoyed by this demand, while
the Germans were irritated by the unwillingness of the Austrians
to move at all. The Italian issue troubled Austro-German relations seriously during the winter of 1914–15. The disappointment in Austria-Hungary over the grave military losses, which
had enabled Russian armies to cross the Carpathians and
forced the Austrians to withdraw from Serbia, led to Austrian
complaints about the lack of German military support in the
initial stage of the war.[3] Actually the terrible reverses the
Austro-Hungarian army had suffered, particularly in the Lemberg
battles in early September 1914, were largely the result of
General Conrad's faulty strategic dispositions. But the German
chancellor knew that the Austrians were deeply discouraged
and considered it not impossible that they might try to reach
peace with Russia by offering the Russians East Galicia and
then turn with their whole might against Italy. In order to make
the cession of the Trentino more palatable to the Austrians
Bethmann-Hollweg offered them the future possession of the
Polish coal-mining district of Sosnovice, adjacent to Upper Silesia. But as we have recently learned from a study by Egmont
Zechlin,[4] he was even prepared to compensate them by Silesian districts. For this astounding move he secured the ap-

proval of the Prussian cabinet, the chief of the general staff, and the emperor.

The offer of Silesian territories proved unnecessary, since Austria-Hungary agreed to the transfer of the Trentino a day or two before Wilhelm II's letter would have reached Vienna. While Germany's intention seemed a sign that she treated the Hapsburg Empire as an equal, this was rather the result of the deep worries over the general military situation. As the German leaders regained their confidence, they grew more imperious toward their allies. In 1915 the Germans took on a substantial part of the defense of Austria-Hungary. The offensive at the eastern front spearheaded by the Eleventh German Army under Mackensen operating from Galicia drove the Russians out of Poland, half of the Baltic provinces, and most of east Galicia and of the Bukovina. In the fall and winter of 1915 the German Eleventh Army took the lead in the total conquest of Serbia. Although the Germans unjustly belittled the contributions made to these successful operations by Austro-Hungarian troops, the fact that German armies were needed not only to drive back the Russians but even to defeat little Serbia gave the Germans an unwholesome feeling of superiority. This sentiment was further inflated when in the summer of 1916 two Austrian armies broke up completely under the onslaught of the Brussilov offensive and the southern base of the eastern front could be stabilized only by the withdrawal of a dozen German divisions from the greatly imperiled western front.

The growth of the internal opposition to the war dictatorship of the Vienna government that led to the assassination of the prime minister, Count Karl Stürgkh, in October 1916, and the increasing signs of resistance and defection among the Slav nationalities of the Hapsburg monarchy were other reasons for the steady decline of Austria-Hungary's capacity for waging war.[5] The death of Emperor Franz Josef in November 1916 and the Russian Revolution of March 1917 intensified the centrifugal forces. All these events made the Germans even more disdainful of their allies, and when they believed they saw indications that the Austro-Hungarians might consider leaving the alliance, they showed outright contempt.

Political friction between Vienna and Berlin developed rather early over the question of war and peace aims. Austria-Hungary had entered the war in order to prove herself a great power and to solve the southern-Slav question. But the Austro-Hungarians knew that even a victorious war would consume many of their limited resources and would further strengthen the preponderance of Germany. Thus, in the change of Europe's political map the Austro-Hungarian statesmen wished to win "the greatest possible accretion of power and security" (Baron Burian). They wanted first of all control of Serbia, Montenegro, and Albania; secondly, of Poland. They tried to confine the German ambitions to Lithuania, Courland, and possibly the Belgian Congo. Austria-Hungary always wished to keep Germany from raising demands that would make the conclusion of peace with France and England impossible, whereas she wanted to carry the war against Russia to any length. She was very suspicious when in the spring and summer of 1915 the Germans explored the possibility of a separate peace with Russia.

Yet the Germans were not swayed by the Austrians. Fritz Fischer, who in his well-known work has given us the most detailed and best history of German war aims, has also shown that throughout the war Germany maintained a program of annexationist war aims in the East and West. While its emphasis and priorities changed according to military and political circumstances, its continuity was quite remarkable. The Germans never allowed the Austrians a clear and precise insight into their war aims and always evaded Austrian attempts at the formulation of a common and all-round program.

German war aims were centered around the creation of a

powerful bloc united by strong political, military, and economic ties. And this implied a solution of the Austrian problem. The Hapsburg Empire was to be made secure by the formation of a political, military, and economic community of Germany and Austria-Hungary. This would have restored and perpetuated in the Hapsburg monarchy the domination of the Germans and Magyars, in which the German statesmen still saw the only hope for the survival of Austria-Hungary as a great power. Actually, however, she would have become merely the biggest satellite of Germany.

The Austrians first got a rough idea of these German intentions when the Austrian foreign minister, Baron Stephan Burian, visited Berlin in November 1915. He was told that Germany would agree to Austrian rule of Poland only on conditions. Germany insisted on the annexation of the so-called Polish frontier strip which was to improve Germany's strategic frontier vis-à-vis Poland and Russia, but, of course, was bound to raise profound Polish resentment. In addition she demanded a controlling influence on the economy of Poland. Moreover, Austria was to receive Poland only if she gave guarantees that the Austro-Germans would retain their dominant position in Cis-Leithania and that Austria-Hungary would remain closely tied to Germany. To this end the Dual Alliance was to be replaced by a more permanent quasi-confederate structure accompanied by a military convention that would give Germany a voice in the organization of the Austro-Hungarian army. Finally the two empires were to form a customs union, in which the Germans, owing to their bigger economy, would play the leading part.

Germany did not offer her ally partnership but rather, poorly veiled, the status of a satellite. The Austrians, feeling indignant at being treated merely as "the German East Mark," rejected these German proposals till the winter of 1916 and stuck to their entreaties for the unadulterated "Austro-Polish solution." When in order to win Polish soldiers the two emperors, in

October 1916, proclaimed their intention to create a kingdom of Poland after the war, no agreement existed between the two governments about the nature of this future state.

Actually the breakdown of the Austro-Hungarian armies at the time of the Brussilov offensive had led to a change of German policy. It was now argued that Austria-Hungary could not be trusted with the defense against Russia and therefore Germany would have to assume control of Poland. In May 1917 the Austrians had to concede Poland to Germany and received instead the prospect of Rumania, where Germany, however, had been quick to establish herself economically. But the closer inspection of Rumania's riches made this country so attractive to Germany that at the time just before and during the Brest-Litovsk negotiations the decision was reversed. What the Germans now proposed as the "Austro-Polish solution" was so loaded with German impositions that it was almost indistinguishable from the so-called "candidate solution," under which no connections between Austria and Poland were created except for the establishment of an Austrian archduke on the Polish throne.

The Austrian statesmen probably could be criticized for being sidetracked by the mad annexationist policies of Germany quite often, even after they had made up their minds that the Central Powers needed nothing but peace. Perhaps the Polish issue was a special one. The Austro-Poles were on friendly terms with the Vienna government, which, in stark contrast to the attitude of the German government toward the Prussian Poles, was prepared to let them unite with a Polish national state. Particularly after the Bolshevist revolution a revived Poland might have found it advantageous to join a Danube empire. Yet the so-called "sub-dualism," i.e., mere autonomy within Cis-Leithania, would not have sufficed. The Poles would have insisted on "trialism," the transformation of the dual monarchy into a tripartite empire. This the Magyars would probably not have tolerated.

The young Emperor Charles and his foreign minister, Count Ottokar Czernin, began to look for peace in December 1916. The first feelers were sent to France through Prince Sixtus of Parma and were followed by a good many other feelers to England and the United States, some of them known to Germany, others not, as was true of German peace moves in relation to Austria. The Austro-Hungarian government was not aiming at a separate peace prior to October 1918, although the Austrian statesmen several times threatened a rupture of the Dual Alliance after the war and, after the conclusion of the war in the East, raised some doubts about whether the Dual Alliance placed Austria-Hungary under the obligation to fight on the side of Germany for aims going beyond the status quo ante. Still, the Austro-Hungarians continued to fight. It was poor judgment on the part of Emperor Charles to write in March 1917 that he would support France's just claim for the restoration of Alsace-Lorraine. It was even worse that Czernin stupidly provoked Poincaré to publish this letter later in April 1918. But the Sixtus letter affair was no act of treason.

After the March revolution in Russia Czernin urged the immediate initiation of peace negotiations. His famous memorandum of April 12, 1917, had an effect beyond governmental conversations which took place behind closed and padded doors. Shown to Matthias Erzberger, the ambitious Reichstag deputy, it helped produce the peace resolution of the German majority parties of July 1917. But just as the revolt at the German home front failed to moderate the policy of annexations, which on the contrary in the next twelve months under Ludendorff's aegis assumed its most extravagant forms, so did all subsequent Austrian diplomatic steps. At the same time the German government became more and more heedless of the desperate situation[6] and the vital interests of Austria-Hungary. In order to humor the Ukrainian puppet government, it assigned the predominantly Polish district of Cholm to the Ukraine, thereby setting off a storm of protest by the Austrian Poles, who withdrew their support from the Vienna government. But also the "Austro-Polish solution" was ultimately thwarted. Poland was now considered the country needed for transit to the Russian market that Germany planned to exploit.

While originally the German policy makers had thought that by giving Poland, if truncated, to Austria-Hungary, they could induce her to join a German-dominated Central Europe, in the late spring and summer they felt that they could achieve this end by high-pressure diplomacy. But Baron Burian was a shrewd and tough negotiator. Political, military, and economic agreements were actually drafted, but Burian made their validity dependent on the realization of the "Austro-Polish solution." As late as September 1918 he fought for a Poland under Austrian rule, and for that matter a Poland unimpaired by German annexations and other liens. Apparently he was convinced that the empire could not be saved without a shining gain. He drew his strength from weakness but also from the lingering tradition of the Hapsburg Empire which had sunk often only to rise again. Burian at least defeated Germany's attempts to bring Austria-Hungary completely under her heel. But at this moment neither the Austrians nor the Germans were able any longer to stave off the imminent military catastrophe that made all these schemes meaningless.

VI DIPLOMATS AND DIPLOMACY IN THE EARLY WEIMAR REPUBLIC

I

THE GERMAN diplomatic service could not pride itself on as old a tradition as the French or English services. In the strict sense a corps of German diplomats came into existence for the first time after the founding of the North Germanic Confederation of 1867. Broadly speaking, only two generations had served in the new Foreign Office when the Bismarckian empire collapsed in military defeat and internal revolution. But even if we consider the German Foreign Office a mere continuation of the Prussian Foreign Office, the German foreign service would not gain a very long or great history. The old Hapsburg Empire had always trusted the diplomat's art as much as military valor, and it had picked its diplomatic representatives from among the high nobility of the Holy Roman Empire, Hungary, Italy, and the Austrian Netherlands. Prussia's rise to a great-power position in Europe was the work of her soldiers and, in a less conspicuous way, of her internal administrators. For these careers Prussia's eighteenth-century kings had trained the uncouth scions of the Prussian gentry. The diplomatic service was subordinate to the major departments of state activity. A good many Huguenots and Italians were used by Frederick II as diplomatic agents because they had linguistic ability and social versatility.

Diplomacy became a more important business in Prussia dur-

ing the age of Napoleon, but it was historically significant that
before Bismarck's day no Prussian diplomat ever rose to the
highest office in the monarchy, as for example Metternich did
in Austria. His Prussian colleague at the Congress of Vienna,
Hardenberg, was undoubtedly an accomplished diplomat, but
he had made his career in domestic administration. Even after
1815 the Prussian diplomatic service did not attract outstanding
talents, nor was the timid Prussian foreign policy, conducted
by reactionary officers and bureaucrats, a school for diplomats.

The chief example of new forces in Prussian diplomacy was
Otto von Bismarck, who proved to the Prussians and Germans
what great diplomacy could achieve. He defined the place of the
diplomats in the pseudo-constitutional system of the new German Empire and became the real father of the German diplomatic service.

In addition to all the intricacies of the constitutional life of
the Second German Empire, two major problems existed in the
formulation of German foreign policy. The army remained the
greatest power in the state and, as in the past, was not under
civilian supervision. It exercised a strong influence on the conduct of foreign policy.[1] In both the wars of 1866 and of 1870
Bismarck fought bitter fights with the military leadership over
war policies. As long as Moltke was chief of the Prussian
general staff these conflicts did not extend in a serious manner
into the peacetime relations of the civilian and military authorities, though cases of friction occurred, which arose chiefly from
the insubordination of the military attachés in the German
diplomatic missions.[2] They increased once Moltke's influence
was superseded by younger men like Count Waldersee and
worsened even more with the appearance of Admiral von Tirpitz' ambitious naval attachés. During the First World War the
army under Ludendorff's ill-starred leadership emerged not only
as dominating the course of German foreign policy but also
as the master of German internal affairs.

But the impact of the constitutionally independent position of the armed forces on German foreign policy cannot be discussed without considering at the same time the power that Bismarck had laid in the hands of the emperor-king. The chancellor was appointed by the monarch and executed officially the policy of the emperor. It was Bismarck's belief that the emperor would normally support the policy framed by his experienced minister with the assistance of an expert staff, the foreign service. Wilhelm I lived up to these expectations though at times violent clashes occurred between chancellor and emperor over issues of foreign policy, as in 1866 with regard to the peace and, in 1879, to the alliance with Austria. But while Wilhelm I was malleable, his grandson proved eccentric and intractable, and there was no obstacle in the Bismarckian constitution against direct monarchical government. Differences on foreign policy were not of major importance in the dismissal of Bismarck in 1890, but the personal regime of Wilhelm II immediately went on a rampage in foreign affairs.

The damage inflicted by the preposterous speeches and ill-considered actions of the emperor on Germany's position in the world was enormous, but Wilhelm II was too deficient in imagination and consistency to become the exclusive director of German foreign policy. Apart from the management of the routine operations, the Foreign Office retained a considerable measure of policy-making authority. What endangered this authority, however, more than purely personal gestures and interventions was Wilhelm's propensity to accept the advice of his military and naval chieftains. The determined and reckless machinations of Admiral von Tirpitz overpowered Wilhelm II, and since Tirpitz was in addition to his diplomacy a master of popular propaganda, the Foreign Office lost the decisive role in the molding of Anglo-German relations. Between 1890 and 1914 the political influence of the German Foreign Office declined rapidly from the height that it had attained under Bismarck.

The First World War completed the breakdown of the policy-making authority of the German Foreign Office. The invasion of Belgium, which made the entry of Britain into the war inevitable, had already been conceded to the military before 1914. But every demand raised by Hindenburg and Ludendorff in the course of the war was granted by the chancellor and the Foreign Office. The proclamation of a Polish kingdom in 1916, which killed all possibility of separate peace negotiations with Russia, and the opening of unlimited submarine warfare in 1917, which made the United States declare war on Germany, present only two illustrations of the eclipse of the German Foreign Office. But Ludendorff, protected by Hindenburg's popularity and assisted by Tirpitz' wily gift of mass manipulation, threw the full power of the army behind a program of annexations that only a military victory over all the enemies of Germany could have realized. Moreover, once Hindenburg and Ludendorff had been given supreme command of the German army, they dictated the policies of the civilian government as well. In July 1917 the military leaders forced Wilhelm II to dismiss Chancellor von Bethmann-Hollweg; in July 1918 they brought about the resignation of the Secretary of Foreign Affairs, Richard Kühlmann. In these months the personal regime of Wilhelm II was buried, but so were the last vestiges of Foreign Office authority. The virtual dictatorship of Ludendorff came to an end only when he had to admit defeat in late September 1918 and suddenly demanded a parliamentary German government to conclude an armistice and peace. Then, the German Foreign Office could recover somewhat from the lowly place to which it had fallen.

Whether the German Foreign Office would have provided Germany with a more intelligent foreign policy if it had retained under the reign of Wilhelm II some of the power that it wielded in Bismarck's days, nobody can say. Undoubtedly, there existed in the German Foreign Office at all times persons who on account of their familiarity with conditions in other countries were conscious of the need for moderation. But though a few of them were ready to take the risk of resignation, none of them showed the willingness to fight for a radical revision of the Bismarckian constitutional system.

This was not surprising. Diplomats are the last people to man barricades, though revolutionaries have often become good diplomats. But the German diplomatic corps that Bismarck created after 1871 was composed of people who supported his constitutional system. Bismarck took great care to make the new German foreign service representative of the new empire. The selection of the German ambassadors to the great powers illustrates his policy most clearly. The post in St. Petersburg was in the hands of the Prussian general Hans Lothar von Schweinitz from 1876 to 1893, while Prince Chlodwig Hohenlohe, Bavarian prime minister in the founding days of the German Empire, became in 1874 ambassador in Paris. Count Georg Münster, the son of the British-Hanoverian minister who in 1814–15 had restored the kingdom of Hanover, was sent in 1873 as German ambassador to London. A younger son of one of the small reigning princely families of Germany, Prince Henry VII Reuss, represented Germany at the Austrian court from 1878 to 1894. When in the 1880's Prince Hohenlohe was made regent of Alsace-Lorraine, Count Münster went to Paris and was followed in London by Prince Paul Hatzfeldt. In Constantinople Joseph M. von Radowitz, the first German specialist on Oriental affairs, attended to German interests.

Each of these six men set a standard of diplomatic performance that compared favorably with that of any ranking member of the older foreign services of other countries. It was obvious that Bismarck tried successfully to expand the Prussian into a German foreign service.[3] Indeed, Swabians and Bavarians were quite numerous in German diplomacy after 1871. There was a European air about Bismarck's ambassadors. By ancestry or marriage many of them were related to the nobility of other countries, and their German national patriotism was tempered by their sense of European responsibility. Up to a point Bismarck also cherished people of independent judgment. He always admonished his diplomatic emissaries to feel themselves not only attorneys of German national interests but also pleaders of the case of the foreign governments to which they were accredited. Bismarck was conscious of profiting from their personal reactions and disregarded, therefore, a certain amount of deviationist opinion. Count Münster, a *grand seigneur* of stubborn individual convictions, caused him particular worries by his staunch opposition to German colonial acquisitions. On the other hand, none of Bismarck's ambassadors was fully initiated into the arcana of the chancellor's over-all policy. After Bismarck's resignation, in the debate over the renewal or nonrenewal of the German-Russian reinsurance treaty, all of them sadly missed the decisive points of Bismarckian foreign policy since they were familiar only with the special problems of their particular posts.

In the diplomatic service of the Second Empire a sharp distinction existed between the "political" diplomats and the rest of the diplomatic service. Nobody was accepted in the political diplomatic service who did not enjoy a private income that was comparable to a high official's salary. Without it he might perhaps be accepted in the consular service or become a legal councillor of the German Foreign Office, but could not normally hope to receive a diplomatic post or enter the political section of the German Foreign Office. In theory at least a separation was maintained among the three sections of the German Foreign Office—the political, the economic, and the legal sections, and their dependent diplomatic and consular careers. In practice the distinction often proved surmountable. Quite a few people who started as dragomans in the Oriental field went through the consular into the diplomatic service. The first under-secretary of the German Foreign Office, Dr. Clemens Busch, and the last imperial foreign secretary, Dr. Solf, were examples of such advancement. There were also in Bismarck's Foreign Office, as distinct from foreign posts, some special experts who enjoyed the confidence of the chancellor. The most important personality in this connection was Lothar Bucher, the friend of Karl Marx, who was brought back from his English exile and served Bismarck in the political division of the Foreign Office chiefly as councillor in charge of Western European affairs. As a rule, however, members of the political foreign service in rotation served in the political division of the German Foreign Office, though also in cases like that of Baron Friedrich von Holstein members never returned from the central office to posts abroad.

A strange dichotomy can be noticed in Bismarck's activities as an organizer and educator. He was very conscious of his responsibility as the founder of the German diplomatic service and took endless pains to help its members perfect their performance. He never tired of warning them that Germany's role was not that of Europe's policeman or schoolmaster. But he went as well into more special problems of diplomatic conduct. Thus he once remonstrated when at a conference one of his ambassadors had apparently let pass a public pronouncement that spoke contemptuously, with reference to Bulgaria, of the machinations of a small nation undermining European peace. "Our judgment and our vote," Bismarck wrote, "have more weight before Europe the more calmly and dispassionately they are presented. Such an expression weakens the impression that German policy is not exclusively the product of cool reasoning but rather of some sort of touchy sentiment . . . the more I agree politically with Your Excellency's interpretation and treatment of the situation the more I would wish that also the form of its expression should be colored by the gentleness and benevolence that we do not inwardly cherish but whose outward appearance will act as the oil in the machine and will not increase the anger of others beyond an unavoidable measure."[4] Admonitions of this type went out to the German diplomats continuously.

Yet at the same time Bismarck wanted to leave the direction of German politics to a young generation imbued with pride in Germany's international position and faith in the worth of Germany's semi-absolutist order. He contributed greatly and deliberately to inflating the autocratic sentiments of Prince Wilhelm, whom he wished to immunize against the liberal tendencies of his father, Emperor Friedrich III, and his mother, the daughter of Queen Victoria. The same policy was noticeable in the 1880's in his selection and preferment of the younger members. His own son, Prince Herbert Bismarck, who was his father's chief assistant in diplomatic affairs during the last years of his reign, already represented a new type of German diplomat, less individualistic and more adaptable to the wind that blew from highest quarters, on the other hand more assertive in international dealings. Herbert Bismarck was profoundly loyal to his father and the Foreign Office tradition that the latter had initiated, but other young members of the service had their eyes on the coming ruler.

Even under Wilhelm II a good many men of original character and high competence could be found in the German foreign service. Count Paul Wolff-Metternich, German ambassador in Britain, proved his statesmanlike qualities in his long political duel with Admiral von Tirpitz. During the First World War Count Johann Heinrich Bernstorff in Washington and Richard von Kühlmann fought with similar fortitude for the recognition of their own ideas. But none of them prevailed in correcting the course of German foreign policy, and altogether there were too few independent men left in the high places of the German foreign service to maintain the distinctive level of the first period. The Foreign Office was internally divided by the factions which were the result of the personal schemes of Baron Friedrich von Holstein, who made himself the actual governor of the office between 1890 and 1906 and drove many of the Bismarckian old guard into the wilderness of peripheral posts or retirement. Wilhelm II on his part liked people of personal wealth who could glamorize the social functions of diplomacy. He encouraged drastic language and sharp demands if incidents occurred that could be construed as reflections on German national honor. But the emperor paid little attention to the advice of highly experienced diplomats. Dashing smartness and languid servility were rewarded instead, and an atmosphere of mediocre cleverness settled over the Wilhelmstrasse. Though the average German diplomat in the age of imperialism was not lacking in self-consciousness, his sense of importance occasionally paled when he had to admit that in the competition with the military and naval coteries for the nod of the imperial majesty, the German Foreign Office more often than not failed to succeed, till during the World War it found itself on the sidelines. "Politics must keep its mouth shut during the war until strategy allows it to talk again," Wilhelm II proclaimed.[5]

II

When Dr. Wilhelm Solf became foreign secretary in the cabinet of Prince Max of Baden on October 4, 1918, the German Foreign Office was charged with the melancholy mission of concluding an armistice and opening peace negotiations after the war had been lost. At least it was no longer seriously hampered in its task by the army. When Ludendorff reversed his political attitude late in October and proposed to break off the armistice negotiations in view of the Allied demands, the new government could depose him without incurring opposition.

But the Foreign Office had to cope with the influences emanating from the political parties. Matthias Erzberger, who had led the Catholic Center Party into the coalition with the Progressive and Social Democratic parties, became the chief German armistice delegate and affected German foreign policy during the whole period very profoundly.[6]

Solf was a liberal and convinced that only democracy could offer Germany a better future. He was a man of considerable learning, wide interests, and foreign experience. Temperamentally he was well-equipped to fit the German Foreign Office into a democratic state. But the November revolution not only swept away the monarchical institutions but also placed the chances of democratic development into grave jeopardy. After November 10 the executive and legislative power fell into the hands of a council of people's delegates formed by three members of each of the Majority and Independent Socialist parties. The Majority Socialists under Ebert and Scheidemann saw in the council only a temporary authority to be abolished as soon as democratic elections for a national assembly could be held. Meanwhile they were anxious to see the old bureaucratic agencies of the federal government, among them the Foreign Office, carry on under their general supervision. The bulk of the Independent Socialists was not fundamentally but only partly in disagreement with these aims. They, too, wanted a national assembly, but at a later date in order first to gain through revolutionary action more positions of economic and political power. In this connection they took also a far more critical, and even at times hostile, view of the professional civil servants, a feeling naturally reciprocated by the latter.

But under the wings of the Independent Socialist Party there also existed extremist groups, which pressed revolutionary action forward and which were willing to do so even in alliance with the so-called Spartacus group, the incipient Communist movement of Germany, then under the leadership of Karl Liebknecht and Rosa Luxemburg. In the local workers' and soldiers' councils and on the streets the radical and Bolshevist groups displayed formidable strength. In the absence of a properly functioning central authority they could embarrass and possibly even overthrow the moderate elements in the council of people's delegates. The struggle that went on in Germany in the three months after November 9, 1918, was fought in the first place for domestic ends, but it had from the outset the strongest possible foreign implications.[7] Adherence to democratic forms would mean the creation of a national government that would have the strongest moral right to speak for the whole German people and could take fullest advantage of the democratic principles that Wilson had promised would guide the peacemakers. A democratic Germany, as an equal among the Western democratic nations, could save not only her national unity but also most of her disputed possessions, such as parts of her Polish and Alsatian provinces and perhaps even some of her African colonies. If such a convenient peace could be achieved the internal German conflict would be eased. The democratic principle would protect the continued existence of a strong German national state. It would simultaneously shield the moderate forces from the accusations of the parties on the right that the left had been the gravedigger of the Reich. It would equally help to quiet criticism from the Socialists that no bourgeois group had ever done anything under the Empire to stop official German foreign policy from building up growing anger against Germany among the nations of the world. The first American diplomatic observer, Ellis Lorring Dresel, who visited Germany after the armistice at the end of December 1918, wrote quite correctly: ". . . there is a strong wish to take up relations again with the United States at the same point where they were before the war, and the hope is cherished that the events of the war will be overlooked and condoned and that by the help of America, Germany will be enabled to rehabilitate herself."[8]

It was with such beliefs and hopes that liberals like Solf placed themselves behind Ebert and the Majority Socialists and appealed for the support of the German bourgeoisie through the founding of the new German Democratic Party, which on January 19, 1919, polled about a third of the non-Socialist vote.[9] But before these elections took place the whole democratic program appeared endangered by the growing might of the radical forces in Berlin as well as by Ebert's seeming unwillingness to free himself from the embrace of the sinister Independent Socialists and to put down the terror of the street by force. On December 9, 1918, Solf appeared at a meeting of the council of people's delegates and caused a scene by accusing Hugo Haase of collusion with the Russians. Both the moment and the target for such an attack were ill chosen. Haase had no sympathy with Lenin and had readily assented to the continued exclusion of a Soviet diplomatic representation from Germany. But even if Haase had not taken an anti-Soviet stand, Ebert at this stage could not have afforded an open break with the Independent Socialists. He hoped to out-vote them easily at the elections and was preparing to meet any attempts at disturbing the elections or refusing to accept their verdict by the use of military force. Solf's sally came too early and he consequently had to be dropped as foreign secretary. As his successor the people's delegates selected Count Ulrich von Brockdorff-Rantzau, who was obviously anxious to direct German foreign policy and whom the delegates considered the finest horse in the stable of professional German diplomats.

Brockdorff-Rantzau was undoubtedly one of the best bred among the old-time German diplomats. Descended from an old noble family of Holstein, which in former centuries had seen many of its sons serve in high places in Denmark, and at German courts—in the seventeenth century a Rantzau even had become *maréchal de France*—the count was an unyielding individualist. The artist George Grosz in one of his satirical cartoons of the early 1920's depicted him with his short moustache, cold eyes, and disdainful look as the model of the aristocrat contemptuous of the democratic mob. During the First World War Brockdorff-Rantzau as minister to Denmark had seen to it that Germany respected the neutral rights of its small northern neighbor. Since the German legation in Copenhagen by the end of the war had become one of the most important among the few remaining German missions abroad, the minister had been able to acquaint himself with the broad aspects of German foreign policy.

Naturally, Count Brockdorff-Rantzau had been brought up as a monarchist, but he became a critic of German policies under Wilhelm II. The emperor's flight to Holland in early November 1918 had in his opinion wrecked the moral reputation of the Prussian-German monarchy forever and he used to speak thereafter of Wilhelm II as "the deserter of Doorn." On the other hand, his twin brother and most intimate confidant, Count Ernst Rantzau, acted in the days of the Weimar Republic as the administrator of the large estates and possessions of Wilhelm II in Germany. Brockdorff-Rantzau was free from a blind chauvinism, prone not to overrate military power in international relations, and a resolute hater of generals meddling in foreign affairs. Apart from a burning German patriotism Brockdorff-Rantzau was motivated by cool reason rather than by sentiment. The Russian and German revolutions impressed him with the strength of the masses and, though he was no genuine democrat, he considered the introduction of democracy as inevitable and as the only bulwark against Bolshevism. As conditions of his assumption of office he demanded from the people's delegates the suppression of the power of the revolutionary councils and the earliest possible election of a democratic national assembly. He also wanted to be heard in internal questions and to be

assured that in certain circumstances he would have the support of the government if he refused to sign the future peace
treaty.[10] From the beginning it was his belief that a united
public opinion had to be built behind the official policy at the
peace conference in order to impress the Allies and to keep
them from imposing humiliating and unbearable conditions. Still
Brockdorff-Rantzau did not gain a marked influence on the evolution of Germany's domestic situation even after he had become
German minister of foreign affairs in the first republican cabinet approved by the German national assembly in February
1919. When the critical phase of the peace negotiations arrived
in May and June 1919, Brockdorff-Rantzau's policy failed to
command sufficient support at home.

Brockdorff-Rantzau realized that he could not become a German Talleyrand. The vanquished Germany could not hope like
the defeated France of 1814–15 to safeguard her position as one
of the great powers by diplomatic finesse. The thought of diplomatic maneuver, in particular between the United States and
European nations but also between Britain and France, was, of
course, by no means entirely absent from the minds of German
diplomats, but the German peace strategy was fundamentally
built upon the loud appeal to world public opinion, which it
was confidently hoped would compel the governments of the
West to adopt a most liberal interpretation of the Wilsonian
peace program. "Open diplomacy," as first practiced in a telling
way by Trotsky at Brest-Litovsk and then officially promulgated
by Wilson,[11] was to become the chief medium of German diplomacy. The Germans expected that now after the Fourteen
Points had been declared as the guiding principles of peacemaking they would have an equal voice in debating and settling
the application of these principles to the concrete issues.

German diplomacy chose to place an interpretation on the
Fourteen Points that favored German claims everywhere. This
attitude was understandable if taken at the opening of the

GERMAN DIPLOMACY IN THE WEIMAR REPUBLIC 177

great debate, but rather dangerous if maintained to the bitter end. The actual meaning of the Fourteen Points was not easily defined. By and large national self-determination was most strongly emphasized, but certain ideas about free trade and access to the sea were also considered valid. Considerations of national security, too, were not entirely excluded from the Wilsonian peace proposals, and in what form a balance between the various elements of thinking could be struck remained uncertain.

But even with regard to specific problems the quest for the exact sense of the Fourteen Points required more than an abstract philosophical acumen. Point 13 said: "An independent Polish state should be erected which should include the territories inhabited by indisputably Polish populations, which should be assured a free and secure access to the sea and whose political and economic independence and territorial integrity should be guaranteed by international covenant." Broadly speaking, the German-Polish settlement of Versailles, though unnecessarily harsh in details, could be depended on as a fair execution of Point 13. The passionate German assertions that Point 13 excluded the cession of the major part of the province of West Prussia that became the Polish corridor and the creation of the free city of Danzig were untenable. One can indeed go so far as to sympathize with the position that the Poles took even after 1919 when they complained that the Versailles treaty did not give them "secure" access to the sea. Already in the summer of 1920, when Russian armies approaching Warsaw threatened the very existence of the new Polish state, Danzig refused to let arms shipments from the West go through its port. All this is not to say that the German-Polish settlement was not open to criticism on other grounds. It was very questionable whether it was practical policy to impose provisions of this sort upon Germany so long as the Western powers were not determined to maintain as close a watch over the Vistula as over the Rhine.

But such an argument has no direct connection with the search for a correct interpretation of Wilsonian political ideals.

German foreign policy and propaganda under Count Brock-dorff-Rantzau represented the Germans as the true champions of pure and politically unadulterated Wilsonianism. The Germans failed to appreciate that their erstwhile enemies would rub their eyes when they saw the Germans appear in the white garb of liberalism and would become greatly suspicious if the Germans were in any way to twist Wilsonian principles. Their failings in this respect weakened their case with Wilson especially. The German Foreign Office had entertained great hopes that the United States, not having special interests in Europe, would moderate the war aims of her European allies. But the Germans lacked any understanding of the peculiar political circumstances in which Wilson had to pursue his policy.

Wilson's peace program, which embodied the aspirations of the liberal sections of the American people, clashed sharply with the war aims of the European allies, as expressed in the secret treaties. An uneasy compromise between the United States on one side and Britain, France, and Italy on the other had been achieved at the time when Germany urged the conclusion of an armistice. As a matter of fact the German intelligence service, which in contrast to Germany's foreign-press analysis was very efficient in this period, had somehow managed to get hold of the key document of these negotiations, the so-called "official" American commentary to the Fourteen Points of October 1918.[12] The document was presented by Colonel House to Clemenceau and Lloyd George to illustrate what the American government considered the practical meaning of Wilson's program as it was to be applied at the conference. It was clear that in all cases the United States would take as benevolent a view of the interests of her wartime allies as was compatible with the letter of Wilson's declarations on peace aims. Nobody, for example, with any political judgment could assume that

Wilson's ideas on the reform of the colonial system would be deemed applicable to the colonies of America's European allies. Lloyd George and Clemenceau had agreed to accept the American principles as regulating the future peace settlement with the defeated Central powers, but not the internal problems of the British and French empires.

Yet the execution of the agreement, reached only under great difficulties, depended to a large extent on the development of the internal political scene. The loss of control over Congress in the November elections of 1918, the fight about American partnership in a League of Nations, and the relative indifference of the American public to all the details of the German settlement narrowed Wilson's freedom of action. Equally grave was the collapse of British liberalism in the British December elections, both in its effects on Lloyd George's own policies and on the cooperation between the prime minister and the president. Brockdorff-Rantzau did not display a clear insight into the political situation on the Allied side and Count Bernstorff, the former German ambassador in Washington who headed the bureau in the German Foreign Office charged with the preparations for the Paris conference, apparently did not correct Brockdorff-Rantzau's notions.[13] The German diplomats had made a certain attempt to define priorities among the German national interests that they proposed to defend at the conference. They did not wish to put up a fight for Alsace-Lorraine or for Poznania and were prepared to make concessions to Denmark in north Schleswig, but they intended to insist on the retention of the Rhineland, including the Saar, and of all the eastern territories except Poznania. On Austria and what was at a later date called Sudetenland, the Germans were to reserve their claims, but they were not ready to push them too far, since they feared that the merger of Austria with Germany was likely to give the French a chance to demand the whole left bank of the

Rhine. Brockdorff-Rantzau also realized that most and possibly all of the German colonies would be lost.

Officially the decision to accept the Allied decision to limit the future German army to 100,000 men was made by the German cabinet and not by Brockdorff-Rantzau. General Hans von Seeckt, who was the chief military member of the German delegation at Versailles, attacked Brockdorff-Rantzau for making the German army an object of diplomatic barter.[14] And though it is true that the German cabinet, chiefly under the influence of Matthias Erzberger, adopted this policy, there is no indication that Brockdorff-Rantzau disapproved of the move that was intended to avoid the appearance of German militarism and instead place the restoration of Germany's economic position first. At the last stage of the peace negotiations the German government even went so far as to offer to forgo the building of all the battleships that the draft treaty had left to Germany in order to achieve the revision of other sections of the treaty. In addition to the territorial integrity of the German Reich within the limits already mentioned a reasonable settlement of the reparation issue was made the major aim of the diplomatic strategy of the German Foreign Office. Also, the immediate participation of Germany not only in the League of Nations but also in the drafting of its constitution was considered a highly desirable end.

In itself this program would not have been unrealistic if it had not been followed through in a doctrinaire spirit. German policy was overrating its chances to defend Germany's eastern frontiers. Its desire to partake in the drafting of the League's covenant was hopeless, the more so since the German proposals aimed at turning the League from a federation of governments into an assembly of peoples, ideas that would have made it even more difficult for Wilson to get acceptance of the League of Nations in the United States. But under Brockdorff-Rantzau the original program was adhered to with the utmost determination and, when it began to meet resistance, German diplomatic tactics became stiff and tough-voiced. It should not be forgotten for a moment that the Allies never tried to take cognizance of natural German pride and feeling. The denial of oral negotiations and the humiliating conditions in which the Germans were placed at Versailles were insulting. Still, it is most doubtful whether Brockdorff-Rantzau did a good service to the German cause when he set the style of all subsequent German diplomatic presentations by the tone of his first speech at Versailles on May 7, 1919. It was probably not so important that he remained seated on that occasion as that he purposely used aggressive language.[15] It was strange to say: "At this conference, where we alone, without allies, face the large number of our opponents, we are not without protection. They themselves have brought us an ally, the law that is guaranteed to us by the agreement on peace principles." While this undiplomatic way of addressing the future partners of negotiations, who had granted Germany the benefit of the Fourteen Points, could perhaps be psychologically explained as an outbreak of honest emotion, other remarks show a rather demogogic attitude. "The hundred thousands of noncombatants who perished since November 11 on account of the blockade were killed with cold determination after our opponents had achieved and secured victory. Of this you ought to think when you talk about guilt and atonement."[16] Now, it was true that the armistice of November 11, 1918—and it was an *armistice* and not a peace—had continued the blockade, but by February 1919 the Allies had agreed to lift the blockade and the further delay was as much due to German unwillingness to employ her idle ships and pay for food imports with her own gold as to Allied hesitation to grant credits.[17] These events were fully known to the German minister, and it was not surprising that his speech caused resentment at Paris.

Obviously, Brockdorff-Rantzau felt even at the beginning of the peace negotiations that he would have to use the threat of the German refusal to sign the peace treaty, and no doubt this was the only weapon left to the Germans at the time. But the minister entertained highly exaggerated notions about the possible effects of such a policy. It required a strong and unified popular support in Germany, and it presupposed on the Allied side lack of confidence in the righteousness of their position. Various means were employed to produce both, but most important and, as we may add, most fallacious in its immediate political results was the use made of the war-guilt question. It was certainly a futile German hope that Allied opinion on Germany's war guilt, the centerpiece of all war propaganda, could be shaken or modified by German arguments, particularly at the very moment when victory had blessed the cause of justice.

On the German side the war-guilt question logically became a moral and political issue at the time of the collapse of imperial Germany. The Germans in their vast majority had also been convinced during the war that the others had been responsible for starting the war. The bellicose nature of the Pan-Slavism of czarist Russia and of British imperialism was singled out for special condemnation. Even most of the German Social Democrats, who before the war had always denounced war as the evil fruit of capitalism and castigated the armaments policy of the German Empire, joined in the general German attitude. They justified their own support of the German war effort by the thesis that war had been forced upon Germany by the other powers and that a Socialist party was bound to play its part in the defense of its own national community. Once committed to this new line, however, they had not only made a full contribution to the German defense effort but had also tolerated the disregard displayed by the government for limited war aims. Not even the peace treaties of Brest-Litovsk and Bucharest of 1918 had aroused the Social Democratic Party to forceful protestations. The tolerant and conniving policy of the majority of the party with regard to the nationalistic wartime policy of the imperial government had led in 1917 to the secession of a group of Social Democratic members who formed the Independent Socialist Party. They asserted that no Socialist party ought to forget in its support of national wartime defense its international and social responsibilities. War was a result of capitalistic competition and likely to feed imperialism. It was the sacred duty of the leaders of the Socialist workers' movement to oppose with all the force at their disposal imperialistic war aims. Thus the Independents became the only party that voted in the Reichstag against the Brest-Litovsk treaties and maintained a sharply critical opinion of German foreign policy before and during the war.

Armistice, revolution, and the ensuing struggle between the Majority and Independent Socialists inevitably brought these problems to the fore and the Independent Socialists endeavored to demonstrate not only the imperialistic character of German wartime policies but to find evidence for the culpability of the German imperial government for the outbreak of war in 1914. The most eminent Marxist scholar of the time, Karl Kautsky, was to devote himself to the perusal of the documents of the German Foreign Office pertaining to the diplomatic crisis of July 1914. In Bavaria, where the revolution had unleashed strong regionalist tendencies, the criticism of the foreign policy of the German Empire was presented with an anti-Prussian bias. It was Berlin that since Bismarck's days had falsified the course of German history through the Prussian centralization of German resources and their reckless use for militaristic purposes. Backed by such popular sentiment Kurt Eisner, an Independent Socialist of doctrinaire complexion whom the foaming Munich revolution had made the temporary master of Bavaria, could open his campaign for a frank German confession of war guilt as the first step toward the purification of German life from the sins of militarism as well as toward the restoration of international confidence in Germany. A repentant democratic

Germany could hope to receive from Wilson a just and democratic peace. Eisner did not confine his agitation to public
oratory but also began to publish secret diplomatic documents
bearing on German policy in July 1914, and he demanded
that the Foreign Office be purged of personnel.

The Bismarckian constitution of 1871 had retained Bavaria's
right to maintain diplomatic missions abroad, which enabled
Eisner to send Professor Friedrich Wilhelm Foerster, one of
the few German intellectuals who was a sincere absolute pacifist
and a radical critic of the German *Machtstaat,* as Bavarian
minister to Berne in Switzerland. Foerster succeeded in making
contact with George D. Herron, an American professor who
served as an emissary of President Wilson. Nothing seems to
have come of all these transactions. Herron apparently was
not received by Wilson in Paris, and it is doubtful whether in
any event Wilson would have been interested in this approach.[18]

While the war guilt was hotly debated in Germany and
used to defame the monarchical system and to criticize the
moderate political parties for their lukewarm opposition to the
vagaries and excesses of German foreign policy in the past,
popular sentiment in the victorious countries was running high
with expression of indignation about the responsibility of the
imperial German government for the war of 1914 and for many
violations of international law in the course of the war. It was
said that retribution for the wrongdoers ought to form the
chief objective of the forthcoming peace conference. This whole
trend was highlighted by the furor of the British election
campaign, which also showed that this emotionalism could
shift governmental policies away from the original agreement on
peace principles. The promises suddenly made by Lloyd George
and his ministerial colleagues about reparations were certainly
not in harmony with the pre-armistice agreement. Internal and
external developments thus conspired to fill the German policy
makers with dark forebodings about the political significance

of the war-guilt question. Within Germany it was an instrument to press the revolution further and to drive a wedge between the radical parties on one side and the moderate as well as the old conservative parties on the other. It also threatened, as Eisner's Independent Socialist and separate Bavarian foreign policy proved, the unity of German foreign policy. Yet even worse was the danger that the war-guilt accusation would be employed by the Allied governments to supplant the Fourteen Points in the drafting of the peace treaty. On November 29, 1918, Solf sent a note to the Allied governments proposing to turn over the examination of the causes of the World War to a neutral commission whose members should be given free access to the archives of all the powers.[19] The proposal met with the rejection of all the Allied governments, who found that it was unnecessary to explore what was self-evident.

This result did not allay German fears. In particular democratic groups felt that the political use of the war-guilt accusation would have a pernicious effect on the moral resistance of the German people and the foundation of a just international peace. The great German sociologist Max Weber, whose influence on the establishment of the Weimar Republic was strong, was also most active in condemning the assertions of a German war guilt raised at home and abroad. A group of democratic political and academic figures, the Heidelberg Association for a Policy of Law,[20] began to address the general public in early February 1919 with manifestoes on the question of war guilt. After that the Germans became more and more preoccupied with the expectation that the Allies would base their demands on the allegation of a German war guilt.[21] Such a belief seemed to be confirmed beyond all doubts when the German government came into the possession of a report of a committee of the Paris peace conference dealing with the "authorship of the war." Count Brockdorff-Rantzau consequently did not hestitate at the meeting of the peace conference on May 7, with the big treaty still lying unopened before him, to talk out: "The demand is made that we shall acknowledge that we alone are guilty of having caused the war. Such a confession in my mouth would be a lie."[22]

The Germans when they examined the treaty were apparently not puzzled about the fact that it contained no statement on the German was guilt where one might have expected it most, in a preamble to the treaty, or to the League of Nations, or in Section v, covering the German disarmament, or in Section vii, dealing with war crimes. A reference to German war guilt could be discovered only in Article 231, which opened Section viii, the reparation section of the treaty. This article was now quickly considered to be the result of the already mentioned committee report and thought to demand from Germany the recognition of her war guilt.

Actually the German delegation was mistaken both with regard to the historical origins and the intended legal meaning of Article 231. The committee "for the responsibilities of the authors of the war and sanctions" had considered but, chiefly under American and English influence, rejected a recommendation for the inclusion of an article on war guilt.[23] They were content to write a summary report on the origins of the war of 1914, the very report that came into German hands. But this was only an opinion and no further official action followed from it. The reference to war guilt slipped into the draft treaty of Versailles unintentionally during the discussions of German reparations by the Reparation Commission and the Council of Four. The drafting of the provision for German reparations started from the conditions of the Lansing note of November 5, 1918, which specifically stated that Germany would make compensation "for all damage done to the civilian population of the Allies and their property by the aggression of Germany by land, by sea and from air." But French and British opposition against this formula was strong, since public opinion in Britain and France expected, and had been made to believe by their governments, that Germany could be forced to make much larger payments than this definition permitted. Lloyd George was also anxious to find a settlement that would give Britain a higher percentage share of the future German reparations than the Lansing note would have made possible. Consideration of Germany's capacity to pay, however, indicated that the actual sum would remain far below popular French and British hopes and be in practice closer to figures that could be derived from the Lansing note.

In order to protect Lloyd George and Clemenceau against the wrath of their parliaments it was decided after long and intricate discussions[24] not to set a final sum that would only cause disappointment. It was also resolved to open the reparations section with a statement that Germany was theoretically responsible for all the loss and damage that the Allies had suffered. But after thus appeasing popular sentiment in Article 231, recognition was taken in Article 232 of Germany's capacity to pay and finally the Lansing formula was reestablished as the ruling principle for eventual German payments and deliveries. However, the appendix to this article, which spelled out the categories of these reparations, expanded the German obligations in an extravagant way by adding war pensions and other items.

Article 231, the first article of the reparations section of the Versailles treaty, was not intended to be a war-guilt clause.[25] It was not designed to pass moral judgment on the foreign policy of Germany before 1914, but was meant to affirm a liability of Germany for damages which she was not requested to repair. These exceeded, however, those contained in the Lansing note; and the wording of Article 231 by people who were all convinced of Germany's war guilt could not avoid moral undertones.

The whole difficulty rested with a single word. Article 231 read: "The Allied and Associated Governments affirm and Germany accepts the responsibility of Germany and her allies for *causing* all the loss and damage to which the Allied and Associated Governments and their nationals have been subjected as a consequence of the war imposed upon them by the aggression of Germany and her allies."[26] The insertion of the word *causing* changed what would otherwise have been only a financial liability into a causal responsibility. Thereby "aggression," a word that in the Lansing note (and in Article 232) described only military actions after the outbreak of the war, could change its meaning so as to include events and plans prior to the war.

The German peace delegation read it in this sense, and in their nervous obsession with the war-guilt question their German translation of the fateful sentences placed the accent entirely on the moral issue. Their passionate pleas with the Allies against the acceptance of this article produced stern rebuttals. The Allies would probably never have attached to the article the sense of a moral war guilt had it not been for the German remonstrance. In a very strict sense not even the Allied notes dealing with German war guilt linked it with Article 231, but they avoided a denial of such connection and since they expressed the Allied conviction of Germany's guilt with heated acrimony, they were taken by the world as proof that the German interpretation was largely correct. It was impossible for the Allied statesmen to retreat, once they were challenged by the Germans. The article had been written to cap a delicate political compromise among themselves which would have been endangered if they had disavowed its text. Moreover in public they would have appeared as betraying a main tenet of common faith. For everybody in the Allied camp was convinced of Germany's war guilt.[27]

The German Foreign Office could not, of course, have known

what had been going on behind the scenes of the conference of the Allies in Paris. But even if the German reading of Article 231 was bound to be different from what the Allied reparation experts had primarily intended to put into it, the German delegation approached the problem in a frame of mind that was conditioned by the singular circumstances of a Germany in revolution and defeat. It was no doubt desirable to set into motion an objective study of the causes of the World War. But the mills of historical research grind slowly and do not easily produce a standardized result. Moreover it takes a long time to acquaint the general public with the findings of historians who in most cases tend to agree rather on the complexity of the issues raised by the past than on their absolute meaning. From the German point of view, however, it was enough to have made it clear that historical problems could not be settled by simple moral verdicts of a victor and that historical truth, at least in a world that recognized the freedom of the human spirit, was not the monopoly of any single power.

It was, however, a different matter to make the war-guilt issue the hub of a radical fight against the acceptance of the peace treaty. Any cool examination of the treaty was bound to show that the practical provisions, including those for reparations, would have been identical with or without Article 231. Obviously, the treaty of Versailles had been drafted by people who believed in Germany's responsibility for the outbreak of the war of 1914, but they were not likely to change their opinions from one day to the other because of German protests. If Count Brockdorff-Rantzau decided upon making Article 231 the official test case of the sincerity of the Allied nations to conclude a democratic peace, he felt confident that by declaring the article a despicable attack upon German national honor the government could rally the great majority of the German people to resist the acceptance of what soon became known in Germany as "the peace of infamy." Even at Versailles, Brockdorff-Rantzau spoke incorrectly of Article 231 as imposing on Germany the *sole* guilt, and Chancellor Bauer repeated this statement from the rostrum of the national assembly in Weimar.[28]

The fight against the war guilt did, indeed, bring the mass of the German people together, but it united them on a very dangerous platform. All the German parties with the exception of the reactionary parties and the Spartacus group had been quite irresponsible in their expectations of what a peace on the basis of the Fourteen Points would be like. The government failed to enlighten them before the beginnings of the Versailles discussions about the true feelings of the Allied countries toward Germany. The American diplomatic observer in Germany, Dresel, wrote on May 10, 1919: "The entirely insincere belief that the armistice was only concluded on condition that President Wilson's peace program, as interpreted for the benefit of Germany, would be enforced, had become general. The people had been led to believe that Germany had been unluckily beaten after a fine and clean fight, owing to the ruinous effect of the blockade on the home morale and perhaps some too far-reaching plans of her leaders, but that happily President Wilson could be appealed to, and would arrange a compromise peace satisfactory to Germany."[29] The announcement of the peace conditions was, therefore, a terrific blow to practically everyone in Germany. It could be said now that the introduction of democracy had not saved Germany from a grim fate and that the imposition of the war guilt made it necessary for the Germans to defend their national past. Such at least was the impact of these events on the many bourgeois people who immediately after the revolution had given their vote to the new Democratic Party, since they hoped that democracy would protect them against Bolshevism at home and foreign nationalism. The Democratic Party left the government before the signing of the Versailles treaty, but its power was spent. In the national elections of 1920 the party lost almost half of its members and declined steadily thereafter. The German bourgeoisie went back to the old parties of the right, the more easily since the specter of Bolshevism had lost in the course of 1919 much of its terror after the new German armed forces, the so-called "free corps," had established order.

Count Brockdorff-Rantzau hoped through the appeal to German national honor to gain the approval of the nation. This policy was unrealistic. The threat that Germany would not sign the treaty was a practical political device. Lloyd George foresaw the high cost that further or even total occupation of Germany would entail. It might kill the chance of ever getting reparations from Germany and it was certain to reopen all the political issues just laboriously settled with France. The British prime minister became the champion of considerable treaty modifications. The most important concessions that the Germans wrested from the Allies were a plebiscite in Upper Silesia and a number of adjustments with regard to the German-Polish frontier which actually foreshadowed subsequent British support of German claims in this field during the postwar period. Other valuable promises of a more anticipatory nature, like the early accession of Germany to the League of Nations, were added to the final reply of the Allies to Germany.

Still it was entirely unwarranted to assume that Germany could have improved the treaty conditions if it had rejected the Allied ultimatum. It was wishful thinking on the part of the German peace delegation to urge in their final report refusal to sign the treaty, because, as Brockdorff-Rantzau expressed it, "if our enemies execute their threat and apply force against us, though we are willing to fulfill all their just demands, we are convinced that the progressive peaceful development of the world will give us soon the objective tribunal before which we shall demand our right."[30] It was an optimism born of despair, but with no basis in fact. We know today what would have happened. The Allied armies would have marched into Germany and have occupied northern Germany as far east as the Weser river, cut off southern Germany, and established contact with Czechoslovakia.[31] Most of the German army had dispersed after the armistice and the revolution. After January 1919, however, new troops had been organized on a voluntary basis and the military balance of power vis-à-vis Poland, though not the West, favored Germany. Allied forces had been depleted between November 1918 and June 1919 from 198 to 39 divisions. General Foch was, however, confident that this force was adequate for the occupation of Germany up to the Weser, an estimate in which the German generals fully agreed.[32] For a push beyond the Weser to Berlin Foch demanded additional troops and the authority to conclude armistices with individual southern and western German states.

There is no question that a final German refusal to sign the Versailles treaty would have meant the end of the unity of the German Empire. Military resistance, Hindenburg and Groener admitted, was of no avail. In such circumstances a policy of refusing to sign the treaty would have been suicidal. Direct cooperation with the Soviet Union might have changed the German position to some extent. In this case Germany ought to have publicly renounced the treaty of Brest-Litovsk and withdrawn her troops from the territories of the prewar Russian Empire. This could have opened the way for some sort of diplomatic cooperation between Germany and the Soviet Union that might have impressed the Western powers. Instead German troops remained in the Baltic states fighting Bolshevism and created a deep gulf between Germany and Russia. Still it was highly doubtful how much assistance Germany could have derived from the economically disorganized and exhausted Russia. The new Russian rulers in 1919 thought in terms of world revolution, and Germany was in their opinion the country that had to be won over first. Lenin would probably have supported with all his might and with all the resources at his disposal a Germany fighting the capitalistic countries with revolutionary means. This, however, would have required a radical workers' government in Germany which would soon have drifted into complete dependency on Moscow. Brockdorff-Rantzau was certainly not planning to promote such a political combination, but for that matter nobody in Germany except the Communists and a few adventurers of the extreme right was willing to take this path. Not even most Independent Socialists were prepared to turn to the East. They denounced the Brockdorff-Rantzau policy of resistance as a revival of German nationalism at the expense of the suffering masses who needed peace and bread.

But would there be peace and bread if the treaty was signed? Did not the treaty contain many provisions which could be used by the victors to commit further hostile acts against Germany, and was not the limitless demand for reparations an absolute block to any economic recovery? And finally would it be possible under such conditions to build a democracy in Germany? These were, indeed, questions that could make any German falter, but there were certain points which could inspire a modicum of confidence. First of all, the unity of the Empire was preserved; second, after a respite one could hope to restore the greatest treasure of the nation, the capacity for hard work. Beyond this one might trust that other countries would learn to appreciate the fact that Europe could not recover if Germany did not regain a reasonable prosperity and that if one wished to talk of a comity of democratic nations, Germany could claim the protection of liberal principles.

This belief won out in the councils of the German Social Democratic and Center parties. After the revolution the Center Party had come under the leadership of its democratic wing. Matthias Erzberger dominated, and this former Swabian village teacher, who had a quick if glib mind, became the chief opponent of Brockdorff-Rantzau on the German political scene. As the chairman of the German armistice delegation he had been in contact with Allied representatives since November 11, 1918.[33] Erzberger converted the Center Party to the acceptance of the treaty. In the Social Democratic Party the sober advice of Hermann Müller finally prevailed. Müller had gone to Paris in the last days of July 1914 to establish a common policy of the French and German Socialists toward the war crisis. Now, five years later, as the German foreign minister he affixed his signature to the Versailles treaty, which showed no influence of the Second International but instead the heavy imprints of nationalism. Even on the German side nationalism had been galvanized into life again by the Allied demands, and German foreign policy had not been conducted with much consideration of the vital internal needs of an infant republic.

III

The actual course of German foreign policy had been finally decided by the parties and not by the old-line diplomats. Hermann Müller was the first German parliamentarian to assume the wheel in 76 Wilhelmstrasse, and ever thereafter in pre-Hitler days the appointment of a professional diplomat to the post signified a nationalistic policy. According to the Weimar constitution, the German Foreign Office was made the sole agency for the administration of German foreign interests. The Bavarian foreign missions were abolished. Another anomaly disappeared. In the old Empire the federal Foreign Office served at the same time as the foreign ministry of Prussia that maintained legations with all the German courts. Through them the Foreign Office exercised a direct influence in German domestic affairs.

One important development was still instigated through the Prussian minister in Munich, Count von Zech, after the revolution. Relations with the Vatican under the Bismarckian con-

stitution were reserved to the states. Since the end of the eighteenth century Prussia had sent a minister to Rome, but the
Vatican had never established a legation in Berlin. The highest
diplomatic representative of the Pope was the legate accredited
to the Bavarian government, who, in 1919, was Eugenio Pacelli.
The Communist revolution in Munich in May 1919 forced him
to take refuge in the Prussian legation; and in the conversations
between the young count and the future Pope, the first steps
were taken that led to an early visit of the legate to Berlin
and to the establishment of a nunciature in the capital of the
German Republic in 1920, an event that strengthened the republic internally and externally.

After the dissolution of the Prussian legations the Foreign
Office had to gain its popular support through the parliament.
The Weimar constitution did not envisage a participation of the
state governments in the formulation of German foreign policy;
but, since the foreign problems were closely related to those
of the internal administration of the states, particularly in the
occupied Rhineland, the prime ministers of the states were often
consulted. The Weimar constitution had taken a leaf from the
book of James Bryce[34] and instituted a special foreign-affairs
committee of the Reichstag that remained in being even between sessions and periods of legislature of the German parliament. Under German conditions the committee was not an ideal
instrument for developing a foreign policy beyond individual
party opinions. The German parties were profoundly divided
in their views on foreign affairs. The presence of Communist
members, moreover, made the committee unsuitable for con-
fidential discussions. In practice, therefore, meetings between
the minister of foreign affairs and leaders of foreign-affairs
experts of the parties forming the government assumed the
functions for which the parliamentary committee had been
created.[35]

The Weimar constitution had given the president of the Reich powers greater than those of the French president. In foreign affairs, they included a decisive voice in treaty-making and in the appointment of the diplomatic officers. Both presidents, Ebert and Hindenburg, guarded these rights jealously but were anxious to avoid friction with the Foreign Office. When Brock-dorff-Rantzau was made German ambassador in Moscow in 1922, he made the curious demand that he should be allowed to report to the president instead of to the foreign minister. This wish, though a departure from the constitution, was granted, but all reports were sent from the presidential palace to the Foreign Office. The Weimar constitution had also made an attempt to raise the position of the chancellor above that of the other members of the cabinet. The chancellor was supposed to lay down the guiding principle of the policy of his cabinet. But all the cabinets of the 1920's were coalition governments over which the chancellors presided as chairmen rather than as directors. Still, in certain matters, a chancellor was able to disregard the foreign minister. The most important case of this sort was Chancellor Joseph Wirth's approval of the independent policy of General von Seeckt in Russia. Since Wirth was simultaneously minister of finance, he could provide the funds for the Russian activities of the *Reichswehr*.

Even under the Weimar constitution, there remained additional agencies that were officially charged with foreign policy, or could unofficially concern themselves with it. Among the other federal ministries it was in particular the ministry of finance and, to a lesser degree, the ministry of economics which were influential in foreign affairs. The old Foreign Office had experience in the negotiation of trade agreements, but in the postwar world economic matters became so intricate and, at the same time, politically so important that members of the ministry of economics were brought into the international negotiations. An even more conspicuous role was assumed in all the endless conferences on reparations and loans by the ministry of finance. The new "financial" diplomacy was over the heads of old-time diplomats. In Germany it found its first accomplished representative in Carl Bergmann.[36]

A strong hand was needed at the helm of the Foreign Office to hold the course through various currents and to weather the storm of popular resentment and dissension. In the history of the Weimar Republic, Gustav Stresemann was the only statesman who, through his great ability as a parliamentary tactician and orator, as well as through his diplomatic talents, could make the office fully his own. Under him the German Foreign Office settled down to the execution of foreign policy in greater calm than in the first five years after Versailles. Immediately after the revolution, people had been unanimous in asserting that the German Foreign Office was in bitter need of a drastic reform. Count Brockdorff-Rantzau inaugurated a new internal organization which was realized under his successors.[37] The political and economic divisions of the Foreign Office were merged and then were reorganized along regional lines into three new divisions. Apart from them, four other divisions remained, dealing with legal, cultural, personnel, and press affairs. The merger of the old political and economic divisions was accompanied by the consolidation of the diplomatic and consular services into a single foreign service. Thereby, the selection for higher positions was placed on a broader basis. The change also tended to compel every member of the foreign service to acquaint himself in some measure with economic and social problems.

The German foreign service was small at the end of the war, owing to the closing of many German missions abroad and to the retirement of a good many of the old monarchists. But a substantial number of the middle-aged and younger diplomats of the imperial office remained in the service. Some, like the former ambassador in Washington Count Bernstorff, who was to represent Germany through many years at the disarmament discussions in Geneva, became members of the Democratic Party; others such as Baron von Neurath, Germany's ambassador in Rome from 1921 to 1930, and in London till 1932, for the time being suppressed their displeasure with the republic. The old guard saw to it that among the young candidates a goodly number of their relatives or members of their own elegant student fraternities were selected.

Some of the best representatives of a liberal Germany came from this group, such as Leopold von Hoesch, the greatest of the German professional diplomats of the interwar period. After the mutual recall of the ambassadors in Paris and Berlin during the Ruhr invasion, Hoesch as chargé d'affaires had impressed Poincaré so much that he asked for his appointment as German ambassador. In his eight years in Paris, and again from 1932 to 1936 in London, the sensitive and devoted man proved himself a master of his craft. Dr. Wilhelm Solf went as ambassador to Tokyo, where from 1920 to 1928 he represented a Germany without colonial ambitions and succeeded in establishing close friendly relations in the cultural and economic field.[38] On all levels of diplomatic rank, this list could be extended, and it must at least be added that in general members of this social group, whether liberal or conservative, were less easily swayed in later years by National Socialism. Some of the German nationalists, such as Admiral von Tirpitz' son-in-law, Ulrich von Hassell, even joined the conspiracy against Hitler. But, in the 1920's, these people radiated considerable ill-will toward a republican foreign policy. It is interesting to see how Baron von Neurath spread the idea that the Fascist government of Mussolini would help Germany in a revision of the Versailles treaty, or to find other German diplomats denouncing German parliamentary ministers of foreign affairs as unfit to head their office. Wipert von Blücher, a member of the eastern division of the Foreign Office in the early 1920's and German minister in Finland later on, could complain even in 1951, despite all that had happened in Germany under Wilhelm II and Hitler, that decisions as such to accept or reject the Versailles treaty could not be made by the discussions of a group of people, such as the cabinet, since "a multitude of people cannot make foreign policy, for which but a singular will is needed."[39] Ernst von Weizsäcker, a naval officer who strayed into the diplomatic service at the end of the war and within a short time acquired the feeling of being a knowing professional diplomat, judged: "The old officials were accustomed from former times to work under the direction of a specialist minister. But . . . the men in charge of the Foreign Office after 1918 were changed frequently and were regarded by us as amateurs. Stresemann was indeed of a higher stature than the general run of foreign ministers. But in the Foreign Office he was held to be too trusting in international affairs, a field in which he was not fully at home."[40]

But in the early years of the Weimar Republic, chiefly on President Ebert's insistence, an effort was made to have Germany represented in eminent diplomatic posts by men who had made their career outside of the German bureaucracy. None proved a failure; on the contrary, most of them were unusually effective diplomats. Friedrich Sthamer, a former mayor of Hamburg, was sent as ambassador to London and his absolute honesty and tactfulness helped to allay British resentment and, at least after Locarno, to give Anglo-German relations a rather cordial note. Even more successful were the three Socialist ministers, a somewhat surprising fact, since the German Socialists prior to 1918 had hardly a chance to acquaint themselves with diplomatic affairs and manners. All three were essentially newspapermen. The Bavarian Adolf Müller acted from 1920 to 1933 as German minister in Berne, and the relations between Switzerland and Germany prospered. His influence reached beyond that. Ebert and most republican German statesmen liked to listen to his wise counsel on foreign policy, and much was done from the German legation in Berne to prepare Germany's way to Geneva.

From 1922 to 1930, the Swabian Ulrich Rauscher held the most thankless post of the German Foreign Service, the embassy in Warsaw, with extraordinary courage and circumspection. The third Socialist diplomat came from Schleswig-Holstein. Adolf Köster came to the Foreign Office as successor to Hermann Müller when the latter became chancellor in March 1920. As German representative at the North Schleswig plebiscite, as minister in Riga from 1923 to 1928 and, until his death in 1930, in Belgrade, he proved his mettle.

A member of the Bavarian People's Party, Wilhelm Mayer-Kaufbeuren, was the first German postwar ambassador in Paris; a Center parliamentarian, Maximilian Pfeiffer, became minister in Vienna; while a board member of the Krupp works, Otto Wiedfeldt, was sent to Washington.[41] It may be mentioned that, after the conclusion of the preliminary trade agreement with the Soviet Union in May 1921, for once in German history an academician was appointed the head of a German diplomatic mission. The selection of Wiedenfeld, professor of economics at Leipzig University, was, however, designed to minimize the political significance of this diplomatic exchange in the eyes of the Western powers.[42]

In spite of the good results achieved by the appointment of public figures to diplomatic positions, this policy was abandoned after 1923. Soon after his arrival in Berlin, the British ambassador, Lord D'Abernon, who had no special prejudice against German conservatives, confided in his diary that he preferred the Germans whom democracy had brought to the fore. He disliked in the old officials what he termed "Teutonic obstinacy or dourness." At the end of his ambassadorship he wrote: "German negotiators may be, and perhaps are, difficult to deal with, slow to be persuaded, pernickety, and disposed to quibble on small points, overcareful, making an infinity of reserves and precise pre-conditions on conjunctures and developments which, in all human probability, will not arise."[43] These remarks should perhaps not be taken too literally, for there were good reasons for moving cautiously in the years after Versailles, but they point up some of the shortcomings of the old-time professional German diplomats who were soon again to set the style of the foreign service. A good many people with greater and lesser gifts had gained accession to the Foreign Office in Berlin in the early years of the republic. How long they survived the trend toward the restoration of professionalism depended largely on their party support. The Center Party was especially anxious to have a number of trusted party members in the office, and, since the Center commanded a pivotal position in German politics from 1920 to 1932, it retained a certain influence on the personnel policy of the Foreign Office. The Social Democratic Party never gained representation in the inner councils of the central office after 1920. The examination for admission to the foreign service was stiffened, but this reform did not amount to the introduction of a merit system, since the examination could be taken on invitation only. Moreover, the candidates could not feel certain that, even after passing the entrance examination, their future career would be commensurate with their ability.

Stresemann cared about these problems, but he was not a great administrator nor quite able to see through the cunning of bureaucrats. The tremendous burden of internal and foreign problems that he carried in a continuous struggle with his failing health forced him to leave the internal administration of the office to the secretary of state. Carl von Schubert, a slightly gruff, methodical, and immovable Junker, held this position from 1924 to 1930.[44] Under him the restoration of the German professional diplomat was fully achieved. The German foreign service had acquired a somewhat broader social and political basis, but its character was determined by the conservative professional diplomat. To secure his dominance Bismarck's IA division, a division to deal with high policy questions, was reintroduced in an oblique fashion. So far as the existing six divisions were not directed by old-line diplomats, a deputy director of that ilk was appointed, who received instructions from, and could directly report to, a newly created office of the minister, the *Büro Reichsminister*, which centralized all matters considered of first-class significance.[45] Thus, even in the organizational sense, the old guard, and those who wished to perpetuate the old tradition, had come back. Probably only one group had a greater influence than it used to exert in the days of the imperial office. In a time when so much of the German foreign policy was a fight over the interpretation of the Versailles treaty, the legal division under its ambitious director, Friedrich Gaus, exerted an influence on the formulation and often even the execution of German foreign policy that went far beyond the functions of legal advice.

IV

The internal development of the German Foreign Office in the five years after the revolution reflected closely the general political history of the Weimar Republic. During the period from the middle of 1919 to the middle of 1920, the forces which had supplied the strength for the building of a German democracy lost what earlier had seemed an irresistible momentum. The dramatic weakening of the Democratic Party in the elections has already been mentioned, but even more important was the crisis of the Social Democratic Party. In the elections of June 1920, it lost about a third of its 1919 vote, which went to the Independent Socialists instead. With the great losses which the two democratic parties had suffered, and with the doubling of the rightist vote in favor of the German People's Party and the German Nationalists, the political position of the democratic wing of the Catholic Center Party grew precarious. Fehrenbach, a conservative member of the Center Party, became chancellor and formed a government consisting of the Center, the Democrats, and the German People's Party, with the latter exercising preponderant influence.

The attempt to have a German republic under the leadership of the German workers' movement was shattered and had no actual chance of being renewed for another twenty years or more. It has become a definite tenet of German Social Democratic "self-criticism" that their willingness to accept the Versailles treaty and to support a pacific foreign policy in the period of the Weimar Republic was a major cause in the collapse of their influence on German affairs. This is not true. The German Majority Socialists lost their dominant position in German politics because they utterly failed to give their followers the feeling that they were in dead earnest about abolishing the authoritarian state in Germany, and about preparing the way to a Socialist economy in accordance with what they had preached for almost half a century. The members of the working class would have forgiven their leaders for the original delay of any decisive action in the social field, since they agreed with them that the conclusion of peace must take precedence over all other political aims. But once the peace had been signed, the Socialist workers expected active leadership directed toward the goals of democratic Socialism which the party had inculcated upon its following for many decades. When the Social Democratic chiefs did not take action even after the first open counterrevolutionary move, the Kapp *Putsch* of April 1920, the workers wandered to the Independent Socialist Party.

Foreign policy, therefore, was not the major reason in the decline of the Majority Socialist Party, and the German worker wanted nothing so much as peace then and later. But he was not easily ready to bear the suffering that the German defeat forced upon him in order to vindicate the honor of a past Germany which had denied him full citizen's rights. During the First World War and again during the resistance to the French occupation of the Ruhr, the vast majority of the German workers proved their willingness to make sacrifices for a foreign policy in which they believed. But the leadership of the Majority Socialist Party was unable to formulate a program for a German foreign policy that would have defined the vital interests of a democratic nation and, at the same time, boldly sketched out the practical ideals and obligations of a worldwide society of nations. The foreign policy of the Social Democratic Party appeared to many of its followers as just another version of the policy of the right parties, while the latter could decry its pacifism as sheer supineness. The lack of a clear foreign policy on the part of the Majority Socialists, therefore, was a contributing element to the rise of the Independent Socialists and subsequently of the Communists. In this connection, it should not be forgotten that democratic Socialism had been confounded everywhere by the World War and by the advent of the Third International. And both France and England emerged from the war as bourgeois states.

The direction of German foreign policy fell into the hands of the German bourgeois parties after 1920, and among them the German People's Party assumed a crucial position, not only because it had startlingly increased its popular vote in the elections, but because it represented the bulk of the German industrialists, including most of the coal and iron magnates of the Ruhr district. Hugo Stinnes, who had just expanded his family holdings into one of the greatest industrial and commercial empires, was the chief political spokesman of this group. There was a streak of the gambler in his nature that appeared even in his business enterprises, which collapsed shortly after his death in 1924. In politics, he was reckless and erratic. The new constellation of German party relations made it impossible to stabilize the German currency.[46] It was asserted from now on that in any event inflation maintained high employment in Germany while on the other hand demonstrating Germany's incapacity for making large reparations. Stinnes even argued that it would be desirable to refuse outright the payment of reparations, even at the risk of an Allied occupation of the Ruhr district. He disregarded the impact that the resulting coal shortage would have on the economic life of the rest of Germany and contended that a military occupation of the Ruhr would prove, once and for all, that nobody could collect reparations from Germany with bayonets.

The policy of negotiating reparations with a stiff upper lip was temporarily defeated when, in May 1921, the Allies, through the London ultimatum, presented an exorbitant bill for reparations and a demand for immediate cash payments, which Germany up to then had not made in any considerable size. The Fehrenbach cabinet resigned and, for another year and a half, the so-called "Weimar coalition" of the Center, Democratic, and Majority Socialist parties returned to office. But they ruled largely by sufferance of the right, which did not as yet feel ready to launch its policy of firmness and which retained sufficient power even outside of the government, since it could rely on its influence on industry, the bureaucracy, and the army. The assassination of Walter Rathenau, the foreign minister of the Wirth cabinet, in June 1922 was a dreadful symptom of the demoralization of the fanatic nationalists. Chancellor Wirth and Rathenau had proclaimed Germany's willingness to fulfill the terms of the London ultimatum and had hoped to be able to show through this "policy of fulfillment" the impracticability of the Allied demands. This hope proved fruitless, and, in November 1922, a government of the right under Wilhelm Cuno took the reins again. By this time, Poincaré was set on the enforcement of French claims for reparations and he expected through the occupation of the Ruhr district to solve France's security problem, which the nonratification of the mutual-assistance pact of 1919 with the United States and Great Britain had left unsettled.

The Cuno government called for passive resistance, but within a period of eight months the French administration slowly succeeded in establishing control over the occupied area, while the fantastic super-inflation brought Germany to the brink of complete chaos. The danger of the loss of the Rhineland, as well as the Bolshevization of the rest of Germany, was very real. The ultra-radicals of the right, like Hitler, would have transformed the passive into an active resistance, but the military situation was hopeless in the judgment of the chief of the German army, General von Seeckt. Thus, the *Reichswehr* marched to stamp out the supposed centers of left Socialist and Communist agitation in Thuringia and Saxony. At the same time, it snuffed out the revolutionary flame that Hitler tried to kindle in Munich. The stage was thereby set for a new approach to the major political problems of Germany. Now the liberal leader of the German People's Party, Gustav Stresemann, could persuade the German industrialists to assist in the stabilization of the mark and attempt to reach an understanding with the foreign powers. This led to the Dawes plan on reparations of 1924, the Locarno treaty of 1925, and Germany's entrance into the League of Nations in 1926.

This survey of German foreign policy with regard to its most urgent questions in the years after Versailles clearly indicates how little of it was or could have been made by diplomatic action. The great decisions, as far as they were at all in German hands, were inherent in the outcome of the internal social struggle. However, to regard the reparation problem exclusively, as we have done, from a German perspective is much too narrow a view. On the evolution of French and British thinking about reparations the Germans could exert but a moderate influence. It depended on the economic and political developments of the Western countries, and was also to be determined by the mutual political relations of the wartime Allies in the postwar years. Last but not least, the future policy of the chief creditor nation of the world, the United States, was always to be considered. The size of future American capital export or, for that matter, of American imports from Europe, as well as American preparedness to draw conclusions from the practical interrelations between German reparations and inter-Allied war debts, were all contingent elements. It would be a serious error to overrate the role of German foreign policy in bringing about the Dawes plan.

In the immediate postwar years, German officials had always urged the establishment of the total German obligation, instead of accepting an interim plan of reparation payments for a number of years. It was argued that, so long as the final sum was left undetermined, Germany was not likely to receive those credits that were needed to restore the German economy and enable it to produce reparations. Obviously, the argument was self-defeating if the total sum were placed at a very high level, as happened with the 132 billion gold marks of the London ultimatum. The Dawes plan stuck officially to the London figure, but defined a payment schedule only for a limited period. This was done, however, at a time when as a result of the settlement under discussion the influx of foreign capital could be anticipated. The example illustrates the baffling complexity of the reparation question and the novel problems that it presented to modern diplomacy. It is difficult to see how the German government could have managed the reparation question without the active mediation of the British ambassador, Lord D'Abernon, sometimes referred to in those years as the lord-protector of Germany. The Dawes plan was no solution of the reparation question, as later events were to reveal. But thereafter it was impossible for France to use the reparation issue as a means to achieve political and military aims which the peace settlement of Paris had denied her. The active participation of American financiers in the discussions of reparations strengthened the belief that Europe's economic ills could be cured in spite of reparations, a faith to which Americans themselves subscribed in the

form of loans and credits of which Germany became the chief
beneficiary.

The solution of the reparation question was the foremost task
of German policy all through the 1920's and, even more than
the military occupation, it brought German foreign policy under
the predominant influence of the Western powers. But ever since
May 7, 1919, the general aim of German foreign policy was
the revision of the treaty of Versailles. It was popular with every
party from the extreme right to the extreme left and, one
may say, with every individual German. Revision, however,
meant all things to all men. There was, in the first place, the
division of opinion on whether the revision should be sought by
peaceful means alone or ultimately by military action. In the
latter case, it had to be discovered how a situation of war
between the major powers might develop in which Germany
could join as an ally of one party and thereby regain a role
in world affairs. On the other hand, those who saw the threat
of a new war to Europe and Germany took the view that
bilateral understandings should only serve for diplomatic, as
against military, cooperation.

All these attitudes were reflected in the actual German foreign
policy, or rather policies, in the years after the First World War.
The prevailing sentiment in Germany discovered the divergence
of French and British foreign policies soon after the war. Lloyd
George had already fought for amendment of the draft treaty
of Versailles. After the signing of the treaty, British diplomacy
had continued to assist in its amelioration, in the drafting of
a statute for the free city of Danzig, and in forgoing the
extradition of German war criminals to Allied courts.[47] British
occupation policy in the Rhineland was not overbearing and,
in addition, tried to resist unwarranted French schemes of oppression. Again, after the plebiscite in Upper Silesia, Lloyd
George favored Germany's political wishes. To be sure, Britain
insisted upon the strict execution of the disarmament provisions

of the treaty and displayed no willingness to waive her own claim for German reparations, but she showed an interest in the economic recovery of Germany, and her ambassador was using suave words about German disarmament at an early moment.[48] It was clear that Britain did not wish to see France as the absolute ruler of the continent and would, therefore, back Germany as a counterbalancing force.

It became a fundamental principle of German political thought, outside the Communist Party and a very few other small groups, that the main endeavor of German diplomacy was to be directed towards ingratiating Germany with England in order to induce her to champion the German cause vis-à-vis France. Moreover, Britain seemed to own the best key for opening some doors to American help in European affairs. Practically nobody in Germany questioned the priority of the cultivation of Anglo-German relations on the agenda of German foreign policy. Ebert and most of the ministers were convinced that Britain's support for Germany had to be won by all means. But Ebert's opinion was shared by most of the German rightists as well. Grand Admiral von Tirpitz led the procession of the former England-haters who confessed that, after the lost war, a new German attitude toward Britain would be in order.[49] After the acceptance of the Versailles treaty by the national assembly, Count Brockdorff-Rantzau had not joined the ranks of those who persecuted his successors with reproaches and calumnies. In July 1919, he was already warning that Germany, once she had signed the treaty, must abstain from any secret schemes to blow it up. "Where the treaty is incapable of execution, it must be proved to our opponents."[50] And Brockdorff-Rantzau, too, had his eyes on Britain.

As early as 1918 there were, as we shall see in more detail further on, some military men who thought that they could build a close Anglo-German alliance by offering German military strength to Britain for the overthrow of Bolshevism in Russia. Ludendorff and General Max Hoffmann carried this propaganda into the postwar years, accompanied by the journalistic pleas of Arnold Rechberg, a wealthy industrialist and amateur politician. Adolf Hitler's foreign program was reared in the same camp, though he placed greater emphasis upon the necessity of an internal transformation, which in his opinion would make Germany strong enough to pull Britain in the right direction.[51] But the belligerent anti-Bolshevism lost out in the practice of German foreign policy after 1920. General von Seeckt's refusal to cooperate with the group was especially important in this connection.

On one point, however, all the German schools were in agreement. The attempt at an Anglo-German rapprochement was the most promising method of working toward the diplomatic, and perhaps eventually even the military, isolation of France. The opposite idea that the most logical way to achieve an alleviation of the treaty burdens on Germany was a firm understanding with France had only a handful of advocates in Germany in the Social Democratic and Democratic parties, and it was not the official policy of either party.[52] But the political and psychological difficulties on both sides were so great that it would have been impossible to base German foreign policy upon an early Franco-German reconciliation. The economic approach, as tried by Rathenau in his negotiations with Loucheur in 1922, might have created some of the preconditions for easing the tension between the two nations, but in both countries the majority of the politically powerful industrialists opposed cooperation. In these circumstances, London acquired an even greater control over German foreign policy than could have occurred if even a remote chance for a direct Franco-German understanding had existed.

It is most doubtful whether German diplomacy could have brought such a chance into being during the years between 1919 and 1925, but there is certainly no indication that German diplomats ever thought seriously about the implications of the situation thus created. They were preoccupied with the hope that the friction between Britain and France would grow into such an antagonism as to force Britain to bury the entente and to side with Germany. In 1922–23 these hopes reached their highest pitch. Not only the altercations over Germany but also the clash of French and British policies in Turkey and Greece as well as in Morocco and Tangier appeared from the German perspective as definite proof of the irreconcilable nature of British and French interests. It was a bitter disappointment to these Germans when the Mediterranean and Near Eastern conflicts were composed at the time of the Lausanne conference, which wrote the new Turkish peace treaty replacing the treaty of Sèvres. When British resistance to the French policy in the Ruhr remained lukewarm, it was said that the British government had acquired the oil of Mosul by giving away the Ruhr coal. But then these unhappy events showed even more clearly that Germany must not lose contact with Britain. Stresemann's decision to form a government that could end the Ruhr struggle and work out a compromise with France, under British mediation and guarantees, was greatly affected by the disappointment over British policy.

The Germans, who believed in incompatibility of future French and British policies, made very serious errors in their appreciation of Anglo-French relations. They disregarded the imponderables entirely. Although popular anti-German feeling in Britain lost its shrill emotionalism rather quickly after June 1919, the popular British attitude toward Germany remained reserved for a good many years. It is difficult to decide how much genuine popular sympathy existed between Frenchmen and Britishers, but both knew that they had immensely benefited by the entente cordiale; and from this practical experience stemmed the readiness to tolerate some friction and to stop it before it poisoned their relations. But even the ponderable po-

litical factors should have indicated that the British had no need
to fear France. The Germans, with the French upon them, were
inclined in those years to overrate the strength of France.
Britain was conscious of the security that her vast naval superiority afforded her, and she was also aware of her incomparable
economic preponderance over France.

There was never any panic in Britain over the political and
military position that France had gained as a consequence of the
Paris peace settlement. The British government was not willing
to commit too much British strength on the European continent
particularly after the withdrawal of the United States. If France
ruled the continent within the regulations of the Paris settlement
and with reasonable regard to British sensitivities in Western
Europe, Britain would be content to devote herself to her own
far-flung and knotty imperial problems. Poincaré, however, was
unmindful of the British conception of the Anglo-French entente. French policy became an embarrassing nuisance but not
yet a dangerous threat, the less so since some soul-searching
brought out past British mistakes in the treatment of the French.
Outstanding among them was the gingerly way in which the
British had dealt with the French demand for a British guarantee
of the Rhine frontier after the draft treaty of June 28, 1919, had
come to naught as the result of America's refusal to ratify. British
policy would have to be more generous than in the past in
order to keep France from adopting a unilateral policy in Europe that would be ruinous to the rehabilitation of the continent,
to the collection of any reparations, and to the restoration of
European markets, which was needed for the economic recovery
of Britain. In one respect, the German resistance in the Ruhr
was of great consequence. The expense to which the French
were put led to a long-overdue crisis of their public finances
and of the stability of the franc. Internally it weakened the
confidence of the high bourgeoisie in the government and gave
the parties of the left fresh influence, while demonstrating

how dangerous it was for France to play a singlehanded game in world affairs. The moment had arrived when British diplomacy could intervene and redefine the European power relationships.

One can say that the British Foreign Office under Austen Chamberlain never intended to steer an anti-French course. On the contrary, the whole British policy was often described as a return to the entente cordiale. Chamberlain refused to accept the Geneva protocol that would have meant a British obligation to act in any conflict arising out of the peace settlement, but in the Locarno treaty France received a British guarantee of the Rhine frontier. On the other hand, if Germany received the same guarantee against an act of French aggression, this signified in the first place the French renunciation of a unilateral policy going beyond the treaty of Versailles. No doubt the double-sided British guarantee of the Rhine border had, from the German point of view, a certain prestige value as seemingly joining Germany to the great powers on a basis of equality. In general, the British were now convinced that a stronger Germany was needed to insure not only the recovery of Europe but stricter French adherence to the general ideas of British policy. "Desiring the maintenance of the Anglo-French entente, I am compelled to desire the existence of a strong Germany," said Lord D'Abernon.[53] He might have gone a good bit farther than official British policy did or could go. For the Versailles provisions were not changed. Germany had to accept the cession of Alsace-Lorraine and, more important, to subscribe voluntarily to the demilitarization of the Rhineland. She had to do so without the evacuation of the Allied troops from the occupied western regions. It was true that the Rhineland was eventually freed of Allied occupation, five years before the final date set by the Versailles treaty. But it had already been stated by the Allied statesmen at Versailles that, once Germany fulfilled her treaty obligations, an earlier evacuation would be possible. In these circumstances, it seemed frustrating that the occupation should come to an end only five years after Locarno and after lengthy negotiations, during which the British had not exerted the harsh pressure on France for which the Germans had hoped. Nor did the British show themselves easy bargainers in reparation questions. Germany's admission to the League of Nations afforded her new political opportunities to plead her case before the world, but it was a promise on her part not to seek revision by extra-legal methods and to work in peaceful cooperation with the other League members. In this respect League membership tied Germany closely to the international system that the Western powers represented, and it compromised her in other directions. But those Germans who criticize the courageous policy of Stresemann still have to show how Germany could otherwise have overcome the grave consequences of the lost Ruhr struggle of 1923.[54] Other gains accrued, too. The foreign loans which flowed to Germany in the second half of the 1920's enabled her to build the most modern industrial plant of any European country. Of greater significance yet was the fact that Germany was now being listened to in her new position in world affairs. By 1933 no nation, not even France, was willing to rise to the total defense of the Versailles treaty, which had lost its moral justification in public opinion.

But the Western powers made important concessions to Germany at the time of Locarno and of Germany's entrance into the League which in the eyes of many Germans made these events the starting point for a new German foreign policy that no longer depended exclusively on the Western powers and that was the genuine expression of German national interests. Before we can discuss the concessions of the Western powers to Germany in Eastern European and Russian affairs, we must briefly review German policy in the East since the armistice of November 1918. In this field, the German Foreign Office could develop a greater initiative than in Western European matters. Whereas the Western division of the Foreign Office was continuously under the pressure of the foreign powers and domestic controversies, the Eastern division could plan and execute in an atmosphere of greater calm. However, it had a competitor or pacemaker in the German army, which was under less observation in the East than it was in the West, and which was determined to take full advantage of this situation.

At the time of the armistice German troops in the East were spread as far as the Ukraine and the Caucasus in the south and Finland and the Baltic provinces in the north. They flooded back to Germany in great disorder and dissolved on their march at home.[55] The hostile attitude of populations such as the Polish was a major element in this disintegration, as was the influence of the German revolution upon army discipline. In the Baltic provinces—called the Baltikum by the Germans—a somewhat different situation developed. German military and political authorities had worked closely together during the war with the German nobility, which formed a small minority in these countries but owned most of the land dearly coveted by the indigenous peasantry. But the retreat of the German troops from the northern Baltikum laid the country open to easy conquest by the Russian Bolshevists, and not only the Baltic Germans but also the democratic national movements were anxious not to lose German military protection. Some German troops remained in the Baltikum, and, beginning early in 1919, they were reinforced by a division sent by the high command of the German army and, subsequently, by a stream of volunteers hired with the promise of land settlement in the region. In addition, Russian prisoners of war in Germany were induced to serve in the fight against the Bolshevist desecrators of the Russian Empire.[56]

The German high command under Hindenburg and Groener moved to eastern Germany in February 1919 in order to defend the old frontiers of Germany against Polish infringements and Bolshevist dangers. General von Seeckt was in command of the defense of East Prussia from January to April 1919 and was chiefly responsible for the army's decision to make the province secure by creating a protective zone in the Baltikum. His thoughts ranged beyond this immediate aim. In East Prussia and the Baltikum, it might be possible to rebuild a strong German army which would make its weight felt in the peace negotiations at Paris. But other German leaders entertained even bolder dreams, especially after the military situation in the Baltikum developed favorably and the Paris conference entered its critical stage. Could the Baltic bastion perhaps become the military base for a decisive military action against Bolshevist Russia through the capture of Leningrad? If such a coup were successful, it could be assumed that Britain would join Germany in the anti-Bolshevist struggle. But even if Britain refused to ally herself with Germany one could expect a counterrevolutionary Russia to side with Germany.

All these dreams came to nothing. As in the past, the Germans disregarded the national movements of the Lithuanians, Letts, and Estonians and their White Russian companions treated the Baltic countries as provinces of Russia. The Baltic peasant and middle classes waited only for the moment when they could acquire full national freedom by ridding themselves of the Germans. The hour arrived at which the Western powers had gathered sufficient military and naval strength. Since February 1919 they had been demanding the withdrawal of the German troops; in the fall they saw to it that their orders were obeyed. The whole German Baltikum adventure had to be liquidated. For a while the German Foreign Office still endeavored to keep the White Russian troops of Colonel Bermondt in being and to relate them somehow to the Allied-supported armies of intervention. German diplomatic officials also cultivated relations with prominent Russian refugees. General von Seeckt, who became chief of the *Reichswehr* in the spring of 1920, was the leader in a revision of German policy.[57]

Already during his command in East Prussia it had dawned upon Seeckt that the German military effort in the Baltikum was doing a job for the Allied rather than the German cause. He had always lived in the Bismarck-Moltke tradition and viewed friendly German-Russian relations as the keystone of German security and France as the implacable enemy of the Empire. The general, however, was also a child of the age of Wilhelm II and Tirpitz and had considered the defeat of England to be the major objective of the First World War. Even after the war, he remained cool to the British, who showed no indication of giving Germany a sizable army. Considering the hostile attitude of the Western powers, Seeckt judged that Germany could not afford to incur the enmity of Russia. Bolshevism in Germany would have to be fought relentlessly, but it was imperative to restore the natural contact between Russia and Germany. The German Empire had no real interest in the new Eastern European states; on the contrary, the annihilation of the new Poland and the restoration of the Russo-German frontiers of 1914 should form the main goal of German foreign policy. Thus, he welcomed the opportunity for conversations with Soviet emissaries, which were brought about by the intercession of Enver Pasha, the military leader of the Young Turk revolution of 1908 and of the pro-German groups in Turkey during the World War. In 1920 Enver Pasha had gone to Moscow, originally working for a Russo-German-Turkish alliance against the West.

Seeckt remained seemingly unmoved when the Russians approached Warsaw in the summer of 1920. He expected a total Russian victory. It is impossible to say whether Seeckt felt confident that the Russians would not cross the frontiers of 1914 into Germany or whether he hoped that, in the case of a Soviet threat to Central Europe, Germany would receive arms from the Allies. In any event, after "the miracle of the Vistula," Seeckt proceeded to set up in the war ministry the section R that

was charged with directing the activities of the German army
with regard to the Soviet Union. The innermost concern of
General Seeckt was the building up of German military strength.
To all those Germans who since 1918 believed that economic
recovery came before military power, he had replied that without swords plowshares were of no avail.[58] In his opinion, German diplomacy should have centered its struggle for a better
peace in Paris around the retention of a German army of
300,000 men. Instead, Count Brockdorff-Rantzau appeared in
sheep's clothing, inveighed against imperialism, and fought in
the first place for the economic existence of Germany. The general despised the count for his cowardly policy. After June 1919,
Seeckt pressed the German government to request a change of
the disarmament provision of the Versailles treaty from the
Allies, an entirely hopeless demand that tended only to worsen
the atmosphere in which the discussion of the reparation question had to take place.

When the Allies finally turned down the German demand
for a moderation of the Allied conditions for German disarmament, and when the London ultimatum on reparations had led
to the formation of the Wirth cabinet, General von Seeckt persuaded the new chancellor to allow the *Reichswehr* the use
of whatever facilities the Russians would provide for the production of armaments forbidden to Germany under the terms
of the Versailles treaty. With public funds, though through the
channels of private industry, armament factories were developed
in the Soviet Union for the output of artillery, ammunition, tanks,
and planes. The ominous plan of building also a factory for the
production of gas weapons seems not to have been realized.
But the industrial rearmament was accompanied by mutual ex-
changes of officers for training in staff work and the tactics of
large formations. Although information on the details of the
German-Russian defense cooperation is still lacking, we may
well judge that it did not assume the form of a military alliance

or planned cooperation for war, but was aimed only at mutual assistance in strengthening the war potential of each nation.

The Foreign Office followed suit on the path opened by the diplomacy of the army. Among the old professional staff of the office, Baron Ago von Maltzan emerged as the most powerful member after the war. He quickly rose from chief of the Russian section to chief of the eastern division and secretary of state in the Foreign Office. He came from Mecklenburg Junker stock and became related by marriage to industrial circles. With great personal means at his disposal, he made his pleasant home the center of enjoyable and interesting social gatherings in the midst of inflation-ridden Berlin. At the Maltzans', distinguished foreigners ranging from the papal nuncio to the Soviet commissar met and rubbed elbows with important Germans from all political camps. Exactly where Maltzan stood on the hard-fought issues of German domestic politics, nobody has ever found out, and he epitomized well the deflation of ideologies which was an aftermath of years of war and revolution. Maltzan used his wide connections exclusively with a view to improving the international position of Germany, and after a brief period of hesitation he accepted Seeckt's ideas on the practicability of a German-Russian rapprochement. The negotiations were carried on through the only diplomatic line that had survived the rupture of German-Russian diplomatic relations in early November 1918. Both in Moscow and Berlin commissions for the repatriation of prisoners of war had been created.

As a consequence of the conversations, the Soviet Union and Germany, on May 6, 1921, concluded a trade treaty which laid the foundation for extensive economic intercourse between the two countries. The treaty followed a trade agreement between Britain and Russia of March 1921 and failed to cause any remarkable international reaction. But the German-Russian treaty was in the technical diplomatic sense far-reaching. The repatriation commissions were entrusted with the execution of commercial activities and received all the rights and privileges of diplomatic missions. A bridge had been constructed over the gulf that had separated the two governments since the days of the treaty of Brest-Litovsk.

This is not the place to speculate over all the motives that induced the Soviet government to move closer to Germany. The two countries were undoubtedly pariahs among the nations at that moment, but Soviet policy was never noticeably affected by sentiment. The German talent in military industries were welcome in Russia on the eve of the inauguration of the New Economic Policy. But Germany was weak and, worst of all, poor. The centers of world politics and world finance were in the West. The Soviet Union would have liked to gain recognition by the Western powers. In the West the impact of the postwar depression had created an appetite for new markets, and projects for the opening of the Russian market were freely discussed. Rathenau was not the first to propose such plans, but in his prolific mind the proposal for an international syndicate, supported and financed by all the Western nations and Germany, took definite shape. The expansion of European production and trade, so Rathenau thought, would make German reparations bearable. Rathenau won Lloyd George over for an international discussion of the plan which was to take place at Genoa in April 1922.[59] The idea, as Maltzan apparently felt beforehand, was much disliked in the Soviet Union. It tasted of capitalistic exploitation, which was made even less palatable by the formation of such a union of capitalistic governments.

To break up the common front of the Western powers was the main objective of Soviet diplomacy. But to the German delegation this front did not seem real. They found themselves left out of the discussion and became afraid that the French might falsify the whole plan by offering the Soviet Union a share in German reparations. Article 116 of the Versailles treaty had reserved possible Russian claims against Germany. It was a great relief to Maltzan that Chicherin offered to sign a separate treaty with Germany, in which Russia and Germany renounced all their mutual claims arising from war damages and war expenses. Beyond this, the treaty that was signed in Rapallo on the morning of Easter Sunday, April 16, was in the nature of a general treaty of friendship. It envisaged, as the most important practical step, the immediate establishment of embassies in Berlin and Moscow.

The treaty was not drafted in Genoa. So far as content went, it had been the result of negotiations in the months before. Chicherin had offered to sign the treaty in Berlin on his way to Genoa, but Rathenau did not wish to do so before the conference. There, on Russian insistence, the treaty had been consummated and turned into a demonstration against the diplomatic plans of the Western powers. Rathenau was most reluctant to proceed behind the back of Lloyd George, and it was Maltzan's persuasiveness that dragged the minister along. Rathenau's position in reparation discussions was at least temporarily weakened, and the breakdown of the conference, though it did not inspire Poincaré's decision to use sanctions against Germany, brought the Ruhr invasion a few steps nearer.

The precipitate action of the German conference delegation made President Ebert angry. He saw in it a violation of his constitutional authority and was concerned about the reaction of the German parties. Apart from the Communists, no German party supported a Russian orientation of German foreign policy. The Social Democratic Party was opposed to it; the Center Party very cool; and even the German Nationalists were against close relations with the Soviet Union. Of course, this was true of the militant anti-Bolshevists, but, in addition, the agrarian interests in the party feared Russian economic competition. Genuine popular support came chiefly from a few groups in the German Nationalist, German People's, and Democratic parties. But these few people, supported from the background by

General von Seeckt, succeeded in getting the Rapallo treaty easy passage through the German parliament. Public opinion was friendly, because, after so much submissive toleration of Western demands, Rapallo seemed a defiant gesture of German dissatisfaction.

Count Brockdorff-Rantzau was sent to Moscow as German ambassador. He was not in agreement with Seeckt about the aims of German policy in Russia. During the summer of 1922, the two imperious men fought a furious battle of memoranda.[60] There were many misunderstandings between them. Seeckt's critique of Brockdorff-Rantzau's opinion was an expression of unmitigated contempt for the man of 1919, who "cannot understand that ultimately every political activity rests on power." But the count was a passionate hater, too; he was so aroused that he would have liked to challenge the general to a pistol duel. Brockdorff-Rantzau and Seeckt were in agreement that German foreign policy should aim at the isolation of France and that a British alliance was desirable. Both misjudged the state and trend of Anglo-French relations. The ambassador argued that it was dangerous to have military arrangements with the Soviet Union, since the mere suspicion of such cooperation would bring the British and French closer together. He also warned against Soviet blackmail and wanted to see German-Russian relations confined to the economic field. Seeckt, on his part, denied that the German military activities in Russia would affect the course of British policy. He believed that the clash between France and Britain would come as the result of overseas conflicts and that a Germany strengthened by her rearmament would be more *bündnisfähig*.

Count Brockdorff-Rantzau went to Moscow in 1922 as a "Westerner." While he let his great gift for personal diplomacy work on Chicherin in many conversations in the hours after midnight, Seeckt continued to operate his own wires to Moscow. But practically, though not formally, the two German foreign policies turned into parallel directions. Brockdorff-Rantzau came to find greater value in general cooperation between Russia and Germany.[61] When Germany was about to accept the Locarno treaty, the German ambassador almost joined forces with Russian diplomacy in its storm against Berlin. It seems improbable that he shared the Russian fears that Germany would become in the League the tool of an anti-Russian coalition and especially a vassal of Britain. It is more likely that Brockdorff-Rantzau, in memory of Versailles, was dumfounded by the prospect of close Franco-German cooperation. He was, therefore, little impressed by the concessions made by the Western powers which finally made it possible to conclude the German-Russian treaty of Berlin of April 24, 1926.[62]

Germany was exempted from participation in possible sanctions against the Soviet Union taken by the League of Nations under Article 16. Her special diplomatic situation vis-à-vis the Soviet Union was thereby officially recognized. The significance of this event was greatly heightened by the absence of a British guarantee for the postwar frontiers in Eastern Europe. Whereas Germany accepted the Rhine settlement of Versailles, she was free to press for revision in the East, though only by peaceful means. The political moderation and circumspection, as well as the strong fortitude of heart, that Gustav Stresemann had shown were the greatest single factor in achieving for Germany this new position in the world. She could feel a new sense of relative independence and at the same time of self-chosen participation in European affairs. For a short period German foreign policy was almost as largely consolidated in the hands of the Foreign Office as in the days of Bismarck. However, this influence of the Foreign Office rested as much on the balance of the domestic social and political forces as upon the gains made in the foreign field. The age in which the professional diplomat could preside over the formulation of foreign policy had passed long ago.

VII ORIGINS AND POLITICAL
CHARACTER OF NAZI IDEOLOGY

I

"IDEOLOGY IS intolerant and cannot be content with the role of 'a party among other parties.' It imperiously demands its own, exclusive, and unqualified recognition as well as the complete transformation of the whole public life according to its views."[1] With these words Hitler in 1926 proclaimed his determination not to tolerate any ideology other than the National Socialist one. Only pure ideology can engender the "fanatic" faith that will build the "movement" and the "racial community" (*Volksgemeinschaft*). In the last weeks before his death, in what he called "the last quarter-hour" of the Third Reich, Hitler said that the Allies would now erase the German people as well as the National Socialist ideology.[2]

But in spite of the emphasis laid not only on ideology but also on pure and correct ideology, there existed few canonic National Socialist writings. The party program of 1920, written by the engineer Gottfried Feder, contained among its twenty-five points more economic than political demands, some of which soon became meaningless, since they were geared to the peculiar conditions of Germany in the first years after World War I. In 1925 after Hitler had returned from prison, discussions on a new party program were held, for which apparently Gregor Strasser had prepared a draft. But Hitler, anxious to restore his leadership of the party, opposed a new program and insisted that the program of 1920 should be publicly pronounced "unalterable." Just the same, it was changed later by the dubious reinterpretation of certain points, while others were simply shelved after 1933.

Hitler's *Mein Kampf* is by far the most important source for Nazi ideology. He opened the second volume, written in 1925 with the subtitle "The National Socialist Movement," with a chapter on "Ideology and Party." It is noteworthy that Hitler never mentions any of Feder's points specifically, although he starts the chapter with a glowing reference to the first National Socialist mass meeting, at which Feder's program was adopted by acclamation, and goes on to explain that a program is to a party what dogma is to a church. Hitler obviously was cautious not to commit himself to very specific objectives which were likely to limit the appeal of National Socialism to groups that he hoped to win over. His bombastic and rambling book remains fragmentary in many respects and does not offer a systematic presentation of Nazi ideology. This again is partly due to political considerations. To give only one example, although Hitler's radical anti-Christian attitude was well established and a careful reader could sense it most distinctly, the issue of National Socialism versus the Christian churches is covered up in the book.[3] Other political calculations are revealed in the changes made in the text after 1933. Whereas the first and early editions said: "the movement stands . . . for the principle of a Germanic democracy: election of the leader, but absolute authority for him . . ." the passage later reads: "the movement stands . . . for the principle of the absolute authority of the leader, coupled with the highest responsibility. . . . The leader is always appointed from above and at the same time endowed with unlimited power and authority. . . ."[4]

But although political and propagandistic reasons of the moment explain many omissions as well as the obliqueness of many references, the unsystematic character of *Mein Kampf* is essentially the true expression of Hitler's peculiar mind. His was an unkempt and primitive mind that lacked the power of discrimination but excelled in reducing simple ideas to even simpler terms while believing thereby to have achieved a higher wisdom. On this account he considered himself an original thinker and never cared to give credit to any person from whom he had borrowed his ideas. Moreover he was interested only in those ideas that through propaganda would build organizations. The growth of the Nazi movement became to him a criterion of the truth of the Nazi ideology.[5] He did not pay any attention to the subsequent systematic expositions of National Socialist ideology. Thus he did not read Alfred Rosenberg's *The Myth of the Twentieth Century* (1930), taken by most people as the official treatise on Nazi philosophy,[6] nor any of the other theoretical writings of the Nazis and Nazi fellow-travelers.

The quality of Hitler's mind and the tactical nature of all of his statements make it necessary even for the study of ideology to analyze his actions and the political reality created by them, as Franz L. Neumann was the first to do in his *Behemoth*. Yet at the time Neumann wrote his still important book only two canonic writings were known to Hitler's followers and the world at large, the party program, which is of only limited value, and *Mein Kampf*, while by now we have a wealth of authentic Hitler material, spread over the years down to April 1945, which allows us to describe the Nazi ideology as well as the motivation of Nazi action rather exactly.[7]

II

What stands out most clearly today is the consistency and continuity of Nazi ideology. Hitler was a great opportunist and tactician, but it would be quite wrong to think that ideology was for him a mere instrumentality for gaining power. On the contrary, Hitler was a doctrinaire of the first order. Throughout his political career he was guided by an ideology, parts of which were played down or even publicly denied occasionally or even for a considerable length of time because they seemed to frighten people whom he intended to subject to his will. But step by step he realized his basic ideas, which from 1926 onward do not show any change whatsoever.

Fundamental in his thinking was the conception of life as an eternal struggle for survival and domination. Hunger and love he called the elemental forces behind this process.[8] Struggle rules supreme within peoples and among peoples. This crude Social Darwinism is then linked up with an equally primitive racism; not peoples but races are the primordial forces of history. Hitler admitted that there are no pure races and that, for example, the Germans mixed with peoples whom they conquered and with invaders they later absorbed.[9] But as a rule that did not keep him from asserting the superiority of pure races.[10] The strength of the Germanic race may be sapped by the admixture of other races, and Hitler ascribed the individualistic party spirit of the Germans to this fact. Once the true Germanic elements will have gained full power over the people, it will be possible to eliminate racially inferior groups and to enhance the breeding of the superior racial stock.

Among the races the Nordic or Aryan race is the highest and its chief representative is the German people. It deserves the satisfaction of all its needs for life and growth. Since agriculture cannot raise production beyond the present level, Germany needs a greater *Lebensraum,* which can only be gained by war and the expulsion, if necessary even annihilation, of other peoples. Already in *Mein Kampf* racist nationalism looks to the East for the conquest of *Lebensraum,* and Hitler never modified these ideas which led to his ultimate doom.[11]

Hitler's biological materialism tolerated no ethics. In the pursuit of its struggle for power, which is the dictate of the blood, the racial people may use any means. Any restraint is

Gefühlsduselei, silly sentimentality. Hitler gloated that his conception of race was the true revolutionary principle of the twentieth century, as the idea of nation had revolutionized the preceding century.[12] In this connection he used almost Marxist terminology in deriding the stupidity of the bourgeoisie and the old upper classes for being hampered by humanitarian scruples and for their inability to conceive of better programs than the restoration of the German frontiers of 1914. Only "dynamic" or "fanatic" people fully believing in "race" would be able to fight without being bothered by humanitarian and traditionalist inhibitions. Hitler readily admitted that this fact called for barbarians.[13]

Anti-Semitism was the major instrument in this policy of barbarization.[14] Through the vilification, torture, and mass murder of the Jews the ruthlessness was produced that Hitler wanted to inculcate in his followers. He described quite often the practical political value of anti-Semitism, particularly in the sense that in order to arouse hatred among people it was essential to personify the enemy.[15] But it cannot be stressed enough that Hitler himself was a passionate believer in extreme anti-Semitism. The anti-Jewish demonstrations and pogroms of April 1, 1933, and of November 8–9, 1938 (*Reichskristallnacht*), were carried on in public, but when in 1942 Hitler ordered the physical extermination of all the European Jews, he knew that this "final solution"[16] of the Jewish problem would frighten most Germans and it was therefore secretly executed. It was a personal act of Hitler. But anti-Semitism was only part of Hitler's racism. While the Jews were to him subhuman, there were also low human races, such as the Slavs, whom he did not propose to destroy but to deprive of further growth and of their national education. The Nazi occupation policies in Eastern Europe provide indications of these intentions.[17]

The use of terror against enemies of the party and regime was another means of barbarization, but not even terror and violence were mere instruments of power. Hitler believed in their permanent value. People do not have a natural herd instinct, he said[18]; if left alone they will rather fight among themselves. Only the fear of an authority commanding and using force can create a community.

The National Socialist ideology, which Hitler did not wish to be called "the myth of the twentieth century" but "the science of the twentieth century,"[19] included the self-esteem and worship of its prophet. In him the Germanic race has come to full consciousness of its inner self and of its mission in the world. With the deepest insight he combines the greatest will-power, hallmarks of the born leader. Therefore he must demand complete obedience from the whole people.

The Nazi ideology was quite rigid. Its activist racism and totalitarian authoritarianism contained distinct and immutable principles for a political theory and even for specific policies. We must assume that Hitler had acquired a faith in the main body of these ideas before he left Austria and a good many years before he decided to enter politics. These crude ideas were originally his personal revenge on the old society of property and education, in which he, in his own eyes a budding genius, had been a misfit. In all his intimate conversations one can sense a profound contempt of generals, of the bourgeoisie, and especially of professors, which changed to outbursts of fiery hatred when the underlying feeling that these gentlemen considered him an upstart welled up in him. This social resentment made him embrace the basic ideas from which the Nazi ideology developed. Its conception of "people" or "race" leveled down all social classes and attached no significance to educational differentiation.

Essentially, this was all that Hitler's "Socialism" meant. Equality was his idea only in the abstract sense that everybody was a racial tribesman, for each person was placed immediately into a hierarchical system of military subordination that makes equality a sham. The rise to higher rank was made less dependent on class than before and more on service and loyalty to the party and leader. Equality was not linked to any specific economic system. Hitler was quite ignorant of economic affairs. He was originally concerned only with agriculture as the source not only for the physical survival of the people but also as the ideal breeding ground for pure race and the right ideology that goes with it. There is little in Hitler's statements about the artisan and craftsman, but obviously they were considered creative producers. This attitude carried over to industry, whereas big commerce and finance smelled of profiteering and exploitation.

Such general sentiments were inadequate foundations for a principled economic policy. Hitler's vacillations in this respect reflected his lack of knowledge as well as interest. Prior to 1933 he subordinated economics to propaganda, as shown by his reinterpretation of Gottfried Feder's program. After he had come to power he followed an economic policy that seemed to promise him the maximum of war production. He quickly stopped the activities of the party in favor of artisans, small businessmen, and the like, and before very long gave up the attempt at building a corporative state. What came into being is probably best called a "command economy," a term coined by Franz L. Neumann.[20] It was not corporatism, nor Socialism, nor state Socialism or state capitalism, but an economy more and more directed by the state. The process of integrating the economy into the totalitarian state was in the beginning slower than the imposition of totalitarian controls on other activities, but it was accelerated by the approaching war and in the end equally far-reaching. But Nazi economic policies were less directly affected by Nazi ideology, except insofar as the latter was bent on war.

III

The discussions of the origins of Nazi ideology have often neglected to reduce the pattern of ideas to those that served the double function of a political ideology, namely, to win through propaganda a people as well as to set up a model of ultimate political action. I have tried to confine my definition of Nazi ideology largely to those elements of Hitler's political thinking that constantly and decisively determined his general course of action. It also is a common mistake to describe Nazi ideology as the summary of all the ideas that came to the fore in Germany in the period before 1933. There can be no doubt that some of the ideas of the so-called conservative revolution, in the first place Moeller van den Bruck's "Third Reich," were taken over by Hitler and made part of the official ideology. But actually van den Bruck's conception assumed an entirely different meaning in the context of genuine Nazi ideology. Other "conservative" ideas were left uncensored, because Hitler or Goebbels thought they would gain for National Socialism the support of groups not otherwise easily accessible to Nazi ideology or because they thought it useful to throw sand into the eyes of their opponents.[21] Although naturally all these ideas are of the highest importance for the study of the acceptance of National Socialism by the German people and particularly by a large section of the German intelligentsia in 1933, they are of secondary importance for the understanding of the origins of the genuine Nazi ideology. Italian Fascism, too, was of no significance for the growth of Nazi ideology. Mussolini's actions, particularly the march on Rome, made a profound impression on Hitler, but Fascist ideology was too nebulous and volatile to change Hitler's ideas. The adoption of corporatism by Italian Fascism found some imitation among the National Socialists, but it did not become official policy after 1933.

We still do not know enough about the reading Hitler did in his formative years and down to 1926. It is clear, however, that it was neither very extensive nor critically selective nor systematic. Some books obviously were only read in part, others were misunderstood or not understood at all. There is no indication that books helped him to improve his abominable style, which remained to the last turgid and full of clichés, and aimed at impressing his readers or listeners by stuffing an unbearable number of overworked metaphors into a single sentence.[22] One of the signs of a half-educated person, the preference for words borrowed from foreign languages and their occasional use in the wrong place and with the wrong meaning, is characteristic of Hitler.[23] With this evidence we are well advised not to look for any original philosophical or literary works as the immediate sources of Hitler's first ideas. As a matter of fact, he received them from the political marketplace and even lowlier sources.

The Pan-Germanism of Georg von Schönerer and the Christian Social movement under Vienna's Mayor Karl Lueger gave Hitler his first notions about anti-Semitism and its potential power to move the masses. His theoretical enlargement on anti-Semitism in this period derived from the cheap little *Ostara* pamphlets, issued by a former monk who called himself Lanz von Liebenfels[24] (alias Adolf Lanz) and who peddled a racist "theozoology" of his own concoction. These tracts, sold at tobacco stands, and probably similar sheets, together with certain newspapers,[25] provided his chief literary fare. He no doubt read Richard Wagner's political and anti-Semitic writings and found in them the confirmation of the racist and anti-Semitic faith that he had adopted in his Vienna years. Richard Wagner was to Hitler the conclusive proof that the right ideology would produce the highest art. Hitler was familiar with the book by Richard Wagner's English-born son-in-law, Houston Stewart Chamberlain, *Foundations of the Twentieth Century*, the widely read racist interpretation of world history. He knew, of course, about Count Arthur de Gobineau's *Inequality of the Human Races*, although it is doubtful whether he ever did more than dip into it. Passing on to original thinkers, I have been unable to discover any specific reference to Nietzsche.[26] Whether, if he ever read him, he was repelled by the philosopher's contempt for anti-Semitism and Germanism no one can say. We have, however, a statement by Hitler on the deep impression that Schopenhauer had made on him. Yet he was quite incapable of indicating what was the special fascination of Schopenhauer's philosophy or what concretely he had learned from it. Even Wagner had misunderstood Schopenhauer in many respects, but Hitler's whole thinking did not show the slightest impress of Schopenhauer; it was indeed a world apart from a philosophy strongly opposed to man's being submerged in the state and looking for salvation from the ills and sufferings in the negation of the will for life.

It was on the basis of his limited reading in popular and often cranky and murky writings that Hitler formed his original racist and anti-Semitic ideas. In this respect he did not add any new ideas during his years in Germany.[27] But Hitler experienced the full impact of German militarism and imperialistic nationalism. The Austrian Pan-Germanists prior to World War I were chiefly concerned with the merger of the German parts of the Hapsburg Empire with the German Empire. There are some signs that Hitler's dreams were already in these prewar years going beyond the mere realization of a Greater Germany; his migration to Germany in 1912, his obvious reluctance to report for obligatory military service in Austria prior to 1914, and, by contrast, his enthusiastic welcome of the outbreak of World War I as well as his immediate volunteering in a Bavarian regiment point in this direction. But irrespective of what conclusions Hitler may have drawn from the Pan-German propaganda before 1914, only the outbreak of the war made it possible to think of an early realization of the Pan-German demands for world power. Hitler undoubtedly came into close contact with these ideas which since August 1914 not only constituted the war-aims program of the German rightist parties but colored the policies of the parties further to the left. Within the German army, particularly after Ludendorff had become its leading spirit in the fall of 1916, intensive indoctrination of the troops was carried on in which the alleged superiority of the German people over the degenerate French, the mercenary English, the brute and servile Russians served as the justification for German conquests sufficient to make any future aggression against Germany impossible and to establish her as a world power.[28]

There was already talk in public and in government councils about removing foreign populations in lands adjacent to Germany for the settlement of Germans. Hindenburg promised the soldiers land for settlement after the war. The peace treaties of Brest-Litovsk with the Ukraine and Soviet Russia as well as subsequent military and political actions created a vast orbit of German satellites and colonies that reached from the White to the Black and Caspian Seas. These experiences of World War I emboldened Hitler to draw the most extreme consequences from his racist nationalism. Besides, we may surmise that four years of participation in the slaughter of that war stirred up the ferocity that was in his nature. The loss of World War I by Germany confirmed his belief in his own political mission.

While Hitler adopted some of the major objectives and methods of the imperialistic German nationalism of World War I, he also firmly rejected others. Although his great scheme of eastern expansion was clearly a continuation of the Pan-German aspirations of World War I, he sharply criticized the German government and the German nationalists for simultaneously aiming at the acquisition of colonies overseas, thus antagonizing England. Yet he was even more critical of the methods by which the imperial German government had expected to achieve its ends. He radically disapproved of its mismanagement of internal affairs, particularly by its toleration of opposition parties and a critical press. In this situation a mass movement such as the Fatherland Party with its four million members was doomed to failure. The Fatherland Party, founded by Admiral von Tirpitz and Wolfgang Kapp in order to mobilize popular support for the Pan-German war-aims program, by claiming to be a national movement above the existing political parties, was a direct forerunner of the Nazi Party. Hitler must have watched it with great interest and found it wanting. The Fatherland Party, though heightening the patriotic sentiment of its bourgeois membership, did not produce determined fighters against the double enemy at home and abroad. When the revolution came, they surrendered to the internal enemy and broke off the war.

Although Hitler in his propaganda against the Weimar Republic made the utmost use of the "stab-in-the-back" legend and of the "November crimes," he was always convinced that the old regime was responsible for its own downfall. Its national ideology was weakened by liberalism and by lack of knowledge about the vital needs of the nation. Moreover, the Pan-German ideology, even if adequately propagated—and this should have begun years before the war—was not likely to integrate all classes. Something more elementary and robust was needed. Hitler believed that in his own ideology he possessed the right principles for building a powerful Germany that would resume the battle for German supremacy. Before this war could be won abroad, it first had to be won at home by the destruction of liberalism, Socialism, and Communism as well as by the implementation of a common ideology that would make the

German people immune to foreign propaganda and ready to fight with unmatched determination for *Lebensraum* and race superiority. Hitler made another correction in the World War I ideas of Pan-Germanism. To be sure, anti-Semitism had been a strong ingredient of the movement from the beginning, but, as everywhere else in Central Europe, this anti-Semitism aimed at taking full citizenship away from the Jews and inflicting other humiliating conditions on them. Its intention was to harry the Jews, not to exterminate them. Only National Socialism proceeded to that level of crime. It is impossible to say exactly at what particular moment Hitler set his mind on the physical destruction of the Jews. But the racist nationalism developed by him during World War I to feverish pitch was bound to give his anti-Semitism the highest radical note.

Hitler derived his ideology from few sources, all of them of a rather low type. Many German writers during the Nazi period endeavored to relate Hitler to the great classic tradition of German philosophy—Leibniz, Kant, Fichte, and Hegel—or even linked him with Luther. National Socialism then appeared as the crowning achievement of the German spirit. Outside Germany this view has often been expressed, though usually in polemics against Germany. But all the evidence that we possess forbids this interpretation. Not even the fact that a large segment of the German intelligentsia fell for Hitler's ideas in 1933 can be explained in such manner. Actually, this event cannot be traced back ideologically beyond the 1840's and must be explained largely in political and social terms. The phenomenon of Hitler himself also calls chiefly for a political and social interpretation, since he was satisfied with the mere rudiments of an ideology that allowed him to act as the charismatic leader of the German people.

VIII THE GERMAN OPPOSITION
TO HITLER

———◆———

OPPOSITION TO THE regime existed all through the years of the Third Reich. Its earliest demonstrations came directly from the political parties that had fought Hitler's rise to power. In free elections the National Socialist Party had at best gained 37 percent of the popular vote, and even in the elections of March 5, 1933, which were dominated by Nazi terror, this vote reached only 43.7 percent. Thus, the 8 percent of the German Nationalist Party were needed to give the Hitler cabinet a majority. It was impressive to see that with all their violently oppressive methods, the Nazis failed to inflict significant losses on the Social Democratic Party (SPD) and Center Party. Obviously many members of these two parties were able to act, or at least to think, politically even when not guided by firm leadership or by party organization. There is good reason to believe that a large number of Social Democrats did not change their political outlook throughout the Hitler period. This was also proved by the quick revival of the SPD in 1945–46, an event made possible by the fact that in practically every city some active members of the old party could be found. As early as early 1946 the old rank-and-file members of the Berlin SPD made a decisive contribution to the defeat of the Russian attempt to impose Communist control on the people of Berlin by forcing a merger of the Social Democratic and Communist parties.

In the early period of the Third Reich, the Social Democrats were amazingly active in producing and distributing subversive political propaganda. But the losses suffered by these "unsung heroes" at the hand of the totalitarian state apparatus were horrifying, and after 1934 the Social Democratic opposition was driven largely underground. The emigration of the top leaders of the SPD, the incarceration of the remaining leaders and functionaries as well as the absolute regimentation of the worker's life through the Nazi Labor Front further contributed to cutting political activity down to attempts to form a network of small groups of like-minded people. They could, however, do little more than keep the Socialist spirit alive among themselves and prepare for the day when the Third Reich would collapse. The large numbers of Social Democrats thrown into concentration camps in all these years suggests that such circles or cells must have been widespread. But it seems doubtful whether these groups had many contacts among each other and also whether prominent Social Democrats who joined the Beck-Gördeler conspiracy of July 1944 had managed to make connections with many of these groups. We shall probably never get a full knowledge of these popular movements, although a closer study of Nazi police and intelligence reports than has been undertaken so far may enable us to make a more exact estimate of the actual extent and intensity of this political activity.

Fewer Communists than Social Democrats survived the persecution, but the Communists were better trained in secret operations and possessed more of a central direction. In the years of the Nazi-Soviet alliance, 1939–41, however, even bold Communist actions became ineffective. Except for some cells of members of the former Christian trade unions, little was saved of the Center Party. Still, in their church the Roman Catholics possessed an institution that, although powerless to serve as a shield for the political activities of its members, was a dam against the disintegration of the Catholic society in Germany.

These were the major sources of a popular German opposition that still sprang from the Weimar period and continued—no doubt in varying strength—from 1933 to 1945. The opposition did not constitute a serious threat to the regime, since it was without arms and was not likely to subvert the loyalty of the Nazi Party, the army, and the government service, on which the regime based its absolute power.

New forces of opposition were awakened by the National Socialist fight against the Christian churches. The issues involved were not only the defense of the legal position of the churches, which Hitler had promised to maintain, but also the preservation of the fundamentals of the Christian faith in view of the threatening suppression by a pagan philosophy that cynically disregarded all the rights of the individual and law itself while deifying the Aryan race and its leader.

The challenge to the totalitarian claims of the Nazi government by the churches found the support of people who had been willing to adjust themselves to the new regime or even had helped it into the saddle. In the first place, conservative elements, both Catholic and Protestant, were shocked by the Nazi attacks on the churches and Christian religion. To be sure, there were a good many liberal intellectuals who formerly had not particularly cared about church and religion and were now attracted by the church resistance, because it seemed the last base for saving individual rights. Belonging to a group of dissenters strengthened the capacity of a good many people for holding firmly to their inner rejection of Nazidom.

Thus the church struggle aroused ill-feeling against the regime in many quarters, among them social groups that Hitler still considered necessary for the accomplishment of his political aims. This meant above all the army and to some degree the old expert bureaucracy. Hitler's ultimate intention was the complete de-Christianization of Germany, though the realization of this objective was left to the future, finally to the period after the victorious war. Yet in the meantime Hitler wanted to disorganize the churches and to cut the public spread of their teachings as much as possible. The Nazi persecution of the churches was cruel. Hundreds of priests and ministers perished in the concentration camps. But occasionally, as for example in the case of the medical mass killing of what the Nazis decreed to be worthless human lives, Hitler yielded to the moral pressures that the churches exercised.

The members of the clergy confined their resistance to religious and ecclesiastical problems while supporting Hitler's general policies. Only in the last years of the Third Reich did some members of the clergy come to believe that Christian religion in Germany could be saved only by the overthrow of the Hitler regime, and they cooperated thereafter with those who actively prepared the liquidation of National Socialism. The church opposition never directly imperiled the Nazi government, but just because it was not merely an issue of traditional political partisanship, the conflict between state and church affected even people who had originally welcomed the arrival of the Nazis. Moreover, the defense of the freedom of religion posed problems of individual conscience which demanded clear personal answers and moral commitments. Many activists of the political and military opposition, to whom we shall turn our attention immediately, derived their fearless determination from these experiences.

Two events could have wrecked Hitler's totalitarian government: a split of major proportions within the Nazi Party or a radical conflict between the party and the army. The former happened only once, and the solution chosen by Hitler was designed to stave off the second danger as well. The "blood purge" of June 1934 was Hitler's answer to the challenge that Röhm and his cohorts posed to his party leadership, but he also saw in it the only way of avoiding the brewing clash between party and army. His authority was never questioned by the party thereafter. It is true that a great deal of empire-building and feuding went on among his lieutenants. The phrase "the authoritarian chaos" was coined early in Germany. One of the chief members of the plot of July 1944, Johannes Popitz, entertained the vain hope that Himmler could be persuaded to desert Hitler, and he thereby jeopardized the whole Beck-Gördeler plot. Professor H. R. Trevor-Roper has even denied that the Third Reich could be called a totalitarian state. But actually Hitler played off Göring, Himmler, Goebbels, Ley, Bormann, and the rest against one another, and in the last resort none of them was able to rule unless he enjoyed Hitler's favor.

No rising against the Nazi government had any chance of success without the collaboration of the army. Only the army was capable of subduing the SS and thereby breaking the iron hold that the Nazis had on the country. But for a revolt against the regime civilians were also needed who held crucial positions in public life or at least had held them and maintained the contacts that enabled them to learn what was going on in the upper councils of state and of economy. Without these civilians the army leaders would not have been able to get full political information and make preparations for the formation of a new government. Actually both in the army and in the high echelons of the bureaucracy oppositional currents developed.

Among the civilian agencies of the government the most important center of oppositional elements was the Foreign Office. In the early years of the Third Reich the Foreign Office had been able to ward off the addition of too many Nazis to its staff. But even when the Foreign Office seemingly came under the sway of the Nazis with the appointment of Ribbentrop as minister in 1938, the under-secretary of state, Ernst von Weizsäcker, together with a number of younger diplomats, actively worked at frustrating Hitler's schemes for war. Although in the interior administration no center of resistance comparable to the Foreign Office came into existence, in practically all its branches individual opponents of the Nazi regime could be found. The same was true with regard to the industrial and commercial organizations.

In the civilian sector Carl Friedrich Gördeler emerged as the chief driving force in mobilizing and organizing active resistance to the National Socialist state. He had risen to prominence as a municipal administrator and become lord mayor of Leipzig in 1930. He had served as price commissar under Brüning and as late as 1934–35 under Hitler as well. It would have helped Gördeler in his fight against the totalitarian government if he could have held on to his office. But this would have compelled him to identify himself at least in public with Nazi ideas and policies, which he abhorred, and would have given him the reputation of an unprincipled opportunist among anti-Nazis. Thus he resigned in 1937 in protest against a particularly stupid anti-Semitic measure of the Nazi-dominated city council. Thereafter he devoted himself with unflagging energy to winning new members for the opposition and infusing into the opposition some of his optimism and idealism. Most of all, however, he was busy preparing decisive action against the Nazi rulers. Gördeler's contacts were particularly numerous among the bureaucracy and the business world, but he was also in touch with the oppositional church leaders and the active resistance leaders of the former Social Democratic Party and its trade unions as well as of the Christian trade unions. Although Gördeler did not have relations with all the cells of active resistance, he had more than any other person, and this fact, together with his experience in government, singled him out as the central figure of the future government.

Yet the civilian opposition, as was said before, was powerless without the army. Hitler's ascendancy over the army needs no retelling. He had already won the first round in the game with the appointment to the war ministry of Blomberg and the latter's deputy Reichenau, in 1933. Reichenau was the leading spirit on the military side in preparing the downfall of Röhm and the SA. In the blood purge of June 30, 1934, Hitler not only killed off his own henchmen but also, by the cold-blooded murder of Generals von Schleicher and Bredow, was set on humbling the military as well. Still, Blomberg and Reichenau were prepared to condone everything that happened on June 30, which was in reality the final demise of the *Rechtsstaat*, i.e., government by law, in Germany. Yet although the hideous attack on Dollfuss on July 25 showed that National Socialism was ready to carry assassination even beyond German frontiers, the heads of the German army cooperated in the violation of the remaining constitutional rules by allowing Hitler to assume the succession of Hindenburg. Reichenau formulated the oath, hurriedly taken by the whole army, that placed every soldier under absolute obedience to Hitler personally. Thereafter most German officers felt themselves chained to Hitler's chariot.

The equanimity with which the German officer corps by and large viewed the events of 1934 and the relative ease with which Hitler was able to disperse waves of dissatisfaction in the army and finally gain full control of it must be explained chiefly by the contentment of the officers with the rebuilding of a strong German army. But if they so lightly overcame misgivings that undoubtedly again and again welled up against the methods and manners of the Nazis, this also had its cause in the profound aversion to what they conceived to have been the situation in Germany prior to 1933. To all of them the Weimar Republic was not only the child of national defeat but also of treason. Its beginning was the "stab in the back" of 1918, and the republic had continued to lower national and soldierly ideals. It had crippled German strength by the internecine conflict of parties, and consequently Germany had been exploited by foreign powers. Against this dark backdrop of recent German history the present Nazi age could be judged an improvement by almost everybody. Moreover, to use the army for the correction of political conditions would imply treason, and even General Ludwig Beck as late as 1937 declared that the word *treason* was not to be found in the vocabulary of a German soldier. Thus most, if no longer all, officers comforted themselves with the belief—or was it wishful autosuggestion?—that Hitler and the Nazi Party were not identical and that in due course the dubious practices of the party would be ended by the leader.

Hitler's intention to go to war against Czechoslovakia, announced in the summer of 1938, induced General Ludwig Beck, the chief of staff of the army, to declare his open opposition to these plans, which in his opinion were bound to lead to a new world war of ultimately catastrophic consequences for Germany. His attempt to persuade the army commanders to confront Hitler with a common refusal to conduct such a war failed largely on account of the timid attitude of General Walther von Brauchitsch, the commander in chief of the army. Beck alone resigned. He had already foreseen that a sitdown strike of the generals was likely to lead to a showdown between the army and the SS, and plans for such an eventuality had been drafted by the army. Through the elimination of the SS Hitler was to be reduced to a merely honorific position.

Beck's successor, General Franz Halder, continued these efforts in September 1938. From a technical point of view the projected *coup d'état* of 1938, which now envisaged the arrest of Hitler, was, in my opinion, the most promising of all the plots hatched by the German opposition. But as a prerequisite of such an action Halder demanded from the British government an unequivocal declaration that Britain would go to war if Germany attacked Czechoslovakia. Chamberlain and Halifax had already decided upon appeasement. They totally misjudged Hitler and thought of the German opposition that promised to remove him as a group of German Jacobins. Chamberlain stated this view, probably without much reflection. After the outbreak of war in September 1939, Chamberlain hoped that a blockade and *Sitzkrieg* strategy would be sufficient to convince the Germans that they could not win the war, and that they would then make a revolution against Hitler.

While it seems correct to say that the British government did not possess clear criteria for judging the internal conditions of Germany, it must also be emphasized that after all the German army, and equally the German diplomats, had done since 1933 it was not surprising that no non-German government could easily be persuaded that a German opposition of sufficient strength and determination had suddenly come into existence. The situation called for deeds, not merely for diplomatic conversation, and actually the course of events would have given the military opposition the opportunity for action if they had been determined to overthrow the Hitler regime. The crisis that followed the Godesberg meeting between Hitler and Chamberlain led to the mobilization of the British fleet and an acute tension that was more than Halder's emissaries had asked for in London a month before. Halder and his friends could have acted at once. But their intention was to keep Hitler from starting a war, and thus they waited for orders to march into Czechoslovakia before moving against Hitler. Then, on September 28, the news came that Chamberlain would fly to Munich, and all preparations had been in vain.

The vindication of Hitler's political acumen by the annexation of the Sudetenland and subsequently of rump-Czechoslovakia, as well as the popularity of a reconquest of the Polish Corridor while such German war policy was protected by the Soviet pact, inhibited any attempts of the army chiefs to block Hitler's attack on Poland in September 1939. Only in the winter of 1939–

40 did the members of the army high command discuss projects of how to forestall an offensive in the West, which they realized would make a world war inevitable and, particularly if begun with the violation of the neutrality of Belgium and the Netherlands, would arouse a worldwide hostility against Germany that would eventually prove fatal. But Brauchitsch and in the end Halder as well were hesitant and eventually frightened by Hitler. No doubt, a coup had become more difficult than before. Most of the active anti-Nazis among the ranking generals had been weeded out, and the attitude of the mass of junior officers was a growing handicap for any revolt.

For a while the dazzling victories in the West in 1940 made all active opposition impossible. The idea of an active revolt was kept alive in the years 1940–42 chiefly by the civilian opposition. The field marshals, who were considered indispensable for the revolt, refused to cooperate, although they listened to the entreaties of the conspirators without ever giving them away. Only Field Marshal von Witzleben always remained ready to act, and in the summer of 1944 Rommel joined the opposition. General Beck, who, however, was without a command, never wavered.

The motives of his resistance changed somewhat as National Socialism gained its triumphs on the battlefield only to be forced into the defensive that was bound to end in total defeat. It became clear that the overthrow of the Hitler government could no longer save Germany from disaster. But might not the accusation of the "stab in the back" be pinned on the opposition if it ended the war while the majority of the Germans were still blind to the approaching fate? Only the conviction that National Socialism was an absolute evil that had to be fought without regard to the practical consequences could provide the needed strength. Beck had begun his resistance against Hitler not exclusively for national reasons, in fear for Germany's future; he was also anxious to prevent a war that in his opinion was likely to wreck the historical foundations of the family of European nations. In subsequent years, when resistance became the simple commandment of conscience, Beck placed ever greater emphasis on Europe.

What happened to Beck happened even more clearly to the group of men, most of them thirty to forty years of age, who beginning in the summer of 1940 had banded together around Count James von Moltke in Kreisau, a Silesian estate that the Prussian king had given after 1871 to the former's great-grand-uncle, the old field marshal, in recognition of his services in the wars of German unification. The Prussian nobility was strongly represented in this "Kreisau circle," which in addition contained members from all the other opposition groups, including the trade unions. Moltke had not originally intended this circle to become a center of active resistance. He wished to have fate take its course and to build a program for a new beginning thereafter. An intensive and fruitful search for new political and social philosophies transcending the conflicts of the old German parties was carried on at the meetings, and the members of the circle moved away from an interpretation of history in terms of national states. The circle, however, did not remain for long a mere academic forum but became increasingly involved in the work of active resistance, which in the military sector, too, was represented by younger men.

Brauchitsch retired in December 1941 after the loss of the battle of Moscow, for which he was made the scapegoat by Hitler. Halder resigned a few months later. Among the military opponents the generation of colonels became the most activist group and first among them was Klaus Schenck, Count von Stauffenberg. His position as chief of staff of the home army gave him access to Hitler and control over military forces. Actually he carried much too great a burden in the plot of July 20, 1944, by first planting the bomb in Hitler's East Prussian headquarters and directing the revolt in Berlin thereafter. The hours of his transit to Berlin were a decisive factor in the failure of the *Putsch*. But one may raise more fundamental doubts. The conspirators of 1944 were certainly not very crafty revolutionaries, and for the success of their action they relied too much on the continued order and subordination of the army. It is questionable whether the army, even after having been freed from its oath to Hitler, would have accepted a Beck-Gördeler government. The air force, navy, and, most important, the SS forces at the front and at home would presumably have shown some resistance. The opposition's intention to rule for a considerable time with dictatorial methods underrated the explosive social forces the downfall of the Nazis was likely to ignite. For the mobilization of popular forces the Beck-Gördeler-Stauffenberg group had no plans.

Any such appraisal will necessarily remain speculative. Another issue, however, can in my opinion be clarified with greater certainty. There is no evidence that the Casablanca declaration of unconditional surrender issued in January 1943 had a major impact on the internal developments of Germany. The German opposition, though naturally greatly worried by it, even in 1943 was trying to kill Hitler, and not the Casablanca declaration but the failure of earlier attempts and the difficulty of invading Hitler's headquarters delayed the final *Putsch* till July 1944. On the other hand, the Germans would have fought on, as they actually did, as long as Hitler was in command, irrespective of any Allied declarations. This is not to say that the demand for unconditional surrender was the wisest policy even with regard to strengthening the alliance with the Soviet Union, which was one of the chief purposes of Roosevelt's move. But although the possibility of a separate peace between Stalin and Hitler was greatly overrated in Washington, it is impossible to see how the United States and Britain could have made any advances to a German opposition after Pearl Harbor. It is quite likely, however, that the Allies might have used the German opposition if it had succeeded in removing Hitler.

This did not happen, and the German opposition made no direct contribution to the defeat of Hitler. But the members of the German opposition reached true human greatness in their final action and death. Their hopes for political gains were small. What might become of Germany they did not know. They trusted that their undertaking might at least bring an earlier end to the senseless carnage and destruction. Most of all, however, they wanted to demonstrate that the consciousness of justice and human decency was still alive in Germany and that in order to win freedom no human sacrifice was too great.

IX AMERICAN PLANNING
OF THE MILITARY GOVERNMENT
OF GERMANY DURING WORLD WAR II

THE OUTBREAK of war between the United States and the Axis powers in December 1941 compelled the political and military leaders of America to set into motion plans for the exhaustive mobilization of resources and manpower. This urgent need of infinite complexity remained for some time their pressing preoccupation and kept them from giving much thought to the exact nature of the postwar international order. Diplomacy, too, it was felt, should in the circumstances contribute to the immediate demands of the shooting war by molding the anti-Axis powers into a closely cooperating fighting team in order to win an early victory.

In this connection the relations between the Western Allies and the Soviet Union constituted the major problem. They were difficult in view of their dismal interwar history and were encumbered after 1941 by the delay in the opening of the promised second front in the West. Therefore it seemed chiefly necessary to convince the Russians of loyal and generous support by the Western nations, as was done through lend-lease, and of the determination of the United States and Britain to enter the battle in full force, as was demonstrated by the Casablanca declaration demanding the unconditional surrender of the Axis powers. In contrast, to reach a clear understanding on the concrete issues of the aftermath of the war might lead to new controversies and chill the spirit of military collaboration. Only as victory came in sight were some questions raised, but they were questions of procedure rather than substance.

The treatment to be meted out to the vanquished Germany was by far the greatest concern of all the anti-Axis powers. Whether the United States, Britain, and the Soviet Union would agree on a common policy vis-à-vis Germany was bound to be the acid test for the continuation of the wartime cooperation in the postwar world. It is doubtful at what time such a joint policy should have been formulated. If the hope that a basic agreement could be achieved and would be adhered to was not utopian from the beginning, there can be no doubt that the right moment was before the end of the fighting while the Russians still felt the need for Western military cooperation and lend-lease. Theoretically it might even have been possible to reach an understanding at Potsdam soon after the German surrender when the memory of the joint war effort was still fresh. But then an agreement would have required much greater American concessions, for it had already become clear that the only real interest that the Western powers and the Soviet Union had in common was the defeat of Hitler's Germany. Once this had been accomplished the powers quickly drifted apart. Yet considering to what extent the future peace of the world depended on the state of East-West relations, the attempt had to be made to find a bridge that would lead from cobelligerency to friendly coexistence. Firm arrangements for a common policy in Germany should have been an essential part of such a program.

Franklin D. Roosevelt was indeed profoundly anxious to wrest from the terrors of the war as the highest prize of victory the establishment of a peaceful international order based on law. Roosevelt was Wilsonian in his belief that the rule of law could be established only through a worldwide system of security. Regional security would mean the creation of spheres of interest, which had led so often to arms rivalry and armed conflict. The balance of power, as history had shown, would never create a secure foundation of peace. To win Russia's participation in the building of a new and more efficient League of Nations became the major diplomatic endeavor of the president in the war years and was accompanied by parallel action on the home front. Roosevelt was anxious to avoid a repetition of the events of 1919-20, when the League had become the football of party politics and popular support for America's entrance into the League rapidly evaporated after the end of the war. Roosevelt, with the help of Senator Vandenberg, gained the full commitment of the two parties to the erection of the permanent United Nations. When at Yalta Stalin reluctantly and with reservations accepted the project, Roosevelt was satisfied with the realization of his major war aim and optimistic that the chasm between the Western nations and Russia would begin to close.

Stalin's accession to the United Nations plan shows that he was willing to make substantial concessions as long as he felt that he needed American assistance. For there was no question, as even the Washington government should have known in 1944-45, that the Russian approach to postwar problems was the opposite of American universalism. The Russians wanted national security, and this meant that they intended not only to keep what the Nazis had given them in the pact of 1939 but also to create a belt of friendly states to the west. As it turned out, no state was judged sufficiently friendly that did not conform to the Communist pattern. The Russians also desired to get means for the speedy rebuilding of their cruelly devastated country, and this meant reparations from Germany. Obviously the Russians never intended to have these war aims, which in view of their own tremendous sufferings and sacrifices must have appeared to them perfectly natural, cut by their wartime allies on the strength of abstract universal principles, such as national self-determination or other liberal-democratic ideas. As the crowning act of war and a dearly bought victory, Russia would impose on her western neighbors the conditions considered necessary for her national security. The contrast between the "regionalist" and "universalist" approach to postwar security was to become one of the chief sources of the reviving East-West conflicts which led to the Cold War. And although the historian cannot be expected to find an answer to the question, one must wonder whether at least an early substantive agreement on Germany might not have sustained Allied military government instead of producing first a stalemate of joint operations and then the division of Germany into two parts.

Roosevelt's inclination to give the quest for a universal security system the highest priority, which was strongly backed by Cordell Hull and Harry Hopkins, made it possible to delay the solution of the concrete issues of future peacemaking. If there was agreement on the ruling principles, all these problems could be left to a peace conference. The slogan "Let us win the war first," which was often used by the military chiefs who were under great strain building and sending overseas big armies, appealed to the political leaders as well, although it should have been obvious that ultimately he wins the war who wins the right peace, and the basis for a peace, particularly in a war of coalition, is largely laid during the fighting war. As it was, however, all thinking about the postwar order in Washington remained somewhat tentative.

Without an understanding of this general political setting a fair appraisal of the attempts to develop an American postwar policy with regard to Germany cannot be made. It was a tortuous process, due partly to the inability of the various agencies of the government to work together smoothly in the evolution of foreign policy. It was not the absence of earnest good will but rather the lack of apprehension of the functions and operational methods of the sister agencies that caused difficulties. Probably this weakness would have been overcome if institutions had existed that had brought these agencies together for continuous consultation and joint decision-making. Ideally the president ought to have formed a special war council on which all the agencies concerned with military and foreign policies were represented. In Britain, where civilian and military authorities, largely on account of the common execution of colonial policies, were accustomed to close cooperation, the war cabinet early created such a center of collaboration. Its subcommittee for postwar affairs under the chairmanship of the deputy prime minister Clement Attlee was the supreme agency for all postwar planning. Roosevelt, however, preferred to conduct and win the war with the joint chiefs of staff, and he reserved to himself all the great decisions, political as well as military, in foreign affairs. He did not make much use of the State Department. This disregard of the Department was reflected in the fact that it did not receive from the White House a transcript of the Teheran negotiations nor did it learn about a good many decisions affecting postwar policies that Roosevelt made with the chiefs of staff.

Already prior to the outbreak of war the United States had declared its hostility to the Nazi regime. In the Atlantic Charter of August 1941 Roosevelt and Churchill had envisaged a world in which no nation would seek self-aggrandizement, in which national self-determination would be respected, economic collaboration practiced, and peace made secure by collective measures. In the United Nations Treaty and Declaration of New Year's Day 1942 these goals were made the official war aims of the anti-Axis alliance. It was in the same treaty that these powers promised each other to use all their military and economic resources for the defeat of the Axis and agreed not to make a separate armistice or peace. The declaration did not contain any statement about the future after the defeat, as could hardly be expected at this moment. The first specific political steps against Germany were announced in the so-called Allied declaration on German war crimes, of January 13, 1942, which proclaimed that the Allied powers would hold the perpetrators of war crimes responsible for their misdeeds.

In January 1943 the Casablanca declaration of unconditional surrender added another most important Allied war aim. Unconditional surrender as applied to Germany could only mean the removal of any German government and the taking over of supreme power by the Allied conquerors. This was bound to assume the form of military government. One substantive war aim, though essentially a negative one, was implied in the demand for unconditional surrender. That was the goal of absolute denazification.

In March 1943 President Roosevelt and Sir Anthony Eden had conversations of a noncommittal nature dealing with the future of Germany. Eden reported to the president on this occasion that in his opinion Stalin had a deep-seated distrust of the Germans and would insist that Germany be broken up into a number of states. President Roosevelt made the mystifying statement that he hoped they would not use the methods discussed at Versailles and also promoted by Clemenceau to divide Germany arbitrarily. He suggested that the Allies should encourage the movements for separation that would spring up within Germany and in effect seek a division that represented German public opinion. The president and Eden agreed, according to Hopkins' notes, that under any circumstances Germany and particularly Prussia must be divided into several states. The Prussians could not be permitted to dominate all Germany. It was in connection with these conversations that President Roosevelt urged Cordell Hull to develop a plan for dealing with Germany and Italy during the first few months after Germany's collapse. This might thereafter be discussed with the British, and if enough common ground was found the matter could be taken up with the Russians as well.

As a matter of fact, the State Department had started to consider plans for the postwar treatment of Germany in the spring of 1942. An advisory committee on postwar foreign policy, into which were drawn not only members of the State Department but prominent experts in foreign affairs from outside the government as well, discussed for a month the question of the dismemberment of Germany. Although the committee was under the chairmanship of the Secretary of State, Under-Secretary Sumner Welles played a great role in the deliberations, attempting to gain the approval of the committee for the dismemberment of Germany, of which he was a staunch champion. Hull was "from the first" against dismemberment, but he did not take part in the deliberations of the committee as intensively as Sumner Welles did. The expert staff of the Department of State was strongly opposed to dismemberment, as were some eminent private members of the advisory committee such as Hamilton Fish Armstrong, editor of *Foreign Affairs*, and Isaiah Bowman, president of Johns Hopkins University. But largely owing to the resistance of Welles, who knew that he had the president behind him, it took a long time before the committee was officially recorded as being opposed to dismemberment. The committee recommended on the other hand a long-range policy for preventing German rearmament and developing democratic institutions as well as reducing or controlling Germany's economic power in Europe. In July 1943 the advisory committee on postwar foreign policy was suspended by Hull "in order to enable the technical staff to carry out the work of intensive preparation for a more definitive round of discussion." Actually, the advisory committee and its subcommittees were never reconvened. Instead, the technical staff of the Department of State wrote policy summaries on all of the subjects with which the subcommittees had dealt.

The work on Germany within the Department of State was reorganized and placed under the so-called interdivisional country committee on Germany, which consisted of the staff that had been assembled for doing research for the advisory committee and of the chiefs of the various geographic and functional divisions of the Department concerned with the German questions. This group briefed Secretary Hull for the first Quebec conference of August 1943, and for the Moscow conference of October 1943. Thereafter it serviced the American representative, Ambassador Winant, on the European Advisory Commission. The group closely hewed to the original line of the State Department expert staff. It opposed dismemberment of Germany. It did not oppose a relatively brief period of stern and punitive action in Germany after the surrender, but it favored a moderate peace in order to encourage the growth of democracy in Germany. Democracy and internal decentralization seemed to the members of the State Department the best guarantee for the evolution of a peace-loving Germany.

In August 1943, Secretary Hull attended the first Quebec conference (QUADRANT). It was the only summit conference outside of the United States that Hull attended, and even in this case he was not included in the meetings of the combined chiefs of staff. Hull learned from Eden that within the British government the pressure for a forced partition of Germany was great but that he personally was opposed to it.

On October 4 and 5, Hull, accompanied by some of his staff members, had discussions with the president in preparation for the conference of foreign ministers at Moscow, at which he wanted to have ready some preliminary ideas about the treatment of Germany. President Roosevelt expressed himself in favor of the partition of Germany into three completely separate states, a plan Hull and his associates opposed. They stated the standard view of the State Department: partition would necessitate extensive controls in addition to those in any case required for the enforcement of economic and military disarmament. In fact, the economic and military controls would have to be so stringent that they would "evoke a greatly increased resentment on the part of the German people to the serious detriment of the ultimate reconciliation with the peace settlement." Roosevelt replied that the argument that occupation controls could cause the German people to desire national unity more strongly was exaggerated. On the basis of his own personal experiences in Germany, he had concluded that the Germans were deeply divided. But later on in the conversation the president pointed out that the occupation policy would have to be one of trial and error and that one might discover that partition would not work.

At Moscow the future treatment of Germany was discussed for the first time on a tripartite basis. Secretary Hull presented two memoranda "for discussion purposes," and the ideas they set forth found the general approval of Molotov and Eden. Agreement was expressed that the terms of the unconditional surrender should be enforced by an inter-Allied control commission rather than by the forces of the individual powers. Agreement was also apparent with regard to the extent of the power of such an inter-Allied control commission. It was to extend over the Germany of 1937, including the Saar district but excluding all subsequent Nazi conquests beginning with Austria. Consequently, the three ministers issued a declaration that proclaimed Austria to have been the first victim of Nazi aggression and therefore not a country to be conquered but one to be liberated.

The memoranda proposed the radical and permanent disarmament of Germany. Whereas the aim of military disarmament in the narrower sense left no room for different interpretation, the goals for industrial disarmament of Germany were somewhat ambiguous. The memoranda proposed that "arms manufacturing facilities be dismantled, importation and manufacture, including all types of aircraft, be prohibited." This could be stretched to justify virtually the full destruction of German heavy industry. Actually, the State Department planners had in mind only the control of heavy industry. Although they stated that reparations for physical damage inflicted by Germany would be set by a commission for that purpose, they wanted to see in the end a viable democracy and as a prerequisite demanded "a tolerable standard of living; restriction of matters of control to the requirements of general security; and harmony of policy and purpose among the British, Soviet, and American governments." They envisaged a Germany purged from Nazi influences. Germany was to become "a broadly based democracy operating under a bill of rights." For that reason "freedom of speech and religion, and of the press, freedom to organize political parties other than those of Nazi-Fascist doctrine, cultural associations and trade unions" should be admitted until, ultimately, free elections could be held for a central German government.

Certain problems were treated in the memoranda with some vagueness and uncertainty. The State Department planners did not wish to promote President Roosevelt's dismemberment ideas. For that reason they did not mention definite occupation zones. They were afraid that these might be taken as lines of partition. Before Moscow, the idea had even been ventilated in the Department of State to occupy only certain strategic points in Germany, employing combined Anglo-American-Soviet units. The memoranda presented in Moscow indicated that the Allied forces would be placed in different sectors, but at the same time it was stated that the problem of dismemberment was still under discussion, while decentralization was called a useful means of improving international security. The problem of dismemberment was actually the only problem of the immediate post-hostilities period that was more concretely argued by the three ministers. And each of them confessed that his chief of

government was in favor of dismemberment while they themselves and their foreign-ministry staffs opposed it. There was
no further discussion. Instead, the three ministers agreed that
an inter-Allied agency should be created to deal with these
problems. It was called the European Advisory Commission
(EAC), with its seat in London and a mandate to "study and
make recommendations to the three governments upon European questions connected with the termination of hostilities."

The frame of reference of this commission lent itself to varying interpretations. There could be no doubt that it was no
policy-making body but had only the function of examining
issues and proposing solutions to the governments. Moreover,
the delegates could negotiate only on the basis of instructions
from their governments. On the other side this dependence also
meant that proposals on which the commission had agreed
were likely to be approved. The commission was therefore important to the extent that the governments were prepared to
assign to it significant political tasks.

The British hoped to make the European Advisory Commission an organ of tripartite policy coordination and planning
for all European problems in the immediate post-surrender period. John G. Winant and his American associates in London,
although not expecting quite as much as the British, were
persuaded that the EAC should be used for gaining Russian
adherence to common Allied policies in Europe and especially
in Germany in the post-hostilities period. But Washington
wanted to confine the EAC to the questions that would arise at
the time of the termination of hostilities, such as what form the
document of unconditional surrender was to take, how zones of
military occupation should be apportioned and machinery of
Allied control constructed. President Roosevelt eyed the EAC
with grave suspicions. He was afraid that it might become an
embryonic peace conference and particularly "arrogate to itself
the general field of postwar organization," the president's chief

war or peace aim. He was determined to see to it that the
postwar United Nations Organization was to be built in America
and was afraid of "the possible long-term repercussions on
American public opinion should the impression be gained that
this Commission sitting in London is secretly building the new
world." Nobody, as far as can be seen, intended to use the EAC
for drafting the blueprints of the United Nations. What some
American diplomats urged was an early tripartite discussion of
the regional problems of Europe. But the latter could wait, in
the opinion of President Roosevelt, and also of Secretary Hull.
They consequently wished to give the EAC only a modest role.

At the Teheran conference in November 1943, the Big Three
discussed among other things the future of Germany. They all
expressed themselves in favor of the dismemberment of Germany. But Stalin was not favorably disposed either to the
partition proposals that Churchill made or to those presented by
Roosevelt. The matter remained unsettled and was turned
over to the European Advisory Commission for further deliberations. Shortly thereafter, the Big Three appointed their
representatives on the EAC. They were the two London ambassadors, John G. Winant and Feodor Gusev, and Sir William
Strang, a senior member of the British Foreign Office.

The EAC held its first formal session on January 14, 1944.
Ambassador Winant had to receive his instructions from the
Department of State, but these instructions required the concurrence of the War and Navy Departments. The State Department therefore proposed to set up in December 1943 the
so-called Working Security Committee in order to coordinate
policies and reach decisions on political and military problems
among the State, War, and Navy Departments. It was rather
late to establish such a coordinating committee, because without the knowledge of Secretary Hull or the Department of
State the question of zones of occupation in Germany had al-

ready been studied at some length by President Roosevelt, Prime Minister Churchill, and the combined chiefs of staff.

But before taking up the military negotiations on the problem of zones it will be necessary to describe briefly the organizations of the army that dealt with the problems of civil affairs and military government. In April 1942, the army had established a school of military government at the University of Virginia in Charlottesville. Such a school was foreseen in the original war plans of the army. It was the result of the experiences of the American army in 1918. Then the army had been entirely unprepared for the task of military government after the armistice. It had been forced to use the proclamations that came down from the headquarters of Marshal Foch and had to employ officers of combat units for the performance of military government in the towns and cities of the Rhineland. With the opening of the school of military government, the army did not raise a claim to the administration of liberated or conquered countries much beyond the end of hostilities. On the contrary, the first aim in the creation of a small core of civil-affairs and military-government officers was to assist the army in the fulfillment of its military mission. By organizing the civilian population in such a way as to make possible the exploitation of the resources of an invaded country for the benefit of the American army, the civil-affairs and military-government officers were to contribute directly to the success of the army's combat mission.

Nevertheless, in October 1942, Secretary of the Interior Harold L. Ickes complained to the president about the Charlottesville school. He considered the exercise of governmental functions in foreign countries by army officers as conflicting with American traditions. Although Stimson clarified the character of the school, the president expressed his preference for the use of top civilian talent in the administering of foreign territory. On November 18, 1942, President Roosevelt gave to the Secretary of State full authority over all economic, political, and fiscal questions in liberated, as distinct from occupied, areas. A little later, however, General Eisenhower, who was in command of the invasion of North Africa, ran into serious trouble. The invasion had been hastily planned and hardly anything had been done about civil affairs. Soon life was made very difficult for Eisenhower and his military staff in North Africa by the conflicting aspirations and claims of the Allied civilian agencies, particularly concerning the direction of relief for civilians. The general sent strong complaints to Washington, for he wanted the army to have full control over civil affairs in the combat and communication zones. Roosevelt accepted this demand and on November 10, 1943, directed that the army should have undivided responsibility for civilian relief in each area so long as the fighting continued and for six months thereafter.

As a consequence of the North African experiences, the War Department decided to establish a central agency on the top level to deal in the future with all activities of the army with regard to civil affairs and military government. The Civil Affairs Division was set up on March 1, 1943, as part of the War Department's special staff. A month later the joint chiefs of staff accepted the CAD as the agency that would coordinate the planning and administration of civil affairs in most occupied areas. The director of the Civil Affairs Division, Major General John H. Hilldring, was in this respect wearing two hats, serving the joint chiefs of staff and the War Department. But this made him by no means an independent agent. In all its actions the Civil Affairs Division had to have the concurrence of the Operations Division of the general staff, which occasionally imposed considerable modifications on CAD plans for logistic or other technical military reasons. It was also not always easy to extract decisions from the Operations Division, or for that matter the joint chiefs of staff themselves on matters that belonged to a stage of operations for which the joint chiefs had not completed their planning. On the civilian side the CAD had to work with and through the Assistant Secretary of War, John McCloy, who was in charge of the relations of the War Department with the civilian agencies.

When Hilldring was appointed director of CAD in April 1943, Secretary Henry L. Stimson told him that the army was not supposed to have anything to do with the making of policy, although he himself, as a member of the president's cabinet, might become involved in policy-making. General Marshall, too, calling civil affairs "the most sacred trust of the American people," expressed himself as opposed to having the army take a lead in political planning. General Hilldring, an open-minded, shrewd, and forceful soldier, strictly adhered to these instructions. He gave the Department of State and the other civilian agencies to understand that military government was the responsibility of the army, but that the army made no claim to originate the policies that were to be executed. It regarded itself only as the agent of national policy, and even this merely on a temporary basis during the period of combat and "in the wake of battle." In a mediative way the army would exercise an influence on the formulation of directives. They were not to imperil the chief mission of the army, that of fighting the enemy and winning the war, by adding tasks that would overtax the potential of the military forces. The commander in the field should also retain the freedom of decision on the time when complex civil-affairs assignments should be executed.

The Civil Affairs Division was a staff division and confined its activities to planning and supervision. The operating arm of the army was the Military Government Division of the provost marshal general's office. The foremost aim of CAD activities was the support of the commanders in the field by securing for them general civil-affairs directives, keeping at their disposal the necessary trained personnel, and supplying them with the information that was likely to facilitate the execution of the military-government mission overseas. At an early moment CAD tried to unburden the army of some of its government work by turning certain tasks over to civilian agencies, though its representatives in the field came under the control of the theater commander. But soon the army made every effort to be freed from military government altogether. This, however, proved much more difficult than was expected, particularly in view of the eagerness with which the civilian agencies had been pushing for participation in civil affairs as far back as 1943.

Yet even in that year, when Roosevelt made an earnest effort to assign to the civilian agencies a substantial role in overseas operations, they proved incapable of playing their full part. They failed to agree on common policies among themselves. But their chief weakness was their inability to build up an adequate corps of expert foreign operators. Probably they could not have achieved this even when they had started assembling and training such an organization early in the war. With the military draft and the additional recruitment being done for the war agencies, there were not too many people available. As it was, the army developed under its tutelage after V-E Day, if not a civilian organization, at least what looked more and more like an organization of civilians. The army hired an increasing number of civilian experts without putting them in uniform. General Hilldring was made Assistant Secretary of State late in 1946 to prepare the transition of full control from the War Department to the State Department. The plans for this takeover were ready and supposed to become effective on July 1, 1948, when the Russian blockade of Berlin necessitated a year's delay before John McCloy followed the military governor, General Lucius D. Clay, as high commissioner.

The founding of the Civil Affairs Division in Washington also induced General Eisenhower to make his military-government section into a division of his regular staff, and an assistant chief of staff, G-5, was appointed by him. This was subsequently imitated by the army groups, armies, and divisions. Thus the new type of military-government system was formally adopted into the customary American general-staff organization.

The research-and-analysis branch of the Office of Strategic Services functioned as the chief intelligence organization of CAD. The research-and-analysis branch had the greatest amount of information on the political, social, and economic conditions within the Axis countries during the war. In addition, it had the largest staff of academically trained experts, particularly on Germany. It had already serviced the school of military government. Its biggest single work was the preparation of an extensive and detailed handbook on Germany. This was a purely descriptive work, dealing with all the institutions of German public life and emphasizing the changes National Socialism and finally war conditions had brought about.

In the period immediately after its establishment the CAD was largely preoccupied with the invasion of Sicily and subsequently with Sicilian military government, as well as with the complexities of the Italian unconditional surrender and the government of southern Italy. After the summer of 1943, and to an even greater extent after the fall of 1943, it directed growing attention to the preparation of the invasion of northwestern Europe as well. It went as far as to prepare definite suggestions about the actual execution of military-government operations by its future MG officers in Germany. In November 1943, the Secretary of War created an editorial committee on civil-affairs studies to which the State Department sent a representative. A long list of studies was adopted, covering every field and every key function of military government. Each of these so-called civil-affairs guides dealt with the institutional and legal situations an MG officer would be confronted with when entering upon his task. The guide made concrete recommendations with regard to the suspension of laws, removal of personnel, and the methods to be employed to create the basis for a military-government administration. More than half of these civil-affairs guides were written by the research-and-analysis branch, Office of Strategic Services. The Foreign Economic Administration also made a large contribution, while a few individual guides were written by specialized agencies of the federal government. All these civil-affairs guides were reviewed and eventually approved by the editorial committee.

While this project for the preparation of civil-affairs guides was still a short-term program in the sense that it made only recommendations for actions to be taken immediately, it was the largest planning program that was developed in Washington during World War II. Actually, it incorporated some policies that had never been officially adopted, or in any event did not conform in important respects to the thinking of the highest American policy-makers. Some of these guides, as, for example, those on price controls or rationing, were never issued to the officers in the field. The influence of the whole undertaking should perhaps not be overrated, but it was of some consequence that the future MG officers were presented for the first time with a systematic analysis of the future military-government programs in Germany.

The cooperation between research-and-analysis and the army in military-government affairs was not confined to Washington. The agency was strongly represented in the European theater as well, and military-government problems formed one of the foremost concerns of the OSS people. OSS men participated in the staff seminars in military government held in England prior to the invasion, and others were at the disposal of the planners of military government in SHAEF. It is probably correct to say that much of the thinking that Secretary Morgenthau later objected to originated with the OSS.

Most of the high-level planning in 1943, however, took place between the American and British armies. Both the Mediterranean operations and those envisioned in northwestern Europe were combined operations, and their directives needed the approval of both the American and British governments. For this reason, the Combined Civil Affairs Committee (CCAC) of the combined chiefs of staff was established. It consisted of representatives of the United States joint chiefs of staff and of the British staff mission in Washington. In addition, both the Department of State and the British Foreign Office were represented. All the Italian problems were directly dealt with by CCAC, but with regard to the German case somewhat different methods were applied. After the Casablanca conference of January 1943, it had been decided to set up a military command in Britain to prepare plans for the invasion of Northwestern Europe in the spring of 1944. In place of the appointment of a supreme commander, which was to occur only nine months later, Lieutenant General Sir Frederick E. Morgan was appointed chief of staff to the supreme allied commander (designate). COSSAC, as his office was called, planned what was to become the great Operation Overlord.

When in the summer of 1943 concern arose in the Western capitals that Nazi Germany might abruptly collapse, General Morgan was requested to draw up a plan (designed with the code name Rankin) for the speedy descent of Allied forces on the continent in order to protect the liberated countries and to enforce the unconditional surrender in Germany. This confronted General Morgan with the problem of where the Allied forces should go in Germany. Left without any political directives, he decided on the division of Germany into three large zones. To the Russians, naturally enough, he assigned the eastern zone, to Britain the northwestern, and to the United States the southern one. It seemed logical to assign the southern zone to the United States, since the American forces were deployed from western England and were to form the right wing of the invading army. COSSAC did not propose the military occupation of the whole zones. The plan Morgan presented to the first Quebec conference in August 1943, which was duly approved by the combined chiefs of staff as well as by Roosevelt and Churchill, envisaged only the occupation of the Rhineland as after 1918, with the addition, however, of the Ruhr district and a swath in northwestern Germany reaching to the Kiel canal.

In the meantime the British war cabinet had been busy devising plans for the future of Germany. The Armistice and Postwar Committee of the war cabinet, chaired by Deputy Prime Minister Clement Attlee, presented at the end of the summer of 1943 a report on the occupation of Germany. It argued that a total occupation of Germany was necessary if the country was to be effectively disarmed. The report proposed the joint occupation of Berlin but otherwise recommended the division of Germany into three zones to be occupied by the national forces of the three major victors.

The report divided Germany into three zones. The northwestern zone, to be given to Britain, was to contain Schleswig-Holstein, Hanover, Westphalia, Hesse-Kassel, and the Rhine province. The United States was to receive the southern states of Bavaria, Württemberg, Baden, Hesse-Darmstadt, and on the left bank of the Rhine the Saar district and the Palatinate. The rest of Germany was to form the Soviet occupation zone except for East Prussia, which it was thought would be turned over to Poland. Since under this plan the U.S.A. was to receive the relatively smallest zone, it was suggested the Americans might in addition occupy Austria if they so desired.

When General Morgan learned about the plan of the Attlee Committee, he realized that his Rankin plan would need considerable extension and modification. But before he changed the Rankin plan he first needed the approval of the United States government. He presented a statement of the problems to General Marshall in October 1943, and Marshall passed on this statement to President Roosevelt, who was just about to leave for the conferences of Cairo and Teheran.

On the United States battleship *Iowa* Roosevelt discussed the Morgan paper with the joint chiefs of staff. Roosevelt rather passionately criticized the proposal that the United States was not to receive the northwestern zone. This zone, possibly even expanded to include Berlin, he wished to see as the United States zone. In the assignment of the southern zone, in which the troops would have to rely on supply and communication lines leading through France, he saw a British attempt to compel the United States to carry the main burden in the reconstitution of France and Italy, and possibly even the Balkans. The reconstruction of the Netherlands, Belgium, France, Italy and at least parts of southeastern Europe President Roosevelt considered to be exclusively in the British interest, and he was of the opinion that Britain should assume from the beginning the responsibility and cost of such a build-up of Central and Western Europe. He did not feel that the United States should be involved in this process. He judged that the American army could not stay for more than one or at the most two years on the European continent. Moreover, at least substantial parts of the army would have to be transferred at an early moment to the Far Eastern theater. President Roosevelt therefore insisted that the United States should receive the northwestern zone with its German ports, which offered direct access for American shipping.

A voluminous and at times rather sharp correspondence between Roosevelt and Churchill went on all through the spring and summer of 1944. Churchill remained adamant and declared the president's arguments far-fetched and unconvincing. Under the influence of Stimson, General Marshall, and Admiral King, the president finally accepted the southern zone at the Quebec conference of September 1944. But the southern zone was changed. The Palatinate and the Saar district were transferred to the English zone, whereas the province of Hesse-Kassel was added to the southern zone. Roosevelt refused to have anything to do with the occupation of Austria. In his eyes the British concession on the question of German ports was most decisive. The British agreed that the ports of Bremen and Bremerhaven should be under American control and that the Americans would have free transit between these ports and the American zone. The American chiefs of staff proved very pedantic in defining these rights concretely, and lengthy negotiations with the British military followed. Only on February 6, 1945, when the Russians were already forty-five miles from Berlin, did the arrangement for zones, including the inter-Allied control of metropolitan Berlin, become a formal agreement.

The conflict between the president and prime minister over the occupation zones proved to be a serious obstacle to great progress in the planning for military government in Germany after the surrender. Certain short-term problems were solved. Thus Eisenhower received, on April 28, 1944, directives on military government in Germany prior to surrender. They were drafted by the Combined Civil Affairs Committee and issued to SHAEF as CCS-551. The combined directive dealt with military government chiefly as a means to support military operations. For that reason, military government was to establish some controls over the German economy. The only political goal especially mentioned in the directive was the destruction of Nazism. But even this negative aim was subordinated for the time being to military expediency.

While the combined chiefs of staff still discussed the presurrender directives and the division of occupation zones, the European Advisory Commission (EAC) had started its deliberations. The British hoped to use EAC for the development of a fairly exact tripartite program of Allied military government after the surrender. So did the American representatives at the EAC, but they failed, as we have seen, to gain the support of the policy-makers in Washington. Ambassador Winant and his associates had good reasons for complaints beyond this. The Working Security Committee proved to be an inadequate instrument for turning out a common American policy. It was not a policy-making body but rather a coordinating committee between State, War, and Navy. As has been mentioned, CAD could not approve papers or proposals presented by the State Department unless it gained the approval of the joint chiefs of staff, and they disliked dealing with problems of the future, to which their military planning had not yet proceeded. On the other hand, the State Department was represented on the Working Security Committee only by representatives of the medium echelon. There was no one in the State Department of sufficiently high standing prepared to fight for its policy recommendations. Some of the papers presented by the Department of State had not even full departmental approval and were in the nature of opinions rather than of strict policy directives. The American representatives of the EAC found themselves therefore often without formal instructions. The EAC actually agreed only on a document of surrender, an agreement on occupation zones, and on the organization of Allied control machinery.

The failure to achieve an inter-Allied program for Germany in the pre-surrender period was, however, also closely connected with the internal struggles that arose over this problem in Washington. In August 1944, the imminent collapse of Germany was again considered a distinct possibility. Not only Winant but also Eisenhower urged the formulation of a definite policy directive for occupied Germany. On August 17, 1944, the Secretary of the Treasury, Henry Morgenthau, Jr., had returned from a visit to England, where he had learned about the state of military-government planning in SHAEF. A study of the draft of the SHAEF handbook for military government of Germany had convinced him that the army was aiming at a rehabilitation of the German economy, that both the State and War Departments were disregarding the president's Teheran proposal for partitioning Germany as well as for internationalizing the Ruhr and the Saar, and that in order to continue the cooperation with the Soviet Union a radical reduction of German heavy industry as the basis of Germany's war-making power was necessary. Morgenthau found the ear of the president, with whom he was united by ties of an old friendship. Roosevelt censured the SHAEF handbook and directed Stimson to have it withdrawn.

A little later he appointed Hull, Stimson, and Morgenthau to draft, with the assistance of Harry Hopkins, a final posthostilities policy vis-à-vis Germany. To this committee Morgenthau presented his memorandum of September 1, the first version of what soon became known as the Morgenthau Plan. It was drafted by Harry Dexter White, the Assistant Secretary of the Treasury, and by other Treasury officials. It has often been asserted that Harry Dexter White was the actual author of the plan, but this is entirely wrong. White strongly opposed some of Morgenthau's ideas. As a matter of fact, in this very memorandum White refused to incorporate some of his chief's radical notions.

The Treasury's memorandum, entitled "Suggested Post-Surrender Program for Germany," proposed the complete demilitarization of Germany. "This means completely disarming the German Army and people . . . and the total destruction of the whole German armament industry as well as those parts of supporting industries having no other justification." Secondly, the memorandum pressed for the partitioning of Germany. East Prussia, the southern part of Silesia, the Saar, and the adjacent territories bounded by the Rhine and the Moselle rivers and all Germany north of the Kiel canal were to be incorporated into other countries. The remainder of Germany, excluding the Ruhr, was to be divided into two parts, each becoming a loose federal state. Thirdly, the Ruhr, the Rhineland, and the Kiel canal were to be turned into internationalized zones. Fourthly, reparations out of current production were not to be demanded because they might only help Germany to rebuild her heavy industries. All reparation and restitution was to come from existing German resources and territories or from forced German labor outside of Germany. As a fifth point, a vigorous denazification program was proposed. The only aim of the Allied military government in Germany should be to facilitate military operations. It should not become responsible for such economic problems as price controls, rationing, unemployment, production, reconstruction, distribution, consumption, housing or transportation. It was up to the German people to sustain the German economy with such means as were available under the circumstances. Once Germany was disarmed, it was expected that her continental neighbors would take primary responsibility for policing and administering her. American troops would be withdrawn "within a relatively short time."

It was Secretary Henry L. Stimson who opposed the Morgenthau program in a firm manner. With regard to the transformation of the Ruhr and Saar districts into non-industrialized areas of agricultural land, he commented:

I cannot conceive of such a proposition being either possible or effective, and I can see enormous general evils coming from an attempt to so treat it. During the past eighty years of European history this portion of Germany was one of the most important sources of the raw materials upon which the industrial and economic livelihood of Europe was based. . . .

I can conceive of endeavoring to meet the misuse which Germany has recently made of this production by wise systems of control or trusteeship or even transfers of ownership to other nations. But I cannot conceive of turning such a gift of nature into a dust heap.

War is destruction. This war more than any previous war has caused gigantic destruction. The need for the recuperative benefits of productivity is more evident now than ever before throughout the world. Not to speak of Germany at all or even her satellites, our allies in Europe will feel the need of the benefit of such productivity if it should be destroyed. Moreover, speed of reconstruction is of great importance, if we hope to avoid dangerous convulsions in Europe. . . . My basic objection to the proposed methods of treating Germany which were discussed this morning were that, in addition to a system of preventive and educative punishment, they would add the dangerous weapon of complete economic oppression. Such methods, in my opinion, do not prevent war; they tend to breed war.

Roosevelt, however, failed to see the strength of Stimson's arguments. He called Morgenthau to Quebec, where he met with Winston Churchill in September 1944 and had him present his plan for postwar Germany to the prime minister. In spite of a fiercely negative first reaction Churchill was persuaded by Lord Cherwell to accept Morgenthau's naïve assertion that the suppression of German steel production would be a major contribution to the creation of prosperous British iron industries after the war. He finally even drafted the memorandum that both he and Roosevelt initialed as the "program for eliminating the war-making industries in the Ruhr and in the Saar" with a view to "converting Germany into a country primarily agricultural and pastoral in its character."

The Quebec conference was a victory for Morgenthau, but the diminution of his original plan began at the same moment. The Quebec memorandum did not speak any more of German industry in general but only of the Ruhr and Saar industries. Among these the metallurgical, chemical, and electrical industries were singled out, and, for example, coal mining, which Morgenthau intended to abolish, was not forbidden. Moreover, the meaning of "primarily agricultural and pastoral" was open to many interpretations. Finally Churchill's signature did not as yet signify acceptance by the British government. Even during the Quebec conference Foreign Secretary Anthony Eden threatened to oppose the policy of the prime minister in the British war cabinet, and obviously he prevailed there later. These aspects were overlooked in Washington. Under the shadow of Morgenthau's "victory" the so-called interim directive for General Eisenhower was drafted to deal with the military government of Germany immediately after surrender up to the time when the three powers would work out final directives. The directive allowed the American commander to assure "to the extent that is feasible, the production and maintenance of goods and services essential for the prevention or alleviation of epidemic or serious disease and serious civil unrest and disorder which would endanger the occupying forces and the accomplishment of the objectives of the occupation." This reservation was important and was to remain important beyond the interim period. But otherwise the interim directive enjoined upon the American commander a hands-off policy with regard to the German economy, which was bound to reproduce economic chaos.

The controversies in the cabinet over the future treatment of Germany were discussed in the American press after September 21. The source of the original leak has never been traced. It must have been either in the Treasury or State Department. While press comments on the Morgenthau plan were divided, probably adverse opinions prevailed, particularly if British press reaction is included. In any event Roosevelt and Morgenthau were severely criticized by a number of highly regarded American organs. Roosevelt was quick to deny that he had favored the Morgenthau plan. The work of the cabinet committee was declared to have been preliminary and advisory only. The President dissolved the cabinet committee and in a public letter called upon Leo T. Crowley, the head of the Foreign Economic Administration, to speed up the studies that FEA was in the process of undertaking on the question of what should be done with the German economy after surrender. A public debate on the German problem in the beginning election campaign had to be avoided.

Apparently Roosevelt himself became doubtful about the economic soundness of the Morgenthau plan, but this feeling made him delay all decisions on Germany. He now stated that the time had not arrived when long-range plans for Germany should be made. "I dislike making detailed plans for a country which we do not yet occupy." This attitude of President Roosevelt made it impossible for the Department of State to achieve a drastic change in the document that was eventually to be issued by the joint chiefs of staff as post-hostilities directive to General Eisenhower. In his last weeks as Secretary of State Cordell Hull stuck to his earlier position in German questions. He was piqued by Morgenthau's intrusion into the conduct of American foreign policy at Quebec and expressed himself thereafter more critically on Morgenthau's notions. Hull's deputy and, after December 1944, successor, Edward R. Stettinius, adopted the ideas the State Department experts had developed.

In November 1944, and then again in preparing the Yalta conference, the Department of State made determined efforts to have JCS 1067 replaced by a directive making the short-term policy part of an evolving long-range policy. An agreement among the Allies on these policies, which the department wanted, would inevitably have limited the freedom of the military commanders. The last attempt by the State Department to substitute its own policy for that of JCS 1067 was made when it was directed by the President to execute the decisions of the Yalta conference. The department drafted its own military-government directive of March 10, which was greatly divergent from JCS 1067. It sent this draft directive directly to the White House without first trying to reach an understanding with the War Department. On March 12 the president returned the directive with his formal approval.

But within a few days the document fell by the wayside.

This was to a large extent caused by Morgenthau's intervention. But another equally aggravating factor was the opposition of the War Department, which objected to any substantial changes of JCS 1067 at this late hour. The War Department argued that it would be impossible to negotiate with the Allies a long-range program at the last moment and that in any event the military commanders could not adopt new plans in the midst of the final push into Germany. On March 20 the president canceled the State Department directive. At a meeting with the three secretaries two days later he imposed a compromise that largely restored the principles of JCS 1067. It was the last significant political action of President Roosevelt before his death. The final draft of JCS 1067 was finished by the so-called Informal Policy Committee on Germany (IPCOG), which comprised in addition to the three secretaries, the Foreign Economic Administrator, Leo T. Crowley.

This was the end of the American military-government planning for Germany prior to V-E Day. The chief goals—disarmament, demilitarization, denazification, restoration, and democratization—constituted, except for democratization, largely a punitive program. And there was no indication how the punitive phase of military government was to be eventually transformed into a constructive period in which democracy could take roots and Germany could be reintegrated into the family of nations. JCS 1067/6 also kept the United States somewhat separate in Germany. The Americans had originally hoped that the British would accept it, but they rejected it through the combined chiefs of staff. Although the economic policies for the first period of the occupation on which the Big Three agreed at Potsdam were compatible with the rules of JCS 1067, the American directive as a whole could be applied only to the U.S. zone, and this weakened the cooperation of the three, or with the French joining, four, occupying powers. It is true, however, that the Russians and French were more responsible for the unfortunate development of zonal cleavages in the first two or three years of occupation.

Once adopted it proved difficult to replace JCS 1067 by new directives. For reasons of internal and external policy this did not take place before the summer of 1947. General Lucius D. Clay, by stretching the meaning of the "prevention of disease and unrest" formula in JCS 1067 to the utmost, made the occupation less stringent and prepared the way for a limited recovery. But Germany as late as early 1948 was far from being able to pay her own way and only the currency reform and the subsequent assistance from Marshall Plan funds initiated the "economic miracle."

X THE UNITED STATES AND GERMANY IN WORLD POLITICS

———◆———

THE WORLD in which we live is still faced with the task of working out the consequences of World War II, or perhaps it would be better to say, of the era of the two World Wars. At the same time, it must make the beneficial as well as frightening discoveries of modern science and technology serve future peace. The main political consequence of the two World Wars was the collapse of the political and economic preponderance of Europe, which had seemed unchallengeable in the nineteenth century. The expansion of world trade and world economic growth since the end of the last century suggested that political relationships would also expand. The European nations around the turn of the century were confident that the system of European states would of necessity transform itself into a world system within which Europe would continue to predominate.

The system of European states of the past, however, was by no means a confederated Europe, but rather a grouping of nations in a perpetual state of competition for power; and as they reached out into the non-European world, their conflicts became even sharper. The First World War proved that it was not within the power of the members of the European system to achieve peace either by victory or by compromise. It was American intervention that decided the outcome of the war, a war that had begun as a European war. But neither the victors nor the vanquished were able to learn the lesson taught by these events, which demonstrated the growing inter-connection of the world owing to America's non-participation. The League of Nations, a community too loose and not binding enough, failed to become a world alliance. In the economic field, it is possible to say that the global ties were weaker than prior to 1914. No effective attempt was made to reestablish all the prerequisites for a functioning world economy as it had existed prior to 1914. While reparations and inter-Allied war debts created insecurities and burdens, the nationalistic tendencies, already too manifest in the economic policies of the nations in the 1920's, later, with the great depression, almost destroyed the world economy.

The criminally engineered Second World War inexorably demonstrated the global unity of all states and peoples. This unity, however, at present exists only in the military-strategic area or, to put it in another way, the world has perhaps turned into a single magnetic field, but a field with two magnetic poles of power, both of which lie outside of ancient Europe. One-quarter to one-third of historical Europe is in the bondage of the Eurasian Soviet Union, whereas with the help of America Western Europe has with great effort preserved its independence and assured the survival of its historically based social and cultural order. At the same time the Second World War conclusively brought about a phenomenon the First had only begun, namely, the craving for independence of the colonial nations, which now became irreversible.

To all this the development of science and technology was added. It is not necessary here to describe the technical advances that have made it possible to maintain a growing population on an even higher standard of living, while at the same time destroying the belief that poverty and misery are unalterable facts of life. I will also not go into the progress of transportation, from the stagecoach and horse-drawn carriage to the railway and finally to the airplane. Through them distances were shortened and the world became a surveyable entity. But with the development of atomic and nuclear weapons military geography was also altered. The insular powers, which had enjoyed considerable security when seapower constituted the greatest as well as the most powerful influence, were robbed of their insular security by the development of air weapons, including ICBMs. Neither the Channel nor the Atlantic or Pacific Ocean any longer constitute effective protective barriers, and the Northern Polar Zone has become an open gateway to the North American continent.

It is against this background that the evolution of the American policy of the last twenty-five years has to be viewed. The power of the executive is very strong in the United States, and the president possesses a relatively large degree of independence in the tactical conduct of foreign policy; by contrast, he can make decisions of principle only if popular opinion is on his side. In the 1930's Franklin D. Roosevelt tried unsuccessfully to win sufficient freedom of action to be able to counter Japan and Germany at least on the diplomatic level and thereby perhaps to prevent the coming disaster. But the American people were totally occupied with their domestic affairs and felt safe in the world protected by their oceans; on the other hand, after their experiences in the First World War, they felt rather unsure of being able to realize successfully their capabilities and ideals in contest with the power politics of the old European states.

It was only after the fall of France and face to face with the serious threat to Great Britain that the dream that the security of American institutions and ideals could be maintained by passive peacefulness and in isolation was destroyed. It was during the actual war years, following Pearl Harbor and Hitler's declaration of war, that certain foundations were laid for a permanent American participation in the collective security

of future world peace. Unlike 1919, when Wilson's League of
Nations had been made the object of a ruthless struggle between the two American parties, the principle of a new League
of Nations with much broader authority and much greater
power was conceived and soon accepted by the two parties
in Congress. Similarly, in the economic realm, not only temporary collective organizations (such as UNRRA) were created,
but also permanent institutions such as the World Bank and
the International Monetary Fund were established.

But no matter how radically this turning away from the
concept of isolation was illustrated by these decisions, there
still survived internally the understandable hope that after
several years of transition from war to peace America's active
participation in overseas affairs might be restricted mainly to
diplomatic participation. It was expected that Great Britain
and a reconstructed France would be strong enough to prevent
the influence of the U.S.S.R. from spreading too widely in
Europe and that the ultimate role of America would become
more that of a mediator between the West European and the
Russian allies. The expectations vis-à-vis Asia were a good
deal more uncertain, even if not very different in substance.

All these assumptions were based on analyses containing a
series of more or less sizable errors. Great Britain's power could
not be reconstructed on its prewar basis. The expenditure
of its forces in heroic but almost belated resistance to the Nazi
onslaught had been too great to make this possible. The war
was followed by a far-reaching and inevitable liquidation of
British colonial rule, which, with the exception of Israel and
Cyprus, was carried out by the British postwar governments
with exceptional tact and savoir-faire. Especially the transition
of India and Pakistan from colonial rule to independence was
one of the great achievements of British statesmanship. But to
seize the available opportunity to assume a political and spiritual
leadership of that part of Europe not taken over by the Soviet

Union was beyond Great Britain's capabilities. The United States would certainly not have opposed such an English initiative in the years 1945–47, and the call for European unity that Churchill raised in his Zurich speech of September 19, 1946, found its warmest reception in the United States. But the England of Attlee and Bevin was too preoccupied with the creation of a national and semi-Socialistic welfare state to wish seriously for the unification of Europe. Moreover, both men saw the best hope for reclaiming Britain's big-power status in the intermediary position of England as leader of the British Commonwealth on the one hand, and in partnership with the United States on the other. And this concept was further reinforced when Churchill succeeded Attlee. There is no indication that Churchill as prime minister was willing to let Churchill the prophet of Europe influence his own policies in a decisive way.

However, the assessment of future Russian policy was of decisive importance. It was exceedingly desirable that the joint conduct of the war against Nazi Germany should lead to a serious attempt at bridging the gulf Russia had created between itself and the rest of the world since 1917. But the belief that the Soviet Union, which during the war had largely relied on the national and patriotic feelings of its own masses and at the same time, with the large-scale help of England and America, had for the first time become aware of the advantages of international cooperation, would undergo a certain liberalization under these influences was hardly justified. The total lack of experience with totalitarian governments, coupled with a deep-seated longing for a return to a time in which the United States could disassociate itself from the greatest worries of the world, were responsible for this vain hope. One may see in this a large manifestation of American naïveté, but one should not forget that the European nations, even though they had plenty of experience with authoritarian regimes, did not prove to be much more prudent after 1933.

In any event, the attempt to try to fit the Soviet Union into a world order that corresponded to the optimistic expectations of the war years proved fruitless. To be sure, the Soviet Union accepted the charter of the United Nations, but it enlarged and misused the right of veto of great powers in such a way that it destroyed the value of the United Nations as an instrument of universal peace-keeping. Furthermore, the peace treaties with the enemy states were not under the jurisdiction of the United Nations, and it was on these peace treaties that the nature of any postwar system decisively hinged. The Soviet Union under Stalin initiated almost immediately after the termination of the war an active policy aimed at consolidating all of the militarily won positions into permanent Russian power positions, and went even beyond that: it aspired to expand the Russian and Chinese influence, as far as this was possible without general war, over the entire Eurasian continent.

America was ill-prepared for this Russian policy. Even Franklin D. Roosevelt, who was convinced that the United States could never again return to full political isolationism, still believed that it would be impossible to maintain American troops in Europe for more than two years after the end of the war. But the development after the war was even more critical. No one resented the continued presence of some troops retained in Europe, but demobilization of American military power as a result of the pressure of public opinion in America was undertaken with such haste that at the beginning of 1946 hardly any power was left that could have represented a counterbalance to the Russian military forces in Europe. Actually the possession of the atomic bomb created a certain defensive security of which the American public was hardly aware, as the thought that such a weapon could be used outside of a large-scale war was not even considered in the United States. In the twenty months that followed the end of the war important opportunities and possibilities were neglected, but if one considers the lack of a global political tradition in America, it must at the same time be stated that the Americans learned quickly. As early as September 1946, in his famous speech in Stuttgart, Secretary of State James Byrnes declared that the American military forces in Germany would remain there until a real peace had been established in Europe. The decisive breakthrough, for which the government obtained the complete support of the predominant majority of the American people, occurred in the spring of 1947. The taking over of responsibility for the maintaining of a constitutional government in Greece (a burden Great Britain had carried up to then), as well as American aid to Turkey, were both extensions of the Truman Doctrine, which promised U.S. support to those "free peoples who are resisting attempted subjugation by armed minorities or by outside pressure."

It was a turning point of the highest historical significance. Only the Truman Doctrine and subsequent actions represented the real turning away from the policy of isolation. They underscored especially America's determination to stand by the European nations that had resisted Communism. This goal was not only implemented by military and diplomatic means, but by economic and psychological ones as well. It is possible to say that a total diplomacy was set in motion to counter totalitarianism. Here, too, it is perhaps still possible to discern certain stages, though they follow each other in rapid succession. In the beginning the opinion prevailed that perhaps an intensification of economic aid would be sufficient, but in Greece, as well as a short time later in all of Europe, military and economic measures became more and more intermeshed. At the same time that the Truman Doctrine was proclaimed, the

Moscow conference began, which was primarily supposed to settle the German question. But Stalin did not hesitate to declare that he considered German matters not yet ready for an international solution, and it was clear that the Soviet Union hoped that it would be highly successful in fishing in troubled waters if it left the European countries in extreme uncertainty as to their future and moreover divided them, in order better to be able to exert pressure on them. There was no question that the Russians were counting on a further deterioration of the economic and social conditions of Europe and at the same time were waiting for America to become tired of protecting a ruined Europe.

The American response was not only to restore Europe economically with all available means but also to help it toward a greater development of its energies than Europe had been able to attain prior to 1914 or between the World Wars. This was the basic idea of the Marshall Plan, which was first introduced in June of 1947 and began to function in July of 1948. But it had already been proved in 1948 that economic aid to Europe would be useless if Europe could not be defended militarily, and for a real defense of Europe the active participation of the United States was necessary. America (as well as Canada) was prepared to do this, too, as the NATO agreements of April 1949 bear witness. Here at last America's traditional policy of isolationism had been definitely set aside.

One of the fundamental goals of the Marshall Plan had been the expansion of the European economy by intensifying trade between the individual European states and, if possible, by completely eliminating all trade barriers. This gave the idea of European unification a concrete task and, despite its different composition, NATO, too, has been of great help to intra-European cooperation.

It had been decided in Washington as early as 1947 that West Germany should also partake of the Marshall Plan aid, and it was furthermore decided to abolish the military government on July 1, 1948, and to replace it with a civilian high commissioner whose task it was to create as quickly as possible a German government and to hand over to it his last control rights. While the Berlin blockade delayed the carrying out of this plan for about a year, the restoration of Germany's economic life was immediately translated into action. Through the reform and stabilization of the German monetary system and under the stimulus of Marshall Plan aid, German conditions began to improve. The creation of a sovereign German government and the founding of a German army took another eight years, because, understandably, many Germans were concerned that the creation of a constitution and later of a German army could make the division between West and East Germany permanent. At the same time France wanted to be assured that the war potential of a restored German state could be used only for the defense of Europe.

The delays were considerable, though when seen in retrospect not tragic. While the economic recovery of Germany and Europe steadily advanced, the foundations for the development of a united Europe were laid. The creation of the European Coal and Steel Community was the first step that led finally to the Common European Market. Unification was restricted to the six states formed out of the core of Europe but developed into a force that attracted other European countries.

I am convinced that the final collapse of the European Defense Community project is not regrettable. It is my feeling that it was an artificial project, which would have placed Germany in an extremely precarious position. The final treaties of Paris, which settled Germany's entry into NATO and thereby opened up the way for Germany's sovereignty, seemed to me to be preferable. It is true, however, that the long discussions over the idea of the Defense Community convinced the French not only that they would have to permit the rearming of Germany but that close cooperation between the two nations was essential. The definite reconciliation of France and Germany is one of the best achievements of postwar history, because without a real Franco-German understanding no growth of European unity is possible and the survival of a free Europe is dangerously threatened.

The years from 1947 to 1952 were years of new and fruitful political ideas and constructions. In those years America also began fundamentally and thoroughly to analyze the future problems of the developing countries. Truman's four-point program of 1949, which we will discuss later, was one of the first fruits of this analysis. But at the same time America had to prove by actions its determination to contain the expansion of Russo-Chinese Communism. The Anglo-American airlift of the years 1948–49, which defended West Berlin against the Russian blockade, was only a prelude to the difficult strains and sacrifices that were the costs of the Korean War of 1950–53, and that were carried more than 80 percent by the United States. The result of the war, which was conducted under the authority of the UN, was not negligible. Despite the intervention of Red China the attackers were thrown back to the former boundaries. But the American public was deeply concerned and often embittered over the fact that the aggressors had not suffered a total defeat and that Korea had not been reunited under a democratic constitution. Old wounds reopened which had been inflicted over the loss of China to Mao's armies, an event that was especially difficult for the Americans to overcome. The era came in which demagogy had its heyday, and Senator McCarthy ruthlessly took advantage of this situation, with the consequence that American foreign policy was restricted and the image of America took on a gray color in just those years when the new Secretary of State, John Foster Dulles, was disposed to present the American people to the world as a giant herd of snow-white lambs.

But the United States has also overcome the episode of McCarthyism. However, the new Eisenhower administration was considerably more limited than Truman's as to the international initiatives it could, and would have liked to, have taken. Economically conservative, the members of the Eisenhower administration were especially concerned over the huge increase in military expenditure which during the Korean War had rapidly risen from 12 to 40 billion dollars and henceforth had remained on that level. The conclusions that were drawn from this time were of far-reaching significance. American strategy was based essentially on atomic weapons, i.e., on the strategic air force, which in the case of a renewed attack from the Communist states of Asia and Europe was to hold out the threat of atomic retaliation. It was assumed that a possible enemy attack would essentially resemble the Korean War. It was then necessary only to possess "shield" forces which in the case of an invasion could momentarily hold up the enemy until the "sword" forces in the shape of the air force bearing atomic weapons would bring about a quick decision. America then began to form a circle of alliances around the Soviet Union and Red China: the alliances with Japan, Taiwan, with the Philippines, the Southeast Asian treaty organization, the Baghdad treaty. In the underdeveloped countries of the Middle East and Southeast Asia, money for development aid was used more and more for building armies because no American troops were to be sent there but eventual support was to be provided by the powerful American Seventh Fleet.

This policy was highly questionable. Countries whose immediate political ideas were restricted solely to internal reform and whose rearmament only deepened their social problems were brought into an apparently universal anti-Communist front. A whole list of these states, e.g., Indochina, Iraq, Iran, Lebanon, and finally Laos, have since 1953 proved to be great danger points and Western policy has suffered a number of painful defeats in this region.

One of the reasons for this lay in the fact that after 1953 neither China nor Russia undertook a massive invasion similar to Korea. Mao had learned from the Korean War that China's economic basis was too weak for a large war. The emphasis after 1953 in China was placed on internal modernization, while Russia after Stalin's death was for some time preoccupied with the problems of succession. But the propaganda and the political war continued, and civil wars were supported by Communist weapons-deliveries and diplomacy. The great strategic concept of the West was of little help against the ensuing guerrilla wars.

NATO itself did not flourish to the degree that had been originally hoped for. If NATO was to be only a shield and not a sword, it did not require the large strength in numbers that had originally been set as its goal. But not even the lesser number of forces eventually decided on were met. It should be mentioned here that Germany, faithful to her pledge, assiduously continued to build up her army, an achievement highly appreciated in the United States.

In the course of the years in Western Europe it was said of NATO that it would suffice if it was conceived of as a light tripwire instead of as a shield, since the decision would in any case be brought about by America's strategic air force. The tripwire was to create a warning system which would be set off at the destruction of this symbolic barrier. If this strategy had been a good one, the United States could very well have reduced its troops in Europe to a few thousand men. But in the face of such possibilities, the proponents of these theories in Europe became afraid of their own courage. In any case the number of English troops in Germany was reduced and the impending abolition of the draft was announced. France was forced by the struggle in Algeria to withdraw the larger part of its troops from Germany.

Much worse, however, than the weakening of the common military front were the disagreements that developed between the NATO allies with respect to their political intentions and aims. NATO was entirely oriented toward European questions. Actually, however, many of the allies were colonial powers, not just England and France, but also the Netherlands, Belgium, and Portugal, and in all those years they were engaged in solving the difficult, often vital, problems posed by their colonies. And often they disagreed with or stood in strongest opposition to the American anti-colonialist policy. Indochina, China, Cyprus, and, most of all, Suez are examples of such frictions and conflicts.

This diversity in points of view was dangerously exacerbated by the appraisal of the future of Russia. Disagreements over this question existed not only among the allies but also within the individual countries, including America. The hope that Russia would become liberalized after the death of Stalin was entertained by many people. Intelligent men existed who even thought they could predict such a development on the basis of scientific sociological and economic laws. But even if we want to assume for a moment that the Soviet system should finally decide to opt for a larger production of consumer goods and less military expenditures and simultaneously for a partial dismantling of the police state and the abandonment of imperialistic policies abroad, no one can maintain that this state of affairs must necessarily happen. It is equally possible that the pressure of the class of functionaries or of the masses for a higher standard of living could lead to greater repressive measures or perhaps even to explosive foreign adventures. In other words, nobody can predict the future development of Russia, and even though we should negotiate as much as possible with Russia over concrete questions, we should not consider summit meetings with communiqués, which each side interprets differently, as a solution to any kind of political problem, as happened in 1955 and then unfortunately again in 1959 during Khrushchev's visit to the United States.

When Khrushchev opened up political war on Berlin in 1958 he found the NATO allies partly in disagreement and partly undecided. This gave him the opportunity for worldwide propaganda through his American trip; moreover he forced a new summit conference which, as is well known, fell apart even before it opened. Despite this, Khrushchev waited before using his threat against Berlin, and we must assume that he believed that time was in his favor. The great advances of Russian science and military technology in particular increased his sense of power. And in fact we have entered into a serious danger zone.

The basic strategic concept of 1953 had certain disadvantageous consequences, as previously mentioned, from the very beginning. These initially had to be borne, because as long as the NATO armies did not reach their full capacity, the free world could be protected only by the superiority of American nuclear weapons. The Russian manufacture of the atom bomb and even of the H-bomb still left the United States at a wide advantage in the beginning. It was only in 1956, and perhaps even later, that the Soviet Union had built up a comparable arsenal of nuclear weapons. In addition, it became increasingly evident in the years 1956–58 that Russia was making great advances in the production of missiles, and that especially in the development of ICBMs she was considerably ahead of the United States. In two to three years the Soviet Union will be temporarily superior in rocket weaponry. But this gap is not by itself decisive. America still possesses more nuclear weapons than the Soviet Union, and it possesses air and missile bases that stretch out far across the earth, not to mention the invulnerable firing bases through its Polaris submarines. It also would be possible to keep at least one part of the United States inter-

continental strategic air force continually in the air in order
to be able to use them against a Russian surprise attack.

Even in the case of Russian atomic surprise attack, which
would undoubtedly destroy a large part of the American armament and millions of people, the United States would still be
in a position to carry out terrible retaliatory blows against
Russia. But the use of nuclear weapons threatens both powers
with such enormous losses that the risk can be taken into
consideration only in the utmost emergency. In this situation
conventional military weapons take on a new significance. An
attacker who uses only conventional weapons and who uses
them only against limited targets could hope that the opponent
would not resort to nuclear weapons in retaliation. In any case
a defender would avoid the use of nuclear weapons, provided
that he has at his disposal the conventional military forces
permitting him to restore the military balance. Each power has
the greatest interest in setting the threshold that leads from
conventional to atomic war as high as possible.

It has been said that the conflict between the Eastern and
Western world will eventually be settled by the neutrals. And
it is certainly correct that an essential element in the self-
assurance of the Soviet and Chinese leadership is the belief
that only Communism can raise the productivity of the underdeveloped countries of Asia, Africa and Latin America to a
higher level. In fact, the temptation to throw themselves into
the arms of Communism is very great for many of these peoples.
Only when we have proven that Western ideas and methods
can modernize the societies and economies of these underdeveloped countries rapidly enough can we expect the Communist world to react peacefully toward the West.

The task is huge and requires the common efforts of all
Western nations for an indefinite time. America has quite a
bit of experience in development policy, but has had to pay
dearly for learning its lessons. A successful development policy

is not simply a financial or economic transaction but simultaneously a sociopolitical and pedagogical task which must take different forms according to the starting level of the country. In many cases we cannot expect that countries will be able to assume liberal or democratic forms without interim stages. Western ideals will first have to be demonstrated practically. It was out of this consideration that the Peace Corps was created, which has aroused a great deal of enthusiasm among the academic youth of America. We hope to gain from the services of the young in the developing countries clearer ideas about the particular problems of the different countries and to improve our development policy accordingly.

None of the problems that I have mentioned can be solved by America alone. It can only be done if she wins the support of the nations of the free world.

NOTES

I GERMAN IDEALISM IN THE LIGHT OF SOCIAL HISTORY

First published in German in *Historische Zeitschrift*, Vol. 174 (1952), pp. 359–84. I am most grateful for Professor Robert Herzstein's kind permission to reproduce his translation of the article. He prepared it for a work of his own, soon to be published, on the problems, sources, and interpretations of German intellectual history.

1. An English text of the *Dialogue on Politics* is found in Theodore H. Von Laue, *Leopold Ranke: The Formative Years*, Princeton, 1950, pp. 152–80.

II BISMARCK'S REALPOLITIK

First published in *Journal of the History of Ideas*, Vol. XXI (1960), pp. 84–98.

1. The historical literature on Bismarck is more extensive than that on any other personality in German history except Luther and Goethe. Outside of Germany only Napoleon and Lincoln have elicited a comparable amount of study. The most recent introduction to the Bismarck bibliography is to be found in Walter Bussmann, *Das Zeitalter Bismarcks* (Konstanz, 1957), pp. 251–74 (Vol. III of Brandt, Meyer, Just, *Handbuch der deutschen Geschichte*). In Otto Pflanze's *Bismarck and the Development of Germany: The Period of Unification, 1815–70*, Princeton, 1963, we now possess an outstanding biography of Bismarck.

2. Gustav Adolf Rein, *Die Revolution in der Politik Bismarcks* (Göttingen, 1957), p. 352, uses the term *antediluvianisch* to describe the *unzeitgemässe*—out-of season—character of Bismarck.

3. *Bismarcks Briefe an General Leopold von Gerlach,* ed. by H. Kohl (Berlin, 1896), p. 347.

4. Friedrich Meinecke, "Bismarcks Eintritt in den christlich-germanischen Kreis," *Historische Zeitschrift* 90, pp. 56 ff., reprinted in *Preussen und Deutschland im 19. und 20. Jahrhundert* (Munich, 1918), pp. 296 ff.

5. Besides the above article by F. Meinecke, the most important treatments are still E. Marcks, *Bismarcks Jugend* (Stuttgart, 1909), and Otto Baumgarten, *Bismarcks Glaube* (Tübingen, 1915). The strong criticism recently leveled against Meinecke and Marcks by S. A. Kaehler, "Zur Deutung von Bismarcks 'Bekehrung,'" in *Glaube und Geschichte: Festschrift für Friedrich Gogarten,* ed. by Heinrich Runte (Giessen, 1948), pp. 189 ff., fails to discuss the full evidence. Cf. also A. O. Meyer, *Bismarcks Glaube* (Munich, 1932), the same author's biography of Bismarck, ed. by H. Rothfels (Stuttgart, 1949), and Erich Eyck, *Bismarck,* Vol. I (Erlenbach-Zürich, 1914).

6. *Glaubenslehre* (2nd ed., Berlin, 1830–31), II, p. 476.

7. See Chapter I, "German Idealism in the Light of Social History," pp. 13 ff.

8. Meinecke, "Bismarcks Eintritt in den christlich-germanischen Kreis," *Preussen und Deutschland,* pp. 312 ff., 354 ff.

9. *The State in its Relation with the Church* (London, 1839).

10. Otto Pflanze, "Bismarck's 'Realpolitik,'" *Review of Politics,* XX (1958), pp. 498 f.

11. On this group Friedrich Meinecke's chapter in his *Weltbürgertum und Nationalstaat* is still unsurpassed (4th ed., Munich, 1917), pp. 223 ff.

12. The best brief statement of Luther's conception of the state is in Karl Holl, *Gesammelte Aufsätze zur Kirchengeschichte,* I: *Luther* (2nd ed., Tübingen, 1923), pp. 263 ff. For an amplification of my own views, cf. my *A History of Modern Germany: The Reformation* (New York, 1959), pp. 187 ff.

13. Letter to Friedrich von Preen, April 26, 1872. J. Burckhardt, *Briefe,* ed. by F. Kaphahn (Leipzig, 1935), p. 348.

14. Bismarck, *Die Gesammelten Werke* (Berlin, 1924–35), VIII, p. 459.

15. October 15, 1850, *ibid.*, XIV, p. 175.

16. Egmont Zechlin, *Die Staatsstreichpläne Bismarcks und Wilhelms*, II (Stuttgart, 1929).

17. A. O. Meyer, *Bismarck* (Stuttgart, 1944), p. 712.

18. The term *Realpolitik* became fashionable under the influence of the book *Grundsätze der Realpolitik, angewendet auf die staatlichen Zustände Deutschlands*, published by August Ludwig Rochau in 1853. As a student Rochau had participated in the abortive Frankfurt *Putsch* of 1833. A fugitive from a life sentence he lived for fifteen years in France where he came in contact with the new French sociology. The revolution of 1848 brought Rochau back to Germany. In his book Rochau argued that what gravity is in nature, power is in politics. But although Rochau was an advocate of German unification through Prussian leadership, the power which he had in mind was social rather than military power. The state could gain strength only by allying itself with the strongest forces of society, and power today rested with the bourgeoisie. Rochau wanted to achieve German unification through constitutional reform. It was logical that he became, in 1859, the secretary of the *Deutsche Nationalverein*, which fought and criticized Bismarck until 1866 from a liberal point of view. Cf. on Rochau: H. Lülmann, *Die Anfänge Ludwig von Rochaus, 1810–50* (Heidelberg, 1921); F. Meinecke, *Die Idee der Staatsräson in der Neueren Geschichte* (3rd ed., Munich, 1929), pp. 493 f. (translated by Douglas Scott as *Machiavellism*, New Haven, 1957, p. 396); and recently S. A. Kaehler, "Realpolitik zur Zeit des Krimkrieges," *Historische Zeitschrift*, Vol. 174 (1952), pp. 417 ff., and L. Krieger, *The German Idea of Freedom* (Boston, 1957), pp. 353 ff. In spite of the enthusiastic reception given to it by the young Treitschke, Rochau's book was very quickly forgotten. But the term *Realpolitik* remained current and either denoted a policy contemptuous of all ideals and ideologies and following the interests of the state or it was merely identified with a policy exclusively employing power for the achievement of its ends. The word has become misleading on account of its ambiguities; historically it should not be used, in my opinion, except

for the statesmen who entered the scene in the decade after 1848, and even then it calls for exact definition.

19. Cf. Hans Rothfels, *Bismarck und der Osten* (Leipzig, 1934).

20. Bismarck, *Die Gesammelten Werke*, VIII, p. 106.

21. Bismarck, *Gedanke und Erinnerung*, ed. by Gerhard Ritter and Rudolph Stadelmann, *Gesammelte Werke* (Berlin, 1932), XV, p. 398.

22. *Gedanke und Erinnerung, loc. cit.,* p. 466.

23. Otto Pflanze, "Bismarck and German Nationalism," *American Historical Review*, LX (1955), pp. 548 ff.

24. A curious example of the use of old Germanic mythology is the title which he gave his memoirs. They were published as *Gedanken und Erinnerungen* (*Reflections and Reminiscences*) after his death. But as G. Ritter and R. Stadelmann found out when preparing their critical edition of 1932, Bismarck had given them the title *Gedanke und Erinnerung*, which should probably be translated: *Thought and Memory*. The title had reference to *hugin* and *nunin* (Old Norse), the two ravens which, according to legend, were sitting on the shoulders of Wotan. Germanic scholars have given different translations, but the most widely circulated book in Germanic mythology in Bismarck's days had *Gedanke und Erinnerung*. See Karl Simrock, *Handbuch der deutschen Mythologie* (3rd ed., Bonn 1869), p. 170. (I am grateful to Professor Konstantin Reichardt of Yale for the information about mythology and the identification of the source.)

25. Ernst Troeltsch, *Gesammelte Schriften*, Vol. I: *Die Soziallehren der christlichen Kirchen und Gruppen* (3rd ed. Tübingen, 1923), pp. 537, 596 ff. The distinction between Luther and Lutheranism ought to be more sharply drawn than was done by Troeltsch, though for our problem this is not decisive.

III MOLTKE AND SCHLIEFFEN

First published in *Makers of Modern Strategy*, ed. by Edward M. Earle, Princeton University Press, Princeton, 1943, pp. 172–205.

The extensive bibliography of literature on nineteenth-century strategy is not reprinted here. Among recent studies of Moltke the general historical biography by Eberhard Kessel should be mentioned (Stuttgart, 1959). Gerhard Ritter has given an outstanding appraisal of Moltke's political and strategic thought in the first volume of his *Staatskunst und Kriegshandwerk* (Munich, 1954). Gordon Craig touches on these problems in his *The Politics of the Prussian Army*, Oxford, 1955, and has presented a penetrating and colorful description of the climax of the Bohemian campaign of 1866 in his *The Battle of Königgrätz*, New York, 1964.

Gerhard Ritter published and analyzed the original Schlieffen plan in his *Der Schlieffen-Plan—Kritik eines Mythos*, Munich, 1956 (English translation London, 1958), and also dealt with Schlieffen in the second volume of his *Staatskunst und Kriegshandwerk*, Munich, 1960. An interesting critique of German strategy in 1914 is contained in General Ludwig Beck's *Studien* (ed. by Hans Speidel, Stuttgart, 1955).

IV   RUSSIA AND THE EUROPEAN POLITICAL SYSTEM

First published in *Russian Foreign Policy: Essays in Historical Perspective*, ed. by Ivo J. Lederer, Yale University, New Haven, Conn., 1962, pp. 377–415.

1. For a fuller discussion of the relationship between Russia and Europe see Chapter 1 of my *Political Collapse of Europe* (New York, 1951).

2. For the following see Dietrich Gerhard, *England und der Aufstieg Russlands* (Munich, 1933).

3. *Ibid.*, pp. 31–81, and Douglas K. Reading, *The Anglo-Russian Commercial Treaty of 1734* (New Haven, 1938).

4. Karl Stählin, *Geschichte Russlands*, III, pp. 190–241 (Königsberg-Berlin, 1935) and E. W. Tarlé, *Napoleon's Invasion of Russia, 1812* (New York, 1942).

5. First printed in the appendix of Vol. V, pp. 761 f. of Heinrich von Treitschke, *Deutsche Geschichte im Neunzehnten Jahrhundert* (Leipzig, 1894).

6. *Ibid.*, pp. 756 ff.

7. Karl Stählin, *Geschichte Russlands*, IV, 1 (Königsberg-Berlin, 1939), pp. 264 ff.

8. See the remarks of Bismarck in his *Gedanken und Erinnerungen* (Stuttgart, 1898) and Hajo Holborn, *Bismarcks Europäische Politik zu Beginn der Siebziger Jahre und die Mission Radowitz* (Berlin, 1925), pp. 9 ff.

9. In my opinion wrongly, but he used pressure tactics of doubtful character. The literature on the war panic of 1875 is rather extensive. For Russian opinion, see W. M. Chwostow's [Khvostov's] chapter in W. P. Potjomkin [Potemkin], ed., *Geschichte der Diplomatie, 2,* 2nd ed. (Berlin, 1948), pp. 34 ff., and the article by A. S. Jerussalimski [Erusalimskij], quoted by him. It is surprising that Chwostow asserts that Bismarck's foreign policies were motivated by a deep hatred of Russia. His own treatment of the history of the period does not bear out this judgment, which, incidentally, is uncommon in the Soviet appraisal of modern German history.

10. According to T. G. Masaryk, Germans were represented in the government service in 1881 as follows: Imperial Court Ministry 39 percent, Military High Command 41 percent, Navy Ministry 39 percent, War Ministry 46 percent, Foreign Ministry 57 percent, Post and Telegraph 62 percent: *The Spirit of Russia* (London, New York, 1919), I, p. 158.

11. *Die Grosse Politik der Europäischen Kabinette, 1871–1914,* III, pp. 151 ff.

12. J. V. Fuller, *Bismarck's Diplomacy at Its Zenith* (Cambridge, 1922).

13. A. S. Jerussalimski [Erusalimskij], *Die Aussenpolitik und die Diplomatie des Deutschen Imperialismus Ende des 19. Jahrhunderts* (Berlin, 1954: pub. first in Russian, Moscow, 1948), pp. 282 ff. For the following, see also Valentin Gitermann, *Geschichte Russlands* (Zurich, 1949), III, pp. 191–211, 302–13, 331–41.

14. The trade between Russia and Germany grew, however, more slowly than international trade in general. Russian exports to Germany were considerably larger than imports from Germany.

15. Otto Becker, *Bismarcks Bündnispolitik* (Berlin, 1923), pp. 123 f. and Herbert Feis, *Europe the World's Banker, 1870–1914* (New Haven, 1930), pp. 210 ff.

16. Feis, *Europe the World's Banker.* Of the direct Russian govern-

ment's debts owed abroad in 1914, 80 percent were held in France, 14 percent in Great Britain.

17. Long-term German investments in Russia in 1914 were established to amount to 1.8 billion marks, about as large as those in Turkey. Both Belgian and French investments in Russia were larger.

18. Hajo Holborn, *Deutschland und die Türkei, 1878–90* (Berlin, 1926), pp. 103 ff.

19. See Chwostow in Potjomkin, *Geschichte der Diplomatie*, 2, pp. 216 ff.

20. *Ibid.*, pp. 331 ff. *Die internationalen Beziehungen im Zeitalter des Imperialismus, Dokumente aus den Archiven der Zarischen und der Provisorischen Regierung*, German ed. by Otto Hoetzsch, VI, pp. 193 ff.

21. The literature on Russo-German relations in the interwar period is rather large. The best study in my opinion is Herbert Helbig, *Die Träger der Rapallo Politik*, Veröffentlichungen des Max Planck Instituts für Geschichte, No. 3 (Göttingen, 1958). Also cf. Hans W. Gatzke, *Stresemann and the Rearmament of Germany* (Baltimore, 1954): "Russo-German Military Collaboration During the Weimar Republic," *American Historical Review*, LXIII (1958); Gustav Hilger and Alfred G. Meyer, *The Incompatible Allies* (New York, 1953); and Gerald Freund, *Unholy Alliance* (New York, 1957).

22. Hajo Holborn, "Diplomats and Diplomacy in the Early Weimar Republic," in Gordon A. Craig and Felix Gilbert, eds., *The Diplomats, 1919–1939* (Princeton, 1953), p. 171; see Chapter VI.

V THE POLITICAL COHESION OF THE AUSTRO-GERMAN ALLIANCE IN WORLD WAR I

This unpublished article was written on the basis of a paper presented at the annual meeting of the American Historical Association in Washington in 1964.

1. See Chapter IV, "Russia and the European Political System," pp. 128 ff.; also Chapter II, "Bismarck's Realpolitik."

2. Cf. Hans Rothfels, *Bismarck, der Osten und das Reich* (Stuttgart, 1960), pp. 44 ff.

3. About military cooperation see Gordon A. Craig, "The Military Cohesion of the Austro-German Alliance, 1914–18," in *War, Politics and Diplomacy*, New York, 1966.

4. "Das 'schlesische Angebot' und die italienische Kriegsgefahr 1915," *Geschichte in Wissenschaft und Unterricht*, 1963, pp. 533 ff.

5. The most comprehensive study of these problems is now *The Nationality Problem in the Habsburg Empire in the Nineteenth Century, Austrian History Yearbook*, Vol. III (3 parts), Rice University, Houston, Texas, 1967–68.

6. Cf. my article "The final disintegration of the Habsburg Empire," *Austrian History Yearbook*, Vol. III, part 3 (1967), pp. 189–205.

VI DIPLOMATS AND DIPLOMACY IN THE EARLY WEIMAR REPUBLIC

First published in *The Diplomats, 1919–1939*, ed. by Gordon A. Craig and Felix Gilbert, Princeton University Press, Princeton, 1953, pp. 123–71.

1. Cf. on the relations between military and civilian leadership, most recently Gerhard Ritter, "Das Verhältnis von Politik und Kriegführung im bismarckischen Reich," in *Deutschland und Europa, Festschrift für Hans Rothfels*, ed. by Werner Conze (Düsseldorf, 1951), pp. 69–97. For the older literature see Hajo Holborn, "Moltke and Schlieffen," Chapter III.

2. A number of cases are illustrated by Albrecht Mendelssohn Bartholdy, in *Diplomatie* (Berlin-Grunewald, 1927), pp. 51–77. For a historical analysis see Gordon A. Craig, "Military Diplomats in the Prussian and German Service: The Attachés, 1816–1914," *Political Science Quarterly*, LXIV (1949), pp. 65–94.

3. A good description of the German Foreign Office and foreign service in the Bismarckian period is contained in Joseph Maria von Radowitz, *Aufzeichnungen und Erinnerungen*, ed. by Hajo Holborn (Stuttgart, 1925).

4. J. M. von Radowitz, *Aufzeichnungen und Erinnerungen*, II, pp. 256–57.

5. Otto Hammann, *Bilder aus der letzten Kaiserzeit* (Berlin, 1922), pp. 128 f.

6. For the general history see Arthur Rosenberg, *The Birth of the German Republic* (New York, 1931), and Harry R. Rudin, *Armistice* (New Haven, 1942).

7. Cf. Hajo Holborn, *La Formation de la Constitution de Weimar, problème de politique extérieure* (Paris, 1931) (Dotation Carnegie, Bulletin 6).

8. The interesting reports of the first Dresel mission are printed in *Foreign Relations: Paris Peace Conference*, II, pp. 130–72.

9. In the national elections of January 19, 1919, the Majority Socialists received 37.9, the Independent Socialists 7.6, while the Center Party received 19.7, the Democratic Party 18.6, the German People's Party 4.4, and the German Nationalist People's Party 10.3 percent of the national vote.

10. See his letter and memorandum to Scheidemann of December 9, 1918, in Graf Brockdorff-Rantzau, *Dokumente und Gedanken um Versailles* (3rd ed., Berlin, 1925), pp. 29–35. Obviously, Scheidemann must have been in contact with Brockdorff-Rantzau before the actual Solf crisis.

11. On the historical background of the idea of "open diplomacy" see Hajo Holborn, *The Political Collapse of Europe* (New York, 1951), pp. 80 and 104–5.

12. The document was printed in Charles Seymour, ed., *The Intimate Papers of Colonel House* (Boston, 1928), IV, pp. 192–200. I first mentioned in my *Kriegsschuld und Reparationen auf der Pariser Friedenskonferenz von 1919* (Leipzig-Berlin, 1932, p. 18n.), that the document had fallen into German hands, a fact later on broadcast by Hjalmar Schacht, "Germany's Claim for Colonies," *Foreign Affairs*, XV (1937), pp. 223–34.

13. On the organization of the German preparations for the peace conference see Alma Luckau, *The German Delegation at the Paris Peace Conference* (New York, 1941), pp. 159–86.

14. The event was the origin of the enmity between Seeckt and Brockdorff-Rantzau; see Friedrich von Rabenau, *Seeckt, Aus seinem Leben, 1918–1936* (Leipzig, 1940), pp. 159–86.

15. The incident of the German representative remaining seated in his reply to Clemenceau has been interpreted in many different ways. See for example D. Lloyd George, *Memoirs of the Peace Conference* (New Haven, 1939), pp. 453–54. This author believes that Brockdorff-Rantzau's neglecting to get up was the result of his extreme nervousness at that moment. But the count always supported the myth that he had acted this way deliberately and thereby gave belated justification to the understandable annoyance of the conference. That the German representatives were themselves divided concerning the character of this first German speech before an international audience is shown by the discussion that took place on the evening before among the members of the German peace delegation. See Luckau, *The German Delegation*, pp. 63–65, 213–20.

16. See Brockdorff-Rantzau's speech in Brockdorff-Rantzau, *Dokumente und Gedanken*, pp. 70–73. Also in Luckau, *The German Delegation*, pp. 220–23.

17. W. Arnold-Forster, *The Blockade, 1914–1919* (New York, 1939). Also D. Lloyd George, *Memoirs of the Peace Conference*, pp. 192–99; John M. Keynes, *The Economic Consequences of the Peace* (New York, 1920), and his article on Dr. Melchior in *Two Memoirs* (London, 1949).

18. Mitchell Pirie Briggs, *George D. Herron and the European Settlement* (Stanford, 1932).

19. *Foreign Relations: Paris Peace Conference*, II, 71–75.

20. On Heidelberg Vereinigung see Luckau, *The German Delegation*, pp. 46–53. Also Max Weber, *Politische Schriften* (Munich, 1921), pp. 381 ff., 394 ff., 485 ff.

21. See the report by the representative of the Foreign Office to the committee for peace negotiations of the Weimar national assembly on April 15, 1919, in Luckau, *The German Delegation*, pp. 187 f.

22. *Ibid.*, p. 220.

23. The minutes of this committee were published by Albert de Lapradelle, *La paix de Versailles*, III: *Responsabilités des auteurs de la Guerre et Sanctions* (Paris, 1930).

24. They are excellently narrated and documented in Philip M. Burnett, *Reparation at the Paris Peace Conference* (New York, 1940).

25. This opinion was first expressed by R. C. Binkley and A. C.

Mahr, "A New Interpretation of the 'Responsibility' Clause in the Versailles Treaty," *Current History*, XXIV (1926), pp. 398–400; then again, with better material, in Binkley's "The 'Guilt' Clause in the Versailles Treaty," *ibid.*, XXX, pp. 294–300. Shortly before the Lausanne Conference of 1932 that buried the reparations problem, two eminent French historians gained wide publicity by their study of the problem, Camille Bloch and Pierre Renouvin, "L'Article 231 du Traité de Versailles. Sa genèse et sa signification," *Revue d'Histoire de la Guerre Mondiale*, X (1932), pp. 1–24. Cf. also my treatment in *Kriegsschuld und Reparationen auf der Pariser Friedenskonferenz*. A well-balanced and thorough modern historical statement is found in the introduction of Burnett, *Reparation at the Peace Conference*.

26. Italics mine.

27. See for example Charles Seymour, *Intimate Papers of Colonel House*, IV, pp. 392, 409.

28. Brockdorff-Rantzau, *Dokumente und Gedanken*, p. 70; *Stenographische Berichte der verfassunggebenden Nationalversammlung* CCXXXVII, p. 1115.

29. *Foreign Relations: Paris Peace Conference*, XII, p. 119.

30. Brockdorff-Rantzau, *Dokumente und Gedanken*, pp. 278–79.

31. See the discussions of the Council of Four in *Foreign Relations: Paris Peace Conference*, VI, pp. 501–50. On German military estimates, cf. Rabenau, *Seeckt, Aus seinem Leben*, pp. 181–87. Also a book for which its author received much information from General Groener, E. O. Volkmann, *Revolution über Deutschland* (Oldenburg, 1930).

32. Volkmann, *Revolution über Deutschland*, pp. 278–79.

33. See, on his conversations with American representatives, *Foreign Relations: Paris Peace Conference*, XII, pp. 124–35.

34. See James Bryce, *Modern Democracies* (London, 1921), II, pp. 402 ff.

35. Cf. on the Weimar constitution and foreign affairs Heinrich Pohl, *Völkerrecht und Aussenpolitik in der Reichsverfassung* (Berlin, 1929).

36. See Sir Josiah Stamp in the foreword to the English edition of Carl Bergmann, *The History of Reparations* (Boston, 1927).

37. The details of this organization, which was named in Germany the Schüler Reform after the official in charge, cannot be treated here.

38. On German policy in the Far East cf. Kurt Bloch, *German Interests and Policies in the Far East* (New York, 1940).

39. Wipert von Blücher, *Deutschlands Weg nach Rapallo* (Wiesbaden, 1951), pp. 47 ff.

40. Ernst von Weizsäcker, *Erinnerungen* (Munich, 1950), p. 80; English translation by John Andrews (Chicago, 1951), p. 68. Herbert von Dirksen, *Moskau, Tokio, London* (Stuttgart, 1951), pp. 44, 56–58, is more considerate and restrained in his judgment on this point. So is Erich Kordt, *Nicht aus den Akten* (Stuttgart, 1950), pp. 24–52.

41. Mayer-Kaufbeuren was recalled at the time of the French Ruhr invasion and died in 1923; Pfeiffer died in 1926; Wiedfeldt resigned his post in 1925. About the events leading to his retirement, see Gustav Stresemann, *Vermächtnis* (Berlin, 1932), I, pp. 290–93.

42. Wipert von Blücher, *Deutschlands Weg nach Rapallo*, p. 150.

43. Lord D'Abernon, *An Ambassador of Peace* (Boston, 1929), I, p. 39; III, p. 28.

44. On the Foreign Office at the time of Stresemann's death in 1929, see Julius Curtius, *Sechs Jahre Minister der Deutschen Republik* (Heidelberg, 1948), pp. 146–50.

45. Dirksen, *Moskau, Tokio, London*, p. 54.

46. Cf. C. Bresciani-Turroni, *The Economics of Inflation.*

47. On the history of the revisions of the Versailles treaty, see W. E. Stephens, *Revisions of the Treaty of Versailles* (New York, 1939), and the annotated edition of the treaty prepared at the suggestion of President Roosevelt in the State Department at the end of the Second World War and published as Volume XIII of *Foreign Relations: Paris Peace Conference.*

48. D'Abernon, *Ambassador of Peace*, I, pp. 87, 225.

49. Foreword to Alfred von Tirpitz, *Politische Dokumente*, I: *Der Aufbau der deutschen Weltmacht* (Stuttgart, 1924).

50. Brockdorff-Rantzau, *Dokumente und Gedanken*, pp. 125 f.

51. See on the "anti-Bolshevist" school Max Hoffmann, *Aufzeichnungen*, ed. by Karl F. Nowak (Berlin, 1929), and Chapters 13–15 of the second volume of Hitler's *Mein Kampf*, written after Locarno in 1926.

52. The main organ of this school was a Socialist monthly, *Sozialistische Monatshefte.*

53. D'Abernon, *Ambassador of Peace,* II, p. 238–39. Cf., for the general historical analysis, Arnold Wolfers, *Britain and France Between Two Wars* (New York, 1940); W. M. Jordan, *Great Britain, France and the German Problem, 1918–1939* (London, 1943); Hajo Holborn, *The Political Collapse of Europe* (New York, 1951), pp. 124 ff.

54. Dirksen, *Moskau, Tokio, London,* pp. 75–76 is rather serious in his criticism, while Ernst von Weizsäcker's remarks are insipid, *Erinnerungen,* p. 69.

55. See Forschungsanstalt für Kriegs- und Heeresgeschichte, *Darstellungen aus den Nachkriegskämpfen deutscher Truppen und Freikorps,* I: *Die Rückführung des Ostheeres* (Berlin, 1936).

56. On the military events, see *ibid.,* II: *Der Feldzug im Baltikum bis zur zweiten Einnahme von Riga* (Berlin, 1937). Also Graf Rüdiger von der Goltz, *Als politischer General im Osten* (Leipzig, 1836). On the political side of the Baltikum developments in 1919, see *Foreign Relations: Paris Peace Conference,* XII, pp. 136–227; *British Documents,* 1st series, III, pp. 1–307; Dirksen, *Moskau, Tokio, London,* pp. 29–34; Wipert von Blücher, *Deutschlands Weg nach Rapallo,* pp. 69–86.

57. Cf. Rabenau, *Seeckt, Aus seinem Leben,* pp. 251–53; 305–520; Julius Epstein, "Der Seeckt Plan," *Der Monat,* I, No. 2 (November 1948), pp. 42–50. Cf. also George W. F. Hallgarten, "General Hans von Seeckt and Russia, 1920–1922," *Journal of Modern History,* XXI (1949), pp. 58–71.

58. Cf. Rabenau, *Seeckt, Aus seinem Leben,* pp. 117–19.

59. On the Genoa conference, see, in addition to the works cited above and the memoirs of D'Abernon, Dirksen, and Wipert von Blücher, Eric C. Kollman, "Walter Rathenau and German Foreign Policy," *Journal of Modern History,* XXIV (1952), pp. 127–42.

60. See *Der Monat,* I, No. 2 (November 1948), pp. 42–50; Rabenau, *Seeckt, Aus seinem Leben,* pp. 314–20.

61. Some interesting material on the later years of Brockdorff-Rantzau was brought together after his death in *Europäische Gespräche,* VII (1929), pp. 1–47.

62. Cf. Stresemann, *Vermächtnis,* II, pp. 502–42.

VII ORIGINS AND POLITICAL CHARACTER OF NAZI IDEOLOGY

First published in *Political Science Quarterly*, Vol. LXXIX (1964), pp. 542–54.

1. Adolf Hitler, *Mein Kampf* (3rd ed., Munich, 1928), p. 506.

2. February 6, 1945, see F. Genoud (ed.), *Le Testament Politique de Hitler, Notes Récueilliés par Martin Bormann*, préface de H. R. Trever-Roper (Paris, 1959), p. 65.

3. This largely continued after 1933. A shocking preview of what Nazi policy with regard to the Christian churches would have been after a victorious war can be gleaned from the church policies of the Nazis in the conquered and annexed Polish territories. See Martin Broszat, *Nationalsozialistische Polenpolitik, 1939–45* (Stuttgart, 1961), pp. 167 ff.

4. See Hermann Hammer, "Die deutschen Ausgaben von Hitlers 'Mein Kampf,'" *Vierteljahreshefte für Zeitgeschichte*, IV (1956), pp. 161–78.

5. When in 1932 a group of economists, among them Alfred Weber and Wilhelm Roepke, challenged him to a debate on problems of economic policy, he replied that the professors should first prove their ability to build up something like the NSDAP or SA before he would debate with them.

6. See Hitler's statement in Henry Picker, *Hitlers Tischgespräche im Führerhauptquartier 1941–42*, edited by G. Ritter (Bonn, 1951), p. 275.

7. A bibliography is now readily available in the monumental work of Karl Dietrich Bracher, Wolfgang Sauer, and Gerhard Schulz, *Die Nationalsozialistische Machtergreifung* (Cologne, 1960). Hugh R. Trevor-Roper, "Hitlers Kriegsziele," in B. Freudenfeld (ed.), *Stationen der Deutschen Geschichte* (Stuttgart, 1962), likes to give preference to the "four windows through which light falls into the most recondite thoughts of Hitler at the four turning points of his political career." These are the hours "of his political defeats" (*Mein Kampf*); "of his political triumphs" (Rauschning conversations

1932–34; H. Rauschning, *The Voice of Destruction*, New York, 1940); "of his military triumphs" (*Table-Talks* 1941–42, see footnote 6 above); and "of his military defeat" (Bormann dictations, 1945, see footnote 2 above). To these Trevor-Roper would probably be willing to add G. Weinberg (ed.), *Hitlers Zweites Buch* (Stuttgart, 1961), written in 1928 on the eve of the big expansion of the Nazi Party. But there are many other documents, particularly between 1933 and 1945, which though not as extensive as the aforementioned sources are of primary importance.

8. *Hitlers Zweites Buch*, p. 46.

9. Picker, p. 444.

10. Usually he declared the American people to be inferior for this reason. But occasionally he argued that if it had been possible to create in two hundred years an American nation it was because the immigrants had been the best people, and that meant mostly the Nordic elements of Europe. *Hitlers Zweites Buch*, p. 131.

11. See Wolfgang Sauer in *Nationalsozialistische Machtergreifung*, pp. 744 ff.

12. Rauschning, pp. 231 ff.

13. Rauschning, p. 80.

14. See Hannah Arendt, *The Origins of Totalitarianism* (New York, 1951), and Eva G. Reichmann, *Hostages of Civilization* (Boston, 1951).

15. Rauschning, pp. 235–38.

16. G. Reitlinger, *The Final Solution* (New York, 1955).

17. See Alexander Dallin, *German Rule in Russia, 1941–45* (New York, 1957).

18. Picker, p. 71.

19. *Ibid.*, p. 275.

20. Franz L. Neumann, *Behemoth* (New York, 1942), pp. 293 ff. See also his *The Democratic and the Authoritarian State: Essays in Political and Legal Theory*, edited by Herbert Marcuse (Glencoe, Ill., 1957).

21. See Hitler's curious statement on Rosenberg's *Myth:* "It gives me considerable pleasure to realize that the book has been closely studied only by our opponents," in Picker, p. 275.

22. On Hitler's metaphors see the recent article by Hermann

Glaser, "Adolf Hitlers 'Mein Kampf' als Spiesserspiegel," *Aus Politik und Zeitgeschichte*, Bonn, July 24, 1963.

23. Privately Hitler disapproved of the public agitation of purist Nazi linguists. Picker, pp. 382 f.

24. Wilfried Daim, *Der Mann, der Hitler die Ideen gab* (Munich, 1958).

25. On the Vienna newspapers at this time see William A. Jenks, *The Young Hitler* (New York, 1960), pp. 126 ff.

26. There is a brief reference to Nietzsche's superman in one of the conversations with Rauschning, but it is the latter who introduces Nietzsche. Rauschning, pp. 246 f.

27. Except that the acquaintance with *The Wise Men of Zion* after World War I may have given his anti-Semitism an even more poisonous character. Rauschning, pp. 238 ff.

28. A full view of the war aims of the German government, army, and political parties is presented by a recent historical work that exploits for the first time all the relevant German archives, Fritz Fischer, *Griff nach der Weltmacht* (Düsseldorf, 1962).

VIII THE GERMAN OPPOSITION TO HITLER

This unpublished article was written on the basis of a paper presented to the annual meeting of the American Historical Association in New York in 1960.

The literature on the German opposition is rather large and only a few of the most important studies can be mentioned here. Franklin L. Ford wrote the first critical study: "The Twentieth of July in the History of the German Resistance," *American Historical Review*, Vol. LI (1946), pp. 609–26, followed by Allan Dulles' *Germany's Underground* (New York, 1947), and Hans Rothfels, *The German Opposition to Hitler*, Hinsdale, Ill., 1948. (Revised edition in German: Frankfurt, 1958; English: London, 1958.) Guenther Weisenborn, *Der lautlose Aufstand*, Hamburg, 1953; Gerhard Ritter, *Carl Goerdeler und die deutsche Widerstandsbewegung*, Stuttgart, 1954 (abbr. English tr. *The German Resistance*, London 1959); Maurice Baumont, *La grande conjuration contre Hitler*, Paris, 1963; Eberhard Zeller, *Geist* der Freiheit, der zwanzigste Juli, 4th ed., Munich, 1963; Terence Prittie, *Germans Against Hitler*, London, 1964; Fabian von Schlabrendorf, *The Secret War Against Hitler*, New York, 1965; Gert van Roon, *Neuordnung im Widerstand: Der Kreisauer Kreis innerhalb der deutschen Widerstandsbewegung*, Munich, 1967. Harold C. Deutsch, *The Conspiracy Against Hitler in the Twilight War*, Minneapolis, 1968.

IX AMERICAN PLANNING OF THE MILITARY GOVERNMENT OF GERMANY DURING WORLD WAR II

This article was prepared for a conference on military-occupation policies held under the auspices of the Social Science Research Council in March, 1967, in New York City.

Sources and literature pertaining to this subject are rather large and no full bibliography is offered here. A very thorough and extensive compilation, reaching till 1963, is available in Paul Y. Hammond's study "Directives for the Occupation of Germany: the Washington Controversy," in H. Stein, ed., *American Civil-Military Decisions*, Birmingham, 1963. I mention in the following bibliographical note only books and articles of primary importance. First place should be given to the documents published by the Department of State (Harley A. Nother, ed.): *Postwar Foreign Policy Preparation* (Washington, 1949); the supplementary volumes to *Foreign Relations of the United States* dealing with the big wartime conferences: *The Conferences at Cairo and Tehran, 1943* (Washington, 1961); *The Conferences at Malta and Yalta, 1945* (Washington, 1955); *The Conference of Berlin, 1945* (Washington, 1960). The regular volumes 1941–45 are also relevant; among them are the volumes of 1944 and 1945 which contain the material concerning the European Advisory Commission. Among the private sources the following are the most informative: Cordell Hull, *Memoirs* (New York, 1948); William D. Leahy, *I Was There* (New York, 1950); Robert E. Sherwood, *Roosevelt and Hopkins* (New York, 1948); Henry L. Stimson and McGeorge Bundy, *On Active Service in Peace and War* (New York, 1948); Henry Morgenthau, Jr.,

Germany Is Our Problem (New York, 1945) and "Our Policy Toward
Germany," New York *Post*, November 24–29, 1947; John M. Blum,
From the Morgenthau Diaries: Years of War, 1941–1945 (Boston,
1967); Winston S. Churchill, *Closing the Ring* and *Triumph and
Tragedy* (Boston, 1951–53); Lord Moran, *Churchill* (Boston, 1966);
Sir Frederick Morgan, *Overture to Overlord* (Garden City, New
York, 1950); Lord Strang, *Home and Abroad* (London, 1956).
Strang was the British member of the EAC, on which we also
possess reports by three associates of the U.S. member: Philip E.
Mosely, "Dismemberment of Germany: The Allied Negotiations from
Yalta to Potsdam" and "The Occupation of Germany: New Light
on How the Zones Were Drawn," *Foreign Affairs*, XXVIII (1950),
pp. 487–98 and 580–604; reprinted in *The Kremlin and World
Politics* (New York, 1960); E. G. Penrose, *Economic Planning for
the Peace* (Princeton, 1953); George E. Kennan, *Memoirs* (Boston,
1967).

Among the general studies of wartime policies John L. Snell,
Wartime Origins of the East-West Dilemma Over Germany (New
Orleans, 1959), largely centers around military government. The best
and most detailed analytical treatment of military government planning in Washington is the already quoted Paul Y. Hammond's "Directives for the Occupation of Germany." His aim is not an exclusively
historical one; he wants to gain insight into the problems of coopera-
tion between civilian and military government. His picture of the
War Department, however, is less clear than that of the Department
of State. Of high value are Walter L. Dorn, "The Debate over
American Occupation Policy in Germany in 1944–1945," *Political
Science Quarterly*, LXXII (1957), pp. 481–501, and William M.
Franklin, "Zonal Boundaries and Access to Berlin," *World Politics*,
XVI (1963), pp. 1–31.

X THE UNITED STATES AND GERMANY IN WORLD
POLITICS

Speech given at the opening of the American Week at the University
of Munich in June, 1961.

INDEX

DATE D

GAYLORD		

ALSO BY DAVID BELSON

Tributes and Forms for Public Occasions

Speeches for Every Occasion (with Ruth Belson)

What to Say *for* Every Occasion

MODEL SPEECHES, LETTERS, AND REMARKS

∾

DAVID BELSON

BARNES
&NOBLE
BOOKS
NEW YORK

Published by MJF Books
Fine Communications
322 Eighth Avenue
New York, NY 10001

What to Say for Every Occasion
LC Control Number 2002106261
ISBN 1-56731-541-0

This edition published by arrangement with Citadel Press, an imprint
of Kensington Publishing Corp.

Manufactured in the United States of America on acid-free paper ∞

MJF Books and the MJF colophon are trademarks of Fine Creative
Media, Inc.

QM   10   9   8   7   6   5   4   3

TO MY WIFE, RUTH

Contents

Introduction

Nearly everyone is called upon, at some time or another, to prepare a speech or compose other material to be spoken, read or used in his club, school, community center, religious or other group activity. Incidental to these activities, meetings are conducted; speeches are delivered for various purposes and causes; officers are installed; gifts are presented and accepted; testimonials are tendered to deserving persons; resolutions, scrolls and written documents and data of all kinds are drafted.

Many would like to become active in their community, welfare, fraternal and other endeavors. They would like to exercise their rights and perform their obligations as members of their community. But they are deterred from so doing because they either lack sufficient time to compose and organize the material which is required of them, or they cannot locate a satisfactory source of material; possibly they do not have the essential training to perform the obligations of such group activities.

It is for those who are painfully groping their way

and struggling with the difficulties of composition that
this work holds out a helping hand.

To draft a resolution or compose a speech is an art
and demands the exercise of skill. Every workman in
the exercise of his art should be provided with proper
implements. The author and public speaker employ for
the accomplishment of their purposes, the dictionary,
the thesaurus, and reference books. The lawyer has his
form books without which he would be greatly handi-
capped. While there is no dearth of books on public
speaking, there is an absence of books devoted primarily
to furnishing materials, illustrations and guides. This
work gives a generous amount of such data. It is long
on illustration and short on explanation which is the
function of the books on public speaking.

It is hoped that the character and variety of forms
and illustrations will enable the user adequately to cope
with the usual situations with which he may be confronted. The material furnished will often answer the
queries, "What shall I say?" "How shall I say it?" and
save anxious hours of composing. The user can readily
select out of the collection of material and illustrations
those expressions and examples which are best suited for
his purpose. The models should be modified and con-
formed to the user's personality and his special needs.
Most of these forms, which have been shorn of excess
verbiage, have been used and tested in the public arena.
Many of the forms may be adapted or used for written
statements or letters.

To save space no attention has been given to para-

What to Say *for* Every Occasion

1. Presentations

Here is a speech situation that could confront you on very short notice. The occasion often arises that an officer of your lodge, for example, is retiring and it has been suggested that a gift be presented. You have been selected to make the presentation address. There are two steps in the formulation of the speech of presentation: (1) praise the recipient, and (2) tender the gift.

To aid in preparing the talk, material and complete examples to meet the usual situation are given in this chapter.

Following these examples of the breakdown of the speech of presentation into its two component parts are completed illustrations combining step one and step two, constituting the entire speech of presentation. In every chapter of this book, whenever a formula is provided for organizing a speech, examples of each step will be given, followed by completed illustrations.

Decide which of the illustrations most clearly approaches the requirements of your own assignment. Then adapt it to your special needs.

1. Praise for recipient

You have shown yourself to be a man of courage, humility and integrity as well as great personal charm. Your outstanding contributions to interracial and interfaith movements mark you as a true American in the best traditions of our democracy. To me, you represent the embodiment of what is good, fine, righteous and admirable.

✦

Your deeds speak for you far better than anything I can say. You have devoted yourself unselfishly to a host of humanitarian causes. Your activities have been so extensive it would almost seem one lifetime could not encompass them all. Yet you have found the time and the energy to serve, to work and to lead, shouldering countless burdens with unfailing good humor and grace.

✦

Your many activities have brought you richly deserved honors in the past.

✦

You have been a tower of strength and a strong force for progressive, efficient public service.

✦

In all of our dealings with you, you have always shown patience and tolerance—qualities which you are going to need as president of this great organization.

✦

In the course of your duties, you have earned the respect of all members and officers of our organization for your integrity and sincerity. Your neighbors in the community in which you live have recognized your worth by electing you president of the P.T.A.

◆

You have advanced through every rank. You combine tenacity with dynamic action. You have the reputation of being incorruptible. Your knowledge of the men you worked with and their faith in you has helped to restore public confidence in the force. The community is grateful to you for the public service you have performed.

◆

You are a vital and effective force in the great growth of this Association. To the presidents who came and went, you have been a guide and counselor; to our treasurer, you have been a big brother and helpful associate; to the directors, the chairman and members of our many committees, you have been the aid and mentor; and to our staff, you have been the understanding and directing father. To all of us, you have given your heart and you received in return our boundless admiration and affection.

◆

I am very sorry from a selfish point of view to see Mr. Doe retire. I have depended upon him to so great an extent that I am going to miss him deeply.

◆

You have long been a figure in the public life. You have always taken a keen interest in amateur sports. You are active in fraternal matters and have been honored by the Grand Order. You have merited the commendation of your fellow citizens.

2. Tender of the Gift or Award

Please accept this gift as an expression of our sincere gratitude for all you have done to further the work of our organization. It is our fervent hope that you may long enjoy your new-found leisure.

✦

I have a very pleasant duty to perform and that is to make formal presentation to you of the emblem of your office. I know it will represent for you the fruits of many years of service to this organization. I present this gavel and with it go our best wishes for a successful administration.

✦

We dedicate this plaque as a reminder that these honored dead, through their vigorous and active devotion to American ideals and the American way of life, have set a standard for us to emulate.

✦

I present this to you as a token of my warm affection and esteem and as a remembrance of what has been for me, at least, a uniquely happy relationship. May you find satisfaction and fulfillment in your new position and may you enjoy happiness and good health for many years to come!

✦

I am happy for this opportunity to add my expression of gratitude for your sincere and devoted efforts on behalf of our Association by tendering to you this emblem of your new office.

◆

I take pleasure in presenting to you on behalf of your former associates this desk-set as a token of our respect and admiration for you. May I read the inscription on the marble base? "To our Esteemed Colleague, John Doe, who, in the years of our association, has won our sincere respect, our deep affection, and to whom we extend our warmest wishes for a long life of health and happiness."

◆

On behalf of the Committee of Awards, it is my privilege to confer upon you this medal for conspicuous service in the cause of our servicemen.

◆

The token which I am about to present to you takes the form of a chest of silver. Will you accept this chest as a symbol of our gratitude for the hospitality which you have extended to us on this visit?

◆

We have arranged this meeting for the twofold purpose of saying good-bye to you and offering you some tangible evidence of our appreciation and goodwill. On behalf of your fellow officers, I ask you to accept this token of our esteem.

Illustration 1 — Award

We are proud of this opportunity to honor you for your achievements. We are here tonight to pay high tribute to you not only for what you have done but for all that, God willing, you will achieve in the future. There is no doubt that a man of your abilities is destined for even greater accomplishments and higher service. As a token of our very high regard for you we have prepared this illuminated and engraved award for distinguished service. We present it to you with our sincerest good wishes and hope that you will continue your outstanding public service for many more years and in the even broader fields for which you are so ably fitted.

Illustration 2 — Charter

You and your associates have taken on an important and necessary task. You are to be commended on the nobility of your purpose in forming this local union. You are rendering a service to the members of your industry in attempting to improve their working conditions. I congratulate you for your enterprise and unselfishness. It gives me a sense of satisfaction to turn over to you the charter permitting you to function as a labor union. The charter has been duly signed by the appropriate international officers. Many problems beset a new group which will tax your officers and members. I am confident, however, that by applying your combined talents, energies and ingenuity you will solve these problems. I am sure that all of us who are interested in maintaining high standards in the industry will give you and the members of your local union whatever cooperation lies within our power in the furtherance of your commendable purposes.

Illustration 3 — Citation

What makes a good leader? Courage and loyalty, understanding, initiative and vision, and a saving sense of humor. On your 10th anniversary as Secretary of the organization I salute you as an outstanding exponent of all these qualities. It has been, indeed, a privilege to be associated with you and one which I deeply appreciate. As one of the many in whom you evoke the keenest admiration and respect, I take this occasion, on behalf of your brother officers, to present to you this Distinguished Service Award which reads: "To John Doe: Under your inspired leadership our organization has been built up to a high point of efficiency and to a high standard. You have served in many responsible and honored positions. You have given to our organization the benefit of your many attributes with untiring devotion and fidelity. You have lived a life so full of accomplishments that few can match the honor and respect that is associated with your name." It is an honor for me to be chosen to present to you this Distinguished Service Award.

Illustration 4 — Dictionary

Our guest loves words. He uses them well. He can spend whole days with dictionaries. Accordingly, the officers have gotten together to indulge this foible of his and have bought him the best, biggest, and most unabridged dictionary ever printed. I have at the request of the donors inscribed it: "To John Doe: Not that he needs it, but because he knows how to use it better than anyone we know, this book is presented with the affectionate regard and high esteem of all his colleagues."

Illustration 5 — Gavel

You have worked long and diligently in this Lodge and have richly deserved the honor. If I were to attempt to describe adequately the sterling qualities you possess I would infringe upon the time and patience of the other speakers. It gives me pleasure to present to you the gavel which is the emblem of your authority to preside over this lodge. I know you will wield it in a manner which will bring credit to you and honor to the membership. Each time you rap this gavel I know it will be not to demonstrate your authority but to signify the adoption of another progressive step in the fine work of this organization. I have the highest confidence in your ability and I know the success of your administration is assured. It is with pleasure that I tender to you the gavel of authority and the symbol of your new office.

Illustration 6 — Gift

On the 25th anniversary of your service to our organization I express to you appreciation for your loyalty. You have been part of this organization for more than one half of its existence. Through your long years of service you have done your work with the utmost efficiency and dependability. Please accept this little gift as a token of our sincere gratitude for your faithful service. With it go our best wishes for your continued success and happiness for many years to come.

Illustration 7 — Medal

We recognize fully the great service you are rendering to the community. In recognition of these services, I have a very pleasant duty to perform. It is my privilege and delight to make a presentation to you as a mark of appreciation for your unstinting sacrifice of time and effort. It is not often we bestow this medal upon a resident of this community. In this case we feel that no one deserves it more than you. Therefore, on behalf of the community, it is my privilege to present to you the Gold Citizenship Medal. There is an appropriate inscription engraved on it. It reads: "For truly outstanding work to our Community." I ask you to accept this medal from hearts full of gratitude for all you have done.

Illustration 8 — Portrait

In hanging the picture of a true gentleman whose career has been so full of inspiration, whose accomplishments are an outstanding credit to his calling and whose future still lies ahead of him, we perform an act that is and will become even more significant in time to come. What finer tribute can be paid any man than to say he is a gentleman? The word in itself speaks volumes and embodies all those rich traits of character that thrill one with happiness when they are mentioned and more especially when spoken on an occasion such as this. This is a rare and unusual happening since it marks a gracious expression of appreciation which, according to custom, is usually indulged in only after the completion of a man's activities. It is my cherished privilege to present to you this symbol of our affection and love.

Illustration 9 — Scroll

Seldom do we run across a man of better temperament or a more gentlemanly, more considerate and patient one than our secretary. I don't believe that any one of us has ever seen him angry or upset although the Lord knows he must have had plenty of provocation at times. His services for the past 25 years make us so deeply indebted to him that we ought to give him, now that he is retiring, some written evidence of our debt and gratitude to him—some evidence of our appreciation for his long, meritorious and patient work—some token by which to remember us. I, therefore, present this beautifully illuminated scroll, which I now read:

"To John Doe: In acknowledgment and appreciation of the true, faithful and outstanding service rendered by him to our organization in its steady, sound and rapid growth and progress to its present position of influence and prestige. During his secretaryship, no night has been too cold, nor any day too hot, nor any task too difficult for him, whenever an occasion existed to enhance the interests of a member or the organization. His zeal, his personal sacrifices, his devotion and his allegiance to our organization have known no limits. He is respected, honored and beloved by every member and officer of our order. It is our sincere hope and prayer that he may be blessed with health, strength and increased opportunities for even greater achievement in the noble work of our organization." We are certainly going to miss you. Good luck and many years of good health and happiness.

2. Appreciation, Acceptance and Thanks

In your social, community or lodge life you may be the recipient of honors or gifts. You will want to know how to make a brief and interesting speech of acceptance. Say thank you, praise the donor and say something good about the gift or honor. Follow with an expression of acceptance, telling what benefit or pleasure you expect to derive from it.

1. Expression of Appreciation and Thanks

It is the greatest honor that has ever been bestowed upon me.

◆

I shall never forget this warm and touching expression of your friendship.

◆

It has aways seemed to me that the greatest honor which can come to a man is to be selected by his brothers for the presidency of their lodge.

◆

I regard the gift of this beautiful gavel as symbolic of the power and might of this organization.

◆

This honor realizes one of my life's ambitions.

◆

I am deeply touched that I am the one upon whom you chose to confer this high honor and all I am able to say at the moment is thank you very much.

◆

I am grateful to you for bringing this beautiful memento all the way across the ocean to present to me.

◆

I have the pleasant duty, in the absence of the Mayor, of participating in these ceremonies and of accepting this magnificent gift on behalf of the citizens of this community.

◆

How can I express the full measure of my appreciation that you have chosen to name this school after me?

I am deeply and sincerely grateful for your considera-tin, courtesy and thought in presenting this traveling bag to me. It is a very appropriate "going-away" gift.

◆

I wish publicly to thank the members for the great honor of electing me to this high office.

◆

I extend my thanks to the organization, the members, and to all who spoke in my behalf, to the president for his confidence in me, and to all of you for coming here.

◆

I thank each of you most heartily for making me so inexpressibly happy by your presence on this impressive and, for me, anyway, memorable occasion.

◆

From the bottom of my heart, I thank my good friends for the kind, congratulatory messages which they have sent to me and the high tributes they have paid me.

◆

I thank the newly elected officers for the kindness, consideration and helpfulness which they have shown me since my elevation and I hope that I may continue to receive the benefit of their experience and wisdom.

◆

With gratitude I acknowledge your message of good wishes and thank you for the many tributes you have paid me. Your friendly sentiments are also heartily appreciated.

◆

It is very pleasant to receive such compliments, espe-cially in the presence of one's wife and parents. But they are so prejudiced in my favor that they are likely to believe all they have heard.

◆

I am grateful, indeed, for the high measure of understanding and support which has been given me.

◆

We thank you with all our hearts for the kind welcome, for the great courtesy, for the generous hospitality, which you have shown us.

2. Acceptance

I accept this appointment with pride but also with a sense of humility. I realize full well the responsibilities and importance of this position, and cherish the opportunity to serve.

◆

I deeply sense the great obligations of this position to which I have been appointed and I shall regard it a duty and privilege to advance your policies with the greatest vigor I possess. With the help of God and the cooperation of the members of this mighty organization I shall devote myself unswervingly toward the attainment of your objectives.

◆

I am fully aware of the magnitude of this office and will do my utmost to discharge my duties with credit to those who have confidence in me and to myself.

◆

It is with a feeling of solemnity and a sense of responsibility that I accept this high honor which you have conferred upon me.

✦

I enter upon my duties with a sense of humility, with appreciation of the attendant responsibilities of the office, and with anxiety lest my abilities fail to keep pace with my eagerness to render the service you expect and to which you are entitled.

✦

It is because this welcome gift from you implies that I am considered worthy, that I will treasure and hold it in the greatest esteem.

Illustration 1 — Award

This realizes one of my life's ambitions. I am proud to be the recipient of this Medal of Distinguished Achievement and I accept it with gratitude and a deep sense of humility. I realize, however, that team spirit, hard work and the loyalty and personal sacrifices of my associates have made this recognition possible. I consider this honor as one in a representative capacity to be shared with all my associates.

Illustration 2 — Gift

Please convey my sincere thanks to the Commander-in-Chief of the VFW for this beautiful token. I interpret this emblem as a present to the officers and members of my organization. It shall be considered by me as a symbol of honor presented by your great organization to the membership of my organization. I want to thank you personally for your fine presentation and your organization for the honor of its visit to us. Please assure your Commander-in-Chief of our continued cooperation and support. We will stand with you in the fight for favorable legislation for veterans and we will work together in the future as we have in the past.

Illustration 3 — Plaque

Thank you for this magnificent plaque. It touches me deeply to be so honored. I shall include this beautiful plaque in my valuable possessions as a common heritage handed to me by representatives of this great fraternal organization. I have really done nothing more than in my own humble way to serve this fine fraternity as best I could. I shall continue to serve as long as I am able.

Illustration 4 — Watch

It would be quite unnatural if I were not deeply touched by this evidence of your good will. I know I will make frequent use of this valuable watch. When I look at it, I will be reminded of the many happy hours I spent in this room. I will recall the time 20 years ago when I was privileged to join the club. This club was then small. Its treasury was insignificant. But its members were enthusiastic and friendly. I will recall the many events that brought the club to the position of influence and prestige that it now enjoys. I will recall the many lasting friendships that began in this club room. I will recall the many happy experiences I enjoyed here. For your thoughtfulness, your kindness, for the sentimental as well as the practical value of your gift, my sincere thanks.

3. Appeal for Funds

In your community or public activities the occasion will frequently arise requiring you to make an appeal, either for funds or for some action. There are two steps in organizing a letter or speech appealing for funds: (1) a statement of the cause, purpose or urgency, and (2) the request for a contribution to the cause or participation in the particular activity, as, for example, voting for the proposition being advocated.

1. Cause, Purpose or Urgency

Cancer has become a national problem which requires national attention and action. No sex or age is safe.

✦

The Cardiac Home is the only place people suffering from heart disease, in desperate need of convalescent care and rehabilitation, can turn to for help.

✦

We respectfully call your attention to the seriousness of the problem of chronic diseases. We wish to emphasize the importance of the work of one of the most needed institutions of its kind in the country—Hope Hospital.

✦

The community strives to provide essential services for the young and the old. Such services include better care for children, summer camps, supervised recreation for youngsters, and programs for the care of the aging.

✦

Not many persons realize the sacrifices your volunteer firemen make to provide fire protection for you. This protection helps to keep your insurance rates down and your taxes lower.

✦

The Police Boys Clubs are important not only to the boys—they are also important to you. They help to keep our community a good place in which to live. The police force knows that a wholesome, friendly respect for law and order must be taught youngsters while they are growing up. Boys who get a chance to know their neighborhood policemen as human beings do not generally turn to juvenile delinquency.

◆

In the Police Athletic League the community has a powerful weapon in the fight against juvenile delinquency. Working at the grass roots level among children who do not belong to any other youth organization, PAL is in a position to prevent delinquency before it gets started.

◆

The high incidence of polio in the past few years has created a national as well as local public health problem. The victims of polio must be aided and the research scientists enabled to continue their work until an effective preventative and cure is found.

◆

If catastrophe strikes, the task of the Red Cross will be gigantic. It must be ready with trained volunteers, nurses, doctors and equipment.

◆

The primary function of the Salvation Army is to fill the gap in services not provided by other organizations. The Army establishes good liaison with churches, schools, fire department associations and clubs so that these organizations may refer to the Army problems which they themselves are not equipped to handle.

◆

It has always been a part of our great American heritage to extend a helping hand to those less fortunate than ourselves. Repeatedly we have taken to our hearts and opened our purses to the sufferers from other lands seeking haven in this country. Is it too much to ask that they be given an opportunity for rehabilitation and a new start in life?

2. Request for contribution or participation

This is a cause that merits our generous support, our most devoted efforts. I, therefore, earnestly urge you to send a generous contribution to the campaign. Please send it in today.

◆

It is by your generous contribution that they may be assured of that opportunity. Think of them now and act.

◆

Please add a lonely child—a troubled person—to your Christmas list by sending a special gift to the Fund. It will spread happiness throughout the year.

◆

Will you help us to ameliorate this suffering? Will you make a contribution now to help these children? Enclosed is a leaflet which tells you what we do for needy children and what you can do to help.

◆

Please subscribe as much as you possibly can. Of course, you will be saving yourself a substantial amount of tax money in the end. But your greatest satisfaction will come in knowing that you are giving these children a real, helpful break. Your cooperation will be long remembered.

Your assistance will make larger facilities possible to help those who have not had a chance to develop their bodies. Your contribution helps to sustain not only these children but also ensures that the Community Service will continue to be able to meet the growing needs for its many institutional services in the area.

✦

Our representative in Washington would act to appropriate sufficient funds for the cancer problem if enough Americans showed their concern by writing or wiring to their Congressman. Won't you please write or wire him at once?

✦

I know how many times a year you are called upon for help. I can readily appreciate the strain on your budget. Nevertheless, I ask that you consider giving us a small donation and I assure you personally that these funds will be utilized properly and administered economically.

✦

PAL is now conducting its annual drive to support its many varied activities. This campaign offers the public the opportunity to contribute to a cause which has helped to curb juvenile delinquency and has aided youngsters in building character and good citizenship.

✦

Let us not be too late with too little. We have it within our power to control the destiny of those who have suffered so much. I, therefore, urge you to send a generous contribution to the campaign.

I ask you to show your gratitude to God for your sight by voting for this bill.

Illustration 1 — Blind

Do you realize that 87 percent of our perceptions come through our eyes? This fact tells how much a blind person lost. It tells how important it is for him to have the benefit of help from the rest of us. By careful training the blind can make better use of the perceptions of hearing and touch and thus overcome much of their handicap. Your gift, any amount, will be much appreciated.

Illustration 2 — Blood Donation

A member of my lodge called me. He was frantic and it was with difficulty I got him to talk calmly. His wife was in the hospital bleeding internally from unknown causes. Her bleeding weakened her and she couldn't survive much more loss of blood. She needed a quart of blood each day until her bleeding could be stopped. Would I help? I said, "Of course." Then I reminded myself. My lodge was promoting something known as a blood bank. Some members had contributed blood— enough for a start. Everyone was welcome to use the blood in time of need but he had to pledge to restore a similar quantity. In other words, anybody can borrow blood and have someone repay it later. We have a blank check to draw on the blood bank. The member's wife received all she needed. I am happy to say she is now home and in good condition. If we hadn't had the blood bank the story might not have ended as well as it did. We want more blood in the bank in case we need it. Here's what you do! You, your wife, or any member of your family can go to any Red Cross Blood Donor Station. Tell them, "I want to give blood and I want my lodge to be credited with it." Your biggest sacrifice will be that you must not eat for four hours before you do this. Don't delay too long. You can't tell how badly blood may be needed.

Illustration 3 — Cancer

The enclosed dollar bill, crisp and fresh, should not startle you. We are not giving it away. It is enclosed to dramatize the appeal we are making for the cancer fund. Cancer, as you know, is a terrible scourge upon humanity. It is taking its toll at an alarming rate. The cancer patient needs care, attention, comfort, medication, hospitalization and financial assistance. All too frequently some or all of these needs are denied to him or her by overcrowded hospitals and nursing homes. The cancer fund helps provide all this quickly and efficiently. We are now engaged in a campaign to raise these urgently needed funds. The enclosed dollar bill is to impress you with its importance. Won't you please return it in the enclosed envelope together with your own contribution? Remember, it is better to give a little than nothing at all.

Illustration 4 – Church

Once in a great while a cause so tragic in intensity and so overwhelming in importance is brought to our attention that it transcends any consideration of creed or race. The repair of the damage to our Church as a result of the fire, is such a cause. For 50 years the Church has been a beacon of hope and learning serving the spiritual and communal needs of all residents of the community. We need $50,000 to rebuild the Church. We must insure its continuation for the future. The critical nature of the emergency makes it all the more essential for us to give all we can and as soon as we can. I know that you will not refuse so urgent an appeal. Please mail a generous check with the enclosed blank.

Illustration 5 – Volunteer Fire Department

Your volunteer fire department requires assistance in meeting its operating expenses. Such expenses include death benefits to the beneficiaries of deceased members and cost of recreational and athletic activities, all of which help maintain the morale of the members of your volunteer fire department. Will you please make a generous contribution to those who stand ever ready to make sacrifices for you?

Illustration 6 – Hospital

Almost daily we have been forced to turn away many of the sick and afflicted for lack of the necessary beds and facilities. Hope Hospital must add a new wing to keep pace with the growing demands made upon it for help. Unfortunately, we do not have large endowments but must depend on those who know of the work we have been doing at the hospital for over 50 years. A building fund has been started and we earnestly ask you to add your contribution. We ask of you, in the name of the needy, to give and give more than you have ever given, in gratitude to God for granting you the glorious gift of grace to give, to give to your fellowman, to give for your own self's sake.

Illustration 7 — Needy

You cannot buy happiness. You cannot go to the nearest grocery store and order a pound of happiness as you would a pound of butter. But, since happiness comes from within, you can secure a measure of happiness by your own acts. You can find that feeling of contentment by helping your less fortunate fellowmen. You can help those, who, because of ill-fate, will not have a happy Christmas unless we share with them. During this season of peace and good will, let us not force those in need to look at happiness through our eyes. Rather, let us help them to see and find happiness through their own eyes. Let us not fail the needy and less fortunate of the community.

Illustration 8 — Red Cross

The Red Cross belongs to the people. Major disasters cannot be predicted and when they occur the Red Cross must be ready to throw ample resources into the rescue work. Some of what the Red Cross does is dramatic. A hurricane, a big flood, a burning forest or a burning city stands out as help is mobilized and hurried to the scene. But the Red Cross helps in other ways. If a single burned-out family is in trouble the Red Cross is its neighbor. Disaster service is only one part of the picture. In aiding the veteran and his family, in supplying nursing service, in accident-prevention campaigns, in the national blood donation program, in many other ways, the Red Cross stands ready to minister to all the people. It needs the support of all who can give, and all those who can give only a little can still have the sense of full participation in a great neighborly undertaking.

4. Awards, Citations, Inscriptions, Resolutions, and Scrolls

Awards, citations, inscriptions and scrolls are usually but not necessarily begun by the words:

> "In recognition of"
> "In appreciation of"
> "In tribute to"

then followed by the name of the recipient, words of praise and a brief record of his accomplishments.

Resolutions may be either in simple form beginning "Resolved that" or in the more formal style beginning with the "Whereas" clauses and ending with the "Now, therefore, be it resolved" clause.

A generous amount of material to aid in composing the award, citation, inscription, resolution or scroll is given. Use the material which most nearly applies to your situation and adapt it to your special needs.

Awards, Citations, Inscriptions, Resolutions and Scrolls

(Material for use in awards, citations, inscriptions, resolutions and scrolls.)

✦

He has exercised sound judgment and a wise and kindly counsel and has endeared himself to his associate directors and the office staff.

✦

He is very close to the hearts of his associates who look with pride and satisfaction upon his elevation to the great and exalted position of Grand Master.

✦

He richly deserves the esteem and admiration of his associates. He stands as a shining example of our American way of life. He has conquered handicaps of poverty. Knowing what it means to be poor and underprivileged, he has devoted himself to helping the less fortunate members of our community. We are happy to honor him and we look forward to working with him for the common good and for the welfare of our community for many years to come.

✦

He has rendered efficient, faithful and unobtrusive but invaluable service to our Association.

✦

His passing will leave an unfillable void in the minds and hearts of all those who knew him personally.

✦

For his tireless efforts, unfading loyalty and devotion

on behalf of the fraternity, and the sincere affection he has shown his brothers, we take this occasion on the 25th anniversary of the founding of the fraternity, to tender this scroll as evidence of the high esteem in which he is held by all the members.

✦

For the past 25 years John Doe has rendered faithful, conscientious and valuable services to our organization. Despite the fact that during this period of time, occasions have arisen when his health was impaired, nevertheless, with great personal inconvenience and sacrifice, he carried on his responsibilities. The Board of Directors make formal acknowledgment of its appreciation of the services rendered by him during the years of his leadership and duly acknowledge the substantial contribution which he has made to the organization during the past 25 years. It is the sincere hope of the members, officers and Board of Directors that he will enjoy many more years of good health and happiness.

✦

John Doe, as president of this organization, served for many years with loyalty, honor and distinction; in his official acts he was governed by a keen sense of duty and always showed a unique grasp of human problems; he always sought to aid his fellowman in an hour of need, and for these reasons he gained and maintained the admiration, esteem and affection of members and his colleagues. Therefore, we herewith give expression on behalf of the members of our sense of loss and deep regret on his retirement and extend our best wishes to him for a long and happy life.

For his leadership in gaining public support for the national program of education and service so vitally needed to combat a serious threat to the nation's health. . . . . .

✦

We do appreciate the energy, the enthusiasm, the resourcefulness and the skill with which you served as campaign chairman for the March of Dimes drive. We hereby salute you for the success that crowned your efforts in this noble community project.

✦

His humanitarian sympathies and inspiring efforts during the national campaign to gain public support for research, education and community service made him the individual most responsible for the successful initiation of the program so essential to our nation's health. In recognition of all this, the testimonial is awarded with grateful appreciation.

✦

The Board of Directors extend to you, John Doe, on your birthday, July fifth, many good wishes for your health, happiness and prosperity. It is our fervent hope that you be spared for many years to come so that you may continue to guide the Board of Directors.

✦

In appreciation of the rich contribution made by the Tribunal to the common objectives of enlightened thinking and democratic living through the medium of intelligent, fair-minded journalism.

✦

Sincerely, quietly, modestly and with grace and dignity has John Doe demonstrated his patriotism and his deep interest in the welfare of the members. For his generosity and loyalty to them; for his graciousness, devotion, courtesy and help to the members of the Association, and his many acts of public service, this testimonial is given by his brethren.

◆

His passionate interest in life was to see that the individual was given the freedom to be heard; and to this end he fought relentlessly against all forms of censorship, intolerance, and political, social and economic oppression. He had the courage of his convictions and the ability to exercise them.

◆

Eminent statesman, distinguished teacher, editor and author in the fields of history and political science. Man of noble spirit, humanitarian principles, and one who possesses a compassionate understanding of the suffering and persecuted. His high moral integrity, lofty ideals, broad sympathies, and unselfish devotion to democratic principles has won for him the love and affection of freedom-loving people throughout the world. Saintly in character, liberal in spirit and vigorous in mind.

◆

The Association, cognizant of the unique part Mary Doe has played in advancing its power and prestige, delights to record in this her 60th year the affection and grateful regard in which she is held by all of its officers and members, and to express to her their best wishes for continued health and happiness.

Illustration 1 — Resolution of Praise

RESOLVED, that the Executive Board recognize the long services rendered by John Doe in the various positions held by him in this organization, and appreciating his faithful services therein for the past fifteen years, wishes him all the happiness he so justly merits by his good and loyal conduct during his long connection with it.

RESOLVED, that this resolution be entered into the minutes and a copy be presented to John Doe.

Illustration 2 — Resolution of Praise

WHEREAS, this month marks the completion of the 5th year Reverend John Doe has served Hope Church as its spiritual leader, and

WHEREAS, during these five years Hope Church has expanded its physical facilities with the addition of a new community center and schoolhouse, and has enlarged its services to members and their families, and has extended the curriculum of the religious school, and

WHEREAS, this growth on the part of Hope Church has been due in large measure to the inspiration, zeal, devotion and leadership of Reverend John Doe,

NOW, THEREFORE, BE IT RESOLVED that we, the Board of Trustees of Hope Church, do hereby express our sincere thanks and appreciation to Reverend John Doe for his achievements on behalf of our Church, and it is further

RESOLVED, that this resolution be spread on the minutes of this meeting, be published in the next issue of the Bulletin and also be read at the next annual meeting of the congregation.

Illustration 3 — Resolution of Praise

WHEREAS, John Doe has completed 25 years of service as President of Local 234, and

WHEREAS, by his zeal and generous labors he has helped to improve the working conditions of our members, and by his dignity and sterling character gained the love and esteem of his devoted brothers,

NOW, THEREFORE, BE IT RESOLVED, that the entire membership unite in giving this testimonial to their beloved and honored president as a token of heart-felt appreciation for his untiring efforts.

Illustration 4 — Resolution to Aid Charity

WHEREAS, The Medical Center has always supported the March of Dimes to help fight infantile paralysis, and

WHEREAS, a great majority of those afflicted must look to the National Foundation of Infantile Paralysis throughout the country to provide funds for medical and hospital care to help them on the road to recovery, and

WHEREAS, this care is being provided regardless of age, race, creed or color,

BE IT RESOLVED, by The Medical Center, that we commend to our members the March of Dimes drive for special and extraordinary support, individually and collectively.

Illustration 5 — Resolution of Thanks to Press

WHEREAS, the press has lived up to its highest tradition of accuracy, fairness and comprehensiveness in its coverage of this conference,

THEREFORE, BE IT RESOLVED, that this organization go on record as expressing its deepest thanks to the press.

Illustration 6 — Resolution of Thanks for Hospitality

Resolved, that most cordial thanks be tendered to the Association for the kindly welcome and generous hospitality which have been extended to the delegates, and for the arrangements which have been made for their further reception and entertainment at the places to be visited in the coming weeks. It would be impossible adequately to express the gratitude felt by every member of the delegation for the kindness which has been showered upon all. The delegates can only ask the Association to believe that the sentiments now recorded are expressed with the deepest sincerity and in the hope that they will be regarded as strengthening, renewing and extending the many friendships which were made here.

Illustration 7 — Resolution of Thanks

WHEREAS, John Doe has rendered loyal and faithful services as president for the past ten years, and before that as a loyal member, and

WHEREAS, he has exhibited marked ability, deep interest and uniform attentiveness and has fulfilled his office with credit, and

WHEREAS, the Executive Board wishes to express the sincere appreciation it and the membership feels for the fine and faithful services rendered by John Doe,

THEREFORE, BE IT RESOLVED, that John Doe is deserving of the tributes paid to him, and further,

RESOLVED, that a copy of this resolution be printed in the Souvenir Journal to be published in connection with the Testimonial Dinner to be tendered to John Doe.

Illustration 8 — Resolution of Tribute

WHEREAS, it has been the Will of Almighty God to remove from amongst us Brother John Doe who has been a most valued member, ever active in the affairs of the Club since 1928; one who throughout the years has served the Club loyally, generously and unselfishly,

THEREFORE, BE IT RESOLVED, that the Officers and Board of Governors do hereby record this expression of sincere and enduring grief which has been sustained by the Club of which he was so faithful and prominent a member.

5. Testimonials

Frequently a testimonial dinner is tendered to a deserving person. In conjunction with the dinner a souvenir journal is often printed. Testimonials or greetings, which are messages of praise and tribute, are printed in the journal. Examples of such testimonials are given below.

Illustration 1

It is a privilege to extend to John Doe our sincere greetings in recognition of his many years of faithful service to the organization which he heads. He has served his membership faithfully and deserves the high esteem in which he is held. On behalf of my organization, I extend sincere greetings to him and all those in attendance at this Testimonial Dinner.

Illustration 2

I have known John Doe for the past ten years and have worked with him during that time. His diligent and courageous efforts to bring about better conditions in the industry have been eminently successful. It is because of men like John Doe that we have prospered and I cannot let pass this opportunity to express my sincere appreciation of his achievements. This is my testimonial to a good, sincere labor official.

Illustration 3

I consider it a privilege to greet you on the occasion of this splendid dinner in your honor. During the years I have had contact with you, I have learned to respect the ability and good sense you have brought to your work. As a leader of your community, you have demonstrated courage and vision. Whether at the conference table, in private meetings, or on the platform, your measured words have always produced a keen respect for your wishes and warm, human understanding. I am happy to join with your many good friends in paying tribute to you this evening.

Illustration 4

We send you our warmest congratulations on the occasion of your 25th anniversary and the testimonial tendered to you in celebration of that event. You can well be proud of your quarter century of service. Accept our best wishes for your continued success.

Illustration 5

Congratulations and many happy returns of the day are my wishes for your 25th anniversary. It is not the years a man has lived, but how much he has accomplished, that indicates his usefulness. You are blessed with an irrepressible spirit and a dynamic energy, transmitting your power to others. This is proved by the enviable reputation, influence and prestige of the organization of which you have been such an important part. May you continue to enjoy splendid health.

Illustration 6

It is to you, John Doe, our first president, that we owe the existence of our Association. You were the founder. It was in your brain that the idea of founding an association germinated. To carry out that purpose, you gathered around you a group of distinguished persons whose labors culminated in the organization of the Association. Your interest in the group has never wavered. You have been the guiding hand throughout those vital, formative years. This testimonial is a fitting ribute to you.

Illustration 7

The excellent work done by Mr. John Doe during the many years of his leadership of your organization clearly warrants this Testimonial Dinner. The strength and recognition attained by the organization are a silent tribute to his able efforts.

6. Announcements of Meetings and Functions

In group activities the occasion to tender a testimonial dinner to a deserving person is a frequent occurrence.

The requirements of a letter or statement announcing a testimonial dinner, a meeting or other function are a statement of (1) the purpose, cause or occasion, and (2) the invitation or request to participate.

Illustrations of letters and statements normally used for such occasions appear in this chapter. The complete illustrations follow the material in Step one and Step two.

1. The purpose, cause or occasion

To provide funds for the maintenance and upkeep of the club and to insure a continuance of entertaining monthly meetings, a souvenir journal will be printed in conjunction with our Annual Installation and Dinner.

✦

Here's a chance to have a good time enjoying one of the season's funniest comedies and at the same time help the Community Fund. As you have doubtless guessed, it is a theatre party. The show is "Community Antics," written by Richard Jones.

✦

Once again the opportunity is afforded us as members of the community to participate in its charitable activities. Just such an activity is the dinner which is being given in honor of Sam Brown, on behalf of our hospital fund.

✦

On May 19th at 5:00 P.M. we will have a meeting at the Hotel Main and we want you with us. The purpose of this meeting is to discuss a plan we have formulated to "do something" for our president. We know you are among those who respect and admire our president. We need help to carry out this plan.

2. The invitation or request to participate

It is a real pleasure to extend to you a most cordial invitation to attend your school's Charter Day Celebration to be held in the Main Hall on November 12th at 6:00 P.M.

✦

Since I know that you are a personal friend of our guest of honor, it is my pleasure to extend to you and your wife a cordial invitation to be our guests and enjoy the evening with us at that time.

✦

Please do your utmost to attend and bring with you any of your friends who would be willing to assist us. We want this afternoon to be the beginning of the most successful campaign our community has had. Your presence will help assure this.

✦

The contribution you make above the box office price helps the sick and needy.

✦

I urge you, therefore, in order to help us pay proper tribute to him, to let me know on the enclosed card that you will be with us at his testimonial dinner on December 1st.

✦

I would like, therefore, to have you join us on December 1st, at the Plaza. There will be no engraved invitations and no fund raising. Tickets are $5. We have less than a month to do it in. You know how we put off send-in reservations and such. Would you be good enough to return yours today. Thanks a lot and please let me hear from you.

You may obtain tickets by sending your check to the theatre. Those who cannot find it convenient to attend, may be inspired to make a donation to the Foundation.

✦

Your participation in the past has proved that you are willing to extend your help to the needy. Your active help is needed to make the campaign successful.

The need this year is greater than ever before and we feel that we can rely upon your coöperation to help us make this year's drive an outstanding success.

This is a purely voluntary proposition. Nobody is going to be asked to work or contribute funds unless he offers to do so.

✦

The committee urges every member to attend the December 1st meeting. At this meeting a vote will be taken to determine whether the club favors the establishment of a Housing Authority. If you find it impossible to attend, please cast your vote by returning the enclosed card.

Illustration 1 — Testimonial

I know you will be pleased to learn that a testimonial dinner will be tendered to our esteemed president, Mr. John Doe, on the completion of ten years of service to the Sutton Association. The dinner will be held at the Plaza Hotel on December 1st. Mr. Doe has demonstrated time and again a deep understanding of our problems, and by a fair and just administration he has won the respect and affection of everyone. When the idea for a testimonial dinner was first advanced, the response was so spontaneous and so overwhelming that the plan soon became an accomplished fact. I know that you and your wife will want to join us in doing honor to Mr. Doe.

The dinner will be a delicious one with music, dancing, and a minimum of speeches. Tickets are $10 per person, with the net proceeds going to a charitable organization. Let me know the number of tickets you desire by filling in and returning the enclosed card. Tickets are selling rapidly and the committee wants to make proper allocation of the limited number of reservations available. Let me hear from you very soon, please.

Illustration 2 — Reserve Now!

Because of the splendid coöperation of the members, the outlook for the John Doe testimonial dinner is most favorable. In fact, the possibility is strong that we will be oversubscribed. It would be very unfortunate if we had to turn down any member who wishes to be with us on that gala night. We cannot overcrowd the room. 350 will be our limit. That number can be handled comfortably. Please mark this: We have reservations for over 250. If it is your intention to attend, please send in your reservation early. Mail it to Secretary Smith.

Illustration 3 — Ad for Journal

On Saturday evening, December 1st, the Sutton Association is sponsoring its 20th Annual Entertainment and Dance at the Plaza Hotel. This year we are honoring John Doe's ten years of devoted and loyal service to the association. In connection with the dance we are printing a souvenir journal. A contract for the journal is enclosed. We feel confident that you will want to be represented in this journal. Please return the contract with your remittance to the journal chairman, Mr. Walter Whalen.

Illustration 4 — Greeting for Journal

The Craft Union is tendering a testimonial dinner to Robert Roe, its president, on the occasion of his completion of ten years of service to it. A souvenir journal is being published in connection with the event. You have met Mr. Roe on many occasions, and have had frequent contact with him, particularly during the last mayoralty campaign. It would be appropriate to print your message of greeting to him as Mayor of this city in the souvenir journal. We would appreciate it if you would forward your copy to us so that we can send it to the printer no later than December 1st.

Illustration 5 — Appreciation for Good Wishes

On behalf of the Sutton Association I wish to thank you for your message of congratulations and good wishes upon the occasion of your 20th Anniversary. Your letter symbolizes the fine spirit of friendship and cooperation between our organizations and it is most sincerely appreciated.

Illustration 6 — From Guest of Honor

I am the guest of honor at the charity dinner to be held in the Community Center on Wednesday evening, December 7, at 7 P.M. Ordinarily, when arrangements are being made for an occasion such as this, the guest of honor should be seen but not heard. But everybody knows that charity dinners are different. Here, I am merely a symbol for something more important. The Fund needs money to enable it to carry out its program to maintain the institution for which it is responsible. I appeal to you to consider the problem of the Fund when making your contribution. A reservation card for the dinner is enclosed. Your check made out to the Fund should be in the amount of $5 for each person attending the dinner. I look forward to greeting you there.

Illustration 7 — Dinner Schedule

Final arrangements have been made to assure the outstanding success of the testimonial dinner to Robert Roe. So that you may derive the fullest enjoyment from the evening's events, your coöperation is solicited. All guests must arrive at the ballroom of the hotel no later than 6:30 P.M. on Saturday, December 1st. Dinner will be served promptly at 7 P.M. This schedule must be maintained so that the events of the evening can go on as planned. Yours for a memorable evening.

Illustration 8 — Reservation Acknowledgment

Thank you for your reservations for the dinner in honor of John Doe on December 1st, 6:30 P.M. in the Plaza Hotel. We appreciate the support that you are giving the community and we are sure that the dinner will be made more impressive by your attendance. Please remind your friends about the dinner as it promises to be a memorable tribute to John Doe and a helping hand to the community. Once again, thanks.

Illustration 9 — Reservation Reminder

We have not yet received your reservation to join us at the Plaza Hotel the evening of December 1st to do honor to John Doe for his services to the community. We believe this must be an oversight on your part. Final reservations must be made at least thirty days in advance. Your committee was given until November 15th to pay for all the reservations. We are enclosing a reservation blank and postpaid envelope for your convenience. We would appreciate it very much if you will fill in your reservation and mail it, together with a check payable to the undersigned. We anticipate the pleasure of seeing you at the dinner.

Illustration 10 — Serve on Reception Committee

I have been asked by the officers and directors of the Sutton Association to serve as chairman of the testimonial dinner to honor John Doe. I am writing to ask you to serve on the reception committee to pay a suitable tribute to our guest of honor who has done so much for so many people. The proceeds of this dinner will be contributed to the Fund to erect a clubhouse for thousands of boys in this and neighboring communities. Please let me have your acceptance. Your coöperation will be a source of encouragement to us.

Illustration 11 — Serve as Sponsor

On the occasion of John Doe's 10th Anniversary of service to the community, the members of the Sutton Association and his friends are tendering to him a testimonial dinner. It would be an honor to have you join with us as a sponsor of this dinner and to have your permission to place your name upon our letterhead. The dinner is to be held on December 1st at the Plaza Hotel and I am sure you will want to join us. Your coöperation will aid immeasurably in insuring the success of this affair. We anxiously await your reply.

7. Speech Openings

The audience's first impression is the speaker's chief concern. As he walks on to the platform, greets his audience, gives his first sentences, the audience is forming their first impression of him. He must win the approval of his audience for himself and his subject. The beginning should establish a friendly relationship between speaker and audience and arouse their interest in his subject and its development.

In the next few pages will be found sufficient speech openings to meet the demands of almost any normal situation and help the speaker off to a good start.

It is certainly gracious of you to listen to me at this very late hour. I, in turn, will be as brief as possible in discussing this tremendously important subject now under consideration.

◆

It is hardly necessary for me to say that I consider it a very great honor to be asked to occupy this platform for a few moments.

◆

I appreciate very much this opportunity to meet with you men and women, and I am deeply grateful for the confidence and for the honor that you have done me.

◆

I am deeply honored by the invitation extended to me to address you this evening. It is always a pleasure to come here. I have pleasant memories of my visit about a year ago when I was a guest at your round table conference. I remember vividly the difficult questions that some of you asked then and I hope that I am prepared to answer a few more tonight.

◆

I fully appreciate that at this hour, and after the entertaining addresses we have listened to, it would be an imposition to attempt to hold your attention except for the briefest time.

◆

I regard the privilege of addressing you as imposing upon me two obligations: first, that of being brief; second, that of saying such things only as are calculated to merit the attention of men whose time is as precious as yours is. For breach of the first obligation I should be without excuse but the second involves such difficulties that I must rely upon your kind forbearance if I fall short.

✦

When I have recovered, Mr. Chairman, from your kind but too generous introduction I will, I hope, get my mind sufficiently cleared to make a few pertinent remarks.

✦

It would be very difficult, indeed, for me to express adequately my appreciation of the honor which has been conferred upon me by inviting me to address this great gathering.

✦

We are about to perform one of the most sacred rites incidental to our membership in this great organization, that is, the installation of our newly elected officers.

✦

These induction proceedings are becoming quite a habit, but I think they are very proper because they express the desire of the organization to pay tribute to one who richly deserves the honor.

✦

Agreeable to the established tradition of this organization, the president is expected to make a report. The hour has now come. With your indulgence, I will do so, and I think within 15 minutes it will be over.

✦

I deeply appreciate the privilege of addressing the organization from which in so short a time and from such humble beginnings this vast, influential and strong association has grown. This organization has prestige; it has strength. May it always continue to use its position for the common good!

♦

It is good to be home again. As I have gone about the state I have had many cordial welcomes and friendly receptions but none has touched me as deeply as the heartwarming greetings from my friends and neighbors in this town. There is no place like home.

♦

It is a great joy for me today to be here to introduce the speakers on this very delightful occasion.

My function is to act as presiding officer and to introduce to this audience those who have asked to participate and give expression on this occasion of their regard and affection for our guest of honor.

♦

I have called this conference at this time for the three-fold purpose of, first, meeting you personally and giving you an opportunity to look over your new president; second, to outline briefly the policy I shall adopt in the administration of the organization; third, to set forth the results of my survey of the organization to date and the initial steps upon which I have decided.

♦

I have attended enough conventions to know how you feel after a week of it. You have visited all the museums, art galleries and other cultural monuments of the city and you are beginning to weary. And, of course, you have to listen to speeches, too. I console myself with the thought that this punishment, while cruel, is not unusual.

We are embarking tonight upon a new venture, the formation of a civic group for the purpose of protecting and advancing the interests of the residents and to foster a healthy interest in the civic affairs of the community. Since we are all bound together by a desire to make our community a friendly and wholesome place in which to live and bring up our children, we are all hopeful that our common goal will be attained.

◆

This is the 10th annual dinner, and with no immodesty, it can be said that we have grown in membership, and have become stronger in prestige and influence.

◆

We have met for a special purpose tonight and that is to honor a man whom we all esteem and love, a man who has had a distinguished career. The sentiments of the Association will later be expressed by the one selected for that purpose.

◆

You may have noticed that on our program we have the song we all love so well, "America," and I am going to ask you, after the first toast, to sing that song. I now ask you to rise and drink to the President of the United States.

◆

All of us are agreed that more participation by the citizens in public affairs is not only desirable but imperative. The problem we are here to discuss is how we can achieve that—by what ways and means.

◆

The distinct privilege of opening this pleasant ceremony has been accorded me and naturally I must be brief because of the speakers who are to follow.

✦

It has indeed been a cherished privilege that was accorded me to be the presiding officer of these ceremonies.

✦

I would like to render a somewhat free-style account of my brief stewardship as the Secretary of the organization.

✦

If you will permit me, I will use these few notes, not to encourage the expansion of my remarks but as an anchor to keep me nailed down to a short space of time.

8. Addresses of Welcome

As the presiding officer or his designee you welcome guests and members. It is your duty to be gracious. In most cases you will be acting as spokesman for a group. Make it clear that the greeting comes from all and not from you alone. There are several examples of addresses of welcome in the next few pages. Almost any one of them can be adapted to your needs.

Illustration 1

I want to assure you that our welcome to you is warm and heartfelt. We hope you will enjoy our city and that the friendships made here may grow and deepen. We hope you will have time to enjoy many of the unrivaled beauty spots of the state and its many facilities for recreation. We want to do everything possible to make your visit here memorable. We hear so often that the city is a cold place—but those who live here know that this is not true. We have made arrangements to show you the warmth of hospitality that exists here. May your gathering here be a successful and enjoyable one!

Illustration 2

The Community welcomes you to her heart with all the warmth and fervor which she accords to the homecoming of her own sons and daughters, among whom you are numbered by adoption during the next few days. We hope that your meetings will be so marked with success that you will immediately begin making plans for a return visit to this community. It is our hope that your deliberations may be fruitful of good to all of the peoples represented and that lasting friendships may here be cemented. We greet you not as strangers, not as mere acquaintances, but as friends. We want you to know that we will do everything in our power to make your stay here a pleasant one.

Illustration 3

We are indeed very grateful that you are here. We hope you will enjoy yourselves and that you will return to your homes with pleasant recollections of what you have seen and done here. If there is anything that we can do which we have not already done to make your visit more pleasant, we are yours to command. To be a host to such a gathering is an honor of which any community might well be proud.

Illustration 4

It is a very great pleasure for me, as the Mayor, to extend to you the warm welcome of this City. You have many problems to consider. A glance at your agenda is sufficient to indicate the range. You have not only a heavy task but a great responsibility. Many eyes are upon you today. I hope you will find here the satisfaction and guidance that you wish for, and that your meetings will meet with every success.

Illustration 5

I am performing here today one of the pleasantest tasks of my career: that is, welcoming you to this distinguished organization. It is going to be a pleasant association. I am sure that the organization has never responded more warmly to any appointment than it has to yours. I am sure that the staff will serve under your direction with the greatest of pleasure and with full coöperation. To have you as a co-officer is a matter of great personal satisfaction to your new colleagues.

9. Introductions

The object is to create a desire to hear the speaker you are introducing. The situation requires a brief statement of the speaker's background, his qualifications for handling the subject, and his name. Laudatory remarks are appropriate but should not be overdone. In this chapter are examples of complimentary remarks followed by illustrations of introductions.

HOW TO INTRODUCE IMPORTANT PERSONS

Governor (out of his own state)	"The Governor" "The Governor of New Jersey
Mayor	"Mayor Jones"
Senator (U.S. or State)	"Senator Sampson"
Member of Congress (or State Legislature)	"Mr. Brown, Congressman from Georgia"
Cardinal	"His Eminence, Cardinal Stanton"
Roman Catholic Archbishop (There is no Archbishop in U.S.)	"The Most Reverend, The Archbishop of Chicago"
Bishop (either Roman Catholic or Protestant)	"Bishop Land"

Priest	"The Reverend Father Delaney"
Monsignor	"Monsignor Hogan"
Protestant Clergyman	"Mr. Kirk"
(if D.D. or LL.D.)	"Dr. Kirk"
(if Lutheran)	"Pastor Kirk"
Rabbi	"Rabbi Lane"
(if D.D. or LL.D.)	"Dr. Lane"

Examples of Complimentary Remarks

He is a man of science, learning and skill. His profound knowledge and experience have won for him widespread recognition in his profession. Like many men of accomplishment, he is unaffected and unassuming.

✦

He has performed his official duties with unswerving integrity and fearless determination. His forthright, frank and honest attitude in relation to public matters stamps him as being destined for higher office and responsibilities.

✦

He gives lavishly of his time and effort. His sincerity and integrity have earned him the respect and admiration of all of us.

✦

We are aware that many men who attain high positions continually grow in stature. From the very beginning the career of our next speaker has been one of continuous growth.

He has always been a champion of civic betterment and a tireless advocate of honest government.

✦

He represents a rare combination of judgment, social imagination, immunity to pressure, and fidelity to truth.

✦

Under his leadership we can look forward to a brilliant future and increased success for our association.

✦

He is a fluent speaker, a man of extraordinary vitality and great administrative ability. He is certain to be a source of strength to the administration in the solution of its problems.

✦

He has a knack of taking the audience into his confidence and no audience is proof against his expansive charm.

✦

Through her intellectual force and the warmth of her understanding she has done much to explain the international scene to her audience.

✦

We all admire his penetrating insight into the complexities of the international situation. He is indeed a most remarkable journalist.

✦

His contribution to a better understanding of Europe's problems will not be forgotten. He brings to the muddled international affairs a clarity of thinking and interpretation which is unmatched.

He has performed his arduous tasks with a seriousness, a sense of responsibility, and a feeling for the gravity of the issues involved which deserves the highest praise.

◆

His industry and sincerity have made for him a host of friends and have earned the respect of his colleagues.

◆

He is a man of great character and wonderful temperament who enjoys a splendid reputation for integrity, honesty, and loyalty.

◆

He has many attributes of the successful advocate: a fine presence, quick wit, commanding eloquence, and an enormously persuasive manner.

◆

He is a champion of unpopular causes; a man who never lets the prevailing opinion divert him even an inch from the course he thinks is right.

◆

He has demonstrated his warm-hearted humanity and deep concern for the welfare of his fellowman by unceasing service and devotion to myriad philanthropic causes.

Illustration 1

In introducing the Mayor, I present to you a man who at all times has championed the interests of the civil employee. He has never hesitated to make known his sympathy for the white-collar class, nor has his stand ever been a source of embarrassment to his administration. I am pleased to present Mayor Jones.

Illustration 2

It is a great honor to have with us the Governor of the State of New Jersey. In addition to gracing this occasion by his personal presence, it is a special tribute to our guest of honor. Governor Brown, we welcome you here as a true friend. We are honored to have you with us. It is a privilege to call upon you at this moment. Ladies and Gentlemen, the Governor of New Jersey.

Illustration 3

We are to have the pleasure of meeting and listening to an address by Senator Weston. He responded to our invitation with refreshing speed and enthusiasm. He is a great American, a distinguished member of the Senate and a good friend. I present Senator Weston.

Illustration 4

I am happy to present to you a newly elected member of Congress who made a great campaign when the odds were much against him. I present Mr. Wilson, Congressman from Ohio.

Illustration 5

The next speaker is one of the honored gentlemen of this community. He is widely known as one who has held many important offices and who continues to hold public office. He is a member of the State legislature. I take pleasure in presenting Mr. Samuel Shield.

Illustration 6

I have the great privilege of presenting the Most Reverend, The Archbishop of San Francisco. He is a highly regarded representative of a great religious organization. He is a philosopher, a scholar, and a humanitarian. He has built up to a high point of efficiency the splendid diocese over which he presides. He is loved by all people, regardless of religious affiliation. He belongs to all of us. The Most Reverend, The Archbishop of San Francisco.

Illustration 7

We are fortunate in having the Reverend Father Delaney as guest speaker for our meeting. The subject of his talk is one of which he is exceptionally well qualified to speak, with both wisdom and authority. I know we shall have a stimulating evening. The Reverend Father Delaney.

Illustration 8

I present Bishop Land who will pronounce the benediction.

Illustration 9

I am happy to present Rabbi Lane who has spoken to us before. On the other occasion he made a most favorable and lasting impression upon our hearts and minds.

Illustration 10

I present a member of the Board of Chaplains, Pastor Brown, for the opening prayer. Pastor Brown.

Illustration 11

I now give the audience the real gift of the occasion, the man you have been waiting to hear, our guest of honor, John Doe.

Illustration 12

It is particularly appropriate to have with us tonight a devoted colleague of our guest of honor. I know he did not expect to be called upon, but may I invade his privacy to ask him to say a few words, or take a bow. Mr. Fred Frost.

Illustration 13

Our secretary has rendered most valuable services to our organization. No man has served with a greater degree of integrity and sincerity. We cannot appraise adequately the value of his services, but it far exceeds the compensation we pay him. I present Mr. Samuel Wright.

Illustration 14

I would like to pay my respects to Mr. Bernard Banks, our treasurer. I have had the good fortune of knowing him for many years. I doubt if any organization has a better watchdog of the exchequer than we have. He is what a treasurer should be. He is constantly on his guard to see that no money is spent foolishly. I hope he will consent to address you. Mr. Banks.

Illustration 15

I present to you the able, industrious, and efficient chairman of the ways and means committee, for his report. Mr. Robert Roe.

Illustration 16

We consider it a matter of great good fortune that Professor Stanton has agreed to deliver the first annual lecture. At the risk of carrying coals to Newcastle, I will give you a brief recital of the high points in the career of this distinguished scholar. Professor Stanton is the recipient of last year's scientific award. He represented American engineering and education organizations at two international conferences abroad during this year. He is the president-general of the International Congress on Coastal Engineering. It is with great pleasure and a deep consciousness of privilege that I introduce the lecturer, Professor Stanton.

Illustration 17

I am sure that our distinguished visitor fully appreciates the warmth of the welcome you have extended to

him. I can assure him that we are tremendously happy
because he is here. He is associated with the liberal, progressive, forward-looking people of our country. I am
pleased to present Sir William Church.

Illustration 18

Mr. Samuel Sampson has traveled a long way to bring
you a message that will be both scholarly and interesting.
He comes here especially qualified to speak to us upon
the subject. I present Mr. Samuel Sampson.

Illustration 19

I know you have been looking forward with pleasant
and happy anticipation to the message of a great American. He came here at a great personal sacrifice. I want
to assure him we are pleased and happy to have him
with us. I take great pleasure in presenting Mr. John
Jones.

Illustration 20

What shall I say about Alfred Alton? That he is a
gifted actor? Shall I enumerate the enormous range of
parts he has portrayed? The names of the Broadway hits
in which he has made theatrical history? Shall I tell you
he holds audiences spellbound and that this should be a
truly thrilling experience? Any attempt on my part to
embellish Mr. Alton's accomplishments with superlatives
is unnecessary. His very presence projects his person-

ality. I know what I shall say to you. It is my great privilege to present Mr. Alfred Alton.

Illustration 21

The chair recognizes a most beloved member of the community, who by his own character and attainments, is most worthy to eulogize the late John Doe. I present Richard Roe.

10. Thanking the Speaker

At the conclusion of the speaker's address it is the obligation of the chairman to thank him briefly and graciously. On the following pages are examples of remarks which may be used by the chairman to express appreciation and thanks.

Illustration 1

The audience has indicated in an impressive manner its appreciation of your eloquent and entertaining address. And it was thought-provoking, too. We thank you also for that graciousness, that friendliness of manner which has given so much charm to every moment of your presence with us.

Illustration 2

We are deeply indebted to you for your statesmanlike address. Although I have heard many good talks, I can say sincerely without any attempt at flattery that we have just listened to one of the most constructive and thoughtful speeches, on a subject of major interest, that has been delivered in many years.

Illustration 3

Thank you, Mr. Brown, for your excellent talk and the sincere way in which you delivered it. I know your message has made a deep impression upon our consciences.

Illustration 4

I am sure that I voice the unanimous sentiment of this meeting when I thank Mr. Brown for his contribution to a verv perplexing problem.

Illustration 5

I know we are all deeply impressed by the address of Mr. Smith. It touches us very deeply. He has left an imprint upon our memories which will remain with us for a long, long time.

Illustration 6

Much light has been shed by Mr. Doe on the confusing questions of foreign policy. We all liked his sincere, outspoken and courageous thinking and his refusal to succumb to mob hysteria. Your sincere attentiveness is eloquent appreciation of his talk. Thanks to him for his brilliant and courageous dissertation and thanks to you for being such an excellent and responsive audience.

Illustration 7

You have indicated your appreciation of the masterful address delivered by Congressman Brown better than I could. The people of this district are to be congratulated upon the exercise of fine judgment in electing this splendid, keen and vigorous man as their representative. He has shown vision and an understanding of our problems. The manner in which he delivered his message was most impressive and convincing. I predict for him a great future. We thank you profoundly for your address.

Illustration 8

I wish to add my words of thanks for the very notable talk delivered by Mr. Smith. The particular value of his address lies in the fact that his opinions result from an intimate knowledge of the facts and his experience with concrete cases.

Illustration 9

Senator, the audience has manifested its feelings of appreciation for your eloquent address by the volume of applause. We are grateful to you for your visit with us. Thank you.

Illustration 10

Thank you for expressing so eloquently the feeling that we have for a great leader.

II. Nominations

The elements of a nomination speech are (1) a statement of the qualifications of the candidate, and (2) the placing in nomination.

The nomination should be simple and concise. Under some circumstances, when the qualifications of the candidate are well known, the plain statement, "I nominate John Doe for President," is sufficient.

Material giving parliamentary procedure, and for composing the more embellished speech of nomination is given in this chapter, followed by complete illustrations.

PARLIAMENTARY PROCEDURE

CHAIRMAN: Nominations are now in order.

MEMBER: I nominate John Doe for president (or states qualifications and places in nomination).

(Nominations need not be seconded.)

CHAIRMAN: Are there any other nominations?

MEMBER: I move that nominations be closed.

CHAIRMAN: There being no objection, nominations are closed and we shall proceed to vote.

(After the vote, the newly elected president takes the chair and says: "Nominations are in order for vice-president." In the same manner the other officers are elected.)

1. Qualifications of candidate

There are certain requirements that the leadership of an organization of a thousand members must have and among these qualifications is that humble touch, that down-to-earth approach to problems. John Doe has these qualifications.

◆

He is a champion of minorities, a defender of human rights. He has often raised his voice against bigotry and intolerance. He is loved and revered by members of this organization. He is an asset to it.

◆

Time does not permit me to give a recital of the abilities and accomplishments of the man I desire to place in nomination but I think you know them as well as I do. Ten years ago you elected him secretary. He has served you ably, honestly and capably.

◆

It is not my purpose to deliver an oration regarding his qualifications because they are all well known. He has always placed his great talents at the service of his organization whenever there was a call to duty.

◆

He has been a distinguished public official but that is only part of the story. In both his public and private life he has demonstrated a deep and abiding feeling for those whose opportunities have been limited by circumstances or by cruel conditions imposed on them by events beyond their control. He has more than outstanding ability; he has a sense of compassion. The two together give him his distinction. They explain his sense of kinship with us and ours with him.

✦

It is significant that he has always served in positions where he could help people. The desire to do so must run very deep in the grain of his personality and beliefs. I do not believe that much more can be said for any man.

✦

As a Senator he has raised the prestige of a chamber where simple integrity and common sense have too often seemed at a premium. He has been a spokesman for all that is best in his party and a staunch supporter of the administration.

✦

There is a man in our midst who is endowed with relentless courage, vision, ability, and profound faith in humanity. At all times he has championed the underdog. If ever for a moment we lose faith in the ability of the nation to find capable leaders under emergency conditions we need only to remember that men like him come forth to give us leadership.

✦

Words are inadequate to describe the qualities of the man I will place in nomination. His record of service to the country equals his devotion to the nation.

I can assure you he possesses all the necessary qualifications—learning, patience, experience, a fine personality, integrity, and, of course, ability. He will serve well, if elected, and bring credit to all his admirers and friends, and great satisfaction to the community.

✦

He is a man of tested ability, sound judgment, and keen perception. He is possessed of a fine character. He is a sincere friend and a devoted worker. These are the attributes which qualify him for the office we are about to fill.

✦

John Jones exemplifies the highest ideals and standards of public service as a career. Modest, painstaking, thorough and devoted to his assigned tasks, his reputation for ability and fairness extend far beyond the borders of this community.

✦

While the offices he occupied all brought honor to him, he, in turn, brought honor to them by the manner in which he filled those offices far above any feeling of partisanship or any political advantage.

✦

He will bring to the office competence, a conscience and an understanding heart.

✦

His rise to his present position is the result of intellect, effort, character and integrity. His career, brief as it is, has already left its mark upon our society.

By his integrity and great learning, he has earned for himself a place of great distinction. He has made an enviable record.

2. The placing in nomination

I nominate for president of this organization a distinguished citizen, a peerless leader, Robert Brown.

✦

I deem it a great pleasure to present to you and place in nomination Mr. Robert Brown.

✦

I deem it a personal honor to have the privilege of placing in nomination the name of Robert Brown for reëlection.

✦

I rise to nominate Robert Brown.

✦

The man I place in nomination will follow the example which has been so worthily set by his predecessors. I submit the name of Robert Brown.

✦

My nominee, Robert Brown, will maintain the influence and the standard of this Association and he will discharge all the duties of the office to your satisfaction.

Illustration 1

I have in mind to fill my place, Mr. John Jones. I know him well. He is capable, he is qualified, he is responsible, he is reliable. I speak from experience. I have worked with him for 25 years day in and day out. When he says "yes" he means "yes"; when he says "no" he means "no." He is never on the fence. I feel that he will make an excellent officer. He is my friend, my co-worker, my co-officer. It gives me great pleasure now to nominate him for the position of treasurer.

Illustration 2

I assume that everyone knows whom I will nominate for President of this great organization. I know this man more intimately than any other person in our organization. I have worked with him as closely as two human beings could work together, building the organization, helping him make plans, helping him to create that fine feeling that exists right through our organization today. I have been his assistant, doing whatever I could in every possible manner to make his task easier. You have heard the glowing praise for him from the other speakers. They mentioned his part in the remarkable growth of this organization and the fine leadership that it has enjoyed. Why should I go any further? I nominate for president, John Jones, who is intelligent, an industrious worker, and who possesses a genius for making friends.

Illustration 3

I am not endowed with a great deal of eloquence. Even if I had the skill, I do not believe I could adequately describe the abilities and qualifications of the man

I desire to place in nomination. Such oratorical ability, however, is not necessary for he is well known and appreciated. His services to the Associations and his achievements are common knowledge. I know of no one who has been called upon so often to give service; I know of no one who has given that service as freely as he has. It is a distinct pleasure to place in nomination for the office of president, Brother John Doe.

Illustration 4

The man I am going to place in nomination is known to every active member. He is a friend of the rank and file. His ear and heart are open to all. Nearly everyone has gone to him for guidance and assistance at one time or another. No problem is too small for his thoughtful consideration. For ten years you have elected him to various offices. He has served you well. I deem it a personal honor to place in nomination the name of John Doe for reëlection.

Illustration 5

In order to save time, I nominate for reëlection for the ensuing two years all the incumbent officers to the positions they now hold, and I move they be elected by acclamation.

Illustration 6

I nominate a man who has stood every test. He has measured up to the many responsibilities of his office.

He served his apprenticeship in the junior offices faithfully and his experience now will serve the organization well in these days of stress and strain. It is my pleasure to place in nomination for the office of president, Mr. John Doe.

Illustration 7

Every institution is judged by its elected representatives. This organization has been most fortunate in its officers. They have been loyal men of the very best judgment and of high character. I desire to emphasize the qualities of the man I have nominated. He is able, a man of courage, and loyal to his organization. It is my honor to place before you for the office of president the name of Mr. John Doe.

Illustration 8

I deem it a signal honor to be given the opportunity to submit the name of one of the founders of our Association. He has successfully led our organization for the past few years. He has been a tireless worker and an inspiring leader; he has always been in the top rank of those who have guided us in the performance of our tasks. His colleagues and co-workers have turned to him again and again for advice, for coöperation, for "sacrifice beyond the call of duty"—and never has he failed them. Legwork and brainwork, or just plain hard work—in all of these he has set the example for others to follow. It is because of these qualities, and because he has won the affection and respect of all who know him, that I am privileged to nominate him to succeed himself as president. In reëlecting him we will reward him for his labors for the great cause which has engaged his heart and conscience. I nominate John Jones.

Illustration 9

Yes, words are truly inadequate to describe the qualities of the man I will place in nomination. He possesses all the attributes necessary for the office of secretary. He has worked unceasingly for the betterment of our organization. He has a great capacity for industry. We love him because of his humane attitude and his deep understanding of our problems. He can fill the office as no one else can. Therefore, I present the name of James Jones.

Illustration 10

I nominate for President, Mr. John Doe, a sincere friend, and generous benefactor of our Club. He, more than any one else, is responsible for our beautiful building. Not only did he give money freely but he gave generously of his time, going over every detail of the structure with the architect and the builders. His own good taste is reflected throughout the building. We shall never forget the notable occasion when our building was formally dedicated. It is therefore a cherished privilege for me to be permitted to offer his name for the office of president.

12. Installation Ceremonies, Inaugural Addresses, and Tributes

Installation (Induction) Ceremonies

Examples are given in the pages which follow of rites installing the president, vice-president, secretary and executive board. The ceremony of inducting persons into membership in a union is also given. These forms may be easily converted or adapted to fit similar occasions in other organizations.

Installation (Inaugural) Addresses

The important elements of the installation or inaugural address of an incoming officer are (1) an expression of appreciation for the honor, and (2) a pledge faithfully to perform the duties of the office.

Tributes to Installed Officer

Often one wishes to pay tribute to the person who is installed to office. Such tributes are composed of two elements. The first is praise for the person, and second, good wishes.

Examples of each of the two steps, followed by complete illustrations, are given.

In composing other types of speeches of tribute, this chapter and other chapters of this book will provide an abundance of material.

INSTALLATION (INDUCTION) CEREMONIES

Illustration 1 — Introduction by Chairman

We are gathered here for the purpose of inducting our newly elected president. Many prominent citizens have graced the presidency of this important society. It is a great honor and distinction to become its head. Here we deal not in monetary matters but in protecting the life and liberty of human beings charged with offenses against the law. The office of president of this society requires a man of experience, ability and fortitude, with a knowledge of life, and above all, a heart and mind imbued with a passion for justice. We are fortunate, indeed, that Sam Jones was selected by the membership to this exalted office. By dint of his own energy and ability he has achieved a notable career, and by sacrifice and devotion he has attained a reputation of being one of the most charitable and civic-minded citizens of our community. Small wonder then that so many people have gathered here to pay him tribute. We extend to him a hearty welcome. I predict that he too will become one of our great presidents. I am mindful of the fact that the chairman is not expected to make a lengthy speech so I will proceed at once to the business before us and call on the distinguished personages who have come here to honor him.

Illustration 2 — President (Fraternal)

It is now my function, as it is my privilege and pleasure, to induct our new president into office. As I hand you the emblem of office as president, it is a great satisfaction to me to welcome you as my successor. You are in every way worthy of the honor conferred upon you tonight. For many years you have served us ably and well. I am sure that you have the same great love for our fraternity that I have. I know that the leadership which you now assume is in very safe and capable hands. And now, with my best wishes and every confidence in your success, I turn over to you the presidency and the leadership of our order. May I leave this closing thought with you: "Nothing succeeds like successors."

Illustration 3 — President (Union)

Brother Jones, you have been chosen to preside over the destinies of Local 234 for the next two years. The president's first duty is to lead the local to success and prosperity. Upon your skill and ability depend its honor, reputation, and usefulness. It will be your especial duty to preserve its reputation and dignity. You are to permit nothing to tarnish its excellent reputation. It is your duty to remind the members of the fine traditions of our union, of the sacrifices made that they may enjoy the prevailing terms and conditions of employment. You should be as careful of the reputation of our local as you would of that of your family. It is also your duty and no doubt it will be your pleasure to teach our members to be good unionists, sober, industrious, and to do all things to be a credit to it. A president's paramount duty is to preserve peace and harmony—a matter on which no specific instructions can be given.

The powers you possess are extraordinary powers. You have powers that the presiding officer of no other organization has. You are admonished not to exercise that power in an arbitrary or dictatorial manner, but with a determination to administer impartial justice to the end that peace and harmony may be preserved. The president whose rule is just and fair will gain respect and support even from those who do not agree with him. When necessary, however, authority should be used fearlessly and firmly. The president has a duty to those who follow him to hand down the office with its dignity, its rights, its privileges and its responsibilities unchanged. I will now administer the oath of office: "Do you solemnly promise that you will serve the union as president for the next two years and will perform all the duties appertaining to that office to the best of your ability?"

Illustration 4 — Vice-President

The International Constitution states that the vice-president is to perform all the duties of the president in his absence and to take the chair whenever he requests. You have heard me describe the powers and responsibilities of the president. Those powers and responsibilities are also yours. (Administers oath.)

Illustration 5 — Secretary (Fraternal)

The secretary's duties are substantially of a business character, and are of the highest importance to the welfare of the lodge. Punctuality in attendance at the meetings of the lodge is an indispensable requisite of the secretary. He should be first in his place at its meetings, and the nature of his duties is such that he can scarcely avoid being the last to leave the lodge room. He is particularly charged with the duty of watching the proceedings of the lodge and making a complete record of all things proper to be written; to keep the financial accounts between the lodge and its members; to receive all moneys due to the lodge and pay them into the hands of the treasurer; to prepare the annual reports for the Grand Lodge; to have in charge the seal of the lodge, and to perform all other duties pertaining to the office, as may be ordered by the presidents.

Illustration 6 — Secretary (Union)

The skillful performance of your duties are of the highest importance to the welfare of the union and its members. The qualities which distinguish a good secretary are quick comprehension, prompt attention to business, sterling integrity in all his dealings with the union and its members. Your records as secretary constitute the current history of the events of the union. The records you prepare will be conveyed to future generations and will be the monument by which your work will be remembered. Your own honor and the confidence the members repose in you will arouse you to that faithfulness in the discharge of the duties of your office which its important nature demands. The office of the secretary is the most responsible and important office that the members of this union can confer upon a man. It should be given only to men of the strictest integrity. But once a union has a true and trusted secretary, it should not dispense with his services, but continue to elect him as long as he can be prevailed upon to serve. A union which has secured for this office a man who is as interested in his work as you are will do well to value him highly and retain him in the office until he grows gray in the service. (Administers oath.)

Illustration 7 — Executive Board

Each of you has been elected by the membership to serve two years on the all important executive board.

The responsibility of the executive board cannot be overstated. In the last analysis it is you who make or break a union's efficiency. The executive board is often the court of last resort. You are the court which decides grievances. Every member of the executive board should make a determined effort to gain a reputation for fair dealing. You must try to see the point of view of the member who is being judged by you. Consider each case on its merits. Be willing to accept the logical conclusion flowing from the facts even if it involves some concession on your part. Keep an open mind and listen to both sides. (Administers oath.)

Illustration 8 — Union members

We have been joined together since 19⎯ to build a strong union, to improve conditions, to obtain better working conditions. Great sacrifices were made by our members to realize these aims. The rise of our union has often been compared to the rise of our nation. Every American is acquainted with the story of how thirteen weak colonies won their freedom from the English kings by organizing themselves into a union of states. As it was then, so it is true with us. Hundreds of workers, who were weak by themselves, united to get rid of the sweatshop. These hundreds laid the foundation of our union. But just as the thirteen states—once they won their freedom—grew to forty-eight powerful states composing the greatest nation on earth, so our little union has grown in membership, in prestige, and respect. Our members now enjoy many rights. They cannot be discharged at will. They are guaranteed sanitary conditions, minimum wages, maximum hours, vacations with pay, welfare funds, insurance, sick and health benefits.

Now that you have heard what the union is and does, it is up to you to decide whether you wish to be a member and whether you wish to assume the responsibilities which union membership carries with it. If you so decide, you may take the pledge. Before reading the pledge, I should like to know whether you have any questions. There being none, will you please repeat after me: "I, John Doe, do hereby solemnly and sincerely pledge to obey the laws of the International Union and Local 234 to the best of my ability and to bear true allegiance to my local." You are now members of the union. You will be presented with a copy of our union constitution. Read it; know it; let it be your guide.

INSTALLATION (INAUGURAL) ADDRESSES

1. Appreciation

The honor that has been conferred upon me is a great one. That I should have been thought worthy of this high distinction arouses in me mixed emotions of humility and profound gratitude.

✦

I am sure you realize that I am grateful to you for this honor. I have a sense of my inadequacy to preside over this great organization, but I will do my utmost to justify your faith in me.

✦

This new distinction which is about to be conferred upon me brings up a sense of pride and humility. I renew my resolution to try to merit the confidence which has been reposed in me.

I devoutly hope that I will justify the confidence reposed in me by the Mayor, the political party which nominated me, and the voters who elected me.

✦

I realize the grave duties and responsibilities of the high office to which I have been elected. I enter upon my duties with a sense of humility, with an awareness of the attendant obligations, and with anxiety lest my abilities fail to keep pace with my eagerness to render the service you expect.

✦

To take the oath of office as president is always a solemn occasion. The responsibility of directing the affairs of this great order is never to be lightly undertaken. I am fully aware of the magnitude of the responsibilities of this office. I am alert to the duty I owe the members of this proud organization.

✦

I am so pleased with it all that my cup of happiness is filled to overflowing. This day will remain in my memory forever, brightening every dark moment and lifting any shadow that may cross my path.

✦

May I tell you how grateful I am for bestowing this honor upon me? Your loyalty and faith in me will be my greatest assets in the administration of my new office.

✦

The enthusiastic support which has come from the membership has been inspiring and a stimulant to me.

l extend to them, my heartfelt thanks for this highest honor in their power to grant.

✦

Let me say without hesitation that I accept this great honor. I accept it with pride and gratitude and a full heart. Most of all I thank you for the confidence you express in me. Today, I thank you in words. After today, I hope to translate my appreciation into deeds and conduct.

✦

I am indeed as humble as I am proud of your decision to confer upon me the leadership of this organization. To those who have worked so hard to make this occasion a success I extend my thanks. Your kindness and the warmth of your friendship will not be forgotten. It is great to know you and to work with you. Thank you again.

2. Pledge faithfully to perform the duties of office

I pledge my best efforts as your president to continue the glorious work of our organization. I know I can count on your support and coöperation. With it, I cannot fail.

✦

In this staggering task you have given me I shall always try "to love justice, to do mercy and walk humbly with my God." In the language of my oath of office and in conformity with the spirit of that oath, "I will faithfully discharge my duties to the best of my ability." My every effort will be exerted to justify the expressions of praise and confidence uttered here tonight.

◆

With the help of the Divine Creator, I shall strive to be a capable, conscientious and humble presiding officer.

◆

I will be faithful in the discharge of my duties. I will be courteous and considerate of all. I am fully aware of the duty I owe to the membership and shall discharge that duty to the best of my abilities.

◆

I recognize clearly the weight of the responsibility that you have placed upon me and I assure you that I shall never give short weight to those responsibilities.

◆

I am grateful to you for the confidence which you have in me and I pledge to give to you and to all the members the best that is in me.

◆

I solemnly promise the members that my devotion is to them and only to them. I will try to justify the confidence they have placed in me.

Illustration 1

To all my friends I wish to express my gratitude and thanks for having taken time out to come here, and for the good wishes so many of you have sent to me. I took the oath of office to carry out, to the best of my ability, the duties of president of this great organization. I shall endeavor to do this with, I trust, the assistance and coöperation of my friends and the members of this organization. Once again, I thank you all.

Illustration 2

I assure you that I am touched by your demonstration of confidence, and feel very deeply the responsibilities that rest upon me in this position. These are very trying days, days when all the qualities of constructive leadership are put to a severe test. Therefore, I am under no illusions. While I am very happy over this wonderful expression of confidence, I realize that the work of the ensuing year is going to be increasingly difficult. I renew all promises I made the first time I was elected to this high office. I will apply myself, God willing, to the task and do the best I can.

Illustration 3

Let my first words be those of gratitude to all of you for having elected me as your president. This is a great association and it is a great honor to be its president. But I am very humble when I think of my illustrious predecessors. The power and prestige which it now enjoys reflect so greatly the loyalty and the devotion of their great talents to its cause. Yet, I have complete confidence, despite my own limitations, that this administration will measure up and will carry forward the banner of this association.

Illustration 4

It is not my purpose at this hour to weary you with a long speech. It would be a poor return for the great kindness which you have shown in selecting me as your president. It is an honor that I greatly prize and my only regret is that I may not be able to follow the splendid example of my predecessor—a man who with distinction and success has administered and watched over the affairs of this association during the past year. He has administered its affairs in a way that has made it a subject of regret that he could not be persuaded to continue for another term. It is my distinct privilege to pay him this tribute of friendship. It is a great privilege that you have conferred upon me. Not only because you have selected me as your president, an honor which I cherish greatly, but because my selection has afforded me this opportunity of expressing my respect and admiration for the guest of honor. For your kindness in selecting me as your president for the coming year, from my heart, I thank you.

Illustration 5

I am very happy to be here today surrounded by my family, my colleagues, my co-officers and by the president of the Grand Lodge who has just sworn me in. I want you all to know I am deeply grateful that you are here today. I shall at all times do my level best to justify the confidence you have reposed in me.

Illustration 6

This is the first opportunity I have had to thank you for the very great honor which you have conferred upon me. In this distinguished audience, I take upon myself in all sincerity the obligation to discharge the duties incumbent upon the president of this association to the best of my ability. I know that I shall have your coöperation without asking for it. I hope that we may carry on during the coming year and that we shall all work together for the greater prestige of our association.

Illustration 7

To you, I trust, this has been an impressive ceremony. To me, as you probably realize, it has been doubly so and almost overwhelming. I am especially grateful to the membership for electing me to this high post. I will endeavor as best I can to carry on the position of president in such a manner that the confidence reposed in me by the membership will be justified.

The praise has been overwhelming and overgenerous but after it has been sufficiently discounted it has nevertheless been music to my ears. To all my friends I wish to express my gratification and thanks for having taken time out to come here and for the good wishes so many of you have sent to me.

Illustration 8

You have placed an obligation upon my shoulders and at the same time imposed a trust upon me. The obligation is welcome. The trust, I assure you, will be fulfilled. I want to thank the members for the great honor of electing me to the high office and to my friend, our outgoing leader, for administering the oath of office to me. I thank the officers for many acts of kindness, consideration and helpfulness which they have extended to me since my election. I hope I may continue to receive the benefit of their experience and wisdom.

Illustration 9

I am mindful of all the duties and obligations that go with this office. I would accept it with great misgivings except that I am assured that I am, for a time, to be captain of a ship in which every member of the crew is capable of being captain and in which there is a spirit of coöperation that makes holding office easy and pleasant. Relying on that spirit, I have accepted this position, and it shall be my earnest endeavor while I am captain of the ship to hold it on that fine course which was so ably chartered and so faithfully followed by all my predecessors.

TRIBUTES TO INSTALLED OFFICER

1. Praise for the person honored

Your appointment is cause for deep satisfaction because the office is one of national distinction. The society is to be congratulated upon obtaining the services of so able a man as you are. Your accomplishments and career have left an imprint upon the people of our community whom you have served so faithfully for many years.

✦

He is a great American with faith in the American people and in the democratic processes. His convictions and faith show through everything he has said and has written.

✦

Your distinctive attributes have brought you signal honors as you reach another milestone in life's journey.

✦

You can take pride in the fact that your faithful performance of an exacting and vital duty has contributed much in maintaining the people's respect for our government.

✦

You have the artist's sensitivity to people and situations. You seem to know instinctively how people think and feel and your personality reacts automatically to every change in the atmosphere.

✦

Genial, companionable and cultured, you have endeared yourself to all with whom you have come in contact.

✦

No one in this community exceeds you in the possession of integrity and ability. You are proof that unassuming, able and conscientious public service does attain, at times, its just reward.

You are a true, selfless citizen and a loyal public officer. Your sense of honor and your integrity are qualities which we should all try to emulate.

✦

You are scrupulous, fair and impartial. You are gentle, understanding and considerate. You embrace the principle that loyalty runs in two directions.

✦

The appointment of a man of your attainments is the best assurance that the task will be capably performed. Your acceptance of this post may well be hailed with satisfaction.

✦

You have the rare quality of being able to unite all who work with you into a cohesive unit. This is because you have taken the time to know personally and closely all with whom you have been associated.

✦

I rejoice with you on this wonderful opportunity that has come to you to serve your community.

✦

You have established yourself as a friend of the underprivileged. Your humane philosophy, your capacity for understanding, and your tireless efforts on behalf of those less fortunate are the qualities which endear you to all. You rank very high, indeed, among the friends of the needy.

✦

It is impossible to translate into words the respect and admiration for you that I see etched upon the faces of your friends assembled here to pay you homage.

As you would expect of a man of his breadth of interests, he has been active in all manner of fraternal, civic and philanthropic organizations; so many that I wouldn't attempt to detail them to you.

2. Good wishes

As one of the many in whom you evoke admiration and respect, I take this occasion to wish you every happiness.

✦

In concluding, I want to do my bit to give you a good, big, hearty send-off and to wish you well.

✦

I need hardly express the hope that this will be a stepping stone to even greater honors in the future.

✦

I hope that you will derive from your work the satisfaction that comes to a man from the knowledge that he is serving mankind.

✦

We hope that God's grace will accompany you throughout the remainder of your life and that He may grant you peace and enjoyment.

✦

It is my sincere wish that the relinquishment of the cares which you have borne so faithfully will result in your improved health.

✦

We hope you may live to a ripe old age so that you may enjoy the companionship and society of your family and the satisfaction of knowing that yours was a job well done.

✦

I hope that the future will bring you everything that you could wish.

✦

We wish you good luck and happiness in your new position.

✦

I have every confidence that you will be eminently successful in any enterprise you undertake. God bless you and may you continue to enjoy life at its best.

Illustration 1 — To installed officer

You have demonstrated your ability for leadership; you have shown great industry in your work and eloquence in the meeting room. Your most important quality, however, is your absolute fairness. No man who has ascended to the presidency of this organization has enjoyed a finer reputation than is yours. The membership has deep respect and warm affection for you. On behalf of your co-officers, I congratulate you and wish you long life, happiness, and continued successes.

Illustration 2 — To installed officer

You are exceedingly well equipped for the high office you are about to assume. You are an industrious worker. Your sterling character, great ability, and high integrity are our assurances that you will carry on in the finest traditions of our order. I have no doubt that you, who are possessed of such fine attributes of mind and heart, will enjoy a long, happy and successful career, and that you will be a credit to the organization, to your friends, and to yourself. To me has been assigned the pleasant task of administering to you the oath of office. Please repeat after me: "I solemnly and sincerely promise and swear that I will serve the organization as president for the next two years and will perform all the duties appertaining to that office to the best of my ability." I congratulate you and now pronounce you the president of our organization.

Illustration 3 — To installed officer

This is rightfully an occasion for celebration. It is difficult for me to say what is in my mind and heart without repeating, because everything has already been well said. The privilege of greeting you as our new president thrills me. You have made an enviable record and have won the confidence of the members. You have earned the privilege of leading them for the next two years. My best wishes to you for a successful administration.

Illustration 4 — To installed officer

We, your junior officers, rejoice with you in the fact that you have been chosen for the responsibility of this high office. We know that your judgment, experience, and energy will guide you successfully through the years of your presidency. We pledge ourselves to work in harmony with you to the fullest extent. We cannot think of a more vital message than this: "Go forward with strength and conviction to help you fulfill our highest destiny."

13. Retirement Addresses and Tributes

A retiring officer, such as the president of a club, generally expresses his thanks to the organization and his associates for their support and assistance in carrying out the duties of his office. He begins by expressing appreciation for the honor of serving and the support he has received, and he concludes by offering good wishes to his successor.

The speeches which follow illustrate the ideas presented in this preface.

The farewell speech, is a speech of tribute to the outgoing or retiring officer, follows a similar pattern that is, appreciation for the person who is retiring and good wishes for the future.

1. *Appreciation*

I have stated many times, both publicly and privately, my high regard for the members and my colleagues. I have learned to admire them for their personal qualities and have appreciated the splendid fashion in which they coöperated with me in the performance of my tasks. Nor am I unmindful of their unfailing courtesy at all times and of their loyalty to me.

✦

I want to tell you of my deep appreciation for the wise counsel and unwavering support I have received from you and for your great sacrifice of time and energy.

✦

I am deeply grateful to the membership and to my associates for the confidence which they have placed in me and I pledge myself to give to my distinguished successor, the best that is in me.

✦

I have received your generous support of every part of my program and I, in turn, pledge to my successor who has been a tireless and unselfish worker for the organization, my whole-hearted support and coöperation in the administration of this important position.

✦

I want to express to the members my great appreciation for the coöperation they have given me as president.

✦

May I tell you how grateful I am for your unselfish help during my term? Your faith and loyalty were my greatest assets. I hope I may continue to come to you for inspiration.

✦

I want you to know how greatly I appreciate the splendid support and coöperation which have been given me during my tenure as chairman.

✦

I am grateful to my fellow officers for their confidence in me in the past and particularly during the current year when they were confronted with an issue concerning me personally.

✦

The enthusiastic support with which the members have favored me has been an inspiration and a great comfort. I extend to the membership my heartfelt thanks for their loyal support.

2. Good wishes to successor

To my mind you are the greatest leader the organization has had and my admiration and respect will always be yours. You can count on my all-out coöperation.

✦

It will be a privilege to serve this organization under your inspiring leadership. I have supported and endorsed all your proposals and will continue to do so.

✦

I wish you a successful administration and express the

hope that, should you find that I can be helpful at some time in the future, you will not hesitate to call upon me.

✦

I pledge my fullest coöperation to the new president and his administration. We will make a united effort to meet the present problems facing the organization by the most effective means.

✦

I know you will supply the necessary inspiration and enthusiasm to carry our aims into effect and that your administration will go down as one of the most successful.

✦

I congratulate you and hope that your tenure of office will be happy and successful.

✦

I heartily approve of your program. You are deserving of the highest praise, and will have our consistent support.

Illustration 1 — Retirement Addresses

I can hardly realize that four years have passed since I first appeared before you to take my oath of office as president of this organization. The intervening years have been full and difficult. Busy as they were and great as have been the burdens, I enjoyed my years as president and I am grateful for the friends I have made here. I am particularly indebted to that loyal body of members who have worked so faithfully with me. Their confidence and support made my task easier.

My illustriouṣ successor can count on my whole-hearted coöperation during the four years that lie ahead of him. He is one of the sweetest-natured and most even-tempered men in the organization. It will be a joy to work with him. I know he will give of his real ability, freely, graciously and to the fullest possible degree. He deserves our coöperation.

Illustration 2

I want to express to you, the members of our organization, my great appreciation for the coöperation which you have given me as president. Your support has not been passive or mere approval; it has been spontaneous, active and enthusiastic. You have been loyal and unswerving in your support. I am very grateful. Many of you have willingly accepted difficult committee assignments. Many of you have taken time out from your vocations to render services to the organization at great personal sacrifice and some financial loss. As for my personal staff, no one could have had a more loyal and hardworking one and their devotion to me I shall never forget. The tributes that have come to me are not fully deserved. Nevertheless, it is gratifying to receive this recognition. I trust you will give to my successor that same degree of coöperation you have given me. You are a grand group of men and to each of you I owe my affection, gratitude and respect. God bless you and carry on.

Illustration 3

Two years ago I stood here your newly-elected president and stated that I was fully aware of my own limitations and had no intention of competing with any of my great predecessors in office. I expressed complete confidence that the administration then starting and now ending would fully measure up to our high standards. I based that confidence upon the assistance I was certain would come from the former presidents, the officers, the committees, and above all from the membership. My confidence has been fully justified. Thanks to all, the years have recorded a steady rise in the power and prestige of this association. Each month has been marked by a steady and healthy rise in our membership.

Now I come to the end of the road. The friendly coöperation and the warm comradeship of all of you have dispelled the difficulties; the path proved a pleasant one, and the two years, for me, were memorable and happy. You have answered promptly and wholeheartedly every call I made upon you for service. The two years have heartened me with their enriching experiences. They have brought me many new and wonderful friendships which are now among my most cherished possessions. My heartfelt thanks then to all of my fellow members as I step back into the ranks to serve under one whose record of accomplishments ensures us that under his leadership our beloved association will go forward to greater achievements.

Illustration 4

The many kind words which have been said of me on the occasion of my retirement, make me blush with embarrassment. I could not, without vanity, assume that I merit such praise though I cannot deny that I have tried to discharge my duties to the best of my ability. I can only thank you all for these expressions of your belief that I have made some approach to the ideal of a good president. I am profoundly grateful to the members who helped me to serve them. It is literally true that my service has been a labor of love. Our choice for president for the ensuing two years can, of course, count on our coöperation. In spite of the many demands upon his time, the welfare of the society has always been his prime concern. He deserves all the help we can give.

Illustration 5

It becomes my duty to turn over the emblem of my office to my distinguished successor. I have greatly enjoyed this period of service and have prized the privilege of trying in some way to add to the effectiveness of this organization. The incoming president is one who has long labored as chairman of one of the most important of our committees. His contribution to the organization has been so great I am sure the organization has enhanced its own importance by selecting him as its next president. I venture to say that no one among the members has given more lavishly of his time than has the gentleman who will now take the gavel as president of our organization.

Illustration 6

It is our custom at this stage of the dinner for the retiring president to hand the gavel to his successor in order that the new president may entertain and put the motion to adjourn. We are most fortunate today in electing as the president for the coming year a man of wide experience and great ability. We are assured of a great president. He is also a man of so kind and lovable a nature that it will be a joy all through the year to have him preside over our meetings. I have the greatest pleasure now in handing this gavel to John Jones.

Illustration 7 — Tributes to Retiring Official

I will avail myself of the opportunity to refer briefly to the purpose of this event. We are here as friends and associates of John Doe to express our good wishes and affection for him. John has just completed 25 years of service to our organization. During that time he labored unceasingly as our secretary and has earned surcease from his duties. It is proper that we pay him these tributes he is about to receive. I am pleased to introduce the speakers who will honor him and give him a good start on the road to retirement.

Illustration 8

We are sorry to learn of your impending retirement. You have been a sturdy fixture of our organization in one office or another for many years. You have been a decided credit to us. The many fine tributes which were paid to you are an inspiring manifestation of the high esteem in which you are held. I want to supplement them by adding a personal expression of deep regard for you. Your unfailing courtesy, the high fidelity with which you performed the most difficult tasks, and your great sacrifices on behalf of our organization more than justify all the nice things which have been said about you. God bless you and may you continue to enjoy life at its best.

Illustration 9

Your decision to retire as vice-president has been received by us with deep regret. I regard your retirement as a personal loss. The ties of nearly 20 years are not easily broken. For a man of your vigor and devotion to duty, I know this decision was a difficult one to make. However, you have the satisfaction of knowing that everything you undertook was ably and conscientiously performed. Your service as vice-president has covered a good part of the history of this organization. You participated in planning policies which have more than doubled its membership, increased its efficiency and its prestige. Your faithfulness in attending and participating in the meetings of the Executive Board has not gone unnoticed. My own work as president has benefited from the example and counsel derived from your seniority in years and experience. For that I thank you. It is my earnest wish that the relinquishment of the cares which you have borne so faithfully will result in your improved health. Our selfish feeling of personal loss is tempered by the hope and belief that the change will result in your physical betterment. Therefore, we say: Farewell; we'll miss you. May God bless you and prosper you!

Illustration 10

It is with genuine regret that I feel I must, for the personal reasons you gave, accept your resignation. The loyal service you rendered, the understanding you have shown of all our complex problems, the wise counsel you gave in seeking their solution, make your leaving a sad blow indeed. All the members of our organization, who know the quality and importance of these services, will share my feelings. Few of them, however, can realize the great courage and devotion you have shown in sticking to your post in the face of such compelling reasons of health. They will, I know, share with me the fervent wish for your speedy and complete recovery. It is my earnest hope that I may at some early date call upon you once again to help meet our organization's needs.

Illustration 11

With heartfelt regret and great reluctance, we see you relinquishing the symbol of your office as president of this association. I know how difficult have been the problems to which you fell heir when you took office. With all these problems you have dealt with rare tact and judgment. For all you have done you have earned the thanks of every member. Our regret at your leaving us, before the expiration of your term, is tempered, however, with the proud consciousness that you are soon to assume national responsibilities. I give you the assurance of your brethren that you take with you their entire confidence, their good wishes and their affection.

Illustration 12

Brother Easton, you have been a pillar of the fraternity in one office or another for the past 25 years. On December 31st you will have completed 25 years of service. As everyone here knows, you are a modest individual, very exact in the performance of your duties, a fine personality and a wonderful man. It is regrettable that illness now compels a retreat from fraternal activities. After 25 years of service to us you retire to the quietude of private life. May retirement bring back to you good health and may you enjoy happiness for many years. In saying farewell it is with the hope that it will not be good-bye but au revoir, and that you will come around to see us every time you get a chance.

14. Closing Remarks

As the chairman your function is not concluded until you have adjourned the meeting. You should express thanks for the interest and coöperation of the audience and bid them a cordial farewell. Be brief because the listeners will be making for the exits.

(Parliamentary Procedure: During a formal meeting when discussions are completed it is then proper to adjourn. Any member may rise and say, "Mr. President, I move we adjourn." The motion must be seconded. Then it is stated by the president and voted upon just as any other motion is. The chairman may say, "If there is no objection, the meeting stands adjourned.")

Illustration 1

I will conclude by wishing you good luck and saying Godspeed to all of you. But first I want to thank the chairman of the program committee for the thoughtful and splendid program which he projected and planned. And may I close this meeting with words which, in many languages, in many forms, in many religions, have brought comfort and strength. "May the peace of God, which passeth all understanding, be with us and remain with us always."

Illustration 2

We have come to the closing moments of the program and it falls to the president to say the last words of farewell. May I begin by expressing the deepest appreciation of which I am capable for the trust which has been reposed in me in selecting me to serve as your presiding officer. I have tried to justify your trust. I want to thank you all for coming here and I hope we will have the pleasure of seeing you again. Thank you.

Illustration 3

I ask that we now conclude these memorial exercises by rising for a moment of silent tribute to the memory of our beloved brother.

Illustration 4

I regret that we must conclude this discussion. Thank

you for the interesting and illuminating contributions you have made to our understanding of a most complex issue.

Illustration 5

I think everything that should be said or could be said on this occasion has been ably stated. I am not going to protract these proceedings any further by what would amount to mere recapitulation.

Illustration 6

I now declare this most interesting and inspiring meeting adjourned.

Illustration 7

I regret to say that the time has now come when we must conclude this discussion. Therefore, this discussion is now concluded with renewed thanks to our distinguished speakers.

Illustration 8

The hour is late and you have been most patient, kind and generous. The delay in beginning this ceremony was due to circumstances over which, I assure you, we had no control, and that increases my appreciation and my gratitude for your patience in having remained until now.

Illustration 9

In bringing this meeting to a close, it is with the feeling that much of a constructive nature has been accomplished, and I wish to thank the membership and the officers for making this possible.

Illustration 10

Our meeting has been a fruitful one. I believe we can all go to our homes secure in the knowledge of a job well done. Thank you and good night.

Illustration 11

In closing I want to thank the past presidents without whose inspiration our project, so satisfactorily accomplished, would not have been begun.

Illustration 12

I am advised that all of the business of this convention having been dispatched, my only function as your new president is to entertain and put the motion that this convention now adjourn.

Illustration 13

I now declare this very successful, useful and interesting meeting adjourned.

15. Congratulatory Messages

A message of felicitations and congratulations has three elements, (1) the offer of congratulations, (2) praise for the person, and (3) best wishes for success.

However, in telegrams, where brevity is desirable, not all of these characteristics need be given.

Material and samples of congratulatory messages are furnished in this chapter. If the form does not exactly fit the situation, it can be easily adapted or altered.

1. Offer of congratulations

I offer you my most sincere congratulations upon your success at the polls.

✦

May I add my felicitations to the many you have already received on your election.

✦

I am happy for this opportunity to add my voice to the chorus of congratulations.

✦

The 25th anniversary provides us with an opportunity to extend our warmest congratulations to your organization and its membership on its splendid accomplishments.

✦

I congratulate you warmly on this happy and memorable occasion.

✦

I could not let so memorable an event pass without sending you my hearty congratulations.

✦

I congratulate you and the members of your Association on the wise choice they have made in selecting you to lead them.

2. Praise

There are few men for whom I have the same deep affection and respect that I have for you. You are in every sense a leader of men and an ideal administrator. I am happy to be included among your friends. I am privileged to join the hundreds who on this occasion are paying you small homage, indeed, compared to your outstanding contributions.

✦

Your election is an inspiring manifestation of the high esteem in which you are held.

✦

This recognition is most appropriate in view of your many contributions to the progress of the lodge.

✦

This honor is well earned. It is not only a compliment for the past but reflects upon the future.

✦

This was a unique opportunity to reëlect to the leadership of your fine order one of the most sterling personalities in it. John Doe's wisdom and lofty idealism, combined with his vigor and unequaled experience, will be a tower of strength to you at a time when they are very much needed.

✦

Under your wise, fearless, and strong-hearted leadership the organization will increase in membership and influence.

✦

The excellent work done by you during the past many years clearly warrants this testimonial dinner. The strength and recognition attained by the organization during those years are a silent tribute to your able efforts.

3. Best wishes for success

We hope that you will enjoy a long, happy and successful administration.

✦

Sincere best wishes to you for a successful administration. May you continue to enjoy splendid health.

✦

My best wishes to you for the success of your campaign and for the wonderful work you plan to do.

✦

I hope that, no matter what the future holds for you, God will always shower upon you his choicest blessings.

✦

May Almighty God give you strength and wisdom to fulfill your responsibilities during the next four years.

✦

May you be blessed with good health for many years to come, so that you may continue to give your services to the people of this community.

✦

I pray and earnestly hope that the time is not far off when you will go on to even greater honors.

✦

We rejoice in the recognition which has been accorded to you by this community. We pray that God may grant you the years and health to pursue your arduous duties.

✦

We join with your many friends in renewed assurances of our own high regard.

I wish you well in the years ahead. I remind you that you follow in the footsteps of fine men who have gone from this school and have won well deserved public recognition and acclaim. You have a rich heritage. Preserve it well.

◆

May we have the benefit of your good health, happiness and leadership for many years to come.

◆

We hope that your tenure will be happy and healthful. Your colleagues will do everything to make it a very pleasant one for you.

◆

May the Sutton Association continue to carry on with vigor and effectiveness and may its first twenty years be but a mere beginning of its great service to the life of the Community.

◆

May I offer you my complete support and coöperation in this most important election. I know that the community will rally to your support.

Illustration 1

I congratulate you and wish you long life, good health and happiness. You have earned the gratitude of men and women throughout the City as a great leader in the fight for human decency and honesty in government. Under your inspired leadership I am sure the needs of the City for better housing and fuller employment will be met.

My best wishes for the success of your forward-looking program.

Illustration 2

Warmest congratulations to you upon your election as President. All of us in the association have good reason to be proud of the success you have attained. Sincere best wishes for a successful administration.

Illustration 3

May I add my felicitations to the many you have already received on your election to the Presidency. I think the members of your organization should also be congratulated upon their choice. I know you will be a credit to those who sponsored you. Best wishes for a successful administration.

Illustration 4

I congratulate you upon your appointment. You have always displayed an enlightened policy toward all city employes. You have mediated successfully scores of labor difficulties which otherwise would have resulted in the loss of wages to many workers. You have given the city an honest administration. I hope you will receive the recognition your brilliant skill deserves.

Illustration 5

The people of this City are fortunate to have elected

you as its representative. Your liberal and humane outlook on the problems of our times and your courage and
ability to do something about them, assures a successful
administration. Congratulations and may you continue
to receive ever greater rewards and recognition.

Illustration 6

After another election under our free, democratic
form of government, the people of our City have voted
to continue you in office. I congratulate you. May Almighty God give you good health to fulfill the obligations of your office.

Illustration 7

Your appointment deserves unreserved approval and
congratulations. Your eminence in the community, your
stature as a lawyer, and your notable experience in public
life all assure a continuing contribution. This is the sort
of appointment that inspires confidence in the courts.
The quality of the judiciary depends on the standard of
selection. We can depend upon you to make an addition
that will be widely felt to the general benefit.

Illustration 8

On behalf of my associates and myself, I wish to express our felicitations and congratulations upon your
appointment. When the vacancy occurred a few months

ago, we were glad to see that the appointment went to you. We join in wishing you a long and successful career in this most important office. I wish to add that from ~vhat we have seen of your work since you came here on a ⁺emporary basis, we are certain that you will discharge the duties of your office well and faithfully, and without fear or favor, and that you will do equal justice to the poor and to the rich.

16. Greetings

Greetings for special events are written usually for publication in the magazine or newspaper of an organization. In this chapter are illustrative greetings for the following occasions and holidays:

> Anniversary of organization
> Anniversary of magazine
> Birthday
> Christmas
> New Year
> Passover
> Thanksgiving Day

Illustration 1 — Anniversary of Organization

On the occasion of the anniversary we are celebrating, I wish to extend my greetings to the members whose support and coöperation have made it possible for the leadership to achieve so many notable successes. While our organization enjoys the respect of others, we don't intend to rest on our laurels. We are the first ones to recognize that perfection does not exist and that there is always room for improvement. We are aware that much is yet to be done, and that we cannot afford to remain inert. We must either go forward or backward. It isn't like us to go backward. A progressive organization must look to the future, more than to the past but, lest we forget, from time to time it is also important that we review our achievements and the failures of the past.

Illustration 2 — Anniversary of Magazine

On your 25th birthday a friendly salute, a warm typewriter toast. Through your example of accuracy, honesty and fairness, your magazine has exerted a great influence on the community. Your enterprise, ability, integrity and adherence to the principles of sound journalism are an inspiration to all reputable periodicals. Your courageous stand for truth has long been a fountainhead from which our community has derived nourishment and vigor in its fight for liberty and justice.

Illustration 3 — Birthday

As you celebrate your birthday I look anew, and with ever increasing admiration, upon your distinguished career. Few men in our organization have been privileged to serve in so many important capacities as you have and certainly none has done so with such brilliance and devotion. The officers and members of your organization are proud of you; they know you have used your great talents in the interest of all. May you have many more years of happiness and health and may we continue to have the benefit of your counsel and judgment.

Illustration 4 — Christmas

The spirit of Christmas is in the air. Christmas never fails to bring to mind the divine words "Peace on earth and good will towards men." So, on this Christmas Day, while we exchange good wishes and entertain visions of a better future for us and for everyone else, we solemnly dedicate ourselves to do whatever is in our power for the realization of "peace on earth and good will towards men." Within a few days our entire staff will be at their cheery firesides to spend the holidays with their families. Of the 365 days which constitute a year, none is so heartwarming as Christmas. This year we promise again, as in the past, to drink a toast on Christmas Day to our entire force which shouldered the burdens of the organization throughout the year. We can only conclude by wishing you and yours the Merriest Christmas.

Illustration 5 — Christmas

As we draw near the most joyous season of the year, I offer you our sincerest wishes for a most enjoyable holiday and our warmest and kindest congratulations. May the years which lie ahead bring you deep satisfaction and happiness in your accomplishments. A Merry Christmas to you and to those near and dear to you.

Illustration 6 — New Year

May I extend to you and your family best wishes for a very happy, healthy and prosperous New Year. With another milepost in sight and another year beckoning us with hopes and opportunities for service, we stop a moment to reflect upon our pleasant relations of the year about to close. It is, indeed, with gratitude that I look back upon the past year and thank you for your support and trust in electing me your president. And now at the very outset of the New Year, I appeal to you to attend the meetings. Your presence will be the barometer for our efforts. It will spur the administration on to greater achievements. It will be more than an indication of support; it will be an inspiration for even better programs.

Illustration 7 — Passover

It is again my privilege as Mayor to extend warmest greetings to all my fellow citizens of the Jewish faith on the occasion of the wondrous festival of Passover. As you celebrate your people's emancipation from slavery and their exodus from Egypt—which for 4,000 years has been your inspiration against the forces of evil and tyranny—may you be strengthened in your resolve to preserve the hallowed ideals of the Passover—liberation and freedom. The story of Passover is as fresh and appealing today as when it was first told in ancient times, and its message of freedom is no less moving and significant; for the struggle against tyranny and oppression, which Passover commemorates, is as old as the ruins of the Pharoahs and as new as the latest newspaper headline.

Illustration 8 — Thanksgiving Greetings

With so many other weeks in the year devoted to commercial or charitable purposes, it is good to have a week set aside for giving thanks. Thanksgiving is the time for enjoying the ritual of feast and family assembly. It is a time for counting our blessings and good fortunes. We, in the organization, may wish to add thanks for the privilege of giving service—perhaps one of the greatest privileges of all. Our organization tries to serve the aged, the ill, the needy. We should also add thanks that our forefathers patterned a community to serve the spiritual and material needs of a diverse people. We should give thanks that ours is a land where people can still laugh, and dream, and hope, and speak our minds and worship as we please. We have much to be thankful for.

17. Speeches for Special Occasions

This chapter deals with speeches to stimulate a group of people. The typical situations requiring such speeches are anniversary memorials, dedications, commencement exercises and the like. On these occasions there is the opportunity to recall the traditions and ideals—patriotic, religious and social—and to deepen the reverence and enthusiasm of the audience for the lives and principles of great men.

The examples given in this chapter by no means cover all the situations in which speeches to stimulate and inspire are appropriate. The illustrations given are:

> Birthday of a great person
> Commencement
> Memorial Ceremonies
> Dedication of Home for Aged
> Dedication of Plaque
> Friendship
> Greetings to Forum

Illustration 1 — Birthday of a great person

Yesterday passed quietly here in our wonderful country. Few took time to remember, but it was the birthday of a great American—Franklin Delano Roosevelt. As we think back on his life we realize the importance to all mankind of freedom from want, and freedom from fear, that he fought for so valiantly. He was stricken down fighting for mankind; he was literally killed on the battlefield of freedom. Today, freedom of speech, freedom of religion, freedom from want, and freedom from fear are further from reality than at any time during peace. Whether we have these great freedoms depends on Americans—it depends on whether we keep them inviolate here and let them extend throughout the world. The very thinking that these freedoms inspire destroys prejudice, promotes brotherhood, insures peace, and brings a glimmer of sunlight into the souls of men.

Illustration 2 — Commencement

To receive a degree from this school is an honor which is especially welcome to anyone who entertains—as I do —a profound and abiding faith in our American way of life. Here in Main School you believe in freedom of enterprise and you are dedicated to the proposition that individual success and social responsibility can and should go together. Perhaps that is why the contribution which this small school has made to good citizenship has been out of proportion to its size. Its alumni have achieved some of the highest positions of leadership in business and in the professions. That is a record of which you may well be proud and it explains why I am so happy to receive your invitation to participate in these commencement day exercises.

I am fully aware, however, that anyone who accepts such an invitation has a delicate task to perform. His first duty, of course, is to congratulate the members of the graduating class. For all of you it is my sincere wish that you will find in your business and professional lives a source of great joy and happiness. Today you become part of the world at a time when it is seriously disturbed. Never in our history has there been a greater need for wise, courageous and enlightened leadership than at the present. It is to you, and young men and women like you, that we must look for that leadership. May God speed you. May you find an interesting and satisfying lifework in a world at peace.

Illustration 3 — Memorial Ceremonies

I ask you to please rise for a few moments of silence out of respect to the memory of a man who was with us yesterday, serving with us the needs of the community. My heart is full, full of sadness, and at the same time full of gratitude that it was my privilege, as it was yours, to be associated with him in the work to which he had dedicated himself and to which you are dedicated.

John Jones was not only a devoted and loyal community worker but was much more. He was a good man. A man of integrity, of deep sincerity. He loved his fellowman. No one could help being at ease in his presence. It was his idea to make those around him feel he was their friend. His features instantly impressed one with their kindly expression, and with a warm handshake or a gentle touch on the shoulder he could win the heart of anyone he met. He gave himself to the work in which we are dedicated. He believed as we believe. He felt as we do. He shared with us our ideals, our thoughts and principles, our desires, and our dedicated service.

Now he has passed on. It is with a sad heart and a tearful eye that we prepare for the final farewell. I am sure, if anyone deserved a reward beyond this mundane world, John Jones deserves it fully. He earned it because of his services to his fellowmen in this world.

Illustration 4 — Dedication of Home for Aged

I congratulate the community upon the finishing, the perfecting, the forging of this appropriate and efficient Home for the Aged. The care of our aged is the holiest of all of our obligations. The obligation applies to us all individually and collectively. Our elders must be kept healthy and happy and we should not rely on government alone to take care of them. It is not only a real joy to be able to take care of those who have cared for us and brought us to this time of our lives but it is our responsibility. The average age to which people live has increased. When we live so long some of our later years are spent in declining health and strength. It is hard to dress and get about. We need a little help and later on a little more. Finally a steadying hand is not enough and the wheel chair comes. Many of our people in the seventies and eighties are up and about until the last day of life.

In an infirmary, while getting the help and kindness needed, life becomes pleasant to them to its end. On this day we accept with utmost gratitude and dedicate the Home for the Aged. I wish publicly to express my sincere thanks to the great many people who aided in bringing about the completion of this great work. I owe my thanks to the other members of the board for their very fine coöperation. I owe sincere thanks to our village president who aided me materially in this work. I owe thanks to a great many other men and women who by their contributions made possible this magnificent event.

Illustration 5 — Dedication of Plaque

This organization, for many years, has set aside a day in honor of our departed members. In doing so we are carrying on one of the many high traditions of which we are proud. We pause momentarily to reflect on the many noble deeds of our departed brothers. They helped establish the glorious history of this organization. We today are reaping the rewards of their steadfast loyalty to the principles of the organization and the many sacrifices they made. It is up to us who are here today to see that this great organization for which they laid the foundation perpetuates the good work begun by them.

Today we are assembled here for still another purpose.

That purpose is to erect a perpetual testimonial to the memory of the ten gallant and courageous members of our order who gave their lives to safeguard the principles for which our nation went to war. We dedicate this plaque as a reminder to our present members. I therefore unveil this plaque to their honored memory and the preservation of their patriotic ideals.

Illustration 6 — Friendship

In our lobby is a sign which reads: "The Spirit of Our Club: Under this roof you need no formal introduction. Speak to others as you would have them speak to you and do it first." We want to make this a friendlier environment. The art of making friends is simply to be a friend. To have friends you must be friendly. Many a man wants to extend his hand, wishes to say a cheery word of greeting, desires with all his heart to be "one of the fellows" but is too shy to do it. The root of personal shyness is the fear of being laughed at. No one will laugh at you here.

Friendliness begets friendliness. The man who is cordial will find hands springing out to meet his. He will learn that a genuine interest in a neighbor produces real interest in him. There is a simple formula for spreading the cement of friendship and brotherly love. It is composed of ten ingredients in about equal parts. Arranged in proper order, the first letters of this formula supplies a word which is the key to the whole mystery. I will let you discover the word for yourselves. The formula is frankness, responsiveness, idealism, enthusiasm, nobility of purpose, dependability, selflessness, harmony, industry and patience. And the word is—Friendship.

Illustration 7 — Greetings to Forum

It is my privilege to greet you and to extend a warm welcome to our Civil Liberties Institute. One of the fundamental principles upon which the Institute was founded is that people should be free to develop their faculties. We believe liberty to be the secret of happiness and courage to be the secret of liberty. We believe that freedom to think as you will and to speak as you think are indispensable to the discovery and spread of political truth; that without free speech and assembly, discussion would be futile; that with free speech and assembly, discussion affords protection against the spread of noxious doctrine. We believe that the greatest menace to freedom is an inert people; that public discussion is a political duty; that it is hazardous to discourage thought, hope and imagination; that fear breeds repression; that repression breeds hate; that hate menaces stable government. The Civil Liberties Institute hopes to make some contribution toward implementing these beliefs. We take encouragement and inspiration from your presence here and do indeed bid you welcome!

18. Speeches of Tribute to Deceased; Messages of Sympathy and Condolence; Notices and Announcements of Death

The tribute to one who has passed on, as well as the expression of sympathy and condolence or the announcement for publication, is a statement of (1) shock and sorrow, (2) praise or eulogy, and (3) sympathy and comfort for the family of deceased.

Following are expressions of the three elements which comprise the speech of tribute in which the speaker will recall to the minds of his listeners the virtues and qualities of one who is no longer with them. The illustrations which succeed these component parts are complete speeches of tribute.

The material and ideas presented may be used in composing written messages of sympathy and condolence and also announcements for publication in newspapers and periodicals. When brevity is necessary, as in a telegram, not all the characteristics described need be given.

1. Shock and sorrow

Again, with unexpected suddenness, death has come among us. John Jones has silently closed the door of life and departed from us never again to return. The shock of his death is visibly and profoundly felt by those with whom he had daily contact.

✦

It is with deepest regret that I announce the death of our friend, John Jones. I was grieved beyond measure to learn that death has removed him from our midst.

✦

Sorrow fills our hearts at this sad moment, a sorrow that is deep and personal. The news of the untimely death of John Jones came as a great shock. His departure was sudden, unexpected and particularly distressing.

✦

I wish to pause sadly to announce the passing of a very conscientious officer of our organization. The shocking news of his death has just reached me.

✦

The very sad tidings that Sam Jones had passed to his eternal reward came to my attention late yesterday. His passing was quite sudden.

✦

I was saddened by the news of the death of your devoted husband who was my faithful friend. My heart is heavy. His sudden passing was a great blow to those who knew him.

I could not hold back the tears when I read in the newspapers of the passing of my close friend.

✦

In the death of Joseph Lawton, the Bar mourns the loss of one of its able members.

✦

It is difficult indeed to find words to express our regret at the death of this splendid man.

✦

It is with profound grief that we learn that the inexorable laws of Fate has decreed that our good brother, John Jones, be taken from us and obliged to move through the Celestial Gate to enter that bourn from which no traveler returns.

✦

We interrupt the usual routine of the program to note the passing of a great public servant, an intimate friend and associate. We pause to pay our tribute of love and affection and respect to his memory.

✦

The lodge pauses to note on its minutes its great sorrow at the passing of Robert Smith who was a member for 25 years.

✦

We pause in our activities this evening to pay a richly deserved tribute to the memory of a devoted and highly esteemed officer of our lodge, Brother John Jones, who yesterday passed to his eternal reward.

2. *Praise or eulogy*

Despite his very active life in fraternal activities and the numerous demands upon his time, he was first and foremost a family man. He loved to be with his family. He was a devoted husband to his dear wife. He was an affectionate father to his children.

✦

The character of the life he lived might be summed up in a few words: he was sincere, he was earnest, he was loyal, he was industrious, he was self-sacrificing. I know no one in the fraternity who tried harder to interpret the wishes of the men he led and served.

✦

He was a splendid man, of great intellect and big heart. This loved and loving husband and father was also my friend and colleague through all the years when our work in the capitol brought us into daily association. It was my privilege to know him through most of the years he served as president of our organization. He combined with his charm an unlimited energy and the highest integrity. His genial personality and the generous instincts of this fine man will be missed not only by the officers but by everybody in the organization.

✦

My foremost thought at this moment is that the passing of so great a champion of civil liberties will be felt not only throughout the city but the nation.

✦

Our college will be a living monument to his foresight and his indefatigable devotion to youth, to education and to humanity. No one ever again will embody all his traits—his professional attainment, his courage, his dedication to service.

✦

In closing, I should like to paraphrase the words of the great Abraham Lincoln, who, in a memorable address, said: "The world will little note, nor long remember what we say here, but it can never forget what they did here." In this instance, Samuel Jones, an honored, respected, and revered member of our noble profession, gave of himself unstintingly to the preservation of human rights and liberties and was ever zealous to take and carry through to its ultimate conclusion the cause of those who needed sound, experienced, and wise counsel.

✦

Here was a man of superlatively high standards, complete integrity, and boundless enthusiasm for whatever task he took in hand. No one, whose privilege it was to know him, is likely to forget the candor of his speech, the courage of his faith, the warm and glowing brightness of his friendship. He never dodged a responsibility, never refused to take on a hard job if it needed to be done. What he preached, he practiced. What he believed, he believed with heart and soul. He fought hard for every cause in which he enlisted, and the causes for which he fought were good and right.

✦

He was a quiet, perhaps overly modest man, inclined to be extremely cautious in his personal relationships, acutely conscious of his responsibilities and prone to deprecate his own charms and abilities.

He verily and truly exemplified the spirit of our fraternity: "To help the needy, to succor the distressed, and support everything that is fine and noble."

✦

Her life was the epitome of courage, vision and deep faith—an example worthy of emulation by all who love their fellowmen.

✦

He held positions of trust and died in the full tide of a career which gave great promise of future usefulness.

✦

He was much esteemed in the community in which he lived and was generally recognized as one whose acts and deeds were worthy of emulation.

✦

To all of us in the industry he was and always will be an ideal. The example he set will long continue to influence and inspire us.

✦

We found him at all times a man of understanding, sympathy, learning and integrity.

✦

His untarnished life leaves with us an example and inspiration for higher and nobler deeds.

3. Sympathy and comfort

I extend to you my deepest sympathy.

✦.

There is little I can say that will comfort you in this hour of your bereavement.

Please accept for yourself, and all who mourn with you, our assurance of heartfelt sympathy.

✦

I, his many friends, and the community will miss him. His passing grieves me inexpressibly.

✦

No one can better appreciate than I, who am myself utterly heartbroken by the loss of my own beloved husband, what your suffering must be and I pray you may be supported by Him to Whom alone the sorely stricken can look for comfort in this hour of heavy affliction.

✦

All of us in the fraternity have suffered a heavy loss in his death.

✦

We feel a keen sense of loss in his passing. It is difficult adequately to express our grief.

✦

God bless you and keep you in this your hour of sorrow.

✦

We all felt his severe loss very deeply, but some small measure of consolation may be found in the words of the poet, Walt Whitman:

> He is not gone. He is just away,
> With a cheery smile and the wave of the hand,
> He has wandered into an unknown land,
> And left us wondering how very fair that land
> May be, since he tarries there.

May the bereaved family find solace in the inspiring memories of the exemplary life of the departed.

✦

We are all comforted in the knowledge that he lives in the minds and hearts of everyone. God bless you and keep you in your hour of sorrow.

✦

We join in extending to the members of his bereaved family our heartfelt sympathy and pray that in the years that lie ahead the good Lord will sustain them and give them peace and health.

✦

May his soul rest in everlasting peace and may the Almighty grant solace and consolation to his dearly beloved wife and the members of his grief-stricken family.

✦

His passing leaves a void in our hearts and in the organization that will be difficult to fill. It is with the deepest sorrow and the deepest grief that we learn of his passing.

✦

Words are futile at a time like this to assuage the anguish of his family or of his friends. We can only bow our heads to the will of God, the Father of us all, and say to ourselves:

Is there beyond the silent night an endless day?
Is death a door that leads to light?
We cannot say.

The tongueless secret locked in fate
We cannot know.
We watch and wait.

✦

May he enjoy his eternal rest and the rewards he has earned.

✦

May her family derive some measure of comfort in the knowledge that we share their grief with them.

Illustration 1

We meet tonight under the shadow of a great loss in the passing of our beloved secretary, John Doe. Though the certainty of death and the uncertainty of life is ever with us, each visit of the Grim Reaper brings new sorrow and humbles us in our mad struggle for glory and fulfillment of ambition. Once again, necessarily, we should pause to reflect and consider the life and the work of our friend, and from his achievements seek to gain inspiration and courage to meet the trials and the tribulations of ordinary mortal existence. As a leader of the community, and a man, he built a temple of honor and of virtue, of industry and of unselfish devotion to duty. To the members of the bereaved family we extend our profound condolences, drawing consolation in the fullness of his life's services to his fellowmen.

Illustration 2

Our secretary, John Doe, has been taken from us. Sorrow fills our hearts at this sad moment, a sorrow that is deep and personal.·The news of his untimely death came as a great shock. The simplicity and sweetness of his character have endeared him to us. In his passing I feel a personal loss too great to put into words. May his soul rest in everlasting peace, and may the Almighty grant solace and consolation to his dearly beloved wife and the members of his grief-stricken family.

Illustration 3

The sudden passing of John Doe was a great shock to those who knew him. He was fair, sympathetic, and always sought to do his duty honorably and justly. I can only add to what has already been said, that his loss is one which it will be difficult to overcome.

Illustration 4

It becomes our distressing duty to take notice of the death on Friday of John Doe, whose years of service were distinguished by his integrity and devotion to duty. By his death, his colleagues will miss a rare friendliness and charm of personality; this lodge will be deprived of the services of a valuable officer; and the fraternity will lose a faithful friend.

Illustration 5

It is impossible to speak of John Doe other than in superlatives. Loveable, gentlemanly, scholarly, kindly—

he was a man in the very best sense of that meaningful term. Those who knew him loved him; the better they knew him the more they loved him. He possessed great personal charm; men were drawn to him irresistibly. John Doe now rests in peace, but his noble and resplendent spirit remains to comfort us. He is deep in our hearts, and will continue there, warmly, as long as there is life within us. His sterling qualities and his great works live on.

Illustration 6

In the passing of John Doe I have lost a great and good friend, whose encouragement, counsel and wisdom have meant so much to me over the years. The cause of charity has lost a leader who gave unstintingly of his labor and his time. We shall all miss him. His passing is a great blow to his colleagues on the Board, where intimacy of association added love to the respect entertained for him.

Illustration 7

It was my good fortune to meet John Doe a few years ago. My contacts with him were frequent. He radiated from his personality a charm and sweetness. As we go through this busy life, each striving selfishly to survive, becoming callous to the sufferings of our fellows, it is remarkable and unique to meet a personality like that of John Doe. I know that the impress he left upon me was a durable one. I found him to be one of nature's own noblemen. He touched nothing that he didn't brighten and better. I don't think there is any man who came in contact with him who didn't add to his own determination to be better and more sympathetic and generous to his fellowman. His passing leaves a void in our hearts and in the organization that will be difficult to fill. It is with the deepest sorrow and grief that we conclude this tribute.

Illustration 8

We come together this morning to pay tribute to the memory of one of our members and brothers, John Doe, who has passed through the valley of the shadow of death from which no one ever returns. He was a loveable soul. We, his brothers, who admired him and loved him so much, simplify this ceremony in an expression that has never left my mind. It speaks volumes: "You never lose what you love if you love what you lose."

Illustration 9

Only today I learned your sad news and my heart is with you. I know you are grateful that your father knew no protracted suffering and that he enjoyed a long and full life. Some men ask for death in one way. Some would prefer it in another. John Jones found death in the midst of the discharge of his duties. Also, you have the comfort of knowing that the devotion shown him by you and his. other children enriched his later years. Withal, the loss of a parent is a sad thing and hard to bear. I only wish I knew of some way to help you through this heartbreaking time. I can only hope, that from now on, life will bring you only happy things.

Illustration 10

Let us pause to note that death has struck again. Death has removed from our midst Brother John Doe, a gifted and erudite newspaperman. In his passing, journalism has lost one of the leading editorial writers of this era. His was a career of incredible vigor and forcefulness. He was a relentless crusader for what he believed right. His claim to fame is secure. Sometimes we differed with him politically, but we recognized that he was a genius in his field. He left an indelible imprint on American journalism and the life of this nation. We feel a keen sense of loss in his passing.

Illustration 11

The untimely death of your son, Robert, has been a tragic loss. While no one can fully share the sorrow which the death of a loved one brings, he will be sorely missed by his friends, too. There should be some measure of consolation in knowing that he met death pridefully and manfully in the service of his country. May God bless you and keep you in this hour of sorrow.

Illustration 12

The shocking news of the tragic death of my colleague has just reached me. He was my warm personal friend. His passing grieves me inexpressibly.

Illustration 13

It is a shock to realize that John Doe, who was so good and so gifted, has passed to the Great Beyond. It is with a full heart that I offer you my deepest sympathy.

Illustration 14

I was saddened to learn of the sudden death of John Doe. I wish to convey to you and to the other members of your organization my deep sympathy upon the loss of this remarkable man. It was my privilege to know him through most of the years he served as president of your organization. He was a combination of unlimited energy and highest devotion. All of us in the fraternity have suffered a great loss.

Illustration 15

Though death has removed from our midst our beloved secretary, Harry Horn, his spirit and influence will abide with us and his example will be with us for many years. Our deepest sympathy to you and your family.

Illustration 16

The Community Council deeply regrets the death and feels the loss of the Reverend Father Donald Dolan, the great servant of the Lord in the church life of our community. He was the distinguished friend of all the community, regardless of race, or creed, whom he valiantly supported in their difficult times. They are grateful to him and devoutly bless his memory.

Illustration 17

The officers, Executive Board, and members of the Community Center sorrowfully announce the death of our president, John Doe, who for many years devoted himself unselfishly to the interests of the Center. His friendly and kindly spirit will be greatly missed by all of us who had the privilege of serving with him. Because of his interest in humanitarian endeavors, his loss will be deeply felt by a great many.

Illustration 18

The officers of The Welfare Fund wish to express their grief over the untimely death of Mrs. Mary Roe, who served as chairman of our Executive Board. She gave unstintingly of herself as a leader of women and devoted her life to the cause of philanthropy. The example of her courage will remain as a source of continued inspiration to all of us. To her family and many friends we extend our heartfelt sympathy.

Illustration 19

The founder of our organization, John Doe, our inspiring leader, was identified for 25 years with the struggle for decency, justice and security. He devoted to the cause of labor and to his country a sincerity of purpose and intelligence of outlook which are the hallmark of a great man. His passing removes from the scene a peerless partisan of labor who fought a good fight for trade unionists everywhere, and a dauntless citizen who persevered to achieve a better and more secure America in a better and more secure world. He will be mourned long and sincerely, not only by working men and women throughout the world, but by all who aspire to a better way of life.

Illustration 20

The lodge pauses to note its great sorrow at the passing of Brother John Doe who served as our president for twelve years. Brother Doe had been ill for some time, but he insisted on performing his lodge duties whenever he felt physically able to come to meetings. It was that devotion to duty which brought about several heart attacks culminating in his death. His untimely death at age 60 is probably the result of the tremendous force and energy which he had put into the various offices which he had graced.

John Doe, in his years of efficient service to the lodge and in the high quality of his work as secretary, has merited the commendation of his brothers. The officers and members on this occasion join in paying this tribute to a good and faithful brother. He lives in our memory as a kindly soul who helped his fellowman. May God rest his soul!

Illustration 21

No one has served the Church with more devotion or with such fearless courage as the Reverend Father John Jones. He was a champion of all causes he believed to be right. As a churchman and as a citizen he rendered faithful service. He will be long remembered for his many contributions to the life of our community. Not the least of these is the part he played in the development of the movement for slum clearance and his courageous support of racial justice. We pray the Almighty God may grant him eternal rest.

19. Hints for Effective Speaking

Preliminary Considerations

An effective speech is one in which the speaker accomplishes his purpose of communicating ideas to an audience in a manner pleasing to them. The speaker should strive to make a good first impression. As he walks to the platform, greets his audience, utters his first sentences, his listeners are forming their first impression. He must, in the first few minutes, win the audience's approval of him, his subject matter and its development. He must appear confident, relaxed, and enthusiastic. He must never communicate any apprehension to his hearers. Of course, he must be sincere. There must be honesty in composition as well as in delivery if the speaker is to win over his audience.

Preparation is the best known guaranty against a poor performance. Its lack is the most common cause of stage fright. A contractor would not build a house without a blueprint and a speaker should not venture onto the platform unless he has prepared and practiced his talk. The preparation ought to begin long in advance of the speaking date and the work on the speech should be frequent. It is hard to force the development of a talk; speeches grow and should be given time to ripen.

When a speech has been carefully prepared, the

speaker can face his audience with confidence and assurance that his purpose will be attained.

The actual method of preparation varies with the speaker. Some write out their speeches word for word and then commit the entire speech to memory. Too often the memorized speech results in a stilted, inflexible presentation. Others think through their ideas carefully, writing down only the barest skeleton of an outline. The best course is carefully to plan the speech and to outline it in detail. Writing out a complete draft is helpful but the wording should not be committed to memory. The speaker should practice his speech out loud, choosing his words each time as he goes along.

By practicing a variety of words the speaker will develop a flexibility of expression. The outline should be used to fix firmly in mind the sequence of ideas. With practice the gist and order of the speech will be impressed upon his mind.

As the speaker practices he may feel impelled at various points to gesture and to emphasize certain words and thoughts. Gestures and emphasis so added are all to the good. The value of gestures is that they assist in the communication of ideas, help to hold the audience's attention and serve as an outlet for the speaker's tension, thereby increasing his self-confidence.

To help make a good impression, the speaker should look directly at his hearers. Just as he would do in speaking to a group of three or four, he will turn from one member of the audience to another taking in as many as he can. The speaker must convey the impression that he is talking to his audience individually and not gazing over their heads. The audience want to feel a sense of personal relationship as if the speaker were engaging them in a conversation. Nothing is quite so important a means of establishing personal contact with the audience as the simple device of looking them in the eye.

The speaker, once on the platform, acknowledges the chairman with a pleasant nod or says, "Mr. Chairman," and faces the audience. Then he greets the audience with a smile. Under proper circumstances, his salutation to the audience might be, "Fellow members of the Literary Society," or "Ladies and gentlemen." Then he is ready to begin.

In his opening sentences, to win the confidence and good will of his hearers, he should say something pleasant and agreeable. The guest-of-honor at an installation ceremony in response to expressions of tribute said:

Illustration 1

It is not easy to tell you of the happiness which your presence brings to an already full heart. I shall long remember the sacrifice which you made to come here to greet me. I earnestly hope that this ceremony was not a trespass upon your time and patience.

The effect of such a beginning, sincerely spoken, would tend to commend him to the audience's good-will and kindness.

The Central or Main Idea

Getting across to the audience the central theme or idea is a matter that overshadows practically all else.

Clear organization of the speech is the first essential. If the speaker is making his point in an earnest and enthusiastic way, the audience will not only listen but will overlook many faults in form. The speaker should use specific data and examples of the point he is trying to make. He must be precise. An audience is not likely to accept vaguely expressed ideas. Many of the illustrations given in this book are purposely bare and unadorned. They are thought skeletons, but it is the meat which the speaker puts on that skeleton that will give them body, warmth and reality for the audience.

If, for instance, the speaker is delivering a speech of tribute at a testimonial dinner, the central idea is that the guest-of-honor is a deserving person. Uttering mere platitudes would not impress. The speaker should tell why the guest-of-honor is a deserving person and support the conclusion with facts.

Illustration 2

Robert Roe added strength and stature to the organization when he assumed the presidency. As a result of his forward-looking policies, our membership has doubled in the four years he has been at the helm and our organization has become a powerful force. He accepted what is essentially a thankless job holding no reward but the opportunity to serve. To perform the duties of president Robert Roe has taken time out from a lucrative business and his service to us has been at a tremendous personal sacrifice. He has been a most capable administrator. He succeeded in coördinating the functions of all sections of our order so that they now work together as one cohesive unit. He has stressed competence and good organization. He is not one to make hasty decisions. But once after study and investigation he reached a decision, it was forcefully executed.

He has a long and active record of civic participation and holds a high place in the community. Last year he was chosen to head the drive for the Hospital Fund and the results of his efforts were most gratifying. We can feel a deep and lasting satisfaction in having him as our president. He served us well. His excellent record deserves generous recognition.

If the object of the speech is to inform, the main purpose is to increase the audience's store of knowledge. To do this effectively the speaker must present enough concrete examples and precise information to avoid becoming vague and dry.

The following excerpt from President Eisenhower's State-of-the-Union message to Congress (Jan. 6, 1955) illustrates the speech to inform:

Illustration 3

I believe it would be well to remind ourselves of this great fundamental in our national life: our common belief that every human being is divinely endowed with dignity and worth and inalienable rights. This faith, with its corollary—that to grow and flourish people must be free—shapes the interests and aspirations of every American.

From this deep faith have evolved three main purposes

of our Federal government: First, to maintain justice and freedom among ourselves and, to champion them for others so that we may work effectively for enduring peace; second, to help keep our economy vigorous and expanding, thus sustaining our international strength and assuring better jobs, better living, better opportunities for every citizen; and third, to concern ourselves with the human problems of our people so that every American may have the opportunity to lead a healthy, productive and rewarding life. Foremost among these broad purposes of government is our support of freedom, justice and peace.

THE CONCLUSION

It was indicated that the first impression is a prime concern of the speaker, but the last impression is also important. Many a speech well begun has ended disastrously because of a poor conclusion. Last impressions often erase from memory impressions made earlier. The speaker dare not neglect the conclusion. This is his last opportunity to stress his main ideas. He should permit no one in the audience to leave with any doubt as to what he is trying to say. In the closing sentences, if the speech is to gain action, the speaker will ask the audience to do something, to contribute to some worthy cause, or to participate in some activity.

Illustration 4

I ask you, therefore, not to go away simply feeling satisfied and proud of the national candidates your party has chosen. There is something else to be done and it is up to you to do it. I urge you not to overlook the need to elect the right men to local and state offices. I believe most deeply that the roots of good government in this country lie in clean, honest and efficient local and state government. Many citizens are concerned with electing able, honest men to national office, but, I am afraid they overlook dishonesty and incompetence in their own back yards. We want clean, efficient government in this country from the towns and cities all the way up the ladder to Washington. And the only way to get it is to vote for the right men on election day.

If the object of the speech is one to inform as, for example, a demonstration of the greatness of our Constitution, a sample of the speaker's conclusion follows:

Illustration 5

Be grateful, therefore, for your heritage. Be proud and happy for the benefits the Constitution confers and pray God for a continuance of those benefits.

The ultimate value of training in effective speech will depend upon what the reader does with his knowledge of the principles given here. Skill in speaking grows weaker with disuse; but it develops strength from constant practice. The reader should participate to the fullest extent in the programs and meetings of the organizations to which he belongs. Only by constantly applying the principles studied will they remain fresh in mind and the effectiveness of his delivery will then keep pace with his growing knowledge.

Index